Guide to Housing Benefit

2015-16

Sam Lister and Martin Ward

Guide to Housing Benefit
Peter McGurk and Nick Raynsford, 1982-88
Martin Ward and John Zebedee, 1988-90

Guide to Housing Benefit and Community Charge Benefit
Martin Ward and John Zebedee, 1990-93

Guide to Housing Benefit and Council Tax Benefit
John Zebedee and Martin Ward, 1993-2003
John Zebedee, Martin Ward and Sam Lister, 2003-12
Sam Lister and Martin Ward, 2012-13

Guide to Housing Benefit and Council Tax Rebates
Sam Lister and Martin Ward, 2013-14

Guide to Housing Benefit
Sam Lister and Martin Ward, 2014-17

Sam Lister is policy and practice officer at the Chartered Institute of Housing
(email: sam.lister@cih.org) and a founding director of Worcester Citizens Advice Bureau
and Whabac. He has specialised in Housing Benefit and social security since 1993.

Martin Ward is an independent consultant and trainer on housing and benefit related
matters *(e-mail: mward@info-training.co.uk)*. He has provided consultancy services
and training for several national organisations as well as many local authorities and
large and small housing providers across the UK since 1982.

ISBN 978 1 905018 97 0

Edited and typeset by Davies Communications *(www.daviescomms.com)*

Printed by The Russell Press Ltd, Nottingham
(www.russellpress.com)

Shelter

Shelter helps over a million people a year struggling with bad housing or homelessness – and we campaign to prevent it in the first place.

We're here so no-one has to fight bad housing or homelessness on their own.

Please support us at *shelter.org.uk*

For more information about Shelter, please contact:

> 88 Old Street
> London
> EC1V 9HU
>
> Telephone: 0300 330 1234
>
> Website: *shelter.org.uk*

For help with your housing problems, phone Shelter's free housing advice helpline on 0808 800 4444 (open from 8am to 8pm on Mondays to Fridays and from 8am to 5pm on weekends: calls are free from UK landlines and main mobile networks) or visit *shelter.org.uk/advice*

Chartered Institute of Housing

The Chartered Institute of Housing (CIH) is the independent voice for housing and the home of professional standards.

Our goal is simple – we want to provide everyone involved in housing with the advice, support and knowledge they need to be brilliant.

> Chartered Institute of Housing
> Octavia House
> Westwood Way
> Coventry
> CV4 8JP
>
> Telephone: 024 7685 1700
>
> E-mail: *customer.services@cih.org*
>
> Website: *www.cih.org*

Contents

Preface

This guide explains the rules about housing benefit as they apply from 1st April 2015, using the information available on that date.

We welcome comments and criticisms on the contents of our guide and make every effort to ensure it is accurate. However, the only statement of the law is found in the relevant Acts, regulations, orders and rules (chapter 1).

This guide has been written with the help and encouragement of many other people. Much material remains as written by John Zebedee. This year we thank the following in particular:

Linda Davies and Peter Singer (editing and production), Kem Herbert, Jonathan Reid, Martin Scott and John Zebedee as well as staff from the Department for Work and Pensions and the Rent Service. Their help has been essential to the production of this guide.

Sam Lister and Martin Ward

May 2015

List of tables

Table		Page

Abbreviations

The principal abbreviations used in the guide are given below.

CTB	Council tax benefit
CTC	Child tax credit
CTR	Council tax rebate
DLA	Disability living allowance
DSD	The Department for Social Development in Northern Ireland
DWP	The Department for Work and Pensions in Great Britain
EP	Extended payment
ESA	Employment and support allowance (including ESA(C) and ESA (IR))
ESA(C)	Contributory employment and support allowance
ESA(IR)	Income-based employment and support allowance
GB	England, Scotland and Wales
GLHA	The DWP guidance local housing allowance
GM	The DWP HB/CTB Guidance Manual
HB	Housing benefit
HMRC	Her Majesty's Revenue and Customs
HMCTS	Her Majesty's Courts and Tribunals Service
IB	Incapacity benefit
IS	Income support
JSA	Jobseeker's allowance (including JSA(C) & JSA(IB))
JSA(C)	Contribution-based jobseeker's allowance
JSA(IB)	Income-based jobseeker's allowance
NI	Northern Ireland
NIHE	The Northern Ireland Housing Executive
OG	The DWP HB/CTB Overpayments Guide
PIP	Personal independence payment
SDA	Severe disablement allowance
SI	Statutory instrument
SMI	Support for Mortgage Interest
SPC	State pension credit (including guarantee credit and savings credit)
SR	Statutory rules (Northern Ireland)
SSI	Scottish Statutory Instrument
UC	Universal credit
UK	England, Scotland, Wales and Northern Ireland
WTC	Working tax credit

Key to footnotes

Each reference applies to Great Britain only unless otherwise stated.
If prefixed by 'NI' (e.g. NIAA) it applies to Northern Ireland only.

AA	The Social Security Administration Act 1992 [section number]
AC	Appeal Cases, published by The Incorporated Council of Law Reporting for England and Wales, London
All ER	All England Law Reports, published by Butterworths
art	Article number
BC	Borough Council
BMLR	Butterworths Medico-Legal Reports
CA	Court of Appeal for England and Wales
CBA	The Social Security Contributions and Benefits Act 1992 [section number]
CC	City Council
ChD	High Court (England and Wales) Chancery Division
COD	Crown Office Digest, published by Sweet & Maxwell
CPR	The Housing Benefit and Council Tax Benefit (Consequential Provisions) Regulations 2006, SI No. 217 [regulation number]
CPSA	The Child Support, Pensions and Social Security Act [section number]
CS	Court of Session, Scotland
DAR	The Housing Benefit and Council Tax Benefit (Decisions and Appeals) Regulations 2001, SI No. 1002 [regulation number]
DAR99	The Social Security and Child Support (Decisions and Appeals) Regulations 1999, SI No. 991 [regulation number]
DC	District Council
ECJ	European Court of Justice
EEA	The Immigration (European Economic Area) Regulations 2006, SI No. 1003 [regulation number (UK reference)]
EWCA Civ	Court of Appeal Civil Division for England & Wales (neutral citation)
EWHC Admin	High Court for England & Wales, Administrative Court (neutral citation)
FTPR	The Tribunal Procedure (First-tier Tribunal) (Social Entitlement Chamber) Rules 2008, SI No. 2685 [rule number

HB	The Housing Benefit Regulations 2006, SI No. 213 [regulation number]
HB60+	The Housing Benefit (Persons who have attained the age for state pension credit) Regulations 2006, SI No. 214 [regulation number]
HBRB	Housing Benefit Review Board
HC (Admin)	High Court for England and Wales, Administrative Court
HL	House of Lords
HLR	Housing Law Reports, published by Sweet & Maxwell
IAA99	Immigration and Asylum Act 1999 [the section number (UK reference)]
LBC	London Borough Council
MBC	Metropolitan Borough Council
NIAA	The Social Security Administration (Northern Ireland) Act 1992 [section number]
NICBA	The Social Security Contributions and Benefits (Northern Ireland) Act 1992 [section number]
NICPR	The Housing Benefit (Consequential Provisions) Regulations (Northern Ireland) 2006, SR No. 407 [regulation number]
NICPSA	The Child Support, Pensions and Social Security Act (Northern Ireland) 2000 [section number]
NIDAR	The Housing Benefit (Decisions and Appeals) Regulations (Northern Ireland) 2001 SR No. 213 [regulation number]
NIDAR99	The Social Security and Child Support (Decisions and Appeals) Regulations (Northern Ireland) 1999 SR No. 162 [regulation number]
NIED	The Housing Benefit (Executive Determinations) Regulations (Northern Ireland) 2008 SR No. 100
NIHB	The Housing Benefit Regulations (Northern Ireland) 2006, SR No. 405 [regulation number]
NIHB60+	The Housing Benefit (Persons who have attained the age for state pension credit) Regulations (Northern Ireland) 2006, SR No. 406 [regulation number]
NISR	Statutory Rules of Northern Ireland (equivalent to Statutory Instruments in GB)
NISSCPR	The Social Security Commissioners (Procedure) Regulations (Northern Ireland) 1999, SR No. 225 [regulation number]
QBD	High Court (England and Wales) Queens Bench Division
reg	regulation [regulation number]

ROO	In England and Wales, The Rent Officers (Housing Benefit Functions) Order 1997, SI 1984; in Scotland, The Rent Officers (Housing Benefit Functions) (Scotland) Order 1997, SI 1995 [in both cases followed by article number or schedule and paragraph number]
sch	Schedule
SI	Statutory instrument [year and reference number]
SLT	Scots Law Times, published by W. Green, Edinburgh
SR	Statutory rules [year and reference number (apply to NI only)
TCEA	Tribunals, Courts and Enforcement Act 2007 [section number]
UCTP	Universal Credit (Transitional Provisions) Regulations 2014 SI No. 1230 [regulation number]
UKHL	House of Lords, UK case (neutral citation)
UKSC	Supreme Court (neutral citation)
UTPR	The Tribunal Procedure (Upper Tribunal) Rules 2008 SI No. 2698 [rule number]
WLR	Weekly Law Reports, published by The Incorporated Council of Law Reporting for England and Wales, London

Chapter 1 **Introduction**

- Summary of HB and how it is changing: see paras 1.5-19.
- Using this guide (benefit figures, terminology and references): see paras 1.20-27.
- How HB is administered: see paras 1.28-35.
- HB law, guidance and proper decision-making: see paras 1.36-58.

1.1   Welcome to this guide, which describes housing benefit (HB) throughout the UK. The guide is used by administrators, advisers, people claiming HB, landlords and appeal tribunals.

1.2   HB helps you pay your rent anywhere in the UK, and your rates in Northern Ireland. About five million people get HB: see table 1.1.

1.3   For working age claims, HB for rent is gradually being replaced by universal credit (see para 1.15). You can find full details about UC and about council tax rebates in *Help With Housing Costs Volume 1: Universal Credit and Council Tax Rebates,* the companion to this guide.

1.4   The rules in this guide apply from 1st April 2015. The next edition will give the rules from 1st April 2016. Recent and expected changes to the HB scheme are summarised in table 1.2. For basic definitions of the main terminology used in this guide see para 1.22.

Table 1.1 **Key HB statistics**

HB claims in Great Britain on 1st August 2014

Number of cases	4,930,160
Average weekly payment	£92.69

Composition of HB caseload in Great Britain on 1st August 2014

In receipt of passport benefit	63.5%
Claimants aged under 65+	26.0%
Local authority tenants	28.4%
Housing association tenants	38.8%
Private tenant LHA cases	28.1%
Private tenant non-LHA cases	4.6%

HB caseload in Northern Ireland on 1st August 2014

Number of cases	162,760
Claimants aged 65+	21.0%

- Source: DWP, Single Housing Benefit Extract (SHBE); DSD Statistics and Research Agency

Table 1.2 **Summary of HB changes from 2014**

1st Jan 2014 SI 2013/3032 SI 2013/3196 NISR 2013/308	Worker authorisation scheme for Bulgarian and Romanian nationals ends, so they now have the same benefit rights as other EEA nationals. EEA retained worker status limited to six months for those seeking work. EEA nationals entering UK seeking work excluded from JSA for first three months of residence.
13th Jan 2014 SI 2013/2978 NISR 2013/303	In 'targeted affordability funding' cases (certain accommodation sizes in certain areas), LHA figures now set by increasing the previous year's figures by 4% (unless the national LHA cap is a lower figure).
3rd Mar 2014 SI 2014/212	Errors corrected in relation to social sector size criteria.
13th Mar 2014 SI 2014/107	Amendments in England and Wales taking account of same sex married couples.
1st Apr 2014 SI 2014/212	EEA nationals on JSA(IB) excluded from HB unless they have a right to reside unrelated to being on JSA(IB). But people on HB and JSA(IB) on 31st March 2014 remain entitled to HB until their JSA(IB) ends or they make a new claim for HB (e.g. because they move areas or return to HB after a period off HB).
1st/7th Apr 2014 SI 2014/147 NISR 2014/78	2014 annual HB up-rating.
1st/7th Apr 2014 SI 2014/213	Rules introduced about the date on which transferring from DLA to PIP takes effect in HB. Other minor corrections.
10th Apr 2014 SI 2014/771	The HB benefit cap ceases to apply in most supported accommodation cases (or applies in a very limited way).
25th Jul 2014 SI 2014/1667	Councils' HB subsidy claims now have to be submitted to auditors by 30th April. Some new subsidy figures for 2013-14 and 2014-15.
3rd Nov 2014 SI 2014/771 SI 2014/1626	Claimants on UC can get HB in a wider variety of supported accommodation than just exempt accommodation.
3rd Nov 2014 SI 2014/2888 26th Nov 2014 NISR 2014/275	New definitions of 'blind' and 'severely sight-impaired' as requiring certification by a consultant ophthalmologist (replacing old definition of 'registered as blind').
16th Dec 2014 SI 2014/3229	Amendments in Scotland taking account of same sex married couples.

8th Jan 2015 SI 2014/3126 20th Jan 2015 NISR 2015/2	National LHA caps increased, and changes to list of 'targeted affordability funding' cases. Rent officers now set April's LHA figures on the last working day of January.
9th Feb 2015 SI 2015/6 18th Feb 2015 NISR 2015/19	More detailed rules introduced about assessing employed earnings (reversing the effect of [2014] UKUT 369 (AAC)).
1st/6th Apr 2015 SI 2015/30 NISR 2015/124	2015 annual HB up-rating.
2015 onwards	Continuation of gradual replacement (for working age claimants) of HB and the passport benefits by UC, by extending the areas in which UC is available and the groups who can claim it.

Table 1.3 **State benefits before and after the changes**

	Before	After
Help with living costs	JSA/ESA/IS/SPC	UC/SPC
Help with mortgage interest	JSA/ESA/IS/SPC	UC/SPC
Help with rent [1]	HB	UC/SPC
Help with rates in Northern Ireland [2]	HB	RRS
Help with council tax [3]	CTB	CTR

1. HB for rent continues in supported accommodation (para 2.7) for the time being, but will be absorbed into UC at some later date or replaced by a separate scheme in its own right administered by local authorities.
2. HB for rates in Northern Ireland continues for 2014-15, but is expected to be superseded on 1st April 2016 by a new rate rebate scheme (RRS).
3. CTB was replaced by CTR on 1st April 2013.

The HB scheme

1.5   Many people can get HB towards their rent, and/or in Northern Ireland rates. Chapters 2 and 3 give the details about whether you are eligible for HB. This section summarises how much HB you are awarded and other key rules including the changes to HB.

The amount of your HB

1.6   The main rules about the amount of your HB are as follows:

(a) your HB is based on your 'eligible rent', and/or in Northern Ireland 'eligible rates': see para 1.7;

(b) if you are on a passport benefit (para 1.9), you qualify for maximum HB;

(c) if you are not on a passport benefit, your HB depends on how much income and capital you (and your partner) have: see chapters 13 to 15;

(d) if you are not on a passport benefit, it also depends on your 'applicable amount', which reflects your (and your family's) basic living needs: see chapters 4 and 12;

(e) your HB can be reduced if you have one or more 'non-dependants' in your home. These are adults who are expected to contribute towards your housing costs: see chapters 4 and 6;

(f) if you are working age your HB can be reduced if the total income from your HB, out-of-work benefits, child tax credits and child benefit exceeds 'the benefit cap': see chapter 6.

Chapter 6 gives the full HB calculation.

Eligible rent and rates

1.7   The council works out your eligible rent and rates as follows:

(a) in social sector lettings, your eligible rent normally equals the rent payable on your home (reduced in certain cases if the home is larger than you need), apart from any charges included in the rent for services which HB cannot meet (chapters 7, 9 and 10);

(b) in most private sector lettings, your eligible rent is a fixed 'local housing allowance' figure depending on where you live and the size of accommodation you need (chapter 8);

(c) in Northern Ireland, eligible rates equal the rates payable on your home (chapter 11).

The passport benefits

1.8   The 'passport benefits' (para 1.9) can help you meet basic living needs (such as food and heating) and also, if you are not in rented housing, your mortgage interest: see chapter 25.

1.9   The 'passport benefits' are:

(a) income-based jobseeker's allowance (JSA(IB));

(b) income-related employment and support allowance (ESA(IR));

(c) income support (IS); and

(d) guarantee credit (part of state pension credit).

How to get HB

1.10 In England, Scotland and Wales you can claim HB from your local council, or from the relevant government agency in Northern Ireland (para 1.28). Chapter 5 explains how to claim and chapter 17 describes how your HB can change.

Payments of HB

1.11 If you qualify for HB it is paid as:

(a) a rent rebate if you rent from the council or the Northern Ireland Housing Executive (para 16.16);

(b) a rent allowance if you rent from any other landlord (para 16.18);

(c) a rate rebate towards rates in Northern Ireland (para 11.18).

If you are overpaid you may have to repay it: see chapter 18.

Information and appeals about HB

1.12 The council must send you a decision notice about your HB claim, about any later changes to it, and about any overpayments: see chapter 16.

1.13 You can ask the council to reconsider its decision about HB, and/or appeal to an independent tribunal: see chapter 19. This includes decisions about how much HB you are awarded, how it was calculated, when it starts, backdating (para 5.50) and overpayments.

Landlords and HB

1.14 If your HB is a rent allowance (para 1.11), it can be paid to your landlord in some situations instead of you. The rules about this, and about your and your landlord's rights, are in paras 16.34-66.

Universal credit and changes to HB

1.15 For working age claims (para 1.23), universal credit (UC) is gradually replacing:

(a) the passport benefits JSA(IB), ESA(IR) and IS; and

(b) HB for rent (except, for the time being, in supported accommodation: see para 2.37).

1.16 UC can help with basic living needs (such as food and heating) and rent (whether you are working or not), child care costs (if you are working), and mortgage interest (if you are a homeowner and are not working), but not council tax or rates. Table 1.3 summarises the changes.

1.17 If you fall within the UC scheme (whether or not you claim UC or qualify for an amount of UC):

(a) you cannot get JSA(IB), ESA(IR) or IS;

(b) you cannot get HB towards your rent unless you are in supported accommodation (see paras 2.37-39);

(c) you can get council tax rebate in England, Scotland and Wales (see para 1.19).

You can find out which areas in England, Scotland and Wales are covered by the UC scheme online [www]. At the time of writing it is expected that every Jobcentre Plus office in all three countries will be accepting new UC claims by the end of 2015, but only for a limited range of claimant groups.

State pension credit and changes to HB

1.18   For pension age claims (para 1.23), it is expected that state pension credit (SPC) will also be changed at some later date to include help with rent (as well as mortgage interest as at present) and that the rules will be similar to UC. The law allowing the DWP to make this change has already been passed.

Council tax rebates

1.19   Council tax rebates (CTR) are separate from both HB and UC. You may be able to get CTR from the council towards your council tax whether or not you are on HB or UC (paras 1.29-30). For full details see *Help With Housing Costs Volume 1: Universal Credit and Council Tax Rebates.*

Using this guide

1.20   The HB rules in this guide apply from 1st April 2015. For changes during 2014 and 2015, see table 1.2.

HB and other benefit figures

1.21   The figures used in calculating HB are up-rated each April together with other social security benefits and credits, usually in line with inflation. For the exact dates in 2015, see table 1.4, which also gives expected dates for 2016. For the main figures for HB and other benefits in 2015-16, see table 12.1 and appendix 2.

Table 1.4 **Up-rating dates 2015-16**		
	2015	**2016**
For HB for rent if the rent is due weekly or in multiples of weeks	Monday 6th April	Monday 4th April
For HB for rent in all other cases, for HB for rates in all cases (also CTR)	Wednesday 1st April	Friday 1st April
For most other benefits (see also paras 17.39 and 17.44)	Week commencing Monday 6th April	Week commencing Monday 11th April

---

1.17   www.gov.uk/government/publications/universal-credit-national-expansion

T 1.4   AA 150(10); NIAA 132(1); HB 79(3); HB60+ 59(3); NIHB 77(5); NIHB60+ 57(5)

Terminology used in this guide

1.22 In this guide, the following terms are used:

- 'council' or 'authority' means any of the public authorities which administers HB (para 1.28);
- 'tenant' is used to describe any kind of rent-payer (including, for example, licensees);
- 'housing benefit' (HB) means any form of HB for rent or (in Northern Ireland) rates;
- 'rent rebate' means HB for rent for a council or NIHE tenant;
- 'rent allowance' means HB for rent for anyone else;
- 'rate rebate' means HB for rates in Northern Ireland;
- 'eligible rent' and 'eligible rates' mean the amount of rent and rates HB can meet;
- 'local housing allowance' (LHA) is the main way of working out eligible rent in private sector cases;
- 'social sector' and 'private sector' cases are defined in chapters 7 and 8;
- 'family', 'single claimant', 'lone parent', 'couple', 'partner', 'child', 'young person' and 'non-dependant' are all defined in chapter 4;
- 'pension age' and 'working age' are defined in paras 1.23-25 and table 1.5;
- 'state pension credit' refers to either type of pension credit – 'guarantee credit' and 'savings credit';
- 'guarantee credit' is used to refer to any award of pension credit which includes an amount of guarantee credit – whether it is paid with or without the savings credit;
- 'savings credit' is used to refer to awards of pension credit which consist solely of an award of the savings credit.

'Pension age' vs 'working age' claims for HB

1.23 Some HB rules are different between pension age and working age claims, for example in relation to backdating (paras 5.50-58) and the assessment of income and capital (chapters 13-15).

1.24 The main dividing line is the qualifying age for state pension credit (SPC). The law refers to people below that age as being 'working age', people above it as 'pension age'. The qualifying age for SPC is increasing from 60 (before April 2010) to 66 (from April 2020). During the 2015-16 financial year it rises from 62½ to 63, and during 2016-17 from 63 to 63¾ (in each case approximately). A complete list of qualifying ages is given in appendix 3.

1.25 However, people on JSA(IB), ESA(IR), IS or universal credit (UC) are counted as 'working age' regardless of their actual age. Table 1.5 shows whether you count as 'working age' or pension age'.

Table 1.5 **Pension age or working age claim?**

Single claimant/lone parent

- ■ under SPC age   Working age HB claim
- ■ at or over SPC age:
    - ■ not on JSA(IB)/ESA(IR)/IS/UC   Pension age HB claim
    - ■ on JSA(IB)/ESA(IR)/IS/UC   Working age HB claim

Couple/polygamous marriage

- ■ both/all under SPC age   Working age HB claim
- ■ at least one at or over SPC age:
    - ■ neither on JSA(IB)/ESA(IR)/IS/UC   Pension age HB claim
    - ■ one on JSA(IB)/ESA(IR)/IS/UC   Working age HB claim

- ■ Appendix 3 gives a complete list of the qualifying ages for state pension credit ('SPC age').

Abbreviations and footnotes

1.26   The tables at the front of this guide give:

(a)   a list of the abbreviations used in the text; and

(b)   a key to the abbreviations used in the footnotes.

The footnotes throughout this guide refer to the law governing HB. All the references are to the law as amended.

1.27   For example, the footnote for this paragraph (which is actually about the definition of a non-dependant) refers to regulation 3 of the Housing Benefit Regulations 2006, regulation 3 of the Housing Benefit (Persons who have attained the qualifying age for state pension credit) Regulations 2006, and regulation 3 of the two Northern Ireland equivalents, all four of which are similar.

Administering the HB scheme

Who administers the HB scheme

1.28   HB was first introduced throughout the UK in 1982-83. There are different arrangements for administering it in different parts of the UK:

(a)   in areas in England with two layers of local government (county and district/borough), HB is administered by the district/borough councils – also known as the local housing authority;

(b)   in the rest of Great Britain (areas with one layer of local government), HB is administered

---

T1.5   HB 5; HB60+ 5; NIHB 5; NIHB60+ 5

1.27   HB 3; HB60+ 3; NIHB 3; NIHB60+ 3

by English unitary authorities and London boroughs (including the Common Council of the City of London), Welsh county and county borough councils, and Scottish local councils;

(c) in Northern Ireland, HB for rent and rates for tenants is administered for tenants by the Northern Ireland Housing Executive (NIHE) and for owners by the Land and Property Services. More details and exceptions are in table 1.6.

1.29   In Great Britain (except as described in paras 1.30-32), you claim HB from the council in the area where you live (para 5.8). The same council also administers CTR, and you can often claim both benefits on a single application form.

Table 1.6 **Which agency administers HB in Northern Ireland**

Land and Property Services	**Northern Ireland Housing Executive (NIHE)**
Owner occupiers	NIHE tenants
Partners of sole owners	Housing association tenants
Former partners of sole owners	Tenants of private landlords
Former non-dependants of sole owners	People with a life interest
	People in co-ownership schemes
	People in rental purchase schemes

■   The same agency also administers rate relief and lone pensioner allowance.

Out-of-area council tenants

1.30   If a council owns properties outside its area (as is reasonably common in London), the tenants there claim HB from their landlord council – but claim CTR from the council in the area where they live.

Arranging for someone else to administer HB

1.31   Councils in Great Britain may arrange for HB (but not CTR) to be administered on their behalf by another council or by a number of councils jointly. This is very common.

1.32   Councils can contract out the administration of HB (and CTR) to private companies (in other words, pay them to do part or all of their work). They do this under the Deregulation and Contracting Out Act 1994 and the Contracting Out (Functions of Local Authorities: Income-related Benefits) Regulations 2002/1888. When contractors make decisions on claims, they must submit a daily 10% random sample of claims for the council to check.

Good administration

1.33   Under the Local Government Act 1999 councils in England and Wales are required to provide the best value they can, achieve continuous improvement and publish their plans for how they will perform.

1.28   AA 134(1),(1A),(1B),(2), 139(1),(2), 191; NIAA 126(2),(3)

1.31   AA 134 (1A),(5), 191

1.34   The DWP sets councils 'performance indicators' relating to HB (checks on how well they do their work). The key indicators are:

(a) a 'right time' indicator – which is the average time to process claims and changes to entitlement; and

(b) a 'right benefit' indicator – which is the number of changes to entitlement in a year.

The DWP inspects a small number of councils each year and reports on their administration generally and on the prevention and detection of fraud. The *HB Good Practice Guide* provides guidance to help councils manage their services efficiently and is available online [www].

Maladministration

1.35   In individual cases of bad administration by your council, you (or someone else) can complain to the Local Government Ombudsman. Guidance on how to complain, what constitutes maladministration, and recent Ombudsman's reports on HB (and CTR and CTB), are available online [www].

HB law

Acts of Parliament

1.36   The Acts giving the basic rules of the HB scheme are the Social Security Contributions and Benefits Act 1992, the Social Security Administration Act 1992 and their Northern Ireland equivalents, and also (as regards decision-making and appeals) the Child Support, Pensions and Social Security Act 2000 (appendix 1).

1.37   The Data Protection Act 1998 controls the use of, and access to, information about an individual held on a computer or any other retrievable filing system. This Act does not stop disclosure when other law requires it (section 35 of the Act) but authorities are under a duty to protect personal information (GM chapter D3).

1.38   Other Acts affecting HB include the Immigration and Asylum Act 1999 (e.g. s115 about migrants), section 87 of the Northern Ireland Act 1998 (making the social security system UK-wide), the Human Rights Act 1998, various anti-discrimination laws, the Deregulation and Contracting Out Act 1994 and the Local Government Act 1999.

Regulations, orders and rules

1.39   The regulations, orders and rules giving the detail of the HB scheme are all passed under the Acts mentioned above and are listed in Appendix 1. They are known technically as Statutory Instruments (SIs) and in Northern Ireland as Statutory Rules (SRs).

Obtaining the law

1.40   The public has the right to see copies of the relevant legal material (plus details of any local scheme: para 13.18) at the council's principal office.

1.34   AA 139A-139H
         www.gov.uk/government/collections/housing-benefit-performance-support-information

1.35   www.lgo.org.uk (England), www.ombudsman-wales.org.uk (Wales)
         www.spso.org.uk (Scotland), www.ni-ombudsman.org.uk (Northern Ireland)

1.41   The Acts, regulations, orders and rules are available online [www]. For the consolidated legislation, see the DWP's *The Law Relating to Social Security,* volume 8 parts 1 and 2 (also called 'the blue volumes') which are available online [www]. The Child Poverty Action Group's annual publication, *CPAG's Housing Benefit and Council Tax Reduction Legislation,* also contains all the law in Great Britain plus a detailed commentary including references to case law.

Proper decision-making

1.42   This section explains how the council (or the relevant government agency in Northern Ireland) should go about making decisions on HB by working through the following steps:

(a)   identifying what the relevant facts are in any particular case;

(b)   properly considering the evidence that does exist, if the facts are in doubt or in dispute;

(c)   establishing the facts 'on the balance of probability' if this is necessary;

(d)   correctly interpreting the relevant law and applying it to the facts of the case; and

(e)   arriving at decisions that can be understood in terms of the relevant facts and law.

Relevant facts

1.43   The only facts which are relevant to the council are those which affect the HB scheme:

(a)   sometimes the facts are clear and not in dispute. For example, it may be agreed by the claimant and the council that the claimant has a grown-up son living with him;

(b)   sometimes facts are unclear or are in dispute. For example, the claimant may say the son is not living with him (but other things suggest he is);

(c)   sometimes there is no evidence of the facts at all. For example, the claimant may have left all of the 'your household' section of his HB application form blank.

1.44   The law uses two ideas to deal with uncertainty about the facts: 'burden of proof' and 'balance of probability'.

Burden of proof

1.45   The 'burden of proof' is based on the idea that it is up to someone to prove their side of a dispute. It is used when there is something that has to be shown to be the case in order for HB law to apply at all. Two examples are:

(a)   when a claimant first makes a claim for HB, there is at the outset no evidence – and so it is for the claimant to support the claim by supplying the council with all the evidence it reasonably requires (para 5.13);

(b)   when the council says that a recoverable HB overpayment has occurred, the council must have evidence to support this (para 18.11).

1.41   www.legislation.gov.uk
lawvolumes.dwp.gov.uk/
www.dsdni.gov.uk/ law_relating_to_social_security (Northern Ireland)

1.46   The 'burden of proof' is also used when a decision cannot be made by the 'balance of probability' because there is no evidence either way, or the evidence that does exist is exactly balanced. In these cases the side with the burden loses unless they can supply evidence that adjusts the balance of probability in their favour.

Balance of probability

1.47   The 'balance of probability' is based on the idea that in the end a decision has to be made or nothing would ever get done. It is used when there is a disagreement about the facts. In such a case, the council must consider the available evidence to decide what the true position is. The evidence each way must be weighed up and the 'facts' of the case are those supported by the greater weight of evidence. There does not have to be absolute certainty. It is because HB decisions are matters of civil law that the appropriate test is the 'balance of probability' (not 'beyond reasonable doubt', which is a test used in criminal law).

Applying the law

1.48   The HB scheme is governed by law passed by Parliament (paras 1.36-39). The starting point for applying the law is that it means exactly what it says – though many words have special meanings in HB (as described in this guide) and precedents can affect how the law is interpreted (para 1.50).

1.49   Having worked out which piece of law applies and what it means, it must then be applied to the case in hand. For example, whether or not a claimant's son counts as a non-dependant can only be answered by considering the legal definition of 'non-dependant' and applying it to the facts. Part of the definition is that the person must 'normally reside' with the claimant. So if the facts are that the son normally resides somewhere else but visits the claimant from time to time, then as a matter of law he cannot be a non-dependant.

Precedents from courts and Upper Tribunals

1.50   When there are 'precedents' (also called 'case law'), these should be followed. A 'precedent' is a binding decision by a court or an Upper Tribunal (para 19.67) on a case which is relevant to the case in hand. For example, in deciding whether a person 'normally resides' with a claimant (para 1.49) there is a precedent in the decision Kadhim v Brent LBC (para 4.45) which may well have a bearing on other cases. Generally speaking, precedents from one part of the UK are regarded as binding in other parts of the UK (for example Great Britain precedent is taken into account in Northern Ireland: C001/03-04(HB)); and precedents from other parts of the social security system may be binding on similar HB decisions (e.g. on backdating: para 5.55).

1.51   Case law from the courts is given throughout this guide, and the full legal citation and details of how to find the transcript online are found in the footnote to the appropriate paragraph. Most Upper Tribunal decisions are available online [www]. Since 1st January 2010 Upper Tribunal decisions are cited using the 'neutral citation' (e.g. [2011] UKUT 136 AAC – see also para 19.68); the file reference (e.g. CH/3853/2001) is used for older decisions.

1.51   www.osscsc.gov.uk/aspx/default.aspx (Great Britain)
          www.dsdni.gov.uk/index/law_and_legislation/ni_digest_of_case_law/nidoc_database.htm (Northern Ireland)

Judgment and discretion

1.52   Sometimes a decision about HB requires the council to use its judgment. The law uses terms like 'reasonable', 'appropriate', 'good cause' or 'special circumstances' to show that the council has a judgment to make. Examples of judgments are:

(a) whether it is 'reasonable' for the council to award HB on two homes in the case of person who has fled violence (para 3.12);

(b) how much it is 'appropriate' to restrict the rent in exempt accommodation (para 9.29);

(c) whether a claimant has 'good cause' for a late claim (para 5.55);

(d) whether a claimant has 'special circumstances' for their delay in notifying an advantageous change in circumstances (para 17.14).

1.53   And sometimes a decision about HB allows the council to use its discretion. A discretion differs from a judgment in the sense that an authority may choose what to do. The law usually says that a council 'may' do something to show that it has a discretion. Examples of discretion are:

(a) whether to award discretionary housing payments (para 24.4);

(b) whether to recover a recoverable overpayment of HB (para 18.27);

(c) in some situations whether to pay HB to a landlord (para 16.42).

Judicial review

1.54   When using judgment or discretion, councils are bound by the principles of administrative law evolved by the courts. If they ignore these they can be challenged by applying to the High Court (or in Scotland the Court of Session) for 'judicial review'. Examples of when a challenge may be successful are if the council:

(a) fails to consider each case on its merits, instead applying predetermined rules;

(b) takes into account matters which it ought not to consider;

(c) does not consider matters which it ought to take into account; or

(d) reaches a conclusion that no reasonable council could have come to (what is reasonable here means rational rather than what is the best decision).

1.55   For more on judicial review, see *Judicial Review Proceedings,* Jonathan Manning, Robert Brown and Sarah Salmon, Legal Action Group; or *Judicial Review in Scotland,* Tom Mullen and Tony Prosser, Wiley.

DWP guidance

1.56   The DWP (Department for Work and Pensions) is the central government department responsible for HB policy. It publishes guidance on the scheme which is often very useful and is referred to throughout this guide. But (like this guide itself) it is guidance, not law: CH/3853/2001.

1.57   DWP guidance includes the following:

■ *Housing Benefit and Council Tax Benefit Guidance Manual (GM);*

■ *Subsidy Guidance Manual;*

■ *HB Overpayments Guide (OG);*

■ *Guidance on Discretionary Housing Payments;*

■ circulars in the 'A' series (about adjudication and operations);

■ circulars in the 'F' series (about fraud);

■ circulars in the 'S' series (about statistics and subsidy);

■ circulars in the 'G' series (about general matters); and

■ circulars in the 'U' series (about urgent matters).

1.58   The manuals are available online [www] as are the 'A', 'S', 'G' and 'U' circulars. The 'F' circulars are not available to the public. Strictly speaking, DWP circulars do not apply to Northern Ireland although the relevant government agencies there generally accept the validity of 'A' circulars (unless the law in Northern Ireland is different).

1.58   www.gov.uk/government/collections/housing-benefit-claims-processing-and-good-practice-for-local-authority-staff

Chapter 2 **Eligibility for HB**

- Basic conditions for getting HB: see para 2.1-4.
- People excluded from HB: see paras 2.5-16.
- Payments HB can meet: see paras 2.17-36.
- Specified supported accommodation: see paras 2.37-39.
- Liability to pay rent: see paras 2.40-54.
- Contrived lettings and other exclusions: see paras 2.55-74.

Basic conditions

2.1　　To get HB, you must satisfy all the conditions in paragraph 2.2. Once an award of HB is made, it continues until you no longer satisfy all those conditions, at which point it ends (para 17.41).

Eligibility

2.2　　The basic conditions for getting HB are that:

(a) you are liable (or treated by the authority as liable) to pay 'rent' for a dwelling in the UK (paras 2.17, 2.40 and 2.49), (and/or in Northern Ireland rates (chapter 11));

(b) you occupy that dwelling as your normal home (chapter 3);

(c) you (or someone on your behalf) make a valid claim and provides relevant information and evidence (chapter 5);

(d) you are not a member of an excluded group (para 2.5);

(e) your capital does not exceed £16,000 (para 15.4) – but this does not apply if you are on guarantee credit;

(f) any deductions for non-dependants (para 6.17) do not exceed your eligible rent (and/or in Northern Ireland rates);

(g) your income is not too high (para 2.4); and

(h) the result of the HB calculation is that at least 50p each week is payable (para 6.9) – but in Northern Ireland this does not apply to HB for rates.

2.3　　There are also rules about when the authority should treat you as not liable to make payments and therefore not entitled to HB even though you have a legal liability to make payments (para 2.55).

2.2　　AA 1(1),(1A),(1B); CBA 130(1),(4),134(1)(4); NIAA 1(1),(1A),(1B); NICBA 129(1),130(1),(3)

How low must your income be?

2.4   Your income is low enough for you to get HB if any of the following applies:

(a) you are getting JSA(IB), ESA(IR), income support, guarantee credit or (in specified supported accommodation) universal credit, or treated as being in receipt of those benefits (para 6.4 and table 6.1);

(b) you have no income (para 6.7);

(c) your income is less than or equal to your applicable amount (para 6.7);

or

(d) your income is greater than your applicable amount but the 'taper' calculation (para 6.8) still leaves you with an entitlement to HB.

Exclusions from HB

2.5   You can't get HB for rent if you fall into one of the following categories:

(a) you fall within the UC scheme – unless you live in specified supported accommodation (paras 2.7-9);

(b) in many circumstances, if you are aged under 18 and a care leaver (para 2.10);

(c) in many circumstances, you are a migrant or recent arrival to the UK (para 2.14);

(d) in most cases, if you are a full-time student (para 2.15);

(e) members of religious orders (para 2.16);

(f) your housing payments are excluded from HB (para 2.17);

(g) you are not liable to make eligible payments (para 2.40);

(h) your liability is excluded because of the circumstances surrounding your agreement (para 2.55); and

(i) you do not occupy the dwelling as your normal home (chapter 3).

Further exclusions from HB may be introduced in the future (e.g. possibly for certain under-25-year-olds [www]). For HB for rates in Northern Ireland, see chapter 11.

Introduction of UC and SPC-for-rent

2.6   As UC and (possibly from 2017 onwards) SPC-for-rent are introduced across the country (paras 1.15-18), fewer and fewer people will be eligible for HB for rent (paras 2.7-9).

UC cases

2.7   You can't get HB for rent unless you are in specified supported accommodation (paras 2.37-39) if you are a claimant:

(a) on UC; or

(b) who falls within the UC scheme even if you do not claim UC or are not entitled to it.

2.5   www.parliament.uk/briefing-papers/sn06473.pdf.

2.7   UCTP 5(1),(2), 6, 7

2.8 During the transition to UC, you can only get UC if you meet certain gateway conditions. This means only certain categories of claimant, and only in certain local authority areas (and often only certain postcodes within those areas). But the 'once in, stay in' principle of UC (circular HB A19/2013) means that you continue within the UC scheme even if your circumstances change or you move into a different area – and when this happens you cannot get HB (except in specified supported accommodation).

SPC-for-rent cases

2.9 It is expected (para 1.18) that, from a date to be decided but probably not before 2017, the following 'SPC-for-rent cases' will be unable to get HB for rent unless they are in specified supported accommodation (paras 2.37-39):

(a) those on SPC whose SPC assessment includes a housing credit element for rent ('SPC-for rent'); and

(b) those who fall within the SPC-for-rent scheme even if they do not claim SPC or are not entitled to it.

Care leavers aged under 18

2.10 If you are a 16 or 17-year-old who has left local authority care you may not be entitled to HB (paras 2.11-13). Responsibility for providing your support falls on the social services authority.

2.11 Except as described below (para 2.13) if you are a 16 or 17-year-old you are not entitled to HB if you:

(a) have been looked after (in Scotland, looked after and 'accommodated') by social services for a period or periods amounting to at least 13 weeks in total which began after you reached the age of 14 and which ended after you reached the age of 16; or

(b) in England, Wales or Northern Ireland, you would have satisfied condition (a) but for the fact that at the time you reached the age of 16 you were in hospital or detained in an institution as the result of a court order.

2.12 In calculating the 13 weeks, any periods of four weeks or less you spent in respite care are ignored if at the end of each period you returned to the care of your parent (or the person with parental responsibility). In Scotland 'accommodated' includes instances where you were placed under a supervision requirement following a children's hearing.

2.13 The exclusion from HB does not apply:

(a) in England, Wales and Northern Ireland if you were placed with a family for a continuous period of six months or more unless that placement broke down and you stopped living with the person concerned. This rule applies whether the six month period started before or after social services finished looking after you;

(b) in Scotland if you were placed by social services with a member of your family aged at least 18 or with the person who was looking after you before you went into care.

2.10   Children Act 1989 sch 2 para 19B; Children (Leaving Care) Act 2000 s6; Children (Leaving Care) Act (Northern Ireland) 2002 s6; SI 2001 No 2189 (W) as amended by SI 2004 No 1732; SI 2001 No 2874 (E); SI 2004 No 747 (S); NISR 2005 No 221

2.13   SI 2004 No 747 Reg 2 (2)(c); NISR 2005 No 324 Reg 2(2)

Migrants and recent arrivals

2.14   If you are a migrant or recent arrival to the UK you may not be able to get HB for rent or rates (paras 20.1-2 and table 20.1). All the rules about your eligibility in these circumstances are in chapters 20 and 21.

Full-time students

2.15   If you are a full-time student you cannot get HB for rent or rates unless you fall within certain eligible groups (para 22.9 and table 22.1). All the student rules are in chapter 22.

Members of religious orders

2.16   If you are a member of a religious order and fully maintained by it (disregarding any liability you have to make payments for your accommodation) you are treated as not liable and therefore not entitled to HB. This applies for example to monks or nuns in enclosed orders. The DWP (GM A3.257) points out that members of religious communities (as opposed to religious orders) are often eligible for HB since they frequently do paid work or retain their own possessions.

Which housing payments can HB meet?

2.17   This section explains the types of housing payments that can be met by HB and which cannot. (For specified supported accommodation see also paras 2.37-39, and for rates in Northern Ireland see chapter 11.) Payments that can be met by HB all count as 'rent' for HB purposes and are taken into account in the assessment of your HB (para 2.41). Help with housing payments that can't be met by HB may be included in your other benefits (chapter 25).

'Tenant'

2.18   If you make periodical payments to occupy your accommodation as a home (such as rent payments if you are a tenant or a licence fee if you are a licensee) these payments are eligible for HB. This includes such payments made for self-contained or shared accommodation, whether or not furniture, meals or services are provided. The exceptions are given below. In this guide, the term 'tenant' is used to indicate anyone who makes such periodical payments not just tenants but also licensees and others (table 2.2).

Owner-occupiers and long leaseholders

2.19   If you own your home, or your partner does, you are not eligible for HB for rent. This is also the case even if you only have the right to sell the freehold with the consent of other joint owners. It also applies to a long leaseholder. A long lease ('long tenancy') is one which is for more than 21 years when it is first granted, and complies with the legal formalities of being a lease: R(H) 3/07.

2.16   HB 9(1)(j); HB60+ 9(1)(j); NIHB 9(1)(j); NIHB60+ 9(1)(j)

2.18   HB 12(1); HB60+ 12(1); NIHB 13(1); NIHB60+ 13(1)

2.19   HB 2(1) defs: 'owner', 'long-tenancy', 12(2)(a),(c),(f); HB60+ 2(1), 12(2)(a),(c),(f); NIHB 2(1), 13(2)(a); NIHB60+ 2(1), 13(2)(a)

Shared owners

2.20   In Great Britain you are eligible for HB on your rent if you are a shared owner (paras 9.86-87). You are a shared owner (also called an equity sharer) if you are someone who is part-buying and part-renting your home – which can be from a social landlord or from a private firm.

Co-owners

2.21   If you are a co-owner the payments under a co-ownership scheme are not eligible for HB. A co-ownership scheme is one in which you are a member entitled to a payment related to the value of the home when your membership ends.

Co-op tenants

2.22   If you are a tenant of a co-operative you are eligible for HB for your rent if you have no more than a nominal equity share in the co-op (GM A4.170-4.172).

Hire purchase, credit sale or conditional sale agreements

2.23   If you make periodical payments for your accommodation under a hire purchase agreement (for example to buy a mobile home or furniture), a credit sale agreement, or a conditional sale agreement these are not eligible for HB except to the extent that the agreement is a conditional sale agreement for land.

Rental purchase agreements

2.24   A rental purchase agreement is where you acquire ownership of the accommodation by paying the whole or part of the purchase price by instalments over a fixed period of time (GM A4.140). The accommodation remains your landlord's until you make the final payment and become the owner. If you make payments under a rental purchase agreement these are eligible for HB.

Not for profit voluntary organisations

2.25   Payments to these are eligible for HB. Whether a landlord meets this description can involve looking at all the circumstances (not just the landlord's written constitution); and it is a 'commercial reality' that a voluntary organisation is likely to have contracts with profit-making third parties: [2013] UKUT 291(AAC).

2.20   HB 2(1) defs: 'shared ownership tenancy', 12(2)(a); HB60+ 2(1), 12(2)(a)

2.21   HB 2(1) def: 'co-ownership scheme', 12(2)(b); HB60+ 2(1), 12(2)(b)

2.22   HB 12(1); HB60+ 12(1); NIHB 13(1); NIHB60+ 13(1)

2.23   HB 12(2)(d); HB60+ 12(2)(d); NIHB 13(2)(b); NIHB60+ 13(2)(b)

2.24   HB 12(1)(i); HB60+ 12(1)(i); NIHB 13(1)(h); NIHB60+ 13(1)(h)

2.25   HB 2(1) def: 'voluntary organisation' HB60+ 2(1), NIHB 2(1); NIHB60+ 2(1)

Registered charities

2.26   Payments to a registered charity are eligible for HB. A registered charity (while not defined for HB purposes) is one which is registered with the Charity Commission [www] or the Scottish Charity Regulator [www].

Charitable almshouses

2.27   In Great Britain, contributions payable by you if you are resident in a charitable almshouse provided by a housing association (para 7.10) are eligible for HB if they are towards the cost of maintenance and essential services in the association's almshouses.

Crofts

2.28   In Scotland, if your home is on or relates to a croft, payments in respect of the croft land are eligible for HB.

Houseboats, caravans and mobile homes

2.29   Houseboat mooring charges and berthing fees, and caravan and mobile home site charges, are eligible for HB and so is the rent if you rent it. 'Houseboat' can include a canal narrow boat 'fitted out as a dwelling suitable for permanent residence' (R(H) 9/08). There are also rules about when your rent is referred to the rent officer (paras 9.35-38) and how your HB is paid (para 16.15).

Hostels generally

2.30   Payments on a hostel are eligible for HB (but see also paras 2.31-32). For HB purposes a hostel is any building:

(a) that provides domestic accommodation which is not self-contained, together with meals or adequate facilities for preparing food; and which is:

■   managed or owned by a registered housing association (para 7.8); or

■   run on a non-commercial basis, and wholly or partly funded by a government department or agency or local authority; or

■   managed by a registered charity or not for profit voluntary organisation which provides care, support or supervision to help people be rehabilitated or resettled within the community (table 9.1); and

(b) which is not a care home, independent hospital (para 2.34) or Abbeyfield Home.

For specified supported accommodation and local authority hostels, see table 2.1.

2.26   Charities Act 2011, Charities and Trustee Investment (Scotland) Act 2005
        www.gov.uk/government/organisations/charity-commission; www.oscr.org.uk/

2.27   HB 12(1)(h); HB60+ 12(1)(h)

2.28   HB 12(1)(j); HB60+ 12(1)(j)

2.29   HB 12(1)(f),(g) sch 2 para 3(1),(4); HB60+ 12(1)(f),(g) sch 2 para 3(1),(4);
        NIHB 13(1)(f),(g); NIHB60+ 13(1)(f),(g)

2.30   HB 2(1) def: 'hostel', 12(1)(b); HB60+ 2(1),12(1)(b); NIHB 2(1),13(1)(b); NIHB60+ 2(1),13(1)(b)

Bail and probation hostels

2.31   Payments on an approved bail or probation hostel ('Approved Premises') are not eligible for HB because the authority must treat you as not occupying such accommodation as your home. If you are resident in such a hostel you may however be eligible for HB on the normal home from which you are absent (table 3.1).

Night shelters

2.32   Payments on a night shelter are eligible for HB only if the shelter counts as your home (para 3.5).

Tents, etc

2.33   Payments on a tent and its pitch are not eligible for HB but help with these costs may be included in your passport benefits (chapter 25).

Care homes and independent hospitals

2.34   If you are liable to make payments in respect of a 'care home' or 'an independent hospital' you are treated (subject to certain transitional provisions) as not liable to make such payments for HB purposes and are not eligible for HB. In Scotland the equivalent institutions are known as the 'care home service' and 'independent healthcare service' and in Northern Ireland 'residential care homes', 'nursing homes' and 'independent hospitals'. If the residence is temporary see paragraphs 3.21-22, 3.32-34 and table 3.1. In England and Wales an establishment is a care home if it provides you with accommodation, together with nursing or 'personal care', Accommodation is not a care home however unless the care which it provides includes required assistance with bodily functions. Care homes are required to be registered with the Care Quality Commission. In Scotland a 'care home service' is a service which provides accommodation, together with nursing, 'personal care' or personal support for you because of your vulnerability or need.

Crown tenants, etc

2.35   In Great Britain, if you are a Crown tenant or a tenant of a government department you are excluded from HB, unless your home is managed by the Crown Estate Commissioners or the Duchy of Cornwall or Duchy of Lancaster. In Northern Ireland, only tenants of the Ministry of Defence are excluded from HB. If you are excluded by this rule you can get help towards your rent on a passport benefit (chapter 25) or from a voluntary scheme run by your landlord.

Former Crown tenants

2.36   If you are a former Crown tenant (or licensee) you are eligible for HB. This applies when your agreement has been terminated but you are continuing to occupy and liable to pay mesne or violent profits. (See GM A3.213.)

2.31   HB 7(5); HB60+ 7(5); NIHB 7(5); NIHHB60+ 7(5)

2.34   HB 2(1) defs: 'care home', 'independent hospital', 9(1)(k),(4); HB60+ 9(1)(k),(4); NIHB 2(1), 9(1)(k),(4); NIHB60+ 9(1)(k),(4); CPR sch 3 para 9; NICPR sch 3 para 9

2.35   HB 2(1) def: 'Crown tenant' 12(2)(e); HB60+ 2(1) 12(2)(e); NIHB 2(1) 13(2)(c); NIHB60+ 2(1) 13(2)(c)

Specified supported accommodation

2.37 This section is about specified supported accommodation (also called 'specified accommodation' in the law). There are four types of such accommodation, and the definition of each type is given in table 2.1. Accommodation is specified supported accommodation if it falls within one of those definitions or more than one of them.

2.38 If you reside in supported accommodation you are eligible for HB. Two key points apply:

(a) you can get HB even if you are on UC (paras 2.7 and 2.39);

(b) you are unlikely to be affected by the HB benefit cap (para 6.34).

If you live in exempt accommodation (table 2.1), both the above points have applied since April 2013. If you live in other forms of specified supported accommodation (table 2.1), point (b) applies from 10th April 2014 and point (a) from 3rd November 2014.

Table 2.1 **Specified supported accommodation types**

(a) Exempt accommodation[1]

Accommodation provider:[2]

- a housing association, registered or unregistered (para 7.10); or
- a registered charity (para 2.26); or
- a not for profit voluntary organisation (para 2.25); or
- an English non-metropolitan county council.

Condition:

- the accommodation provider, or someone on its behalf, provides you with CSS.[3]

(b) General supported accommodation[4]

Accommodation provider:[5]

- a housing association, registered or unregistered (para 7.10); or
- a registered charity; or
- a not for profit voluntary organisation; or
- an English county council which has a district council for each part of its area.

Conditions:

- you get CSS[3] from the accommodation provider or someone else; and
- you were admitted into the accommodation in order to meet a need for CSS.

2.37-38   HB 75H; UC sch 1 paras 1,3(e),3A; UCTP 15(1),(2),(2A); SI 2014/771

T2.1   HB 2(1) defs: 'hostel' 'housing association' 'voluntary organisation', 75H

(c) Domestic violence refuges

Accommodation provider:[2]

- a housing association, registered or unregistered; or
- a registered charity; or
- a not for profit voluntary organisation; or
- an English county council which has a district council for each part of its area; or
- an authority which administers HB (para 1.28).

Conditions:

- the building (or relevant part of it) is wholly or mainly used as non-permanent accommodation for people who have left their home as a result of domestic violence;[5] and
- the accommodation is provided to you for that reason.

(d) Local authority hostels

Accommodation owner/manager:

- the building must be owned or managed by an authority which administers HB.

Conditions:

- you get CSS[3] from the accommodation provider or someone else; and
- the building provides non-self-contained domestic accommodation with meals or adequate food-preparation facilities (and is not a care home or independent hospital: para 2.34).

Notes

1. *Exempt accommodation:* See paras 9.2-30 and table 9.1. Resettlement places are also supported accommodation (para 9.6).

2. *Accommodation provider:* In exempt accommodation this must be your immediate landlord (para 9.5), and this is likely to be the case in types (b) and (c).

3. *Care, support or supervision (CSS):* See the first part of table 9.1. The cases there are about exempt accommodation, and are also likely to apply to types (b) and (d) (but in types (b) and (d) it need not be provided by the landlord).

4. *General supported accommodation:* This differs from exempt accommodation in two main ways:
   - the CSS can be provided or commissioned independently of the landlord;
   - you must have been 'admitted' into the accommodation in order to get CSS.

5. *Domestic violence:* This is defined as including: controlling or coercive behaviour, violence, or psychological, physical, sexual, emotional, financial or other abuse, regardless of the gender or sexuality of the victim.

2.39   During the transition to UC, if you are in specified supported accommodation you are only likely to be on UC if you were already getting it before you moved in (paras 2.8 and 17.31). Apart from that, you are likely to be among the last group to be brought within the UC scheme. In the long term it is likely that HB for supported accommodation will be replaced by a separate scheme administered by local authorities.

Liability to pay rent

2.40   The general rule is that to be eligible for HB you must be liable (have a legal obligation or duty) to pay rent for the home (or be treated by the authority as so liable).

The meaning of 'rent'

2.41   While the term rent is usually a reference to the payments made by a tenant to a landlord under the terms of a tenancy agreement, for HB purposes all of the types of payment shown in table 2.2 count as rent.

Table 2.2 **Payments counted as rent for HB purposes**

(a) Rent payable under a tenancy agreement, a licence fee, board and lodging payments and payments for 'use and occupation'.

(b) 'Mesne profits' in England, Wales and Northern Ireland or 'violent profits' in Scotland (paid after a tenancy or right to occupy is terminated).

(c) Houseboat mooring charges and berthing fees and caravan and mobile home site charges (even if the caravan or mobile home is owned by you, and in addition to rental if not owned).

(d) Payments under rental purchase agreements.

(e) Payments made by residents of charitable almshouses.

(f) Payments for crofts in Scotland.

For further details, see paras 2.17-39.

2.42   This guide distinguishes between your:

(a) 'actual rent' – this means the total of all payments in table 2.2 which you are liable to pay on your home; and

(b) 'eligible rent' – this means the (often lower) figure used in assessing your HB. It is described in more detail in chapters 7-10.

The nature of liability for rent

2.43   Liability for rent arises under a tenancy, but for HB includes any kind of 'periodical payments' made in return for the right to occupy a dwelling (para 2.40). There is no requirement for a written agreement (GM A3.50): word of mouth alone may be sufficient:

2.40   CBA 130(1)(a); NICBA 129(1)(a); HB 8(1)(a); NIHB 8(1)(a); NIHB60+ 8(1)(a)

2.43   R v Poole BC ex p Ross, QBD 05/05/95 28 HLR 351

R v Poole BC ex p Ross. The landlord normally has a sufficient legal interest in the dwelling to grant you the letting, but circumstances can arise where a landlord does not have such an interest but nevertheless can still create a liability upon which HB is payable: CH/2959/2006 at [21]-[22].

2.44   Most landlords would expect to end the agreement if a tenant does not pay and large arrears may suggest that there is no genuine liability: CH/1849/2007. But the fact that there has been no payment of the rent 'even for an extensive period, does not of itself mean there is no legal liability' [2010] UKUT 43 AAC and nor is this necessarily implied by the fact that the rent actually changing hands is less than the rent on the tenancy agreement.

2.45   It is not possible in law for you to grant a tenancy to yourself: Rye v Rye; nor can liability arise under a tenancy 'granted' to you if you already have the right to occupy that dwelling. For example, if you are one of a couple and are joint owners of a property and your partner leaves, your partner cannot 'grant' a tenancy to you as the remaining occupier.

2.46   If you are unable to act, or are aged under 18, you may have someone appointed to act for you (paras 5.5-7). If you don't and are incapable of understanding the agreement you are entering (lack capacity), this can make the agreement void under Scottish law following a 'transaction by transaction approach' to deciding legal capacity: [2012] AACR 20; but does not do so in the rest of the UK: CH/2121/2006 and [2012] UKUT 12 (AAC).

Illegal and unlawful tenancies and sub-tenancies

2.47   Sub-tenancies created in breach of a clause in the head lease not to sublet or assign the tenancy do not prevent the assignment or sub-letting from being valid between the head tenant and sub-tenant: Governors of Peabody Donation Fund v Higgins (not a HB case). Such lettings are unlawful rather than illegal and expose the head tenant to eviction for breach of the agreement. Given that there is a legal liability for rent it seems that these lettings are eligible for HB, unless it is also a letting to which paragraphs 2.55-74 apply.

2.48   An illegal letting is one in which its creation would necessarily involve committing a criminal offence. An example is where a landlord lets a dwelling knowing it to be in contravention of a Housing Act prohibition order. In contrast to unlawful contracts, illegal contracts are generally not binding and so would not be eligible for HB. Where a letting was not illegal when it was created (e.g. prior to a prohibition order) it seems likely that it remains binding until the end of the next rental period.

Treating you as liable to make payments even when you are not

2.49   If you fit one of the descriptions below (paras 2.50-54) you may be eligible for HB even though you are not liable for rent etc (so long as you meet the other conditions: para 2.2). The law says that you are 'treated as liable to make payments'.

2.45   Rye v. Rye [1962] A.C. 496

2.47   Governors of the Peabody Donation Fund v Higgins 20/06/83 CA (1983) 1 WLR 1091, 10 HLR 82

You are the liable person's partner

2.50 If you are in a couple (or in a polygamous marriage) and only a partner is liable for rent, the authority should normally treat you as liable to make payments. For example, if your partner is the liable person and a full-time student who is not eligible for HB (para 22.9) and you are not liable for rent because your name is not on the tenancy agreement, you can nevertheless be treated as liable and therefore eligible for HB.

Former partners and others and the liable person is not paying the rent

2.51 If the liable person is not paying the rent, the authority should treat you as liable if you have to make payments in order to continue living in the home and you are:

(a) the liable person's former partner (current partners are covered instead by the rule in para 2.50); or

(b) someone else the authority considers it reasonable to treat as liable. An example might be a son or daughter left in occupation where the tenant is now living in a care home or independent hospital.

Examples: Treated as liable to pay rent

Megan has been deserted by her partner Ffion. Although Megan is not the tenant, the landlord will allow her to remain in the property if she continues to pay the rent. The authority should treat Megan as liable if her former partner is not paying.

Logan is the son of a council tenant. He takes over responsibility for paying the rent while his father is working abroad. Logan should be treated as liable to make payments if it is reasonable to do so.

2.52 This rule helps someone who could perhaps arrange to become the tenant (but who has not done so) remain in their home. It can be used if the liable person has been absent for too long to get HB (para 3.32), or has left permanently, and a partner or other person remains. The liable person need not be an individual; they could be a company or other body (R(H) 5/05) – including, presumably, the executors of a deceased tenant. If you claim under this rule you still need to meet the requirements relating to National Insurance numbers (para 5.16), [2013] UKUT 321 (AAC). The test of reasonableness does not apply to you if you are a former partner of the liable person: for you, the rule is automatic. For anyone else claiming under this rule, the test of reasonableness applies. In particular, if the only reason the liable person is not paying is that they are excluded from HB (paras 2.55-74) then it may not be reasonable to award HB to you (CSHB/606/2005).

2.50 HB 8(1)(b); HB60+ 8(1)(b); NIHB 8(1)(b); NIHB60+ 8(1)(b)

2.51 HB 8(1)(c); HB60+ 8(1)(c); NIHB 8(1)(c); NIHB60+ 8(1)(c)

When your rent is waived in return for work you do on the home

2.53 If your rent is waived by your landlord the authority should still treat you as liable – but only:

(a) if the waiver is reasonable compensation for reasonable repairs or redecoration work actually carried out by you; and

(b) for up to eight weeks in respect of any one waiver of liability.

Rent already paid or varied

2.54 If you have already paid your rent wholly or partly in advance you are nonetheless treated as liable for it over the period it is due. If your rent liability is varied during that period you are treated as liable for the revised amount due.

'Contrived' lettings and other exclusions from HB

2.55 The rest of this chapter describes the circumstances in which you cannot get HB, even though you are in fact liable for rent. The law does this by saying that you are treated as not liable to make payments. The term 'contrived' does not appear in the legislation, but is commonly used for the lettings described in para 2.74.

Non-commercial agreements

2.56 You are not eligible for HB if the agreement under which you occupy the accommodation is not on a commercial basis. In reaching its decision the authority must consider whether the agreement contains terms which are not legally enforceable. The regulations do not define what constitutes a commercial basis and how each should be decided but this has been considered by the courts and tribunals. Table 2.3 provides a summary of the case law and guidance.

Table 2.3 **Non-commercial agreements**

■ *General principles in reaching a decision on commerciality:* Each case must be decided on its facts and is a matter of judgment (R(H) 1/03) but the concept is 'notoriously imprecise and difficult' (CH/2491/2007). An arrangement is non-commercial if the main basis on which it is made is not commercial even if the original purpose was commercial, so long as the reasons for the change can be identified: CH/3497/2005.

■ *Relevant matters to be taken into account:* These are not limited to the financial relationship: all the terms of the agreement should be considered (R v Sutton LBC ex parte Partridge). The important factor is whether the arrangements are 'arms

---

2.53   HB 8(1)(d); HB60+ 8(1)(d); NIHB 8(1)(d); NIHB60+ 8(1)(d)

2.54   HB 8(2); HB60+ 8(2); NIHB 8(2); NIHB60+ 8(2)

2.56   HB 9(1)(a),(2); HB60+ 9(1)(a),(2); NIHB 9(1)(a),(2); NIHB60+ 9(1)(a),(2)

length' or more akin to arrangements between close relatives contributing towards their keep or household expenses: R v Sheffield HBRB ex parte Smith.

■ *Sham legal agreements:* The true factual basis of the arrangements is what matters: if they indicate that the letting is a 'truly personal arrangement' then it will be non-commercial even though the written documents give the appearance of legal liability: CH/3282/2006.

■ *Lettings to family members and/or people with disabilities:* A letting by a parent to a disabled child could be commercial. While a family arrangement may indicate that the letting is non-commercial it is one factor and not decisive. The fact that the landlord might not evict but accept a lower rent if HB was not awarded is not evidence that it is non-commercial but bowing to the inevitable. Proper weight should be given to all factors and focusing on one aspect only (such as care and support) is grounds for appeal (CH/296/2004). However, more recent decisions have described the law as 'ill-suited to providing humane outcomes in these cases' and have sometimes found these arrangements to be non-commercial (CH/1096/2008 and CH/2491/2007).

■ *Lettings to former foster children:* The DWP (HB/CTB A30/95) advised that arrangements for paying rent (e.g. when the child reaches age 18) should generally be treated as commercial.

■ *Personal friendship between the parties:* Of itself this cannot turn a commercial arrangement into a non-commercial one (R v Poole BC ex parte Ross and CH/4854/2003). Nor can the fact that the claimant cared for the landlord after an accident: [2009] UKUT 13 AAC.

■ *Arrangements that take into account the claimant's religion:* If an arrangement has all the characteristics of something that is non-commercial, the fact it takes into account the religious beliefs of the claimant cannot make it commercial. Nor does this fact infringe their right to freedom of religion (R(H) 8/04).

Landlord is a close relative residing in the dwelling

2.57   If your landlord is a 'close relative' (para 2.58), or your partner's close relative and the landlord also resides in the dwelling (para 2.60), you are not eligible for HB.

2.58   A 'close relative' is:

(a)   a parent, step-parent or parent-in-law; or

(b)   a brother or sister; or

(c)   a son, son-in-law, daughter, daughter-in-law, step-son, step-daughter; or

(d)   a partner of any of the above.

T2.3   R v Sutton LBC ex p Partridge QBD 04/11/94 28 HLR 315; R v Sheffield HBRB ex p Smith QBD 08/12/94 28 HLR 36; R v Poole HBRB ex p Ross QBD 05/05/95 28 HLR 351

2.57   HB 9(1)(b); HB60+ 9(1)(b); NIHB 9(1)(b); NIHB60+ 9(1)(b)

2.58   HB 2(1) def: 'close relative'; HB60+ 2(1); NIHB 2(1); NIHB60+ 2(1)

2.59   The terms 'brother' and 'sister' include 'half-brothers' and 'half-sisters' (GM paras A3.240-241 and R(SB) 22/87), but not 'step-brothers' or 'step-sisters'.

2.60   For your landlord to count as 'residing in' the same dwelling as you (para 2.57), it is not necessary to share all the accommodation, merely some essential living accommodation: CH/542/2006. Similarly, if you have exclusive possession of one room in a house, this does not mean that the landlord is not residing with you: CH/3656/2004. Despite the slight difference of wording, the definition of 'residing with' (para 4.43) also applies here (GM A3.238).

Renting a former joint home from an ex-partner

2.61   If you separate from your partner and your liability is to your former partner for accommodation that you both occupied when you were together then you are treated as not liable and thus not eligible for HB. This rule also applies if your liability is to your partner's former partner and is in respect of accommodation they both occupied before they separated.

2.62   The rule applies if the informal shared living arrangements changed but the dwelling overall did not, for example, if you are a tenant and you form a relationship with your landlord but then revert to being a tenant. This exclusion does not constitute discrimination under the Human Rights Act: R (Painter) v Carmarthenshire County Council HBRB and [2011] UKUT 301 (AAC).

Responsibility for your landlord's child

2.63   You are not eligible for HB if you, or your partner, are responsible for the landlord's child (i.e. someone under the age of 16). The DWP (GM A3.269) emphasises that 'responsibility for a child' means more than 'cares for'.

2.64   This rule is difficult to interpret as it blurs certain established concepts so far as means-tested benefits are concerned. It appears to apply where the 'landlord' is the parent, or has adopted a child, but where the child is nevertheless considered to be part of your family for JSA(IB), IS or HB purposes. This rule has been found not to be contrary to the Human Rights Act: R v Secretary of State for Social Security, ex parte Tucker.

Certain trusts

2.65   A trust is an arrangement whereby the legal ownership (title) of property is separated from its benefits (such as the right to live in it or get an income from it). The title is held by the trustees who ensure that its benefits are delivered for use by someone else, 'the beneficiary'.

2.61   HB 9(1)(c); HB60+ 9(1)(c); NIHB 9(1)(c); NIHB60+ 9(1)(c)

2.62   R (Painter) v Carmarthenshire County Council HBRB & Anor [2001] EWHC Admin 308 04/05/01
         www.bailii.org/ew/cases/EWHC/Admin/2001/308.html

2.63   HB 9(1)(d); HB60+ 9(1)(d); NIHB 9(1)(d); NIHB60+ 9(1)(d)

2.64   R v Secretary of State for Social Security, ex p Tucker 08/11/01 [2001] EWCA Civ 1646
         www.bailii.org/ew/cases/EWCA/Civ/2001/1646.html

2.66   You are not eligible for HB if your landlord is a trustee of a trust of which one of the following is a trustee or a beneficiary:

(a)   you or your partner;

(b)   your or your partner's close relative (para 2.58) if the close relative 'resides with' (para 4.43) you; or

(c)   your former partner or your partner's former partner.

'Beneficiary' here means someone who could benefit from the trust by occupying the property in question: [2009] UKUT 7 (AAC).This disentitlement does not apply however where you are able to satisfy the authority that the liability was not intended to be a means of taking advantage of the HB scheme.

2.67   You are not eligible for HB if your landlord is a trustee of a trust of which your child or your partner's child is a beneficiary. Unlike in the previous paragraph, this rule has no exception.

Renting from a company of which you are a director or an employee

2.68   You are not eligible for HB if your landlord is a company of which one of the following is a director or an employee;

(a)   you or your partner;

(b)   your or your partner's close relative (para 2.58) if the close relative 'resides with' (para 4.43) you ; or

(c)   your former partner or your partner's former partner.

This disentitlement does not apply however where you are able to satisfy the authority that the liability was not intended to be a means of taking advantage of the HB scheme. Note also that this rule does not apply if you are employed by a company and rent from a director of the company (since a director is not the company itself).

2.69   The DWP advises (GM para A3.271) that a 'company' means a registered company. This can be checked online with Companies House for any part of the UK [www].

Former non-dependants

2.70   You are not eligible for HB if:

(a)   you were, at any time before the creation of the liability, a non-dependant of someone who resided in the dwelling; and

(b)   that person continues to reside in the dwelling.

This disentitlement does not apply however where you are able to satisfy the authority that the liability was not intended to be a means of taking advantage of the HB scheme.

2.66   HB 9(1)(e),(3); HB60+ 9(1)(e),(3); NIHB 9(1)(e),(3); NIHB60+ 9(1)(e),(3)

2.67   HB 9(1)(f); HB60+ 9(1)(f); NIHB 9(1)(f); NIHB60+ 9(1)(f)

2.68   HB 9(1)(e),(3); HB60+ 9(1)(e),(3); NIHB 9(1)(e),(3); NIHB60+ 9(1)(e),(3)

2.69   www.gov.uk/get-information-about-a-company

2.70   HB 9(1)(g),(3); HB60+ 9(1)(g),(3); NIHB 9(1)(g),(3); NIHB60+ 9(1)(g),(3)

Former owners (sale and rent back or mortgage rescue)

2.71   You are not eligible for HB if:

(a) you, or a partner, previously owned the dwelling (including owning it on a long lease: para 2.19); and

(b) owned it within the last five years (even if you subsequently moved out and then back in: CH/3698/2008).

This disentitlement does not apply however where you are able to satisfy the authority that you or your partner could not have continued to live in the dwelling without giving up ownership. Good advice on this is given in DWP circular HB/CTB A5/2009 in the light of the increasing number of these cases, also known as 'sale and rent back' cases.

2.72   Whether you could have remained in the dwelling is a practical test based on fact – and in exceptional cases this can include your perceptions if the stress of the situation you were in forced a quick sale: R(H) 6/07. Authorities are entitled to examine why you gave up ownership and what other options you might have had, such as getting work to finance the mortgage, taking in a tenant, etc: CH/1586/2004. You are not expected to act irresponsibly (e.g. using a credit card to pay mortgage arrears): CH/2340/2008. You may have had no real choice if a mortgage lender would have sought possession and a housing association used a mortgage rescue scheme to buy the property and rent it back to you (GM A3.282-286).

Tied accommodation

2.73   You are not eligible for HB if your, or a partner's, occupation of the dwelling is a condition of employment by the landlord. The DWP advises (GM A3.291) that this test should not be taken to mean 'as a result of the employment'. A retired employee, for example, may continue to live in previously tied accommodation but this would no longer be as a condition of employment by the landlord, and so this rule would not prevent eligibility for HB.

Contrived liability

2.74   You are not eligible for HB if the authority is satisfied that your liability 'was created to take advantage of the HB scheme' (usually called a 'contrived' tenancy). The regulations do not describe what constitutes a contrived tenancy but this has been considered by the courts and tribunals. Table 2.4 provides a summary of the case law and further guidance can be found in GM paragraphs A3.310-319.

2.71   HB 9(1)(h),(ha); HB60+ 9(1)(h),(ha); NIHB 9(1)(h),(ha); NIHB60+ 9(1)(h),(ha)

2.73   HB 9(1)(i); HB60+ 9(1)(i); NIHB 9(1)(i); NIHB60+ 9(1)(i)

2.74   HB 9(1)(l); HB60+ 9(1)(l); NIHB 9(1)(l); NIHB60+ 9(1)(l)

Table 2.4 **Case law on contrived liabilities**

- *Liability and taking advantage of the HB scheme:* These are separate considerations and should not be confused: CSHB/718/2002.

- *The circumstances and intentions of both parties are relevant:* The authority must consider these before reaching a conclusion that the liability is contrived. Particular consideration should be given to the consequences if HB is not paid. If it seems unlikely that the landlord will ask you to leave so that the dwelling can be re-let then this is evidence that the liability is contrived: R v Sutton HBRB ex p Keegan.

- *Letting to relatives:* Except where the liability is excluded from HB by one of the other provisions in this section (paras 2.57-73) accommodation provided by a parent to their children is not of itself evidence of a contrived liability: R v Solihull HBRB ex p Simpson.

- *Letting to people on low incomes generally:* The mere fact that you could not afford the rent cannot be taken as evidence that the liability is contrived although in extreme cases a high rent may support that contention. Before the authority can reach a conclusion that the liability is contrived there must be clear evidence that this is so, it cannot merely be inferred (Solihull case).

- *Letting to people on low incomes to make a profit:* There is no objection to landlords doing this and landlords may even organise their affairs to 'maximise the amounts payable by HB'. In doing so 'the size of the charges and the profit [that results] are relevant [...] only in so far as they show abuse' (see next bullet): CH/39/2007.

- *Charging higher rents to groups outside the normal rent restriction rules:* These types of arrangement may be a factor in considering whether the liability has been created to take advantage of the scheme. For example lettings to vulnerable tenants (para 9.25); or complex arrangements designed to take advantage of specific rules such as 'exempt accommodation' (paras 9.9-12). (R v Manchester CC ex p Baragrove Properties; CH/3933/2006 and CH/136/2007).

T2.4   R v Sutton HBRB ex p Keegan 15/05/92 QBD 27 HLR 92
         R v Solihull HBRB ex p Simpson 03/12/93 QBD 26 HLR 370 & 05/05/94 CA 27 HLR 41
         R v Manchester CC ex p Baragrove Properties 15/03/91 QBD 23 HLR 337

Chapter 3 **Occupying the home**

■ What it means to occupy somewhere as a home: see paras 3.1-5.

■ When you can get HB before moving into your home, after moving out, and on two homes: see paras 3.6-30.

■ The rules about temporary absences from home: see paras 3.31-45.

Occupation as a home

3.1 HB is awarded on accommodation you occupy as a home. This means the dwelling which is 'normally occupied as a home' by:

(a) you; or

(b) you and your family (CH/2521/2002) – if you have a family (para 4.8).

3.2 HB can be awarded on only one home except as described in paras 3.7, 3.12, 3.18, 3.24 and 3.27.

Normally occupied as a home

3.3 Whether a dwelling is 'normally occupied as a home' is a question of fact to be decided in each case, and is not restricted to considering where your 'centre of interests' is (CH/1786/2005). It usually means more than simply being liable for rent: it means being physically present – but exceptions can arise. For example, a claimant aged 87 who had terminated her former tenancy, whose family had moved her furniture and possessions into her new home, but who was unable to move because she was taken ill at the last minute, was held to be 'normally occupying her new home' (R(H) 9/05). However, accommodation you occupy only for a holiday or business purposes is not a home and is therefore not eligible for HB.

3.4 In considering which home you normally occupy, the authority must have regard to any other dwelling you or your family occupy, no matter whether it is here or abroad. The DWP advises (GM para A3.356) that this requirement is not intended to exclude someone who has set up home in this country but whose family, no longer being part of his or her household, remain abroad.

Night shelters

3.5 A night shelter may or may not meet the definition of a 'dwelling [...] occupied as [the claimant's] home.' If it does not, you are not eligible for HB (paras 2.2-3). This is the effect of [2013] UKUT 65 (AAC) which held that 'a person who is allowed to stay overnight (for a charge) at a night shelter but is not allowed to remain there during the day and so has to leave in the morning taking all of his belongings with him, and has no right to stay in any part of the night shelter or indeed right generally to stay there (in the sense that if he turns up late

3.1   CBA 130(1)(a); NICBA 129(1)(a); HB 7(1); HB60+ 7(1); NIHB 7(1); NIHB60+ 7(1);

3.4   HB 7(2); HB60+ 7(2); NIHB 7(2); HB60+ 7(2)

and the shelter is full he will be turned away), is not occupying a dwelling as his home.' This case depended on its particular facts and states that it is not 'intended to prescribe how HB claims for rough sleepers should be decided.'

Moving home and benefit on two homes

3.6 This section describes when you can get HB before moving into your home, after moving out, and on two homes.

Remaining liable for rent on a former home

3.7 Where you have moved home, but remain liable for rent on your old home, you are eligible for HB on:

(a) both the old and new homes, if you are liable on both and liability on both 'could not reasonably have been avoided'; or

(b) your old home, if you are liable only there and that liability 'could not reasonably have been avoided'.

But in each case this applies only for the period after you have moved into your new home, and only for up to four weeks from the date of the move. (See also para 3.9, and for calculation rules para 3.29.)

3.8 The 'two homes' version of the rule (para 3.7(a)) is also called 'the overlapping HB rule'. It often applies when someone in privately rented accommodation is offered social housing at short notice, and has to take up the new letting (and moves in) before notice on the old one has run out (see example 1).

3.9 The 'one home' version of the rule (para 3.7(b)) can apply when you move from a rented home:

(a) to live with relatives (see example 2); or

(b) to a care home – in which case it can follow on from an award of HB during a trial period (R(H) 4/06) (see para 3.32(a), and example later);

(c) to prison when sentenced – in which case it can follow on from an award of HB while on remand (para 3.32(b), table 3.1, and example later); or

(d) other accommodation where no rent is payable (or which is of a kind that is not eligible for HB as described in chapter 2).

3.10 Further considerations for both versions of the rule are as follows:

(a) you must have moved into the new home. If you have a family they must have moved in too, and must be occupying it as a home rather than preparing it for occupation (CH/1911/2006 para 19);

(b) in considering whether liability could reasonably have been avoided, the authority may look at what alternatives were open to you (CH/4546/2002);

(c) DWP advice that the claimant's circumstances should be exceptional (GM A3.682) can mislead authorities, since the only legal test is one of reasonableness;

(d) The rule does not apply when you move out for repairs to be done (para 3.23).

3.7   HB 7(6)(d),(7); HB60+ 7(6)(d),(7); NIHB 7(6)(d),(7); NIHB60+ 7(6)(d),(7)

3.11   The authority may ask you to provide evidence that the conditions for the rule are met (e.g. about liability and reasonableness). But unless you are moving from one authority area to another, there is no legal requirement for you to make a separate claim for the period in question.

Examples: Liable for rent on a former home

1. HB on both old and new homes ('overlapping HB')

Barnaby (already on HB) is living in privately rented accommodation. His rent is due monthly and notice of one month is due if he wishes to leave.

On Thursday 30th April 2015, Barnaby is invited to view a housing association property (in the same local authority area) which he is then offered and accepts. The housing association insists that the tenancy must start on Monday 4th May. On Friday 1st May Barnaby writes to his old landlord giving notice. The landlord insists that Barnaby must pay to the end of May. Barnaby moves in to his housing association home on Monday 4th May.

The authority accepts that Barnaby meets all the conditions for HB on both homes (para 3.7(a)) and awards HB from Monday 4th May for the new address and until Sunday 31st May at the old address; so HB is awarded for both homes for three weeks and six days.

2. HB on a former home

Mildred is on HB and living in housing association accommodation. Her rent is due on Mondays and notice of four weeks is due if she wishes to leave.

On Thursday 1st April 2015 Mildred's brother is found to be seriously ill and Mildred decides to go as soon as possible and live in his house to look after him. She decides to give up her housing association tenancy and gives her notice in on Monday 4th May to expire on Sunday 31st May 2015. She moves out of her housing association tenancy on Wednesday 6th May, handing the keys back the same day.

The authority accepts that Mildred meets all the conditions for HB on the address she has left (para 3.7(b)) and awards HB on the housing association tenancy up till the end of the tenancy (covering three weeks and five days from the day she left till the end of her liability).

Fleeing violence or fear of violence

3.12   You are eligible for HB on two rented homes for up to 52 weeks if you:

(a) have left and remain absent from your former home through fear of violence

   ■   in the home, or

   ■   by someone who was formerly a member of your family; and

(b) have an intention to return to it; and

(c) are liable for rent on both that home and where you are now living; and

(d) it is reasonable to award HB on both homes.

For cases involving both HB and UC, see paragraph 3.28. For the HB calculation rules see paragraphs 3.29, 15.29 and table 15.1. If you are liable for rent only on the home you have left, see paragraph 3.32(b) and table 3.1.

3.12   HB 7(6)(a); HB60+ 7(6)(a); NIHB 7(6)(a); NIHB60+ 7(6)(a)

3.13   You need not have suffered actual violence for the rule to apply. You have only to be afraid of violence occurring. If the authority considers, however, that your fear of violence is not reasonable (CH/1237/2004 para 18) or that you have brought it upon yourself, it may consider it unreasonable that HB should be paid in respect of both homes.

3.14   If your fear is of violence in your home, it need not be related to a family or former family member. It could be related to anyone, so long as you fear that violence could occur in the home. If your fear is of violence outside the home, it must be a former member of your family who poses the threat of violence. This includes not only an ex-partner but also an adult child. On the other hand, someone who is afraid of violence outside the home may well be afraid of it coming into the home.

3.15   The rule applies only if you intend to return to the home you have left. This can include your intention to return when it becomes safe to do so – for example, if you are taking steps to exclude your former partner and intend to return when that has happened. If, from the outset, you do not intend to return, HB can be paid for up to four weeks (para 3.7).

3.16   The DWP advises the authority to check regularly that you intend to return to the previous home (GM A3.631). If you subsequently decide not to return, HB on the former home stops. The HB paid on the former home while you had the intention to return will have been properly paid and is not an overpayment (GM A3.632).

Waiting for adaptations for a disability

3.17   If you become liable for rent on a new dwelling, but do not move into it straight away because you are necessarily waiting for it to be adapted to meet your disablement needs or those of a family member (para 4.8), you are eligible for HB for up to four weeks before moving in, so long as the delay in moving is reasonable. The correct test is to ask whether the change to the dwelling has made it more suitable for the needs of a disabled person. So it is not limited to works that involve a change to the fabric or structure of the dwelling and could include furnishing or redecoration: R (Mahmoudi) v Lewisham LBC.

3.18   In this case, if you are also liable for rent on your old home, you are eligible for HB on both homes during those four weeks. (For calculation rules, see para 3.29.) Whether in the case of HB for one home or two, HB can be paid only after you have moved in and the claim, or notice of the move, must be made promptly (para 3.30).

Waiting for a welfare payment, etc

3.19   If you are liable for rent on a new dwelling but do not move into it straight away you are eligible for HB on that dwelling for up to four weeks before moving in so long as:

(a)   the move was delayed pending the outcome of an application for a social fund payment or similar local authority provisions (table 13.5(j)) to help with the move or with setting up home;

3.13   HB 7(10); HB60+ 7(10); NIHB 7(10); NIHB60+ 7(10)

3.17   HB 7(6)(e); HB60+ 7(6)(e); NIHB 7(6)(e); NIHB60+ 7(6)(e)
        R (on the application of Mahmoudi) v Lewisham LBC 06/02/14 CA [2014] EWCA Civ 284 www.bailii.org/ew/cases/EWCA/Civ/2014/284.html

3.18   HB 7(8)(b)(ii),(c)(i); HB60+ 7(8)(b)(ii),(c)(i); NIHB 7(8)(c)(i); NIHB60+ 7(8)(c)(i)

3.19   HB 7(8)(c)(ii); HB60+ 7(8)(c)(ii); NIHB 7(8)(c)(ii); NIHB60+ 7(8)(c)(ii)

(b) the delay in moving is reasonable; and

(c) you have reached pension credit age (para 1.24), or have a child aged under 6, or someone in your family is disabled in one of the ways relevant to a disability premium or disabled child premium.

3.20 In this case, you are not eligible for HB on your old home as well – a feature of the rule that has been criticised as discriminating against someone moving from a furnished rented home to their first unfurnished rented home. HB can be paid only after you have moved in and your claim must be made promptly (para 3.30).

Waiting to leave hospital or a care home

3.21 If you become liable for rent on a new dwelling, but do not move into it straight away because you are waiting to leave a hospital, care home or independent hospital (para 2.34), you are eligible for HB for up to four weeks before moving in, so long as the delay in moving is reasonable.

3.22 This might arise if your departure from hospital or a care home is delayed. HB can be paid only after you have moved in and your claim must be made promptly (para 3.30).

Moving out for repairs to be done

3.23 If you have had to leave your normal home while it is having essential repairs, and you have to make payments (e.g. rent or mortgage payments) on one but not both the normal home and the temporary accommodation, you should be treated as occupying the home for which payments are made. You are then eligible for HB only on that home (if you are liable for rent there).

Large families

3.24 If your family (para 4.8) is so large that it has been housed by a housing authority (in Northern Ireland, the NIHE) in two separate dwellings, you are eligible for HB on both homes. The DWP (GM para A3.660) advises that both homes should be provided, but not necessarily owned, by the local authority. There is no time limit in this case.

What is 'one' home?

3.25 It is possible for two buildings to be one 'home' for HB purposes, for example if statutory overcrowding would otherwise arise (R(H) 5/09 para 22 and CH/4018/2007). Similar situations have arisen in relation to JSA(IB) and have been approved by the Court of Appeal (Secretary of State for Work and Pensions v Miah reported as R(JSA)9/03). Also, two flats knocked together, though rented from two landlords, might constitute 'one home' (CH/1895/2008).

3.21   HB 7(8)(c)(iii); HB60+ 7(8)(c)(iii); NIHB 7(8)(c)(iii); NIHB60+ 7(8)(c)(iii)

3.23   HB 7(4); HB60+ 7(4); NIHB 7(4); NIHB60+ 7(4)

3.24   HB 7(6)(c); HB60+ 7(6)(c); NIHB 7(6)(c); NIHB60+ 7(6)(c)

Single and lone parent students and trainees

3.26   If you are single or a lone parent and:

(a)   a student who is in the 'eligible student groups' (table 22.1); or

(b)   on a government training course (described below),

and have two homes but are liable to make payments (e.g. rent) on only one, you are treated as normally occupying that one (and are thus eligible for HB on it), even if you in fact normally live in the other one. The training courses referred to are those provided by or via the Secretary of State, a government department, Skills Development Scotland, Scottish Enterprise, or Highlands and Islands Enterprise; or by a local authority on behalf of one of those bodies, either direct or via another organisation.

Student couples

3.27   If you are one of a couple (para 4.10) you are eligible for HB on two homes if one of you is a student in the eligible groups and the other is not a student, or if both of you are students each of whom is a student in the eligible groups (table 22.1). But occupying two homes must be unavoidable and it must be reasonable to pay HB on two homes (para 22.14). There is no time limit in this case.

Two homes: HB and universal credit

3.28   The UC rules about getting a housing costs element for two homes are in some cases similar to those in HB. It is also possible to get a UC housing element for one home and HB for another – but only when the home HB is awarded for is supported accommodation (para 2.38), and only when you are fleeing violence. In this case, the HB test of reasonableness (para 3.12(d)) is whether it is reasonable to award payments (of HB and UC) on two homes.

Calculation of HB on two homes

3.29   In the cases above in which HB is awarded on two homes (paras 3.7, 3.12, 3.17, 3.24 and 3.27), the authority should calculate HB as follows:

(a)   add together the two eligible rents, then

(b)   make any non-dependant deduction(s) only once, then

(c)   subtract 65% of any excess income (para 6.8) only once ([2011] UKUT 5 (AAC) para 23).

If your two homes are in different authority areas, the two authorities must work together to achieve this – making sure in particular that no part of your income is taken into account by both authorities at the same time ([2011] UKUT 5 (AAC) para 33).

3.26   HB 7(3),(18); HB60+ 7(3),(18); NIHB 7(3),(18); NIHB60+ 7(3),(18)

3.27   HB 7(6)(b); HB60+ 7(6)(b); NIHB 7(6)(b); NIHB60+ 7(6)(b)

3.28   HB 7(6)(a)(i)

3.29   HB 80(9); HB60+ 61(11); NIHB 78(10); NIHB 60+ 59(10)

Entitlement prior to moving in: prompt claims

3.30   In the cases above in which HB is awarded before you move in (paras 3.17, 3.19 and 3.21), it is necessary to claim (or notify the move) promptly (i.e. before or in the first week of the new liability for rent) – unless HB is backdated (para 5.50). If the claim is then refused (perhaps because at that time the authority is not sure that you will in fact move in), and you reapply within four weeks, your reapplication should be treated as having been made at the same time as the refused claim. Apart from that, the authority should work out your date of claim in the normal way (paras 5.32-43). However, the payment of HB cannot start until you actually do move in.

Temporary absences from home

3.31   This section describes when you can get HB during a temporary absence from your home.

3.32   Three rules relate to temporary absences. During an absence from your home, you are eligible for HB:

(a)   for up to 13 weeks during any trial period in a care home (or immediately following that: R(H) 4/06) – so long as you intend to return to your normal home if the care home is unsuitable (but the total absence from home must not exceed 52 weeks); or

(b)   for up to 52 weeks if you are absent (in the UK or abroad) for any of the reasons in table 3.1 – so long as you intend to return to your normal home within 52 weeks or, in exceptional circumstances, not substantially later; or

(c)   for up to 13 weeks during an absence (in the UK or abroad) for any other reason – so long as you intend to return to your normal home within a strict 13 weeks.

Table 3.1 **People who can get HB during an absence of up to 52 weeks**

Claimants in prison etc, who have not yet been sentenced (para 3.39).

Claimants in a probation hostel, or a bail hostel, or bailed to live away from their normal home.

Claimants in a care home or independent hospital (para 2.34) who are not trying it out (e.g. during periods of respite care).

Claimants who are patients in hospital, or receiving medically approved* care.

Claimants undergoing medical treatment or medically approved* convalescence or who are absent because their partner or child is undergoing this.

Claimants undertaking medically approved* care of someone else.

3.30   HB 7(9); HB60+ 7(9); NIHB 7(9); NIHB60+ 7(9)

3.32   HB 7(11)-(18); HB60+ 7(11)-(18); NIHB 7(11)-(18); NIHB60+ 7(11)-(18)

T 3.1   HB 7(16)(c); HB60+ 7(16)(c); NIHB 7(16)(c); NIHB60+ 7(16)(c)

Claimants caring for a child whose parent or guardian is absent from home in order to receive medical treatment or medically approved* care.

Claimants following a training course (as defined in para 3.26).

Students who are eligible for HB (e.g. if they have to study away from home for part of their course).

Claimants absent because of fear of violence in their normal home (regardless of who it would be from) or fear of violence from a former member of their family (whether this would occur in the normal home or elsewhere). This applies to people other than those mentioned in paragraph 3.12 because, for example, they are staying with relatives and are not liable to pay rent on two homes but intend to return to occupy their original home.

* Note: 'medically approved' means approved in writing by a GP, nurse or similar – but this need not be in a formal certificate (GM A3.541).

The intention to return

3.33　　Each of the above rules requires you to intend to return to your normal home. It is your intention which is relevant (not, say, the intention of a relative or official) but your intention must be capable of being realised. In one case a claimant desired to return from his nursing home to his housing association property, but the commissioner held that to desire is not the same as to intend (CSHB/405/2005 para 30). It had been found as a fact that it was objectively impossible for the claimant to return, so the absence from home provisions could not apply to him.

Example: Trying out a care home and then deciding to stay there

Betella rents her home and has been on HB for a while. She goes into a care home for a six-week trial period to see if it suits her. Betella remains eligible for HB.

In the fourth week of her trial, Betella decides that this is the care home for her and gives four weeks' notice to her former landlord. The authority is satisfied that Betella could not reasonably have avoided the liability at her old address. She remains eligible for HB for the additional four-week period.

Additional conditions

3.34　　In each of the above cases (para 3.32), you must still be liable for rent on your normal home and the part of the home you normally occupy must not be let or sub-let.

Counting the length of the absence

3.35　　The 13-week and 52-week time limits refer to absences which are continuous: R v Penwith DC HBRB ex p Burt. So if you (with the exception of prisoners on temporary release: para 3.41) return to, and occupy the dwelling as a home, even for a short time, the allowable

---

3.34　　HB 7(11)-(17); HB60+ 7(11)-(17); NIHB 7(11)-(17); NIHB60+ 7(11)-(17)

3.35　　R v Penwith DC HBRB ex p Burt 26/02/90 QBD 22 HLR 292

period of temporary absence starts again. The DWP suggests (GM A3.460) that a stay at home lasting, for example, only a few hours may not break the absence but one that lasts at least 24 hours may do so.

3.36   Depending upon the facts of the case, however, the authority may decide that your normal home is elsewhere for HB purposes (paras 3.3-4). If another person occupying the dwelling starts paying rent in your absence the authority should consider treating that other person as liable and therefore eligible for HB (para 2.49).

3.37   The authority's assessment of whether or not your period of temporary absence is likely to exceed 13/52 weeks has to be made by reference to the date at which you left the dwelling in question (CH/1237/2004 para 12). Continued entitlement has to be judged on a week by week basis. If at any date it becomes likely that the 13/52 weeks will be exceeded, then that is a relevant change of circumstances, allowing a re-consideration of your entitlement (CH/1237/2004 para 12). Once it becomes clear that you are going to be away for more than 13 or 52 weeks, entitlement ends under the temporary absence rule (but see para 3.7(b) for the circumstances in which you may be entitled to up to four weeks' additional entitlement).

3.38   In the case of the absences in table 3.1, if your absence is unlikely to substantially exceed the 52-week period, and if there are exceptional circumstances, the authority must pay up to the end of the 52nd week of absence. DWP guidance (GM A3.532) suggests that the term 'substantially exceed' relates to periods of absence greater than 15 months. It is, however, for the individual authority to interpret the term. The GM illustrates the concept of exceptional circumstances with the examples of someone prevented from returning home by an unanticipated event, and a discharge from hospital being delayed by a relapse. Other circumstances may also be considered.

Absences in prison, etc

3.39   If you are in prison, etc, you can get HB for up to 52 weeks on your normal home until you are sentenced (table 3.1). This means that almost all prisoners on remand can get HB.

3.40   If and when you are sentenced to prison, etc, this counts as a change of circumstances. The relevant question for the authority is then: 'Will you return home within 13 weeks of when you left home?' Only if the answer is 'yes' can you continue to get HB under the temporary absence rule (CH/499/2006) – and this time limit is strict (CH/1986/2009). However, in deciding this, the authority should be aware that most fixed-term sentences qualify for remission, so claimants with a sentence of up to six months (or up to ten months if they are eligible for Home Detention Curfew) are likely to be entitled. Your own prediction of your release date is irrelevant if release could be considered earlier (CH/2638/2006, in which a parole hearing should have occurred earlier than it did). For further guidance see GM A3.512-518.

Prisoners on temporary release

3.41   If you are a prisoner on temporary release ('home leave' or 'ROTL' – release on temporary licence) you are counted as still being in prison, unless you were already eligible for HB immediately beforehand under the above rules (paras 3.39-40).

3.41   HB 7(14)-(15); HB60+ 7(14)-(15); NIHB 7(14)-(15)

Absences on bail

3.42   If you are on bail you can get HB on your normal home for up to 52 weeks (table 3.1). This applies whether you are in a bail hostel or bailed to live anywhere other than your normal home (e.g. at a relative's).

Example: Remand and conviction

Gabriel has been getting HB for a while. He is then arrested and detained on remand pending his trial. The authority should assume that Gabriel will be absent for no more than 52 weeks. He therefore remains eligible for HB.

Fifteen weeks later Gabriel is tried, found guilty, and sentenced to a term of one year's imprisonment. Although he will serve only six months in prison (after remission), and although the 15 weeks he has been on remand count towards this, his total absence from home now exceeds 13 weeks. Gabriel's eligibility for HB under the temporary absence rule ends. The fact that he has been sentenced is a change in his circumstances (chapter 17). (But the HB he was awarded for his 15 weeks on remand was nonetheless correctly paid.) If, however, the necessary conditions are met (para 3.7(b)) Gabriel may be entitled to a further four weeks of HB.

Death

3.43   There is no provision to award HB following your death (see the reasoning in R(IS) 3/04 para 18). HB must stop at the end of the benefit week containing the date of your death under the normal rule about changes of circumstances (paras 17.21 and 17.41). If you have a surviving partner, they may make their own claim. They are not 'covered' by your claim (but see paras 5.35-36). Also, the fact that your estate may be required to pay for a notice period on the property does not mean that you (or the estate) are still entitled to HB.

Informing the authority about a temporary absence

3.44   In any pension age claim you (table 1.5) have a duty to notify the authority of an absence exceeding or likely to exceed 13 weeks. Apart from that, there is no requirement to notify the authority in advance of a temporary absence (CH/996/2004).

Claiming during a temporary absence

3.45   If you are not on HB it is possible for you to become eligible during a temporary absence (e.g. because your income goes down), and in such cases a claim is required in the normal way (chapter 5).

3.42   HB 7(16)(c); HB60+ 7(16)(c); NIHB 7(16)(c); NIHB60+ 7(16)(c)

3.44   HB60+ 69(6)(c); NIHB60+ 65(4)(c)

Chapter 4 **Household members**

- General rules about households and families: see paras 4.1-8.
- Who counts as a couple: see paras 4.9-22.
- Children and young persons: see paras 4.23-38.
- Non-dependants: see paras 4.39-47.
- Lodgers, joint tenants and carers: see paras 4.48-58.

4.1 This chapter explains who counts as a member of your family for HB purposes, and how other people in your home are taken into account. Table 4.1 summarises this.

4.2 Many terms in this chapter have special meanings. For example, 'family' is very precise (para 4.8), unlike in day-to-day life. Others have their ordinary meaning, for example 'household' (paras 4.3-6). These, and other terms, are shared with the passport benefits; important case law from other benefits is therefore included.

Table 4.1 **The occupiers of your home**

(a) **Family members**
- You (the claimant): see para 4.7
- Your partner if you are in a couple (or partners in a polygamous marriage): see paras 4.7 and 4.9
- Children and young persons you or your partner are responsible for: see para 4.23

(b) **Other household members**
- Foster children: see para 4.35
- Non-dependants: see para 4.39

(c) **Other occupiers**
- Lodgers: see para 4.48
- Joint tenants (or joint owners in the case of HB for rates): see para 4.52
- Certain carers: see para 4.54

Membership of a household

4.3 What constitutes your 'household' is not defined in the law. The term should therefore be given its common sense meaning as being a domestic arrangement involving two or more people who live together as a unit (R(IS) 1/99); and this implies that its members nonetheless have a reasonable level of independence and self-sufficiency (R(SB) 8/85). It includes both members of your 'family' (para 4.8) and others such as non-dependants (para 4.39).

4.4   Whether someone is part of your household depends upon the particular facts in each case. However, it requires more than their transitory presence: it requires a settled course of daily living (R(F) 2/81). Someone making a short visit is not a member of your household; they can only be a household member if that is where they spend the major part of their time.

4.5   A person cannot be a member of more than one household at once (R(SB) 8/85). Two people maintaining separate homes cannot be part of the same household (R(SB) 4/83). For couples, see also paras 4.10-11.

4.6   A house may contain one household or a number of households. Two or more people living in the same dwelling are likely to constitute separate households if:

(a)   they have independent arrangements for cooking and storage of food;

(b)   they have separate eating arrangements;

(c)   there is no evidence of family life;

(d)   they arrange their financial affairs independently;

(e)   they have exclusive use of separate accommodation and/or their own obligations for housing costs (even if their liability is to someone at the same address).

Example: Occupiers of a dwelling

A claimant has the following people in his (large) home.

- His partner and dependent children. They are his benefit family (para 4.8).
- A foster child. This child is disregarded in assessing HB (para 4.35), and so is the income from fostering (table 13.5). When the foster child grows up, see table 2.3.
- His parents and his sister. They are his non-dependants (para 4.39).
- His sister has a partner who lives abroad. Because the partner does not live there, the partner is disregarded in assessing HB.
- The sister's baby. The baby is disregarded in assessing HB (para 4.47).
- A lodger who rents a room from him. Part of the income from the lodger is counted (table 13.7).

'Claimant' and 'partner'

4.7   HB law divides claimants into the following kinds:

(a)   you are a 'single claimant' if you do not have a partner and are not responsible for a child or young person;

(b)   you are a 'lone parent' if you do not have a partner and are responsible for a child or young person;

(c)   you are a member of a 'couple' (paras 4.9-19) or 'polygamous marriage' (para 4.20) if you have a partner (or partners) and are responsible for a child or young person.

If you are in a couple or polygamous marriage only one of you is the 'claimant' (para 5.3). HB law calls the other one (or each of the others) your 'partner'.

4.7   HB 2(1) defs of 'claimant', 'couple', 'lone parent', 'partner', 'single claimant'; HB60+ 2(1); NIHB 2(1)

'Family'

4.8   For HB purposes, your 'family' means:

(a) your partner (or partners); and

(b) each child or young person you or your partner are responsible for (paras 4.23-38).

Who counts as a couple

4.9   You are a couple for HB purposes if you are two people who are:

(a) married (opposite or same sex couples) or in a civil partnership (same sex couple): see paras 4.10-11; or

(b) living together as though you were married or in a civil partnership (often called 'living together' cases): see paras 4.10-17.

But if you are in a polygamous marriage see para 4.20, and if your partner is temporarily absent see paras 4.21-22.

All couples

4.10   You can only be a couple if you are members of the same household (paras 4.3-6). This applies to living together cases ([2014] UKUT 17 (AAC)) as well as to married couples and civil partners. You are not a couple for HB purposes, and the other person is not your 'partner', if:

(a) you live in different dwellings; or

(b) you live in the same dwelling but lead separate lives and do not constitute a household (CIS/072/1994).

Even if you are part of the same household you may not be a couple. What matters is the reason why you live together. For example, two people who lived together for reasons of 'care, companionship and mutual convenience' were held not to be a couple (R(SB) 35/85). The HB scheme recognises many other ways two people could live in the same household (paras 4.39-58).

4.11   If your relationship has ended, you are no longer a couple if you now maintain separate households. A shared understanding that a relationship has ended and your actual living arrangements are more important than whether you still share responsibilities and financial arrangements (CIS/72/1994). But by itself a shared understanding may not be enough to show you have separate households if you are married (CIS/2900/1998) or in a civil partnership.

'Living together' couples

4.12   A man and woman who are not married to each other but are 'living together as husband and wife' are a couple for benefit purposes. So are two people of the same sex who

---

4.8   CBA 137(1); NICBA 133(1); HB 2(1) def of family; HB60+ 2(1); NIHB 2(1); NIHB60+ 2(1)

4.10-11 HB 2(1) def of 'couple'; HB60+ 2(1); NIHB 2(1); NIHB60+ 2(1)

4.12   HB 2(1) def of 'couple'; HB60+ 2(1); NIHB 2(1); NIHB60+ 2(1)

are neither married nor civil partners but who are living together as if they were. For decisions about this see the following (paras 4.13-17) as well as the general rules about couples (paras 4.10-11).

4.13   The law does not define the phrase 'living together as husband and wife', nor what it means to live together as civil partners. It does say these are to be decided in the same way mutatis mutandis (with the relevant parts changed). DWP guidance on this says that it is important to consider the changing nature of modern-day relationships (GM C1 annex A para A1.03).

4.14   The first consideration is your purpose in living together (Crake and Butterworth v the Supplementary Benefit Commission). If this is unclear, it can only be decided by looking at your relationship and living arrangements and asking whether they can reasonably be said to be those of a married couple or civil partners. A body of case law has developed. This is considered in detail in vol. 3, chapter 11, paras 1104-11061 of the DWP *Decision Maker's Guide* [www].

4.15   The case law suggests that the following factors need to be considered:

  (a)   whether or not you share the same household;

  (b)   the stability of your relationship;

  (c)   your financial arrangements;

  (d)   the presence or absence of a sexual relationship;

  (e)   whether you share responsibility for a child;

  (f)   public acknowledgment that you are a couple;

  (g)   the emotional element of the relationship.

Points (a) to (f) are in the Crake case (para 4.14) and point (g) is from [2013] UKUT 505 (AAC). See also paras 4.16-17.

4.16   Points (f) and (g) in para 4.15 were emphasised in [2014] UKUT 17 (AAC), which held that 'a committed emotional loving relationship must be established and publicly acknowledged' (reflecting the fact that actual marriage and civil partnership are a public commitment). It also held that the parties' denial that they had an emotional relationship 'itself seriously undermines the notion that there is such a relationship'.

4.17   All the factors in para 4.15 should be considered, but (unless you do not share a household: para 4.10) none of them is by itself conclusive (GM C1 Annex A para A1.02). What matters is the general relationship as a whole (R(SB)17/81). The GM (C1, Annex A paras A1.07-10) provides authorities with advice regarding the information they should gather and the questions they should ask when considering whether two people are living together as husband and wife or as civil partners.

DWP decisions about couples

4.18   If the DWP has treated you as a couple for the purposes of a passport benefit (para 1.9), it does not mean that the council must do so (R(H)9/04). Although the council may regard

---

4.14   www.gov.uk/government/collections/decision-makers-guide-staff-guide
         Crake and Butterworth v Supplementary Benefits Commission 21/07/80 QBD [1982] 1 All ER 498

the DWP decision as satisfactory in the absence of any contrary evidence, if you say that the DWP's decision is wrong the council has to reach its own conclusion (R(H)9/04 para 37).

4.19 If the DWP has awarded you a passport benefit on the basis that you are not in a couple, the council is not normally entitled to take a different view. The exception would be if the council has evidence of fraud which the DWP is unaware of and has not considered (CH/4014/2007).

Polygamous marriages

4.20 A polygamous marriage is one in which a party to it is married to more than one person. The ceremony of marriage must have taken place under the law of a country which permits polygamy. No marriage that takes place in the UK is valid if one of the partners is already married. When a polygamous marriage is formed in the UK, a second or subsequent partner should be treated as a non-dependant (GM C1.42).

Absence of your partner

4.21 If your partner is temporarily living away from you and the other members of your family, they continue to be included as a member of your household, unless:

(a) they do not intend to resume living with you; or

(b) the absence is likely to exceed 52 weeks, unless there are exceptional circumstances meaning they have no control over the length of their absence (e.g. in hospital) and the absence is unlikely to be substantially more than 52 weeks.

4.22 If your partner does not count as a member of your household, their needs, income and capital are not taken into account when calculating your HB. Any money you receive from an absent partner should be treated as maintenance (table 13.6).

Children and young persons

4.23 Children and young persons are members of your family for HB purposes if they meet the following conditions. In particular, you or your partner must be responsible for them (para 4.31), and they must be a member of your household (para 4.34). But if they are temporarily absent, see paras 4.37-38.

4.24 A 'child' means someone under the age of 16.

4.25 A 'young person' means someone aged 16 or over who:

(a) is a qualifying person for child benefit purposes (paras 4.26-30); and

(b) is not on JSA(IB), ESA(IR), IS or UC; and

(c) is not a care leaver under 18 (paras 2.10-13).

When a young person ceases to meet these conditions, they stop being included in your applicable amount (para 12.12) and become a non-dependant (but see table 6.3 for the cases in which no non-dependant deduction applies).

4.20   HB 2(1) def of 'polygamous marriage'; HB60+ 2(1); NIHB 2(1); NIHB60+ 2(1)

4.21   HB 21(1),(2); HB60+ 21(1),(2); NIHB 19(1),(2); NIHB60+ 19(1),(2)

4.24   HB 2(1) def of 'child'; HB60+ 2(1); NIHB 2(1); NIHB60+ 2(1)

4.25-26 HB 2(1) def of 'young person',19; HB60+ 2(1),19; NIHB 2(1),17; NIHB60+ 2(1),17

A qualifying young person for child benefit purposes

4.26   A qualifying young person for child benefit purposes is:

(a) a person aged 16, from the date they reach that age up to and including the following 31st August; or

(b) a person aged 16 years and over but under 20, who is undertaking a course of full-time non-advanced education (para 4.27), or undertaking approved training (para 4.28), which they started before reaching the age of 19; or

(c) in certain circumstances, a person who has left such education or training (paras 4.29-30).

4.27   An education course counts as full-time if the average time spent during term-time in tuition, practical work, supervised study, or taking examinations exceeds 12 hours per week. And a person is treated as undertaking a course during the period between the end of one course and the start of another, so long as they are enrolled on and start the latter course. Non-advanced education is education up to and including GCE (A level), advanced GNVQ or equivalent, Scottish certificate of education (higher level), Scottish certificate of sixth year studies, and equivalents.

4.28   Approved training means training provided under the following programmes (so long as it is not provided through a contract of employment):

(a) in England – 'Entry to Employment' or 'Programme Led Pathways';

(b) in Wales – 'Skillbuild', 'Skillbuild Plus' or 'Foundation Modern Apprenticeships';

(c) in Scotland – 'Get Ready for Work', 'Skillseekers' or 'Modern Apprenticeships'; or

(d) in Northern Ireland – 'Access' or 'Jobskills Traineeships'.

4.29   Someone who has left education or training continues to be a qualifying young person for child benefit purposes up to and including the week including the terminal date; or if they attain the age of 20 on or before that date, the week including the last Monday before they were 20. The terminal date is the last day of February, May, August or November, whichever occurs first after they have ceased education or training.

4.30   In addition to the above, child benefit is extended for 16 and 17 year olds who have left education or training if:

(a) they are registered for work, education or training with the Careers or Connexions Service; and

(b) they are not engaged in remunerative work; and

(c) an application for payment of child benefit during the extension period is made within three months of the date education or training ended.

The child benefit extension period begins on the first day of the week after the week in which education or training stopped and ends 20 weeks later.

Responsibility for a child or young person

4.31   You are considered responsible for any child or young person who normally lives with you. This is usually straightforward; and when it is, receipt (or not) of child benefit is irrelevant. But if a child or young person spends equal amounts of time in different households (e.g. when parents have separated), or if there is doubt over which household they are living in, they are treated as normally living with the person who gets the child benefit. And if no-one gets child benefit, the child or young person is considered the responsibility of:

(a) the person who has claimed child benefit; or

(b) the person the authority considers has 'primary responsibility' if more than one person has made a claim for the child benefit or no claim has been made.

4.32   Recent case law has confirmed that the rules in para 4.31 are lawful, and that they mean a child or young person can only be the responsibility of one person (or one couple) at any one time ([2013] UKUT 642 (AAC); [2014] UKUT 223 (AAC)). A child or young person for whom you are not responsible (for these reasons) is excluded from your applicable amount (para 12.12). They are also excluded when deciding the size of accommodation you need (para 7.39) in both private sector cases (R v Swale HBRB ex parte Marchant; [2010] UKUT 208 (AAC)) and public sector cases ([2015] UKUT 34 (AAC)).

4.33   However, the child or young person does not have to be your son or daughter. They could be your grandchild or the child of a relative or friend, so long as they normally live with you. The example illustrates this and reflects DWP advice (GM C1.70).

Example: Three generations living together

■   A claimant's daughter aged 15 lives with her, as does the daughter's baby. The claimant gets child benefit for them both. The council decides that the claimant is responsible for them both, and includes both in the claimant's family (and thus in her applicable amount).

■   Later, (after leaving school) the daughter claims income support for herself. The council decides that the daughter and baby now form a separate family, and so excludes them from the claimant's family (and applicable amount).

In both cases, the daughter and baby are included in deciding the size of accommodation the claimant needs. Although in the second situation they form two separate families, they are nevertheless part of the same household.

4.34   A child or young person for whom you or your partner are responsible (paras 4.31-33) is always a member of your household, with exceptions only in the cases of fostering, pre-adoption and longer absences (paras 4.35-38).

Fostering, adoption, etc

4.35   A child or young person is not counted as a member of your household if they are:

(a) absent from your home and being looked after by a local authority, or in Scotland or Northern Ireland are in the care of a local authority or the Department;

4.31   HB 20; HB60+ 20; NIHB 18; NIHB60+ 18

4.32   R v Swale HBRB ex p Marchant 9/11/99 CA 32 HLR 856 www.casetrack.com (subscriber site) case ref: OBCOF 1999/0071/C

4.34   HB 21(1),(2); HB60+ 21(1),(2); NIHB 19(1),(2); NIHB60+ 19(1),(2)

4.35   HB 21(3),(4); HB60+ 21(3),(4); NIHB 19(3),(4); NIHB60+ 19(3),(4)

(b) a foster child placed with you or your partner by a local authority or voluntary organisation, or in Scotland and Northern Ireland boarded out with you or your partner; or

(c) placed with you or your partner for adoption or custodianship (though once adopted, they become a member of your household);

(d) placed with someone else for adoption or custodianship.

In these situations, the child or young person is excluded from your applicable amount, and excluded when deciding the size of accommodation you need (para 4.32).

4.36 A child or young person in local authority care who lives with you under supervision must be treated as a member of your household (GM C1.120). So must a child or young person in care who returns to live with you for part or all of a benefit week if, given the nature and frequency of the visits, it is reasonable to do so (GM C1.150).

Absence of a child or young person

4.37 If a child or young person is temporarily living away from you and the other members of your family, they continue to be included as a member of your household, unless:

(a) they do not intend to resume living with you; or

(b) the absence is likely to exceed 52 weeks, unless there are exceptional circumstances meaning they have no control over the length of the absence (e.g. in hospital) and their absence is unlikely to be substantially more than 52 weeks.

4.38 A child or young person who is absent in any other circumstance, for example attending boarding school, should be regarded as temporarily absent and treated as a member of your family (GM C1.140).

Non-dependants

4.39 In broad terms, a non-dependant is someone who normally resides with you on a non-commercial basis (the full definition is in paras 4.41-47). Typical examples are adult daughters, sons, other relatives and friends.

4.40 Non-dependants cannot get HB for any payments they make for their keep. The one exception is that a non-dependant who takes over paying your rent (because you are not paying it) may be able to get HB (para 2.51).

Who is a non-dependant

4.41 HB law defines everyone who 'normally resides' with you (the claimant), or with whom you 'normally reside', as a non-dependant, unless they fall within any of the categories in table 4.2.

4.36   HB 21(5); HB60+ 21(5); NIHB 19(5); NIHB60+ 19(5)

4.37   HB 21(1),(2); HB60+ 21(1),(2); NIHB 19(1),(2)

4.41   HB 3(1),(2); HB60+ 3(1),(2); NIHB 3(1),(2); NIHB60+ 3(1),(2)

Table 4.2 **People who are not non-dependants**

- Members of your family (para. 4.8)
- Foster children etc, who are not counted as being in your household (paras. 4.35 and 4.47)
- Lodgers and members of their household (paras 4.42 and 4.48)
- Joint tenants and joint owners (para. 4.52)
- Certain paid carers (para. 4.54)
- Separate tenants of your landlord, your landlord, and members of your landlord's household (paras 4.44 and 4.57)

4.42 Additionally, if you (or your partner) have a lodger who is not eligible for HB in their own right (because they have a contrived or similar letting: paras 2.55-74), that person is a non-dependant (GM C1.184).

'Residing with'

4.43 To count as a non-dependant, a person must 'normally reside' with you (or you must 'normally reside' with them). So someone who is staying with you but normally resides elsewhere is not a non-dependant (para 4.46).

4.44 For HB purposes a person does not count as normally residing with you if they share only a bathroom, toilet or communal area. Communal areas are defined in para 10.27. So someone in self-contained accommodation, within the same building as you, does not count as a non-dependant even if they share a bathroom and toilet with you.

4.45 Sharing more of the accommodation than a bathroom, toilet or communal area with you is a necessary but not a sufficient condition for deciding that they reside with you (Kadhim v Brent LBC). The person must also have the sort of relationship that could be described as 'residing with' in an ordinary sense. This is more than simply sharing parts of the accommodation.

4.46 Case law has also examined what it means to 'normally' reside with you. In one case the claimant's cousin came to live with her for ten weeks after being deported from the USA. She took him in rather than see him living on the streets as he had no source of income while waiting for his JSA claim. He slept on the sofa. The commissioner decided he was not normally residing with the claimant, so a non-dependant deduction did not apply (CH/4004/2004). In another case, the claimant's mentally ill daughter had been evicted and moved in with her. The tribunal decided that she was not normally residing with the claimant during the first six months of her stay, but that there was sufficient evidence to show that she was after that, so a non-dependant deduction applied only after the six months (CH/3935/2007).

4.42   HB 3(3); HB60+ 3(3); NIHB 3(3); NIHB60+ 3(3)

4.44   HB 3(4), sch 1 para 8; HB60+ 3(4), sch 1 para 8; NIHB 3(4), sch 1 para 8; NIHB60+ 3(4), sch 1 para 8
        Kadhim v Brent LBC HBRB ex p Hamilton 24/01/00 CA [2000] EWCA Civ 344 www.bailii.org/ew/cases/EWCA/civ/2000/344.html

Non-dependants' families

4.47 The partner of a non-dependant is also a non-dependant (but there is only one non-dependant deduction, if any: para 6.25). For children of non-dependants there is usually no non-dependant deduction (table 6.3).

Other occupiers in your dwelling

Lodgers

4.48 A lodger is someone who lives with you on a commercial basis and pays you or your partner 'rent'. HB rules divide lodgers into two kinds:

(a) lodgers who pay an inclusive charge for accommodation and at least some cooked or prepared meals (sometimes called 'boarders');

(b) lodgers who pay a rent which does not include meals (sometimes called 'sub-tenants').

4.49 In the first case above (para 4.48(a)), 'meals' must be provided – for example, breakfast every day is enough. They must be cooked or prepared, and consumed, in the accommodation or associated premises; and the cooking or preparation of the meal must be done by someone other than the boarder or a member of their family.

4.50 Income from a lodger is taken into account in the assessment of your HB (table 13.7). The method is more favourable if you provide meals. A lodger may claim HB in their own right subject to the normal rules.

Lodger vs non-dependant

4.51 Both lodgers and non-dependants may make payments to you and have exclusive occupation of, say, a bedroom. But there are 'many examples… of family arrangements and acts of friendship or generosity not… giving rise to a tenancy even where exclusive occupation is given' ([2012] UKUT 114 (AAC)). The distinction between a lodger and a non-dependant therefore hinges more on whether there is a tenancy or similar commercial arrangement between you and them.

Joint tenants and joint owners

4.52 A joint occupier is someone other than your partner who is jointly liable with you to make payments in order to occupy the dwelling. Joint occupiers include joint tenants (in the case of HB for rent) and joint owners (in the case of HB for rates). You and the other joint occupiers might be three friends or two brothers or mother and daughter (and so on). Joint occupiers are often called house-sharers or flat-sharers.

4.53 Each joint occupier is eligible for HB in their own right (so long as they meet the conditions in the ordinary way); and this often means apportioning the rent or rates (paras 7.21, 8.19-20, 9.9, 9.41 and 11.16).

4.48   HB 3(2)(e)(i); HB60+ 3(2)(e)(i); NIHB 3(2)(e)(i); NIHB60+ 3(2)(e)(i)

4.49   HB sch 5 para 42; HB60+ 2(1); NIHB sch 6 para 44; NIHB60+ 2(1)

4.52   HB 3(2)(d),(3); HB60+ 3(2)(d),(3); NIHB 3(2)(d),(3); NIHB60+ 3(2)(d),(3)

Carers

4.54   If you receive care from your partner, a child or young person, a non-dependant, a lodger or a joint occupier, that person is taken into account in HB according to the category just mentioned. For example, if a claimant's nephew comes to care for her, the nephew is taken into account as a non-dependant and there are no further rules.

4.55   Other resident carers (as well as those in para 4.54) are included in deciding the size of accommodation you need (para 7.39). This can also apply to non-resident carers (para 7.50).

4.56   But a resident carer is excluded from counting as a non-dependant (so there is no non-dependant deduction for them) if:

(a) they live with you to look after you or your partner; and

(b) they are engaged by a charitable or voluntary organisation (not a public or local authority); and

(c) that organisation makes a charge to you or your partner for the services provided.

Separate tenants and resident landlords

4.57   If your landlord lets out rooms in your dwelling separately, the other tenants are not non-dependants (para 4.44) and are not included in deciding the size of accommodation you need (para 7.39). The same applies to your landlord if they are resident in your home, and to members of their household.

Other occupiers

4.58   In nearly all cases, everyone in your home should fall within one of the descriptions earlier in this chapter. Paid live-in staff, for example a nanny or au pair, are an uncommon exception. Like everyone who occupies your accommodation as their home, they are included in deciding the size of accommodation you need (para 7.39), but they are not non-dependants and don't have any other effect on your HB.

4.56   HB 3(2)(f); HB60+ 3(2)(f); NIHB 3(2)(f); NIHB60+ 3(2)(f)

4.57   HB 3(2)(e)(ii),(iii); HB60+ 3(2)(e)(ii),(iii); NIHB 3(2)(e)(ii),(iii); NIHB60+ 3(2)(e)(ii),(iii)

Chapter 5 **Claims**

Making a claim

5.1　　HB can only be awarded if a claim is made. This section explains who makes the claim and how it is made. If you move while you are on HB, see also paras 17.22 and 17.30-31.

Who makes the claim

5.2　　The general rule is that you make the claim yourself, but:

(a) if you are in a couple (or in a polygamous marriage) one of you makes the claim: see paras 5.3-4;

(b) if you are unable to act, someone can make the claim on your behalf: see paras 5.5-7.

Claims by couples

5.3　　If you are a couple (or in a polygamous marriage) your HB claim covers both (or all) of you. But only one of you is the claimant. HB application forms usually make this clear by referring to 'you' (the claimant) and 'your partner'. It is up to you to choose which one of you is the claimant. Your choice does not usually affect your HB, but in some circumstances it can. We explain throughout this guide whenever it could affect:

(a) your eligibility for HB (e.g. paras 20.12, 22.13); or

(b) the amount of your HB (e.g. paras 5.54, 12.5-7).

If you can't agree which one of you is the claimant, the council chooses for you.

Swapping who is the claimant in a couple

5.4　　You should ask the council to let you swap who is the claimant if you would be better off doing so (para 5.3). The law does not give specific rules about this, but in practice the council is likely to agree. You may have to complete a new HB application form, and you can appeal against the council's decision about this (para 19.24).

5.1　　AA 1,5; NIAA 1,5; LGFA sch 1 para 2(5)

5.3　　CBA 134(2); HB 82(1); HB60+ 63(1); NIHB 80(1); NIHB60+ 61(1)

If you are unable to act

5.5   Someone can make a claim on your behalf if you are unable, for the time being, to act. They take over all rights and responsibilities in relation to your HB claim.

5.6   If one of the following has been appointed to act for you, the council must accept a claim from them:

(a)   a receiver or deputy appointed by the Court of Protection;

(b)   an attorney;

(c)   in Scotland, a judicial factor or other guardian;

(d)   in Northern Ireland, a controller appointed by the High Court; or

(e)   a person appointed by the DWP to act on your behalf in connection with some other benefit.

5.7   In any other case, the council may accept a written request from an individual over 18, or a firm or organisation, to be your 'appointee' – for example, a friend or relative, a social worker or solicitor. In doing this the council should take account of any conflict of interests. Once appointed, an appointee has all the rights and responsibilities that would normally belong to you. Either the council or the appointee can terminate the appointment by giving four weeks' written notice.

Claiming HB from the council

5.8   Claims for HB are made to the council – or to someone acting on its behalf (paras 1.31-32, and see also para 5.9). Many councils accept HB claims by telephone or online; and if you claim this way the council can require you to approve a written statement of a telephone claim, or keep written or electronic records of an online claim. In all other cases, HB claims must be in writing on the council's own form (or any other format it decides to accept) and sent to a 'designated office', which can be the council's benefit office, a county council office, a social landlord's address, etc. Application forms must be provided free of charge and give the address of every designated office and optionally an online address. You can ask anyone you like to help you fill in an application form.

Claiming HB via the DWP

5.9   Claims for HB can be made via the DWP in conjunction with a claim for JSA, ESA, IS, pension credit, or IB when it is linked to a former claim (but not UC: para 5.10). These claims are made by telephone to a DWP 0800 number (para 25.16). During the call, you are asked whether you wish to claim HB and if you do information relevant to HB is collected. The information is verified by the DWP if possible at an interview (which can be fast tracked if there is the threat of an eviction) or by post. The DWP then sends the council an electronic 'LAID' (local authority input document, known as 'LACI' in ESA cases), even if you do not qualify for the DWP benefit or withdraw your claim for it. The LAID/LACI is a computer generated claim form with your answers filled in. The DWP also sends the council a 'customer statement'.

5.5   HB 82(6); HB60+ 63(6); NIHB 80(6); NIHB60+ 61(6)

5.8   HB 2(1), 83; HB60+ 2(10, 64; NIHB 2(1), 81; NIHB60+ 2(1), 62

5.9   HB 2(1),83(4),111; HB60+ 2(1),64(5),(5B),92; NIHB 2(1),81(4), NIHB60+ 2(1),62(5).(5B)

5.10   The following are the main exceptions to the above procedure:

(a) You cannot claim HB via the DWP in conjunction with a claim for UC, so if you are claiming UC and live in supported accommodation (para 2.7) you should claim HB direct from the council.

(b) If you make a 'fast track' telephone claim to the DWP (e.g. because you know you wish to claim JSA(C) only), you are not invited to claim HB during the call, so you should claim HB direct from the council.

(c) If you phone the DWP to make a 'rapid reclaim' for JSA or ESA (i.e. within 12 weeks of a previous award ending) the DWP should post you an HB form (HBRR1) and you should send it to the council.

(d) If you claim a DWP benefit other than by telephone (e.g. ESA or pension credit) the DWP should post you an HB form (HCTB1) and you should send it to the council. The DWP also uses form HCTB1 in this way (marked 'CMS contingency') when its computer is unable to accept telephone claims.

Amending or withdrawing a claim

5.11   Before the council makes a decision on your claim, you can:

(a) amend it: the amendment is treated as having been made from the outset;

(b) withdraw it: the council is then under no duty to decide it.

5.12   A claim may be amended by telephone or in writing – to the council, or to the DWP if the claim was made to them. A claim may be withdrawn by telephone if it was made by telephone; otherwise it must be withdrawn in writing.

Information and evidence

5.13   You are responsible for providing 'certificates, documents, information and evidence' which are 'reasonably required by the authority in order to determine… entitlement' to HB. This applies when you make a claim (para 5.22), and also during the course of an award (paras 17.17 and 17.59). The council can ask you to attend an interview, but must not insist on this: R v Liverpool CC ex parte Johnson No. 2. Evidence should be obtained direct from a third party only with your written agreement (GM para D3.400), but this is usually given in the declaration made in connection with a claim.

5.14   The law does not specify (except as described in paras 5.15-16) what information and evidence is required in relation to particular matters. In practice councils require evidence about household members and their status, income and capital (for claimants not on a passport benefit), occupation of the dwelling (when appropriate), rent (in rent allowance cases), and other matters; and usually expect you to provide original documents rather than copies. In written claims, your signature is a reasonable requirement, and many councils also require your partner's signature.

5.11   HB 87; HB60+ 68; NIHB 83; NIHB60+ 64

5.13   AA 5(1); NIAA 5(1); HB 83(1),86(1),(1A); HB60+ 64(2),67(1),(1A); NIHB 81(1),82(1),(1A); NIHB60+ 62(2),63(1),(1A); R v Liverpool CC ex p Johnson (No 2) 31/10/94 QBD [1995] COD 200

Information you need not disclose

5.15 The council must not require any information or evidence whatsoever about the following types of payment, whether they are made to you, your partner or non-dependant:

(a) payments from the Macfarlane Trusts, the Eileen Trust, MFET Ltd, the Skipton Fund, the Caxton Fund, the Fund or the London Bombings Relief Charitable Fund, and in certain cases payments derived from those sources (para 15.42);

(b) payments in kind of capital from a charity or from the above sources;

(c) payments in kind of income (table 13.9(k)) from any source.

National Insurance numbers

5.16 You must either provide your National Insurance (NI) number, and your partner's if you are in a couple, along with information or evidence establishing this; or provide information or evidence enabling it to be ascertained; or make an application for an NI number and give information or evidence to assist with this – even if it is highly improbable that one will be granted: CH/4085/2007. There are two exceptions:

(a) the rule does not apply to you or your partner if you are claiming HB in respect of a hostel (para 2.30);

(b) the rule does not apply in certain cases if your partner is a foreign national (para 20.14).

Matters relating to the provision of an NI number are appealable, including the evidence needed to ascertain one: CH/1231/2004; and the consequences in an HB decision of a refusal to allocate one: 2009 UKUT 74 (AAC).

If you are on a passport benefit, etc

5.17 If you have been lawfully awarded a passport benefit (table 6.1) or universal credit by the DWP, this is binding on the authority as proof that (at the relevant dates) you fulfill the income-related conditions for receiving maximum HB (paras 6.2 and 13.3): R v Penwith DC ex parte Menear and R v South Ribble Council HBRB. If you have been refused a passport benefit or universal credit, this is not binding on the authority: [2013] UKUT 245 (AAC). But If you have been lawfully awarded savings credit, certain figures are binding (para 13.15).

Information gathered by the DWP

5.18 The law requires the council to use information relevant to HB, without verifying its accuracy, if it is supplied by the DWP and relates to a claim for or an award of: attendance allowance, bereavement allowance, bereavement payment, carer's allowance, disability living allowance, employment and support allowance, incapacity benefit, income support, jobseeker's allowance, retirement pension, state pension credit, universal credit, widowed parent's allowance or winter fuel payment. But the council need not use information which is more than 12 months old, nor if the council has reason to believe that the information has changed since the DWP obtained it.

5.15   HB 86(2),(4); HB60+ 67(2),(4); NIHB 82(2),(4); NIHB60+ 63(2),(4)

5.16   AA1(1A); NIAA 1(1A); HB 4; HB60+ 4; NIHB 4; NIHB 60+ 4; R v Penwith ex p Menear 11/10/91 QBD 24 HLR 115; R v South Ribble HBRB ex p Hamilton 24/01/00 CA [2000] EWCA Civ 518 www.bailii.org/ew/cases/EWCA/civ/2000/518.html

5.18   SI 2007/2911; NISR 2007/467

5.19 In practice, the DWP verifies the evidence relevant to a claim for HB made via them (paras 5.9-10) – but there are exceptions (for example, the DWP does not usually verify capital if the claimant says it is below £6,000). The DWP advises that councils 'should accept' that it has 'taken the appropriate action' in relation to such evidence (CMS Guide for local authorities, March 2010).

Nil income claims, etc

5.20 No-one is required to claim HB via the DWP (even when that is the normal procedure: para 5.9); in some situations you may need to claim HB from the council while waiting for a DWP benefit to be assessed. The DWP recommends councils 'do not ask the [claimant] to provide information and evidence that you know will be collected by [the DWP] unless the claim is urgent' (CMS Guide for local authorities, March 2010). However, if there is evidence of your actual circumstances, it is not reasonable (para 5.13) to delay assessing HB to wait for a DWP decision. If you have no income, you qualify for maximum HB (para 6.7) regardless of what the DWP decides: for example if you are living off voluntary payments from friends or relatives, or payments in kind, or your savings.

5.21 Similarly, no-one can be compelled to claim a DWP benefit; in some situations you may prefer to claim HB without doing so (perhaps because you are living off savings or the kinds of payment mentioned above). The council has no power to refuse your claim for HB because it thinks you 'ought' to be on a DWP benefit.

Complete and incomplete claims

What is a complete claim

5.22 Your HB claim is complete if it is made:

(a) in writing or online (para 5.8) and is on an application form approved by the council and completed in accordance with the instructions on the form – including any instructions to provide information and evidence;

(b) in some other written form which the council accepts as sufficient in the circumstances of a particular case or class of cases, having regard to whether the information and evidence provided with it is sufficient;

(c) by telephone (paras 5.8-9) and you provide the information and evidence required to decide the claim.

Dealing with complete claims

5.23 A complete claim (also sometimes called an 'effective' or 'valid' claim) must be decided by the council, as described in para 16.2.

5.22   AA 1,5,6; NIAA 1,5; HB 83(1),(4C),(9); HB60+ 64(2),(5D),(10); NIHB 81(1),(4C),(9); NIHB60+ 62(2),(5D),(10)

Dealing with incomplete claims

5.24　　Your HB claim is incomplete (it is also sometimes called a 'defective' claim) if it is received by the council (or DWP if appropriate) but does not meet the conditions given above (para 5.22). The council should give you the opportunity of doing whatever is needed to make it complete. In the case of a claim via the DWP, however, the DWP may do this (but if it does not, the council must). Depending on the circumstances, this could mean that:

(a)　the council sends you a claim form;

(b)　the council returns a form to you for completion; or

(c)　the council or the DWP requests information and evidence (or further information and evidence) from you.

In all cases, the council must also inform you of the duty to notify relevant changes of circumstances which occur, and say what these are likely to be.

5.25　　You must be allowed at least one month to provide what is required (para 5.30), and must be allowed longer if it is reasonable to do so. In the case of telephone claims, the law specifically permits more than one reminder, and the month is counted from the last such reminder. In the case of written and online claims, some councils send a reminder, allowing a further period for the reply. In all these cases, if you do what is required within the time limit, your HB claim is treated as having been complete from the outset.

Deciding incomplete claims

5.26　　Even if a claim is incomplete it must be decided by the council. In such cases, the council may:

(a)　decide that you are not entitled to HB because you do not satisfy the conditions of entitlement, as you have not provided the necessary information or evidence; or

(b)　make a negative inference (which means 'assume the worst') in order to make its decision. For example, if a claimant's bank statement shows that he withdrew £20,000 three weeks ago, and he refuses to explain this, it might be reasonable to decide that his capital remains £20,000.

In each case, you may appeal to a tribunal (para 19.24).

Claims not received

5.27　　The council has no duty to decide a claim that was not received – for example an application form which is lost in the post. An (attempted) telephone claim in which you do not answer all the questions, or do not approve a written statement if requested to do so (para 5.8), is treated as 'not received' – but in this case the council may nonetheless decide it. An (attempted) online claim which the council's computer does not accept or which is not in the form approved (para 5.8) is treated as 'not received'. In all these cases, if you claim HB again, the council should consider whether the conditions for backdating are met (para 5.50).

5.24　　HB 83(4D)-(4E); (6)-(9), 86(1)(2); HB60+ 64(5E)-(5F) (7)-(9), 67(1),(2);
　　　　NIHB 81(4D)-(4E), (6)-(9), 82(1),(2); NIHB60+ 62(4D)-(4E), (7)-(9),63(1),(2)

5.26　　HB 83(4F),89; HB60+ 64(5G),70; NIHB 85; NIHB60+ 66

5.27　　HB 83(4),(4B),(4C) sch 11 paras 2(7),4; HB60+ 64(5),(5C),(5D) sch 10 paras 2(7),4;
　　　　NIHB 81(4),(4B),(4C) sch 11 paras 2(7),4; NIHB60+ 62(5),(5C),(5D) sch 10 paras 2(7),4

When HB starts

Overview

5.28 Your HB starts on the Monday following your 'date of claim'. But if the 'week-one-yes rule' applies, it can start earlier. The details are in the remainder of this chapter. The main rules are:

(a) your 'date of claim' usually means the date you first notified your intention (to one of the relevant offices) to claim HB – but it can be earlier (para 5.32);

(b) the 'week-one-yes rule' applies if you become liable for rent or rates on a new home (paras 5.46-47).

Duration of award

5.29 There is no fixed limit to an award of HB. Your entitlement may change if there is a change in circumstances (para 17.19). Otherwise it simply continues until you:

(a) stop being entitled – for example, if you gain too much capital or income, die or transfer onto UC (paras 1.15-17); or

(b) fail to respond to a request for information or evidence and then the award is terminated (para 17.75).

Definition of 'month'

5.30 Many of the rules in this guide refer to allowing someone a 'month' to do something in connection with a claim, etc. This means a calendar month, and the month is counted as follows (R(IB) 4/02):

(a) if the council issues a letter on 26th June inviting you to provide something, you have provided it within a month if you get it to the council by the end of 26th July;

(b) if the council issues a letter on 31st January asking you to provide something, you have provided it within a month if you get it to the council by the end of 28th (or 29th) February.

Things sent out by the council (such as requests for information or evidence, decision letters) are counted in the law as being sent out on the date of posting. Things received by the council (such as claims, information and evidence) are counted in the law as being received on the date of receipt. In the case of online communications, this means the date recorded by the computer as the date of sending or receipt unless the council reasonably directs otherwise.

Definition of 'benefit week'

5.31 Many of the rules in this guide refer to a 'benefit week'. A benefit week always begins on a Monday and ends on the following Sunday.

5.28   HB 76(1),(2); HB60+ 57(1),(2); NIHB 74(1),(2); NIHB60+ 55(1),(2)

5.30   HB sch 11 para 4; HB60+ sch 10 para 4; NIHB sch 11 para 4; NIHB60 sch 10 para 4; DAR 2; NIDAR 2

5.31   HB 2(1); HB60+ 2(1); NIHB 2(1); NIHB60+ 2(1)

Date of claim

5.32   The rules about what counts as your 'date of claim' are summarised in table 5.1 (and were confirmed in R(H) 9/07). Further details follow.

Table 5.1 **Date of claim for HB: summary**

Situation	Date of claim
You asked for a form (or notified an intention to claim) and return it, properly completed, within one month of when it was sent out (or longer if reasonable)	The day you asked for the form (or notified the intention to claim)
The claim is made within one month of your partner's death or your and your partner's separation, and your partner was on HB at the time	The day of the death or separation
You or your partner were awarded JSA(IB), ESA(IR), IS, guarantee credit or universal credit and the claim for HB is received within one month of when the claim for that benefit was received	The first day of your or your partner's entitlement to JSA(IB), ESA(IR), IS, guarantee credit or universal credit
You or your partner are on JSA(IB), ESA(IR), IS, guarantee credit or universal credit, and the claim for HB is received within one month of you or your partner first becoming liable for rent or rates	The first day of your or your partner's liability for rent or rates
In any other case	The day the HB claim is received

■ Detailed rules are in paras 5.33-44. See also para 5.50 for backdating.

Notifying an intention to claim

5.33   This rule applies if:

(a)   you notified your intention to claim HB to the council or DWP;

(b)   the council or DWP gave or sent you an application form; and

(c)   you returned the form no more than one month after it was given or sent to you, or longer if reasonable.

5.34   In this case, your date of claim for HB is the day you notified your intention to claim to the office in question. You can do this 'by any means' (which includes telephoning, emailing, writing, texting, visiting or sending a friend: CIS/2726/2005).

5.32   HB 83(5); HB60+ 64(6); NIHB 81(5); NIHB60+ 62(6)

5.33   HB 83(5)(d); HB60+ 64(6)(d); NIHB 81(5)(d); NIHB60+ 62(6)(d)

> ## Example: Date of claim following notice of an intention to claim
>
> On Thursday 23rd July 2015, a claimant realises she might qualify for HB and telephones the authority to ask to claim. The authority sends an application form out that very day. She posts it back and it reaches the authority on Friday 7th August 2015.
>
> Her date of claim is Thursday 23rd July 2015 and (unless the week-one-yes rule applies: para 5.47) the first day of her entitlement to HB is the following Monday, 27th July 2015.

Claims following death or separation

5.35   This rule applies if:

(a) you claim HB no more than one month after your partner's death or your separation; and

(b) your partner was on HB at the time of the death or separation.

5.36   In this case, your date of claim for HB is the date of the separation or death in question, the intention being that there should be no gap in entitlement to HB. The one month time limit cannot be extended, but in some cases backdating should be considered (para 5.50).

Claims following an award of a passport benefit

5.37   This rule applies if:

(a) you or your partner claim and are awarded a passport benefit (JSA(IB), ESA(IR), IS or guarantee credit); and

(b) your HB claim is received by the council or the DWP no more than one month after the passport benefit claim was received by the DWP.

5.38   In this case, your date of claim for HB is the first day of that entitlement to the passport benefit (and in the case of JSA(IB) and ESA(IR) this means the first 'waiting day'). The one month time limit cannot be extended.

Claims following an award of universal credit

5.39   This rule can only arise in relation to HB for supported accommodation (paras 2.37-39). It applies if:

(a) you are awarded UC; and

(b) your HB claim is received by the council (not the DWP) no more than one month after:

- the date the UC claim was received by the DWP, or

- if UC is awarded without a claim, the date the DWP sent notice of the UC award. This can occur if you acquire a partner or separate from your partner while you are on UC, or if you qualify for UC within six months of an unsuccessful UC claim or within six months of the end of a previous UC award.

5.35   HB 83(5)(c); HB60+ 64(6)(c); NIHB 81(5)(c); NIHB60+ 62(6)(c)

5.37   HB 83(5)(a); HB60+ 64(6)(a); NIHB 81(5)(a); NIHB60+ 62(6)(a)

5.39   HB 83(5)(aa)

5.40   In this case, your date of the claim for HB is the first day of that UC award. The one month time limit cannot be extended.

Becoming liable for rent or rates while on a passport benefit or UC

5.41   This rule applies if:

(a) you or your partner are receiving a passport benefit (table 6.1) or universal credit; and

(b) you or your partner become liable for rent or rates for the first time; and

(c) your HB claim is received by the council or the DWP no more than one month after the new liability begins.

5.42   In this case, your date of claim for HB is the first day of that new liability for rent or rates. The one month time limit cannot be extended. (For UC claimants moving into supported accommodation, see also para 17.31.)

Other claims

5.43   If none of the earlier rules applies, your date of claim for HB is the day your claim is received by the council or the DWP (paras 5.9-10). For this rule only, 'council' includes a county council as well as the council administering HB. See also paragraph 5.50 for backdating.

Advance claims

5.44   You may make an advance claim for HB:

(a) up to 17 weeks before you reach pension credit age (para 1.24); or

(b) up to 17 weeks before an event which makes you entitled to HB (pension age claimants); or

(c) up to 13 weeks before an event which makes you entitled to HB (working age claimants); or

(d) up to eight weeks before you become liable for rates (HB for rates only).

In (a) to (c) your date of claim for HB is fixed so that your HB begins on the Monday following the birthday or event in question. In (d) your date of claim is the first day of liability for rates. Rules (c) and (d) do not, however, apply to someone who counts as a migrant or new arrival (chapter 20).

5.41   HB 83(5)(b); HB60+ 64(6)(b); NIHB 81(5)(b); NIHB60+ 62(6)(b)

5.43   HB 83(5)(e); HB60+ 64(6)(e); NIHB 81(5)(e); NIHB 62(6)(e)

5.44   HB 83(10),(11); HB60+ 64(11),(12); NIHB 81(10),(11); NIHB60+ 62(11),(12)

First day of entitlement

The general rule

5.45   The general rule is that your first day of entitlement to HB is the Monday following your 'date of claim' (paras 5.32-44). Even if your date of claim is a Monday, your first day of entitlement is the following Monday. The exceptions follow.

The week-one-yes rule

5.46   The week-one-yes rule applies only if you or your partner become liable for rent or rates in the benefit week (para 5.31) containing your 'date of claim', and move in during or before that week. In such cases, your entitlement begins on the day that liability for rent or rates begins, whichever day of the week that falls on.

5.47   What if you do not 'move in' until a day or so after their liability begins (but within the week in question)? The law appears clear that HB begins on the first day of your liability (within the week in question). The fourth example illustrates this. But many authorities instead pay from the day you move in, causing a day or two of rent arrears in your new home. This may be because of the DWP's choice of words when it advises that the week-one-yes rule 'enables HB awards to match a period of occupancy' (GM para A6.81), or due to older DWP guidance which has been withdrawn (circular HB/CTB A8/2006).

The rule for certain dwellings with daily rents

5.48   This rule applies only applies if you are liable to pay your rent on a daily basis to:

(a) a hostel (para 2.30); or

(b) any other accommodation in which you have been placed as a homeless person and which is board and lodging accommodation, accommodation licensed to the authority, or short-term leased accommodation (with a lease of no more than ten years) outside the authority's housing revenue account.

5.49   In such cases, there is no time limit on when you may claim, and your HB is always awarded back to when you moved into the accommodation. In other words, your first day of entitlement to HB is always the day you moved in. In practice, this rule is likely to be needed only for short periods (as leaving it any longer may mean you are no longer available to provide the information and evidence necessary for your claim).

5.45   HB 76(1); HB60+ 57(1); NIHB 74(1); NIHB60+ 55(1)

5.46   HB 76(2),80(3)(a); HB60+ 57(2); 61(4)(a); NIHB 74(2),78(4)(a); NIHB60+ 55(2), 59(4)(a)

5.48   HB 76(3)-(5); HB60+ 57(2)-(4); NIHB 74(3)-(5); NIHB60+ 55(2)-(4)

Examples: First day of entitlement

The general rule

A man claims HB because his income has reduced. His date of claim is Thursday 17th September 2015.

His first day of entitlement to HB is the Monday following his date of claim, which is Monday 21st September 2015.

The week-one-yes rule: whole weeks

A woman moves into her flat on Monday 1st June 2015, and is liable for rent from that very day. Her date of claim is Thursday 4th June 2015.

Her first day of entitlement to HB is the day her liability for rent begins, which is Monday 1st June 2015. (The answer is the same whether the rent is due weekly, monthly or on any other basis.)

The week-one-yes rule: part weeks

A woman moves into her flat on Saturday 7th November 2015, and is liable for rent from that very day. Her date of claim is Friday 6th November 2015.

Her first day of entitlement to HB is the day her liability for rent begins, which is Saturday 7th November 2015. In her first week she gets two-sevenths of a week's HB (for the Saturday and the Sunday). (The answer is the same whether the rent is due weekly, monthly or on any other basis.)

The week-one-yes rule: claimant does not move in immediately

A man has been living with relatives (and not liable for rent there). He obtains a housing association tenancy which starts on Monday 2nd November 2015. He does not fully move in until Wednesday 4th November 2015, and that is the night he starts sleeping there. His date of claim for HB is Thursday 5th November 2015.

His first day of entitlement to HB is Monday 2nd November 2015 (but see para 5.47).

Backdating

5.50   This section explains how HB can be backdated to cover periods in the past:

(a) for pension age HB claims, backdating for up to three months is automatic (para 5.52);

(b) for working age HB claims, backdating requires you to have good cause and can be for up to six months (para 5.54).

5.51   The following points apply to both age groups:

(a) It is the date of claim which is backdated. So even if you are not currently entitled to HB a backdated award can still be made.

(b) When HB is backdated it is calculated using the rules which applied at the relevant times. Entitlement during the backdated period need not have been continuous or at the same address (or even, arguably, in the same authority's area).

(c) Basing a claim for HB on an application which was (on the balance of probability) received by the council or DWP (paras 5.8-9), but was then mislaid or not acted on, is not backdating (because in fact a claim was made).

Backdating HB for pension age claims

5.52   For all pension age claims (paras 1.23-25), your claim for HB covers any period in the three months before the day your claim is actually received (or the day you notified your intention to claim, so long as you followed that up within the relevant time limits: paras 5.33-34) – but only back to the day you reached pension credit age, or the day you became liable for rent or rates, if these are later.

5.53   You do not have to ask for this rule to apply, and do not have to have 'good cause' (or any reason whatsoever): the rule applies automatically in all cases.

Backdating HB for working age claims

5.54   For working age claims (paras 1.23-25), your HB must be backdated if you (the claimant):

(a) request this in writing (whether on the HB application form or separately later); and

(b) 'had continuous good cause for [your] failure to make a claim' (as described in paras 5.55-58). It is only you who have to have 'good cause', not your partner or anyone else: CH/3817/2004 (see the first example).

Your HB cannot be backdated more than six months before your written request (see the second example).

Example: Backdating for pension age claimants

A claimant aged 73 sends in his first ever claim for HB. It reaches the council on Friday 11th September 2015. He would have qualified for several years for a small amount of HB had he applied.

His date of claim is Thursday 11th June 2015, which is three months earlier, and (unless the week-one-yes rule applies: para 5.46) the first day of his entitlement to HB is the following Monday, 15th June 2015.

Examples: Backdating for working age claimants

Good cause

A claimant aged 53 sends in his first ever claim for HB. It reaches the council on Friday 11th September 2015. He would have qualified for several years for a small amount of HB had he applied. His claim includes a request to backdate his award to Tuesday 7th July 2015 when he was admitted to hospital. He was so ill that it was impossible for him to communicate throughout his time in hospital. He came home from hospital on Tuesday 1st September 2015, but took a few days to start thinking about his finances. He has a grown-up daughter living with him throughout.

Although his daughter could have made a claim for him, this has no effect on his backdating: CH/3817/2004. While in hospital and unable to communicate he could not

---

5.52   HB60+ 64(1),(1A); NIHB60+ 62(1),(1A)

5.54   HB 83(12),(12A); NIHB 81(12),(12A)

claim or ask someone to claim for him, so he had good cause. Taking ten days to claim after such a bad illness is reasonable, so during those ten days he also had good cause.

Because he had continuous good cause, his HB claim must be backdated to Tuesday 7th July 2015, the day he went into hospital. As a result, his HB starts on Monday 13th July 2015.

Time limit

A claimant aged 33 sends in her first ever claim for HB. It reaches the council on Monday 1st June 2015, and HB is awarded to her from Monday 8th June 2015. On Monday 7th September 2015 she writes asking the council to backdate her award as far as possible. The council agrees she has continuous good cause because of incorrect advice she received from her solicitor in 2014.

Even though she has good cause for a longer period, her HB claim can only be backdated to Saturday 7th March 2015, six months before her written request for backdating. As a result, her HB claim now starts on Monday 9th March 2015.

'Good cause'

5.55 Good cause has been explained by tribunals and courts right back to the late 1940s, and this case law is binding: CH/5221/2001. Recent cases are summarised in table 5.2. The following are the main principles.

5.56 Good cause includes 'any fact that would probably have caused a reasonable person to act as the claimant did'; and although claimants are expected to take reasonable steps to ascertain what their rights may be, they 'cannot always be assumed to have an understanding of public administration' (CS/371/1949, quoted with approval in CH/450/2004). However, this 'traditional formulation' has more recently been criticised ([2010] UKUT 64 (AAC)) because:

(a) it does not reflect the language of the regulations;

(b) it introduces subjective elements while what is 'reasonable' is objective;

(c) though ignorance of itself is not good cause, it may be a factor to be taken into account. The law does not 'require a person to be acquainted with the "rules and regulations".'

5.57 The case law shows that you are likely to have good cause if:

(a) you were so ill (physically or mentally) or otherwise unable to act that you could not claim and could not ask someone to claim for you;

(b) someone you should have been able to rely on (such as the council, the DWP, an advice agency and possibly others) advised you that you could not get HB when in fact you could;

(c) there were good reasons for you not believing you could claim, amounting to more than just not thinking or not caring;

(d) some external factor prevented you from making a claim (e.g. failure of the postal services, imprisonment).

But the council's decision about good cause must be based on your individual circumstances, and you may have good cause in other situations.

5.58 Disputes about good cause are appealable to a First-tier Tribunal (para 19.18) – and also to an Upper Tribunal (para 19.90) because they are regarded as questions of law (R(SB) 39/91) as well as fact.

Table 5.2 **Backdating working age HB: case law**

This table summarises case law about backdating HB since 2002.

- *Case law on other benefits:* Case law about other DWP benefits is binding on HB (CH/5135/2001, CH/5221/2001).

- *What constitutes a request:* Backdating does not have to be expressly requested: a claim for a past period is sufficient. For example, it could be a late claim following the end of an earlier award (CH/3402/2005).

- *Backdating if claimant does not qualify during the period:* The question of backdating does not arise if the other conditions of entitlement are not satisfied in the backdated period (CH/996/2004).

- *Backdating if claimant qualifies for only part of the period:* So long as there is good cause, there is nothing to stop HB from being backdated for a period in the past (within the time limit) but then to cease in the past because entitlement ceased (CH/1237/2004).

- *Good cause and illness:* If a claimant was ill, the test of good cause is related not to the severity or seriousness of the illness but to the resulting incapability of the claimant to claim (CH/5135/2001).

- *Good cause and mental incapacity:* In deciding good cause, a mentally disabled person is treated as having their mental age not their chronological age (CH/393/2003).

- *Inability to speak English:* Not speaking English is not in itself good cause, particularly if there is evidence of a growing community with good facilities speaking the claimant's language (CH/3579/2003).

- *Good cause in the case of a couple:* In the case of a couple, it is only the claimant's circumstances that are relevant and the other partner does not have to show good cause (CH/3817/2004).

- *Good cause and a mistaken belief reasonably held:* The claimant (who had mental health problems) had good cause because he had not been careless or sought to obtain benefit to which he was not entitled. He had a firmly held misunderstanding which amounted to a mistaken belief reasonably held (CH/450/2004). Similarly, a reasonably held belief that one cannot get HB if one has not paid national insurance contributions might amount to good cause (CH/2198/2008).

- *Good cause and ignorance:* Though ignorance is not in itself good cause, it may be a factor to be taken into account. The law does not 'require a person to be acquainted with the rules and regulations' ([2010] UKUT 64 (AAC)).

- *Good cause and imprisonment:* The claimant had thought he could not qualify for HB because delays with his parole hearing made his absence greater than 13 weeks. Due to the particular complications in this case, the claimant had good cause (CH/2639/2006).

- *Good cause and failure to receive documents from the council:* A failure to receive a document from the council is not to be dismissed as possible good cause. In all three cases cited here, the document was a renewal claim form (CSHC/352/2002, CH/3009/2004, CH/3402/2005).

Chapter 6 **Calculating HB**

- How HB is calculated: see paras 6.1-10.
- Eligible rent and rates summary: see paras 6.11-13.
- Non-dependant deductions: see paras 6.14-27.
- The HB benefit cap: see paras 6.28-40.
- Converting figures to weekly amounts: see paras 6.41-45.

How to calculate HB

6.1　　This chapter explains how much HB you qualify for. To calculate this, work through the steps in paras 6.2-10. The calculation is summarised in table 6.2.

Maximum benefit

6.2　　The starting point for all HB calculations is your weekly 'maximum benefit'. This is:

(a) your weekly eligible rent and/or rates in Northern Ireland;

(b) minus any non-dependant deductions which apply.

6.3　　Chapters 7-11 define eligible rent and rates, and explain when they are split between joint tenants. For a short summary, see paras 6.11-13. Paras 6.14-27 give the amounts of the non-dependant deductions and explain when they apply.

On a passport benefit or universal credit

6.4　　If you are on a passport benefit you qualify for maximum benefit (para 6.2). You also qualify for maximum benefit if you are in supported accommodation (paras 2.37-39) and are on universal credit. Table 6.1 lists who is on a passport benefit.

Capital

6.5　　If you have capital over £16,000 (assessed as in chapter 15) you do not qualify for any HB. (But being on a passport benefit over-rides this.)

6.3　　CBA 130(1),(3)(a),130A; NICBA 129(1),(3)(a),129A; HB 70; HB60+ 50; NIHB 68; NIHB 60+ 48

6.4　　CBA 130(1),(3)(a),130A; NICBA 129(1),(3)(a),129A; HB 2(3),(3A),(3B) sch 5 paras 4,5, sch 6 paras 5,6; HB60+ 2(3),(3A), 26; NIHB 2(3),(3A) sch 6 paras 4,5, sch 7 paras 5,6; NIHB60+ 2(3),(3A), 24

6.5　　CBA 130(1),(3)(a),130A; NICBA 129(1),(3)(a),129A

Income and excess income

6.6   In all other cases, your weekly income (chapters 13-15) is compared with your applicable amount (chapter 12), as follows.

6.7   If you have no income, or your income is less than your applicable amount, you qualify for maximum benefit (para 6.2).

6.8   If your income is more than your applicable amount, the difference between the two is called 'excess income'. You qualify for maximum benefit (para 6.2) minus a percentage of this excess income. The percentage – also called a 'taper' – is:

■   65% in calculating HB for rent;

■   20% in calculating HB for rates in Northern Ireland.

Minimum benefit

6.9   If the amount of HB calculated as above is less than the 'minimum benefit' figure, then it is not awarded (but see para 6.33 in HB benefit cap cases). For HB for rent the figure is 50p per week. There is no minimum figure for HB for rates in Northern Ireland.

Other calculation rules

6.10   The amount of HB can be reduced to recover an overpayment (para 18.41) or administrative penalty (para 18.73). For working age claims, HB is also subject to a benefit cap (para 6.28).

Table 6.1 **Passport benefits**

You count as being 'on a passport benefit' if you are:

■   on guarantee credit (or would qualify but for the minimum payment rule: para 25.25)

■   on income support – IS

■   on income-based jobseeker's allowance – JSA(IB)

■   on income-related employment and support allowance – ESA(IR)

■   entitled to JSA(IB) or ESA(IR) but not receiving it because of a sanction

■   in the 'waiting days' before your JSA(IB) or ESA(IR) start – or would start apart from a sanction

■   subject to a restriction in your JSA(IB) or IS as a result of breaching a community order.

6.6   CBA 130(1),(3),130A; NICBA 129(1),(3),129A

6.8   CBA 130(1),(3),130A,131(5),(8); HB 71; HB60+ 51; NICBA 129(1),(3),129A; NIHB 69; NIHB60+ 49

6.9   CBA 131(9);HB 75; HB60+ 56; NIHB 73; NIHB60+ 54

T6.1   As para 6.4

Table 6.2 **Amount of HB: summary**

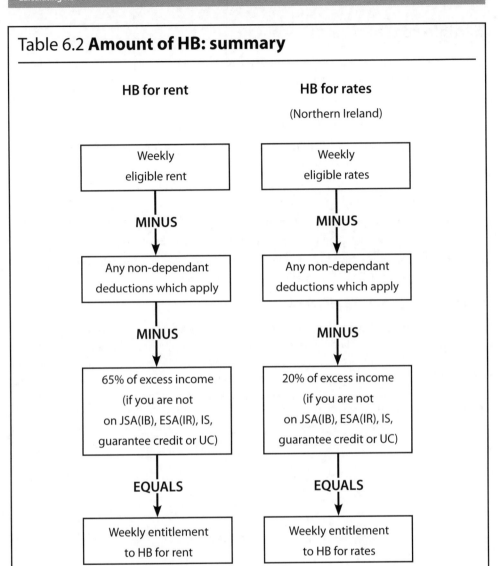

HB for rent

HB for rates

(Northern Ireland)

Weekly eligible rent	Weekly eligible rates
MINUS	**MINUS**
Any non-dependant deductions which apply	Any non-dependant deductions which apply
MINUS	**MINUS**
65% of excess income (if you are not on JSA(IB), ESA(IR), IS, guarantee credit or UC)	20% of excess income (if you are not on JSA(IB), ESA(IR), IS, guarantee credit or UC)
EQUALS	**EQUALS**
Weekly entitlement to HB for rent	Weekly entitlement to HB for rates

■ For the HB benefit cap see para 6.28.

Eligible rent and rates

6.11   Your 'eligible rent' can be equal to or lower than your actual rent: see paras 6.12-13. In Northern Ireland your 'eligible rates' can be equal to or lower than your actual rates: see para 11.14.

Eligible rent for social sector tenants

6.12   If you are a council, NIHE or registered housing association tenant, your eligible rent is the actual weekly rent on your home, but:

(a)   amounts are deducted for any ineligible services (and/or in Northern Ireland rates) included in the rent;

(b)   a further amount is deducted in working age claims if you are under-occupying; and

(c)   the result is split between the joint tenants if you have a joint letting.

The details for these and other social sector lettings are in chapter 7 and (for service charges) chapter 10. Variations for special types of case are in chapter 9.

Eligible rent for private sector cases

6.13   If you are a private tenant, your eligible rent is the weekly local housing allowance (LHA) figure for an appropriate size of dwelling in your area, or your actual rent if it is a lower figure. The details for these cases are in chapter 8. However, different rules apply to: charitable landlords of supported housing ('exempt accommodation'); boarders; certain older (pre-April 2008) claims; and other special cases (hostels, caravans, etc) and these are in chapter 9 and (for service charges) chapter 10.

Examples: Calculating HB

Claimant on a passport benefit

A claimant is on a passport benefit (JSA(IB), ESA(IR), IS or guarantee credit).

She has no non-dependants. Her eligible rent is £105.00 per week.

Claimants on a passport benefit get maximum benefit – which equals their eligible rent.

Eligible rent equals weekly HB	£105.00

Claimant not on a passport benefit

A couple are not on JSA(IB), ESA(IR), IS, guarantee credit or UC. They have no non-dependants. Their joint weekly income exceeds their applicable amount by £20.00. Their eligible rent is £130.00 per week.

Claimants with excess income get maximum benefit minus a percentage of their excess income.

Eligible rent	£130.00
minus 65% of excess income (65% x £20.00)	£13.00
equals weekly HB	£117.00

Claimant on ESA(IR) with working non-dependant

A claimant is on ESA(IR). Her eligible rent is £100.00 per week. Her 26-year-old son lives with her. He earns £450 per week gross for a 35-hour week.

Claimants on ESA(IR) get maximum benefit, which in this case involves a non-dependant deduction. The son works at least 16 hours per week and the level of his gross income means the highest deduction applies in HB (table 6.4).

Eligible rent	£100.00
minus non-dependant deduction	£93.80
equals weekly HB	£6.20

Claimant on ESA(IR) with non-dependant on JSA(IB)

The son in the previous example loses his job and starts receiving JSA(IB).

The calculation is as above, except that now the lowest deduction applies in HB (table 6.4).

Eligible rent	£100.00
minus non-dependant deduction	£14.55
equals weekly HB	£85.45

Non-dependant deductions

6.14 A non-dependant is, in broad terms, a grown-up son, daughter, friend or relative who lives in your home (para 4.39). The calculation of your HB assumes they will contribute to your rent or rates. This contribution is called a 'non-dependant deduction' – because it is deducted from the eligible rent (and/or rates) in the calculation of maximum benefit (para 6.2). This section explains when non-dependant deductions apply, and how much they are.

When no deduction is made

6.15 There is no deduction for any non-dependant listed in table 6.3. Nor is there for anyone who is not a non-dependant (table 4.2).

6.16 Also, there are no deductions for any non-dependant at all, if you or your partner:

(a) are blind or severely sight-impaired or have recently regained your sight (paras 12.51-52); or

(b) receive the care component of disability living allowance; or

(c) receive attendance allowance (or related benefits in para 12.50);

(d) receive the daily living component of personal independence payment.

But (b) to (d) do not apply if the benefits mentioned cease – for example, if you or your partner have been in hospital for four weeks.

Table 6.3 **Non-dependants with no deduction**

A non-dependant who is:

- aged under 18
- in certain circumstances, in receipt of a passport benefit, universal credit or savings credit – see table 6.4 for details
- a youth trainee
- in prison or similar forms of detention
- a patient who has been in hospital for 52 weeks or more
- a temporary resident or visitor or any other person whose normal home is elsewhere
- in England, Scotland and Wales, a member of the armed forces (regular or reserve) away on operations
- a full-time student during their period of study (para 22.18)
- a full-time student during their summer vacation (para 22.18) and they are not in remunerative work
- a full-time student and you (the claimant) or your partner are aged 65 or over.

6.14   HB 3; HB60+ 3; NIHB 3; NIHB60+ 3

6.15   HB 3(2),74(7),(8),(10); HB60+ 3(2),55(7)-(9); NIHB 3(2),72(7),(8),(10); NIHB60+ 3(2),53(7)-(9)

6.16   HB 2(1),74(6), HB60+ 2(1),55(6); NIHB 2(1),72(6); NIHB60+ 2(1),53(6)

When a deduction is made

6.17   In all cases not mentioned above (paras 6.15-16) there is one non-dependant deduction per non-dependant (or per non-dependant couple: para 6.25), as follows:

(a) if the non-dependant works at least 16 hours per week (para 6.19), the amount of the deduction depends on the level of their gross income (para 6.21);

(b) if the non-dependant works less than 16 hours per week or does not work, the amount of the deduction is always the lowest amount.

The details and the weekly figures are in table 6.4 (for HB for rates see table 11.2).

Table 6.4 **Non-dependant deductions: 2015-16**

If non-dependant is on certain benefits:

◼ on JSA(IB)/IS aged under 25	£0.00
◼ on ESA(IR) aged under 25: assessment phase	£0.00
◼ on UC aged under 25 without any earned income	£0.00
◼ on pension credit (either kind)	£0.00

If non-dependant works 16 hours/week or more and has gross income of:

◼ £408.00 or more per week	£93.80
◼ £328.00 to £407.99 per week	£85.45
◼ £246.00 to £327.99 per week	£75.05
◼ £189.00 to £245.99 per week	£45.85
◼ £129.00 to £188.99 per week	£33.40
◼ under £129.00 per week	£14.55

Any other non-dependant:	£14.55

Notes:

See paras 6.19-20 for working 16 hours/week or more.

See also table 6.3 and paragraphs 6.15-16 for when there is no deduction.

T6.3   HB 74(7),(8); HB60+ 55(7),(8); NIHB 72(7),(8); NIHB60+ 53(7),(8)

6.17   HB 74(1),(2),(8),(10); HB60+ 55(1),(2),(8),(9); NIHB 72(1),(2),(8),(10); NIHB60+ 53(1),(2),(8),(9)

T6.4   As para 6.17

Assuming the amount of a non-dependant deduction

6.18   Councils often assume the amount of a non-dependant deduction until they know what your non-dependant's actual circumstances are; and the law specifically permits the use of the highest deduction if they work at least 16 hours per week (but not if this is unlikely to reflect their actual circumstances: CH/48/2006). In all such cases, once the council has evidence showing what the true deduction should be, it should award any arrears of HB that are due as a result (but see paras 17.11-12 if you take more than a month to provide this evidence).

Working at least 16 hours per week

6.19   The rules about when a non-dependant counts as working at least 16 hours per week are the same as in paras 14.69-72 (but read 'a non-dependant' instead of 'you' in those paras). The law calls this 'remunerative work'.

6.20   In particular, a non-dependant does not count as working at least 16 hours per week while they are on maternity, paternity, adoption or sick leave (see para 14.72(e),(f). So the lowest non-dependant deduction applies during those periods.

Gross income

6.21   If a non-dependant works at least 16 hours per week their 'normal weekly gross income' is assessed (see para 6.17). This means gross income from all sources except those in para 6.24.

6.22   Although the law does not give a list of what income to include, councils are likely to include the following in full:

- ▪ earnings (before tax, national insurance, etc have been deducted);
- ▪ self-employed net profit (after the deduction of reasonable expenses but before tax, national insurance, etc have been deducted);
- ▪ social security benefits, pensions and credits (except those in para 6.24);
- ▪ state, occupational and private pensions;
- ▪ rental income;
- ▪ maintenance;
- ▪ charitable and voluntary income;
- ▪ interest on savings.

6.23   The law does not give rules about averaging a non-dependant's income. Because it is their 'normal weekly gross income' which is assessed, short-term variations are likely to be ignored, but longer-term changes are taken into account. For example, a non-dependant who is a school assistant could count as working at least 16 hours per week throughout the year (see para 14.70(c)) but changes in their income may mean different levels of non-dependant deduction in term-times and holidays.

6.18   HB 74(1)(a); HB60+ 55(1)(a); NIHB 72(1)(a); NIHB60+ 53(1)(a)

6.19   HB 2(1) def of 'remunerative work', 6; HB60+ 2(1), 6; NIHB 2(1), 6; NIHB60+ 2(1), 6

6.20   HB 2(1) defs of 'adoption leave', 'maternity leave', 'paternity leave', 6(7); HB60+ 2(1),6(7); NIHB 2(1),6(7); NIHB60+ 2(1),6(7)

6.21   HB 74(1),(2); HB60+ 55(1),(2); NIHB 72(1),(2); NIHB60+ 53(1),(2)

6.24 The following are disregarded in full in assessing a non-dependant's gross income:

- disability living allowance (either or both components);
- personal independence payment;
- attendance allowance (or any of the related benefits in para 12.50);
- payments from (or originally derived from) the Macfarlane Trusts, the Eileen Trust, MFET Ltd, the Skipton Fund, the Caxton Fund, the Fund, the Independent Living Funds and the London Bombings Relief Charitable Fund (para 15.42).

Non-dependant couples

6.25 In the case of a non-dependant couple (or a polygamous marriage), only one deduction applies, being the higher (or highest) of any that would have applied to the individuals if they were single claimants. In appropriate cases, there is no deduction (e.g. if they are both under 18). For the purpose of the various gross income limits in table 6.4, each non-dependant partner is treated as possessing the gross income of both of them.

Non-dependants of joint tenants

6.26 The following rules apply if you are a joint tenant of your home (with someone other than your partner), and there is also a non-dependant living there:

(a) If the non-dependant is part of your household (para 4.3) but not part of any other joint tenant's household, the whole non-dependant deduction is made in the calculation of your HB.

(b) If the non-dependant is part of another joint tenant's household but not part of your household, no non-dependant deduction is made in the calculation of your HB.

(c) If the non-dependant is part of the household of more than one joint tenant, the non-dependant deduction is shared between them, so each of you gets a share of the non-dependant deduction.

The share mentioned in (c) need not be equal: the council should take into account the number of joint tenants concerned and the proportion of rent each of you pays (para 7.21).

Delayed non-dependant deductions if you are aged 65+

6.27 The following rule applies if:

(a) you or your partner are aged 65 or more; and

(b) a non-dependant moves in, or there is any change in a non-dependant's circumstances which causes an increase in the amount of the deduction.

In such cases the change in your entitlement to HB is not implemented until the day 26 weeks after the change actually occurred. But if that is not a Monday, it is implemented from the following Monday.

6.24   HB 74(1),(2),(9); HB60+ 55(1),(2),(10); NIHB 72(1),(2),(9); NIHB60+ 53(1),(2),(10)

6.25   HB 74(3),(4); HB60+ 55(3),(4); NIHB 72(3),(4); NIHB60+ 53(3),(4)

6.26   HB 74(5); HB60+ 55(5); NIHB 72(5); NIHB60+ 53(5)

6.27   HB60+ 59(10)-(13); NIHB60+ 57(12)-(15)

The HB benefit cap

6.28   This section describes how the 'benefit cap' can reduce your HB so that the total of your HB and certain other 'welfare benefits' (para 6.32 and table 6.5) does not exceed a fixed weekly figure (para 6.30). The benefit cap only applies if you are a working age claimant (paras 1.23-25). Exceptions are given in table 6.6 and for supported accommodation see paragraph 6.34. The Court of Appeal has held that the benefit cap does not amount to unlawful discrimination: R(SG) v SSWP.

6.29   The benefit cap is in force throughout Great Britain. However, no council is required to apply the cap and reduce HB until it receives notice from the DWP (para 6.38). At the time of going to press, the benefit cap does not apply in Northern Ireland [www]. General guidance on the benefit cap is given in DWP circular HB A15/2013. See also paragraph 24.9 for discretionary housing payments in benefit cap cases.

The amount of the benefit cap

6.30   The benefit cap is:
- (a)   £350 per week for single claimants (para 4.7);
- (b)   £500 per week for lone parents, couples and polygamous marriages.

The amount of the HB reduction

6.31   The reduction in your HB is calculated as shown in table 6.5 (see example 1 on page 55). If you qualify for HB on two homes (chapter 3) add the two amounts of HB together at step (a) in the table. The DWP advises any resulting reduction is apportioned pro rata (HB A15/2013 para 50).

6.32   Table 6.5 lists all the welfare benefits included in the cap. If a welfare benefit is received at a reduced rate because of sanctions, recoveries of over-payments or third party deductions, the cap calculation is based on the gross amount payable before such deductions. In practice, councils are expected to use welfare benefit figures supplied by the DWP's Benefit Cap Calculation Team (HB A15/2013 para 12 onwards).

Minimum payments

6.33   If the result of the calculation in table 6.5 would be:
- (a)   nil (or a negative figure); or
- (b)   less than the 50p minimum HB award (para 6.9),

your entitlement to HB is the 50p minimum award. This is so that you are eligible to claim a discretionary housing payment (para 24.6).

6.28   WRA ss96-97, SI 2012 No 2995, HB 75A-75G;
        R(SG) v SSWP [2014] EWCA Civ 156 21/02/14 CA www.bailii.org/ew/cases/EWCA/Civ/2014/156.html

6.29   www.nidirect.gov.uk/benefit-cap

6.30   HB 75G

6.31   HB 75A, 75C, 75D, 75G

6.33   HB 75D

Table 6.5 **Calculating HB benefit cap reductions**

For each benefit week (para 5.31):

(a) Start with your entitlement to HB in that week, using the amount of entitlement before any reductions for recoveries of overpayments or administrative penalties. But for supported accommodation start with nil (para 6.34).

(b) Add your and your partner's entitlement in that week (para 6.32) to:

■ bereavement allowance	■ carer's allowance
■ child benefit	■ child tax credit
■ guardian's allowance	■ incapacity benefit
■ income support	■ jobseeker's allowance
■ maternity allowance	■ widowed mother's allowance
■ widowed parent's allowance	■ widow's pension
■ employment and support allowance	■ severe disablement allowance

(c) If the total exceeds £350/£500 (para 6.30) your HB is reduced by the amount of the excess.

(d) This gives your entitlement to HB for that week (but see para 6.33 for minimum payments).

Supported accommodation

6.34 The benefit cap applies if you live in supported accommodation (paras 2.37-39 and table 2.1) but (as table 6.5 shows) the amount of your HB is excluded from the calculation. The DWP has advised that 'the vast majority' of supported accommodation cases will therefore not be affected by the cap (HB A15/2013 para 65). (See example 2 on page 55.)

Exceptions

6.35 Table 6.6 lists the circumstances in which the benefit cap does not apply (and see also para 6.29). In practice, the DWP's Benefit Cap Calculation Team is expected to notify councils when these exceptions apply, apart from those relating to war pensions (HB A15/2013 paras 23, 29 and 52).

T6.5   HB 75A, 75C, 75D, 75G

6.34   HB 75C(2)(a)

Table 6.6 **When the HB benefit cap does not apply**

The HB benefit cap reductions do not apply in any of the following cases:

- Pension age claims (paras 1.23-25).
- In calculating an extended payment of HB (para 17.46).
- When you or your partner (including any partner in a polygamous marriage) are getting:
    - universal credit (because a benefit cap will instead apply to UC itself)
    - main phase ESA with a support component
    - disability living allowance
    - personal independence payment
    - attendance allowance
    - industrial injuries benefit
    - a war pension, or
    - working tax credit (or are entitled to WTC but not receiving it).
- When a child or young person in your family is getting:
    - disability living allowance or
    - personal independence payment.
- When any of the above would be getting disability living allowance, personal independence payment, attendance allowance or a war pension, but are not doing so because they are in hospital or a care home.
- During the 39 week 'grace period' after ending work: paras 6.36-37.

The 39 week grace period after ending work

6.36   The HB benefit cap does not apply during the 39 weeks beginning with the day after you or or your partner's last day of work if the following conditions are met (para 6.37). The DWP calls this time limited exception a 'grace period'. If you are a couple, either you or your partner must meet all the conditions; and if you each meet all the conditions from different dates, both grace periods apply.

6.37   The conditions are that you/your partner:

- (a)   have ceased work; and
- (b)   for at least 50 of the 52 weeks before the last day of work, were engaged in work for which payment was made or expected, and were not entitled to JSA, ESA or IS; and
- (c)   in the last full week of work, worked for 16 hours or more.

For these purposes, being on maternity, paternity or adoption leave, or getting statutory sick pay, counts as being in work.

T6.6   HB 72E, 73E, 75E

6.36   HB 72E, 73E, 75E

6.37   HB 75E(1)(b),(2), 75F

Applying and changing the benefit cap reductions

6.38 In any particular case, the council need not apply the benefit cap or change the amount of any reduction until it receives notification from the DWP's Benefit Cap Calculation Team. The council may however do either of these on its own initiative if it has the relevant information and evidence to do so.

When benefit cap reductions take effect

6.39 A benefit cap reduction may be made as part of deciding your HB claim. Claims wrongly decided as to a reduction may be corrected at any time.

6.40 A benefit cap reduction may start, change or end during your award of HB. When a benefit cap:

(a) starts or increases, HB changes from the date the council makes the decision to do so (this prevents overpayments of HB occurring solely as a result of a reduction);

(b) reduces or ends, HB changes from the date entitlement to the relevant welfare benefit (table 6.5) changed (so you get your resulting arrears of HB).

Examples: The HB benefit cap

1. The general rule

A single claimant aged 42 rents his home (but it is not supported accommodation). Before the benefit cap is applied, he is entitled to:

HB	£210.00 per week
Other benefits listed in table 6.5	£170.00 per week

Because the total of £380 per week exceeds the benefit cap of £350.00 per week, his HB is reduced by the difference (£30.00 per week) to £180.00 per week.

2. Supported accommodation

A single claimant aged 42 rents supported accommodation. Before the benefit cap is applied she is entitled to:

HB	£290.00 per week
Other benefits listed in table 6.5	£130.00 per week

The amount of her HB is excluded from the calculation, and her other benefits do not exceed the benefit cap, so her HB is not reduced.

6.38   HB 75B

6.39   DAR 4(7H)

6.40   DAR 7(2)(r), 8(14F)

Conversion to weekly amounts, etc

Rent, rates and service charges

6.41   Whenever a weekly figure is needed for rent, the following rules apply. The same rules apply to service charges; and in Northern Ireland to any rates payable with the rent:

(a) for rent due in multiples of weeks, divide by the number of weeks it covers;

(b) for rent due calendar monthly (or in multiples of calendar months), divide by the number of months (if necessary) to find the monthly figure, then multiply by 12 to find the annual figure, then divide by 52 to find the weekly figure;

(c) for rent due daily (or, in any case other than above, in multiples of days), divide by the number of days (if necessary) to find the daily figure, then multiply by seven to find the weekly figure.

Rent-free periods

6.42   No HB is awarded during rent-free periods, including in Northern Ireland rate-free periods where rates are paid with the rent. HB is awarded only for periods in which rent is due (and if a rent-free or rate-free period begins or ends part way through a benefit week, the eligible rent and rates that week are calculated on a daily basis: para 6.41).

6.43   During the periods in which rent is due, the calculation factors (i.e. applicable amount, income and any non-dependant deductions) are adjusted as follows:

(a) if rent is expressed on a weekly basis: multiply the calculation factors by 52 or 53, then divide by the number of weeks when rent is due in that year;

(b) if rent is not expressed on a weekly basis: multiply the calculation factors by 365 or 366, then divide by the number of days when rent is due in that year.

Income

6.44   Whenever a weekly income figure is needed, the following rules apply:

(a) for an amount relating to a whole multiple of weeks, divide the amount by the number of weeks it covers;

(b) for an amount relating to a calendar month, multiply the amount by 12 to find the annual figure, then divide the annual figure by 52;

(c) for an amount relating to a year, there are two rules. For working age claims, divide the annual amount by 365 or 366 as appropriate to find the daily figure, and then multiply the daily figure by seven. For pension age claims, simply divide the annual amount by 52;

6.41   HB 80; HB60+ 61; NIHB 78; NIHB60+ 59

6.42   HB 81(1),(2),(3); HB60+ 62(1),(2),(3); NIHB 79(1),(2),(3); NIHB60+ 60(1),(2),(3)

6.44   HB 33; HB60+ 33; NIHB 30; NIHB60+ 31(a)

(d) for an amount relating to any other period longer than a week, divide the amount by the number of days it covers to find the daily figure, then multiply the daily figure by seven;

(e) for an amount relating to a period less than a week, that is the weekly amount.

But for income in a self-employed person's assessment period, divide the amount by the number of days in the assessment period to find the daily figure, then multiply the daily figure by seven.

Rounding

6.45 The council may 'if appropriate' round any amount involved in the calculation of HB to the nearest penny, halfpennies being rounded upwards.

6.45 HB 80(8); HB60+ 61(7); NIHB 78(8); NIHB60+ 59(7)

Chapter 7 **Eligible rent: social sector**

- Who counts as a social tenant: see paras 7.2-16.
- Eligible rent: see paras 7.17-22.
- The social sector size criteria: see paras 7.23-38.
- Size criteria: general rules: see paras 7.39-63.
- Eligible rent: protected groups: see paras 7.64-71.

Basic rules

7.1 Your HB is worked out by reference to your eligible rent. The higher your eligible rent is, the more HB you get (the calculation is in chapter 6). This chapter explains how your eligible rent is assessed if you are a social sector tenant. Different rules apply if you are a private tenant (chapter 8) and in certain special cases (such as if you live in supported housing) if you are a social tenant (chapter 9).

Who counts as a social sector tenant

7.2 Except where you have a protected tenancy or shared ownership tenancy (paras 9.78-85) you count as a social sector tenant if your landlord is:

(a) a council which runs the HB scheme in England, Scotland or Wales;

(b) the Northern Ireland Housing Executive (NIHE) in Northern Ireland; or

(c) a registered housing association (in all four UK countries).

This section gives further details and exceptions.

Meaning of 'landlord' and managing agent

7.3 The method of assessing your eligible rent is usually determined by the status of your landlord (e.g. public, private or not-for-profit). The details are in paras 7.4-16. 'Landlord' means immediate landlord but does not include a managing agent. So, for example, properties owned by a private landlord but managed by a housing association are treated as private, but properties leased by a housing association from a private landlord are assessed as housing association lettings.

Tenants of 'social' landlords treated as special cases

7.4 The following lettings are treated as special cases and are described in chapter 9:

(a) if you occupy 'exempt accommodation' (paras 9.4-6) your eligible rent is always assessed as in para 9.9;

7.3   HB 13C(5),14(1),(2), sch 2; HB60+ 13C(5),14(1),(2), sch 2; NIHB 14C(5),15(1), sch 3; NIHB60+ 14C(5),15(1), sch 3

(b) if you are a shared ownership tenant your eligible rent is assessed as in para 9.87 whoever your landlord is;

(c) if you are housed by the council in temporary accommodation (other than its own housing stock) to meet a homelessness duty, your eligible rent is assessed as in paras 9.88-94;

(d) if your letting is a stock transfer tenancy your eligible rent is usually assessed in the same way as for a council tenant – see para 7.6;

(e) if you have a protected tenancy (paras 9.78-83) that does not fall in any of the above categories, your eligible rent is assessed as in para 9.85.

In any other case, if your landlord is not the council/NIHE or a registered housing association (para 7.8) see paras 7.14-16.

Council/NIHE tenants

7.5   If you are a tenant of the HB authority (i.e. in Great Britain a council tenant or council ALMO tenant, or in Northern Ireland a NIHE tenant) your eligible rent is assessed as a social sector tenant (paras 7.17-38) and your home cannot qualify as exempt accommodation. (But see para 7.15 if you are a tenant of an English county council.)

Former public sector tenancies (stock transfer tenancies)

7.6   If you have a former council/NIHE tenancy that was part of a stock transfer to a housing association (or other body) your eligible rent is also assessed as a social tenant (paras 7.17-38). The only exceptions are as follows:

(a) if your letting qualifies as 'exempt accommodation', your eligible rent is always assessed as in para 9.9;

(b) if the above does not apply and your letting is a protected tenancy (paras 9.78-83), your eligible rent is assessed as in para 9.85;

(c) if neither of the above apply and the council considers your rent is unreasonably high, your eligible rent is usually assessed as a rent referral case: see table 7.1 for details.

Tenants of registered housing associations: the general rule

7.7   If you are a tenant of a registered housing association (paras 7.8-10) your eligible rent is assessed as a social sector tenant – except in stock transfer cases (para 7.6) and in the cases described in para 7.11.

7.5   HB 11(1),12B(2),12C(2),12D(2); HB60+ 11(1),12B(2),12C(2),12D(2); CPR sch 3 para 5(1); NIHB 11(1),13A(2),13B(2),13C(2); NIHB60+ 11(1),13A(2),13B(2),13C(2); NICPR sch 3 para 5(1)

7.7   HB 13C(5)(a)-(c),14(1),(2), sch 2 para 3; HB60+ 13C(5)(a)-(c),14(1),(2), sch 2 para 3; NIHB 14C(5)(a)-(c),14(1),(3), sch 3 para 3; NIHB60+ 14C(5)(a)-(c),14(1),(3), sch 3 para 3

Table 7.1 **Assessing the eligible rent for stock transfer tenancies**

Former public sector stock transferred on or after 7th October 2002

If your letting is a former local authority, new town or NIHE property, and was transferred to the new owner on or after 7th October 2002, it is a rent referral case (para 9.31) only if:

- ■ there has been a rent increase since the transfer took place; and
- ■ the council considers that your rent is unreasonably high.

Otherwise your eligible rent is assessed as a social sector tenant (paras 7.17-18).

Former public sector stock transferred before 7th October 2002

If your letting is a former local authority, new town or NIHE property, and was transferred to the new owner before 7th October 2002, it is a rent referral case (para 9.31) only if:

- ■ there has been a rent increase since the transfer took place; and
- ■ the council considers that either
    - ■ your rent is unreasonably high; or
    - ■ your accommodation is unreasonably large.

Otherwise your eligible rent is assessed as a social sector tenant (paras 7.17-18).

'Registered housing association' and 'housing association'

7.8 'Registered housing association' means a housing association (para 7.10) that is:

(a) in England, registered with the Homes and Communities Agency;

(b) in Scotland, registered with the Scottish Government;

(c) in Wales, registered with the Welsh Government; or

(d) in Northern Ireland, registered with the DSD.

7.9 In Scotland and Wales, registered housing associations are known as 'registered social landlords'. In England they are known as 'private registered providers of social housing' (often shortened to 'registered providers'). 'Private' here simply means non-council (because councils are also registered providers).

7.10 'Housing association' means a society, body of trustees, or company:

(a) whose objects or powers include the power to provide, manage, construct or improve housing; and

(b) which does not trade for profit or, if it does, is limited by its constitution not to pay interest or dividends above 5%.

A 'housing association' may (or may not) also be a charity registered with the Charity Commissioners.

T7.1   HB 13C(5)(a), sch 2 para 11; HB60+ 13C(5)(a), sch 2 para 11; NIHB 14C(5)(a), sch 2 para 5; NIHB60+ 14C(5)(a), sch 2 para 5

7.8   HB 2(1) – def of 'registered housing association'; HB60 2(1); NIHB 2(1); NIHB60+ 2(1)

7.10   HB 2(1) – def of 'housing association'; HB60+ 2(1); NIHB 2(1); NIHB60+ 2(1)

Tenants of registered housing associations: exceptions to the general rule

7.11   The exceptions to the general rule (para 7.7) for a tenant of a registered housing association are as follows:

(a)   if your letting qualifies as 'exempt accommodation', your eligible rent is assessed as in para 9.9 (but see para 7.13 if the council considers the rent to be reasonable);

(b)   if your letting is not exempt accommodation, and the council considers your rent is unreasonably high, your eligible rent is assessed as a rent referral case (para 9.31) (including in England, if your landlord is profit-making and your dwelling is 'social housing': para 7.12);

(c)   in England only, if neither of the above apply, and your landlord is profit making and your dwelling is let at a market rent (i.e. is not 'social housing': para 7.12), your eligible rent is assessed under the LHA rules (chapter 8).

7.12   For the above purposes (para 7.11), a dwelling is 'social housing' if it is 'made available to people whose needs are not adequately served by the commercial [...] market' and either it is let below a market rent (such as part of the Affordable Rent Programme) or it is a shared ownership tenancy (para 9.86).

7.13   If your letting is exempt accommodation and the council considers your rent to be reasonable, your eligible rent is assessed in the same way as for a council tenant (but the source of the law is different: 'old' regulation 13 applies). The crucial difference from other social sector cases is that social sector size criteria do not apply to exempt accommodation (para 7.26).

Tenants of charities and other not-for-profit landlords

7.14   If you are a tenant of any other 'social landlord' (para 7.15) that is not a registered housing association, your eligible rent is treated in exactly the same way as any other private tenant and is assessed under the local housing allowance rules (chapter 8). The only exceptions are in para 7.16.

7.15   For the above purpose (para 7.14) 'social landlord' includes all (or a combination of) the following: a housing association that is not registered (para 7.10), a registered charity, an English county council (i.e. not the HB authority) or any other not-for-profit body.

7.16   The exceptions to the general rule (paras 7.14-15) are as follows:

(a)   if your letting qualifies as 'exempt accommodation' (para 9.4) your eligible rent is always assessed as in para 9.9;

(b)   if the above exception does not apply and your letting is a protected tenancy (paras 9.78-83), your eligible rent is assessed as in para 9.85;

(c)   if the previous two exceptions do not apply and your letting qualifies as a hostel (para 2.30), your eligible rent is assessed as a rent referral case with the special rules that apply to hostels (paras 9.41 and 9.46, and table 9.2);

7.11   HB sch 2 para 3; HB60+ sch 2 para 3; CPR sch 3 para 4(1)(b); NIHB sch 3 para 3; NIHB60+ sch 3 para 3; NICPR sch 3 para 4(1)(b)

7.12   Housing and Regeneration Act 2008, s68-70

(d) if none of the above apply but

- you have been on HB continuously at the same address since before 7th April 2008 (see also paras 9.80 and 9.84), or
- your dwelling is a caravan, mobile home or houseboat, or
- you are a boarder,

your eligible rent is assessed as a rent referral case (paras 9.40-41).

In any other case your eligible rent is assessed under LHA rules (chapter 8).

Eligible rent

7.17 If you are a tenant of the council/NIHE or a registered housing association and the general rule applies (paras 7.7 and 7.11), your eligible rent is:

(a) the actual rent payable on your dwelling (subject to limits and any apportionment: paras 7.19-22);

(b) minus an amount for service charges which are ineligible for HB (table 10.2) and in Northern Ireland an amount for rates unless you are billed separately (para 11.11).

But in many cases a deduction is made from your eligible rent and this lower figure, 'the maximum rent social sector', is used to calculate your HB (para 7.18).

7.18 A 'maximum rent social sector' is calculated in working age claims if your home is considered to be too large: the rules are described in paras 7.23-38.

Example: Eligible rent for a council tenant

A claimant rents a council flat. His actual rent is £65 per week. This figure includes £5 per week for the cleaning and lighting of communal areas and £12 per week for the use of an emergency alarm service.

His eligible rent is calculated as follows. The charge for the communal areas is eligible for HB. However, the charge for the emergency alarm service is not eligible, so this has to be deducted from his actual rent to find his eligible rent. His eligible rent is therefore £53 per week.

Restrictions on unreasonably high rents

7.19 In all social sector cases the council has an over-riding power to reduce the eligible rent (para 7.20) if it considers it to be too high. In practice it is hardly ever used, though it is a possibility even for council tenant cases (Burton v Camden LBC).

7.20 The power exists when 'it appears… that in the particular circumstances of the case the eligible rent… is greater than it is reasonable to meet by way of HB'. If it is, the eligible rent is reduced to 'such lesser sum as seems… to be an appropriate rent in that particular

---

7.17   HB 12B(2); HB60+ 12B(2); NIHB 13A(2); NIHB60+ 13A(2)

7.19   HB 12B(6); HB60+ 12B(6); NIHB 13A(7); NIHB60+ 13A(7); Burton v Camden LBC 17/12/97 CA 30 HLR 991

7.20   HB 12B(6); HB60+ 12B(6); NIHB 13A(7); NIHB60+ 13A(7);
        R (Laali) v Westminster CC HBRB 08/12/00 QBD www.casetrack.com subscriber site case reference CO/1845/2000)

case'. This requires the council to use its judgment (para 1.52), and to take your personal circumstances into account (R v Westminster CC HBRB ex parte Laali).

Joint tenants

7.21   If you are a joint tenant (para 4.52), the eligible rent for your dwelling is apportioned between you and the other joint tenants. To do this, the council must decide how much of the actual rent is fairly attributable to each of you, taking into account the number of joint tenants, the proportion of rent paid by each and any other relevant circumstances – such as the size and number of rooms each occupies, whether there is any written or other agreement between you – and also the presence or absence of the joint tenants (CH/3376/2002). The eligible rent is apportioned among all the joint tenants including those who are students (or otherwise ineligible for HB) (Nagshabandi v Camden LBC).

Example: Joint tenants

Tom, Dick and Harry

Three unrelated friends in their thirties, Tom, Dick and Harry, jointly rent a three-bedroom housing association house, where the rent for the whole house is £150 per week (and this does not include any service charges). They have a bedroom each and share the kitchen and all other facilities. They have each contributed one-third of the rent in the past. Harry loses his job and claims HB, saying that his share remains one-third.

Harry's eligible rent is very likely to be regarded as £50 per week. It is possible that a fairer split would be something other than one-third each, but unlikely based on the information given.

Tom moves out

Tom moves out. He is not replaced. Dick and Harry agree between them that they should contribute equally to the rent.

Harry's eligible rent is now very likely to be regarded as £75 per week – unless the authority considers that this new figure is unreasonable and has the power to restrict his eligible rent (paras 7.19-20).

Other considerations

7.22   For the rules about service charges see chapter 10. For other items included in setting rents (overheads, management costs, garages, land, business premises and space for a carer) see paragraphs 10.57-62.

The social sector size criteria

7.23   This section explains how the social sector size criteria affect HB. The rules about this have applied in Great Britain since 1st April 2013. Similar rules are expected to be introduced in Northern Ireland during 2015-16 but with a compensation scheme that provides full or partial mitigation. Supporters of the rules say they end a 'spare room subsidy'; opponents say they amount to a 'bedroom tax'.

7.21   HB 12B(4),12C(2); HB60+ 12B(4),12C(2); NIHB 13A(4),13B(2); HB60+ 13A(4),13B(2)
          Nagshabandi v Camden LBC HBRB 19/07/02 CA [2002] EWCA Civ 1038 www.bailii.org/ew/cases/EWCA/Civ/2002/1038.html

Overview of the rules

7.24   The main features of the social sector size criteria are as follows:

(a) the rules apply if you are a working age claimant (para 7.26) and are a social sector tenant (para 7.2);

(b) they say how many bedrooms you are entitled to;

(c) if you have more bedrooms than that, your eligible rent is reduced – so you get less HB;

(d) but there are exemptions and protections if you fall within certain groups.

7.25   The reduced eligible rent (called the 'maximum rent social sector' in the law) represents a notional rent for a dwelling that would be the right size for you and your household. The policy intention is to broadly mirror the size criteria for private tenants – although there are a number of differences in the way the rules work.

Exemptions and exclusions from the social sector size criteria

7.26   No reduction applies under the social sector size criteria (para 7.24) if:

(a) you are a social sector tenant (para 7.2) and; either

■   you or your partner have reached state pension credit age (para 1.24) – and it is age alone which counts and not other factors such as whether you get JSA(IB);

■   you have a shared ownership tenancy (paras 2.20 and 9.86-87); or

■   you live in temporary accommodation (para 9.90-92);

(b) your landlord is a registered housing association; and

■   you occupy exempt accommodation; or

■   you fall under the LHA or rent referral rules instead (high or commercial rents: para 7.11).

7.27   If you are a tenant of any other kind of not-for-profit landlord (such as a charity and/ or a housing association which is not registered) your eligible rent is assessed according to the rules in paragraph 7.16 instead. If you have a stock transfer tenancy (para 7.6) the rules depend on who your current landlord is (i.e. if you are a social tenant the rules in paragraph 7.26, in any other case the rules in paragraph 7.16).

Protected groups: when the reduction is delayed

7.28   When the above exemptions do not apply, there are two protected groups for whom a reduction is delayed. In broad terms:

(a) if you could previously afford your accommodation (i.e. were not on HB) you are protected for 13 weeks;

(b) if you have had a death in your household you are protected for 12 months.

The details are in paras 7.64-71.

7.26-27 HB 12B(1), 12BA(1), A13(2); CPR sch 3 para 4(1)(b)

When a reduction applies: tenants who are under-occupying

7.29 A reduction applies if you have more bedrooms in your accommodation than the social sector size criteria say you are entitled to. This is often referred to as 'under-occupying'.

7.30 No reduction applies if you occupy accommodation with the same number of bedrooms as you are entitled to, or fewer bedrooms.

How many bedrooms you are entitled to

7.31 Table 7.2 shows how to work out how many bedrooms you are entitled to. Paras 7.39-63 explain which occupiers in your accommodation are taken into account and when an extra bedroom is allowed.

Table 7.2 **The social sector size criteria**

General rules

For who counts as an occupier for these purposes, see para 7.40.

One bedroom is allowed for each of the following occupiers, each occupier coming only within the first category which applies to them:

- each couple (para 4.10);
- each other person aged 16 or over;
- two children under 16 of the same sex;
- two children under 10 of the same or opposite sex;
- each other child.

Additional bedrooms

One or more additional bedrooms can be allowed for:

- a foster parent;
- an overnight carer;
- a disabled child who needs their own bedroom.

See paras 7.39-45 for which occupiers are included and paras 7.46-63 for when an additional bedroom is allowed.

What counts as a bedroom

7.32 There is no definition in the HB regulations of what counts as a bedroom, but Upper Tribunals have given a number of decisions relating to this. The leading case (at the time of writing) is [2014] UKUT 525 (AAC) (SSWP v Nelson), which was decided by a panel of three judges (para 19.68). It and other decisions are summarised in table 7.3.

7.29 HB B13(2)(b)

7.31 HB B13(5)-(9)

T7.2 HB B13(5)-(9)

7.33   The council is entitled to use its judgment in deciding whether a room is or is not a bedroom (para 1.52). Initially it is likely to base this decision on how your landlord has categorised the rooms in your home (circular HB/CTB A4/2012), but it is not bound by this and should consider each case on its individual details.

7.34   Possible considerations about whether a room is a bedroom include:

(a) the potential or actual use of the room;

(b) how the room was described by the landlord when the accommodation was let, or on the building's plans;

(c) practical considerations including the room's size;

(d) in limited cases, issues relating to overcrowding.

For further details see table 7.3.

Examples: Social sector size criteria

Tenant is under-occupying: deduction applies

A tenant lives with his partner in a four bedroom council house. The weekly rent is £80.00. They have four children, two boys aged 15 and 5 and two girls, both aged 12.

The size criteria apply as follows: one bedroom is allocated for the tenant and his partner, one for the two girls and one for the two boys. They are deemed to be under-occupying by one bedroom so their eligible rent is reduced by £11.20 (14% of £80.00). The maximum weekly HB (para 6.2) used to calculate their HB entitlement is £68.80 (£80.00 – £11.20). Any deductions for non-dependants or tapered excess income (table 6.2) are made from this figure to arrive at their weekly HB.

Tenant is not under-occupying

A lone parent lives in a four bedroom house which she rents from a registered housing association. The weekly rent is £120.00. She has four children: three girls aged 12, 12 and 5 and one boy aged 15. Under the size criteria she is entitled to four bedrooms: one for her, one for the two older girls, one for the boy (no other boy aged under 16 to share with) and one for the remaining girl. She is not under-occupying and so her maximum weekly HB is £120.00.

How much the reduction is

7.35   The amount of the reduction is calculated as follows:

(a) if your dwelling has one bedroom more than your household requires (as judged by the social sector size criteria), your eligible rent Is reduced by 14%;

(b) if your dwelling has two or more bedrooms more than your household requires, your eligible rent is reduced by 25%.

7.35   HB B13 (3)

Table 7.3 **What counts as a bedroom: case law**

- *Applying the undefined term 'bedroom'.* The word 'bedroom' has its ordinary or familiar English meaning. It should not be paraphrased, but should be understood and applied 'having regard to the underlying purpose of the legislation' which is 'to limit the HB entitlement of those under-occupying accommodation'. Like an 'elephant', a 'bedroom' is capable of description rather than definition. And in an individual case, the council's understanding of what is a bedroom 'is best provided by the reasons given for [its] decision'. ([2014] UKUT 525 (AAC) paras 19-24.) The description of bedroom required by an overnight carer (see para 7.55) as a room with a bed or beds in and/or a room suitable for sleeping in ([2014] UKUT 48 (AAC)) is unlikely to be a conclusive general definition.

- *The potential and actual use of the room.* The council should consider the potential use of the room by any of the adults or children referred to in the regulation (the occupiers and overnight carers: see paras 7.40-63). Actual, former or planned occupation is less likely to be relevant. The assessment of the room is 'essentially of a property when vacant'. ([2014] UKUT 525 (AAC) paras 27-28.)

- *The description of the room by the landlord or in the building's plans.* The council can take account of the description of the room by the original or current landlord (for example in the letting agreement or marketing materials) or in the plans or designs for the building. But this is 'a starting point' and is not conclusive. ([2014] UKUT 525 (AAC) para 30.)

- *Relevant practical considerations.* The council should consider practical factors including '(a) size, configuration and overall dimensions, (b) access, (c) natural and electronic lighting, (d) ventilation, and (e) privacy'. For example, it should not be necessary to 'jump from a passage through an outward opening door in order to get into bed'. It should be possible to get into bed from within the room, and there should be somewhere to put clothes and a glass of water. These factors are 'case sensitive' (in other words, based on the individual circumstances) and take account of the adults and children referred to in the regulations (see paras 7.40-63). ([2014] UKUT 525 (AAC) paras 31-44.)

- *Underoccupation and overcrowding.* Underoccupation is not 'the flip side of overcrowding'. The two sets of rules are different, and overcrowding law takes account of living rooms as well as bedrooms (Housing Act 1985 s326, Housing (Scotland) Act 1987 s137). But overcrowding rules (for example if a room has very small dimensions) can sound 'warning bells' that a room may not be a bedroom. ([2014] UKUT 525 (AAC) paras 53-55.) In practice, direct conflict between overcrowding law and the HB size criteria is rare.

- *Discrimination, human rights, and discretionary housing payments (DHPs).* The Court of Appeal and Upper Tribunals have given decisions that the HB size criteria do not amount to unlawful discrimination (under human rights and/or equality law) against disabled people (R(MA and others) v SSWP (CA), Rutherford v SSWP) including couples whose disabilities mean they cannot share a bedroom (R(MA and others) v SSWP (QBD)), parents with shared care of a child (Cotton v SSWP), or people with overnight carers ([2014] UKUT 467 (AAC)). In those cases DHPs were being paid (see para 24.5) and in one case this 'completely compensated' for the reduction in HB (Cotton v SSWP). In another case the Upper Tribunal gave a similar decision in relation to a period before DHPs began to be paid ([2014] UKUT 465 (AAC)). It seems likely that a similar decision may also apply if DHPs stop being paid (Cotton v SSWP suggests this but does not decide it).

The reduction for joint tenants

7.36   If you are a joint tenant the reduction (of 14% or 25%) is made from the eligible rent of the whole dwelling. The resulting figure is then apportioned between you and the other joint tenants as described in para 7.21.

Eligible rent after a reduction

7.37   The reduced eligible rent is used in calculating your HB. Any non-dependant deduction(s) and/or excess income taper are deducted from the reduced eligible rent (table 6.2).

The reduction and further restrictions

7.38   It is possible for the council to further restrict your eligible rent, though this is very unlikely. This is done after (not before) the 14% or 25% reduction has been applied, and only if the resulting figure 'appears… greater than it is reasonable to meet by way of HB'. In other respects the points in paras 7.19-20 apply.

Size criteria: general rules

7.39   This section explains which occupiers are taken into account for the purposes of the HB size criteria, and when an extra bedroom is allowed for carers and people with disabilities. It applies to:

(a) social sector cases – in deciding how many bedrooms a working-age claimant qualifies for (para 7.31 and table 7.2);

(b) LHA (private sector) cases – in deciding how many bedrooms any claimant qualifies for (para 8.15 and table 8.2);

(c) rent referral cases – in deciding how many bedrooms and living rooms any claimant qualifies for (para 9.68 and table 9.5).

The footnotes give separate references to the law for social sector and LHA cases when these differ (for rent referral cases see para 9.68).

T17.3 R(MA and Others) v SSWP CA 21/02/14 [2014] EWCA Civ 13 www.bailii.org/ew/cases/EWCA/Civ/2014/13.html
         R(MA and Others) v SSWP QBD 30/07/2013 [2013] EWHC 2213 www.bailii.org/ew/cases/EWHC/QB/2013/2213.html
         Rutherford v SSWP 30/05/14 EWHC (Admin) [2014] EWHC 1631 (Admin) www.bailii.org/ew/cases/EWHC/Admin/2014/1631.html
         Cotton v SSWP 22/10/14 EWHC (Admin) [2014] EWHC 3437 (Admin) www.bailii.org/ew/cases/EWHC/Admin/2014/3437.html

7.36   HB B13 (2)(c)

7.37   HB 12B (1)(a)

7.38   HB B13 (2)(a),(4)

Which occupiers are included

7.40   The size criteria take account of the occupiers of your dwelling. This means:

(a) you (the claimant) and members of your family (partner, children and young persons: para 4.8);

(b) non-dependants (para 4.39);

(c) lodgers (para 4.48);

(d) joint tenants – but only in social sector and rent referral cases (not in LHA cases); and

(e) any other person who occupies your dwelling 'as their home'.

Further details and special cases are given below (paras 7.41-63).

7.41   The council decides who is an occupier. In doing so it should have regard to the general HB rules about this (chapter 3); and even though some of the law was written to apply to claimants and partners, it should be adapted to apply to non-dependants (for example): [2010] UKUT 129 (AAC). A decision about which occupiers are included is appealable to a tribunal: [2010] UKUT 79 (AAC).

Children and young persons

7.42   The size criteria take into account children and young persons for whom you, your partner or someone else in your household is responsible (para 4.31), including those who are temporarily absent (paras 4.37-38).

7.43   The following are not included:

(a) children in care etc who are not counted as a member of your household (para 4.35). But for fostering see para 7.48;

(b) children who are the primary responsibility of someone outside your household, such as their other parent (para 4.32).

Students and others gradually leaving home

7.44   When a student starts at a university and lives in a hall of residence, coming home frequently, it is correct to include them as an occupier of the parent's home: [2009] UKUT 67 (AAC), [2010] UKUT 129 (AAC). By perhaps the second year, especially if the student has taken on the rent of a flat or house, this is less likely to be the case. There is no fixed rule, each case depending on its facts.

Armed forces absences

7.45   In England, Scotland and Wales, if your or your partner's son, daughter, step-son or step-daughter is in the armed forces (regular or reserve), he or she continues to count as an occupier of your home during an absence on operations, so long as he or she:

7.40   Social sector: HB B13(5) LHA: HB 13D(3),(12); HB60+ 13D(3),(12); NIHB 14D(3),(10); NIHB60+ 14D(3),(10)

7.42   Social sector: HB 2(1)) – defs of 'child' etc, B13(5)(ba)-(e)
        LHA: HB 2(1), 13D(3)(ba)-(e); HB60+ 2(1), 13D(3)(ba)-(e); NIHB 2(1), 14D(3)(c)-(e); NIHB60+ 2(1), 14D(3)(c)-(e)

7.43   Social sector: HB B13(5)(ba)-(e), 21(3)
        LHA: HB 13D(3), 21(3); HB60+ 13D(3), 21(3); NIHB 14D(3), 19(3); NIHB60+ 14D(3), 19(3)

7.45   Social sector: HB 2(1) – def of 'member of the armed forces away on operations', B13(8) LHA: HB 2(1), 13D(12); HB60+ 2(1), 13D(2)

(a) was a non-dependant (paras 4.39-46) before that absence (regardless of whether a non-dependant deduction then applied); and

(b) intends to return to reside in your dwelling when that absence ends.

Additional bedrooms: carers and disability

7.46   The size criteria allow an additional bedroom for:

(a) a foster parent with or without a placed child (para 7.48);

(b) an overnight non-resident carer (para 7.50);

(c) a disabled child who needs their own room (para 7.58).

7.47   In social sector and rent referral cases, the maximum number of additional bedrooms anyone could qualify for is:

(a) except in Northern Ireland, one as a foster parent, or in a joint tenancy one for each single foster parent or foster parent couple amongst the joint tenants; plus

(b) one for an overnight carer, or in a joint tenancy one for each single person or couple amongst the joint tenants who requires overnight care; plus

(c) one for each disabled child who needs their own room.

The same applies in LHA cases but omitting the references to joint tenants.

Fostering/kinship and pre-adoption

7.48   In England, Scotland and Wales, one additional bedroom is allowed if you (the claimant) or your partner are a 'qualifying parent or carer' (para 7.49). In the case of a couple this means one additional bedroom, not two, even if both of you are qualifying parents or carers. In social sector and rent referral cases, one additional bedroom is allowed for each single joint tenant or joint tenant couple who meets this condition. Apart from that, no additional bedroom is allowed for anyone else in the dwelling (e.g. a non-dependant) who is a foster parent, etc.

7.49   You are a 'qualifying parent or carer' if you:

(a) have a child or young person placed with you as a foster parent or kinship carer or prior to adoption (in any of the circumstances described in para 4.35); or

(b) have been approved as a foster parent or kinship carer but have not yet had a placement – but in this case only for 52 weeks.

Overnight carers

7.50   One additional bedroom is allowed if you (the claimant) or your partner 'require overnight care' (paras 7.51-56). In the case of a couple this means one additional bedroom, not two, even if both of you require overnight care. In social sector and rent referral cases, one additional bedroom is allowed for each single joint tenant or joint tenant couple who meets

---

7.47   Social sector: HB B13(5)(ba),(7) LHA: HB 13D(3)(ba),(3B); HB60+ 13D(3)(ba),(3B); NIHB 14D(3); NIHB60+ 14D(3)

7.48   Social sector: HB B13(6)(b),(9) LHA: HB 13D(3A)(b); HB60+ 13D(3A)(b)

7.49   HB 2(1) – def of 'qualifying parent or carer'; HB60+ 2(1)

7.50   Social sector: HB B13(6)(a),(9); LHA: HB 13D(3A)(a); HB60+ 13D(3A)(a); NIHB 14D; NIHB60+ 14D

this condition. Apart from that, no additional bedroom is allowed for any other adult in the dwelling (e.g. a non-dependant) who requires overnight care (but for children see para 7.58).

7.51   You or your partner 'require overnight care' only if the following conditions are met (paras 7.52-55).

Overnight carers: the first condition

7.52   The first condition is that you or your partner:

(a)   are in receipt of the highest or middle rate of the care component of disability living allowance, or attendance allowance, or the daily living component of personal independence payment; or

(b)   provide the council with sufficient evidence to satisfy it that you or your partner require overnight care.

Either (a) or (b) is sufficient. For example, if you get the lower rate of the care component of DLA, you do not meet (a), but you could meet (b), and the fact that you get the lower rate can be used as evidence of this: [2014] UKUT 325 (AAC). Or if you have not claimed any of the benefits in (a), you could meet (b).

Overnight carers: the second condition

7.53   The second condition is that the council is satisfied that you or your partner reasonably require, and have in fact arranged, that one or more people who do not occupy your dwelling as their home:

(a)   is engaged in providing the overnight care; and

(b)   regularly stays overnight in the dwelling for that purpose; and

(c)   is provided with the use of a bedroom for that purpose which is additional to those occupied by the people who occupy your dwelling as their home.

7.54   This could be because you or your partner always have the same overnight carer, or have a rota of overnight carers. But it is not enough to require a carer only by day. The carer must stay overnight regularly. 'Regularly' does not mean normally, ordinarily or at reasonably even intervals, but is closer to habitually, customarily or commonly; so the question is whether the need for overnight care 'arises steadily and often enough to require a bedroom to be kept for the purpose', and a minority of nights can be enough: [2014] UKUT 325 (AAC).

7.55   There must be an actual bedroom provided for the carer, and it must be additional to the bedrooms occupied by you, your partner and the other members of your household. In this context, the Upper Tribunal has held that a bedroom means a room which has a bed in or is used for sleeping in: [2014] UKUT 48 (AAC). In that case, the claimant rented a two-bedroom bungalow. He qualified for one bedroom for himself and his wife (table 7.2), but on medical advice they slept apart – one in each bedroom. Their daughter was an overnight carer, and she slept in a portable bed or sofa in the lounge. This met the condition for an additional bedroom. This is the same as if the daughter had slept in one of the two bedrooms and the husband or wife had slept in the lounge. For further considerations about what is a bedroom, see paras 7.32-34 and table 7.3.

7.51-56 HB 2(1) – def of 'person who requires overnight care'; HB60+ 2(1); NIHB 2(1); NIHB60+ 2(1)

Overnight carers: temporary absence or waiting to move in

7.56   The second condition is also met if you or your partner (whichever requires the care) do not currently occupy the dwelling, but the council is satisfied that:

(a) the dwelling has the additional bedroom; and

(b) you or your partner will in due course arrange for it to be used as described above.

This could apply if you or your partner are temporarily absent (para 3.31), or are waiting to leave hospital or a care home (para 3.21).

Resident carers

7.57   A resident carer who occupies your accommodation as their home (whether they are a relative or not and whether or not they are paid) is included as an occupier (paras 7.40(e) and 10.61). A bedroom is allowed for them under the general rules (table 7.2, 8.2 or 9.5).

Disabled children who need their own bedroom

7.58   In England, Scotland and Wales, one additional bedroom is allowed for each 'child who cannot share a bedroom' (para 7.59), even if the general rules (table 7.2, 8.2 or 9.5) mean the child would otherwise be expected to share a bedroom. This applies to any child under 16 who occupies your dwelling as their home (para 7.40). It does not apply to over-16-year-olds because they qualify for their own bedroom under the general rules.

7.59   A 'child who cannot share a bedroom' means a child who:

(a) is entitled to the highest or middle rate of the care component of disability living allowance; and

(b) due to their disability is 'not reasonably able to share a bedroom with another child'.

7.60   In LHA and rent referral cases (but not in social sector cases) there must actually be an additional bedroom in the claimant's dwelling. For further considerations about what is a bedroom, see paras 7.32-34 and table 7.3.

7.61   If there are other children in your dwelling, the rules are as follows:

(a) first allow a bedroom for each disabled child who meets the above conditions;

(b) then allow a bedroom for the other children using the general rules (table 7.2, 8.2 or 9.5).

7.62   DWP advice on this rule is in circular HB A21/2013. This focuses on whether the child requires overnight care and advises authorities to 'keep in mind the policy intention which is to safeguard the wellbeing of children and prevent them being put at risk of physical harm or having their sleep frequently and significantly disrupted by... sharing a bedroom when it is inappropriate to do so because of severe disability' (HB A21/2013 paras 10-11).

7.58   Social sector: HB B13(5)(ba); LHA: HB 13D(3)(ba); HB60+ 13D(3)(ba)

7.59   HB 2(1) – def of 'child who cannot share a bedroom'; HB60+ 2(1); NIHB 2(1)

7.60   HB 13D(3); HB60+ 13D(3)

7.61   Social sector: HB B13(5)(ba)-(e); LHA: HB 13D(3)(ba)-(e); HB60+ 13D(3)(ba)-(e)

7.63 In England, Scotland and Wales, the above rule about disabled children has applied since 4th December 2013. Similar considerations have applied throughout the UK since 15th May 2012 (Burnip v Birmingham CC and another), but the details were not then set out in regulations.

Eligible rent: protected groups

7.64 The HB rules can mean that a claimant's eligible rent is lower than their actual rent, leaving them to pay the shortfall or get into rent arrears. This section explains how certain groups of claimant are protected against these eligible rent restrictions. It applies to:

(a) social sector cases – when a working age claimant occupies accommodation larger than appropriate (paras 7.23-38);

(b) LHA (private sector) cases – when the LHA figure is lower than the claimant's rent (paras 8.5-21);

(c) exempt accommodation cases – when the claimant occupies unreasonably large or expensive accommodation (paras 9.13-30);

(d) rent referral cases – when the rent officer's or NIHE's rent determination is lower than the claimant's rent (paras 9.40-44).

7.65 The two protections described below (paras 7.66-71) apply to all types of HB case. One further protection applies only to exempt accommodation cases and is described in paragraphs 9.25-27. The footnotes give separate references to the law for social sector and LHA cases when these differ. (For exempt accommodation and rent referral cases see paras 9.23-24 and 9.42.)

People who could formerly afford their accommodation

7.66 You fall within this protected group if:

(a) you or any combination of the occupiers of your home (para 7.70) could afford the financial commitments there when the liability to pay rent was entered into (no matter how long ago that was); and

(b) neither you nor your partner have received HB for any period in the 52 weeks prior to your current claim.

The protection in such cases lasts for the first 13 weeks of your award of HB. This may give you time to move without the additional pressure of having insufficient HB.

7.63   Burnip v Birmingham CC 15/05/12 CA [2012] EWCA Civ 629 www.bailii.org/ew/cases/EWCA/civ/629.html

7.66   Social sector: HB 12BA(6)-(8)

7.67 While the protection lasts, your eligible rent is:

(a) the full actual rent payable on your dwelling;

(b) minus amounts for services which are ineligible for HB (worked out in the same way as for social sector rents: chapter 10) and in Northern Ireland an amount for rates unless you are billed separately.

People who have had a bereavement

7.68 You fall within this protected group if:

(a) any of the occupiers of your home (para 7.70) has died within the last 12 months (including occupiers who were temporarily absent); and

(b) you have not moved home since the date of that death.

7.69 The protection in such cases lasts until 12 months after that death. During that period it works as follows. If you were on HB at the date of the death, your eligible rent must not be reduced to below whatever it was immediately before that date (it is, however, increased if any rule requires this). If you were not on HB at the date of the death, your eligible rent is worked out in the same way as in para 7.67.

Occupiers relevant to the protected groups

7.70 For the purposes of the above protected groups, the only 'occupiers' taken into account are:

(a) you (the claimant) and members of your family (partner, children, young persons: para 4.8); and

(b) any 'relative' of you or your partner (including non-dependants, lodgers and joint occupiers) who has no separate right to occupy the dwelling.

In the law, the term 'linked persons' is also used to refer to the above occupiers.

Who is a 'relative'

7.71 A 'relative' is defined for all HB purposes as:

(a) a parent, daughter, son, sister or brother;

(b) a parent-in-law, daughter-in-law, son-in-law, step-daughter or step-son, including equivalent relations arising through civil partnership;

(c) a partner of any of the above (by marriage or civil partnership, or by living together as a married couple or as civil partners); or

(d) a grandparent, grandchild, aunt, uncle, niece or nephew.

7.68   Social sector: HB 12BA(3)-(5)
        LHA: HB 12D(3),(4),(7)(a); HB60+ 12D(3),(4),(7)(a); NIHB 13C(3),(4),(7)(a); NIHB60+ 13C(3),(4),(7)(a)

7.70   HB 2(1); HB60+ 2(1); NIHB 2(1); NIHB60+ 2(1)

7.71   HB 2(1) – def of 'close relative', 'couple', 'relative'; HB60+2(1); NIHB 2(1); NIHB60+2(1)

Examples: The protected groups

Redundancy

A claimant makes a claim for HB after he is made redundant. His actual rent is high. He moved to this address when he was in a well-paid job and could easily afford the rent and outgoings. He has not been on HB in the last 52 weeks.

Because of the protection for people who could formerly afford their accommodation, his eligible rent must not be restricted in any way for the first 13 weeks of his award of HB. During those weeks, his eligible rent is his actual rent minus amounts for any ineligible services.

Bereavement

A claimant makes a claim for HB after the death of her husband. She has not moved since her husband's death. Her actual rent is high.

Because of the protection for people who have had a bereavement, her eligible rent must not be restricted in any way until the first anniversary of her husband's death. Until then, her eligible rent is her actual rent minus amounts for any ineligible services.

Chapter 8 **Eligible rent: private sector (LHAs)**

- Overview: see paras 8.1-4.
- Eligible rent in LHA cases: see paras 8.5-14.
- Sizes and categories of dwelling: see paras 8.15-21.
- How the LHA figures are set: see paras 8.22-39.

Overview

8.1　　This chapter explains how to work out your eligible rent if you rent your home from a private landlord. Apart from the exceptions described in paragraph 8.3 and table 8.1, this means your claim falls under the local housing allowance (LHA) rules.

8.2　　The LHA scheme was introduced nationally on 7th April 2008 and has since been amended several times. LHA rates apply from the beginning of April each year (para 8.11); though they can change whenever there is a change in the size of your household and in certain other circumstances (para 8.12).

Who falls within the LHA scheme?

8.3　　If you rent your home from a private landlord your eligible rent is always calculated using the LHA rules unless you fall within any of the exceptions in table 8.1. As that table shows, you only fall within the rules if your HB claim started on or after 7th April 2008, or if you moved home on or after that date.

Key features of the LHA scheme

8.4　　If your claim falls within the LHA rules the key features of your claim are:

(a) your eligible rent simply equals the LHA figure that applies to your household;

(b) except that your eligible rent can never be more than your actual rent;

(c) the LHA figures are set by the rent officer (or in Northern Ireland by the NIHE);

(d) the LHA figures are calculated by the rent officer from their rental evidence database;

(e) the LHA figures depend on the size of home that applies to you and on the area you live in;

(f) for each size category the LHA is based on the highest market rent paid in your area for that size home that falls within the cheapest 30% of rents, subject to an overall national cap figure;

(g) the LHA figures for each market area are published online.

You can appeal matters covered in the first part of this chapter (paras 8.5-21) to a tribunal (para 19.18 and table 19.2). Disputes about how the LHA figures are set (paras 8.22-39) cannot be appealed, but see paragraphs 8.37-38.

8.3　　HB 2(1), 13C(1),(2)(a)-(c); HB60+ 2(1), 13C(1),(2)(a)-(c)

Table 8.1 **Exceptions to the LHA scheme**

Your claim cannot fall under the LHA rules if any of the following apply to you:

(a) you are a council/NIHE tenant (in other words if your HB is awarded as a rebate: paras 7.5 and 16.16);

(b) your tenancy was part of a stock transfer from the council/NIHE to a housing association or other landlord (para 7.6 and table 7.1);

(c) your landlord is a registered housing association – except, in England, if they are a profit-making registered provider (paras 7.11-13);

(d) you live in a mobile home, caravan or houseboat (para 9.41);

(e) you live in a 'hostel' (paras 9.41 and 9.46);

(f) the rent officer/NIHE has decided that you are a boarder (para 9.73);

(g) you have a protected tenancy (paras 9.78-83);

(h) you have a shared ownership tenancy (para 9.86);

(i) your home qualifies as 'exempt accommodation' (your landlord is not-for-profit and provides you with care, support or supervision: para 9.4);

(j) you have lived in your home since 7th April 2008 and your HB award started (para 5.32) before that date (para 9.38).

Eligible rent in LHA cases

8.5   If your claim falls under the LHA rules, unless you qualify for protection (para 8.8) your eligible rent (also called 'maximum rent (LHA)' in the law) is simply the LHA figure for the size or category of dwelling appropriate to your household (paras 8.22 onwards) that applies in your area.

8.6   However, if your actual rent is lower than the LHA figure, your eligible rent is your actual weekly rent. This is the case even if your rent includes services which – in other HB cases – would be ineligible for HB (para 10.3).

8.7   Also, your council has the power to reduce your eligible rent further (i.e. below the LHA figure) if 'it appears… that in the particular circumstances of the case [your] eligible rent… is greater than it is reasonable to meet' through HB. If it is, your eligible rent is reduced to 'such lesser sum as seems… to be an appropriate rent in your particular case'. The council must use its judgment (para 1.52), and take your personal circumstances into account when it does this (R v HBRB of the City of Westminster ex parte Laali).

T8.1   HB 2(1),13C(5)-(6); HB60+ 2(1),13C(5)-(6)

8.5   HB 13D(1); HB60+ 13D(1); NIHB 14D(1)

8.6   HB 13D(4),(5),(12); HB60+ 13D(4),(5),(12); NIHB 14D(4),(5),(12)

8.7   HB 12B(1),(6), 13D(4)(b),(12); HB60+ 12B(1)(6), 13D(4)(b),(12)
         R (Laali) v Westminster CC HBRB 08/12/00 QBD www.casetrack.com Subscriber site case reference: CO/1845/2000

Protected groups

8.8 In certain circumstances you can be protected from the LHA rules being used to calculate your eligible rent for a limited period. The effect of the LHA figures on your eligible rent (paras 8.5-7) is delayed if:

(a) you could previously pay your own rent (i.e. you were not on HB) (protection lasts for 13 weeks);

(b) you have had a death in your household (protection lasts for 12 months).

The details are in paragraphs 7.64-71.

When the LHA starts to apply to your claim

8.9 If your claim falls under the LHA rules, the authority uses the LHA figure which applies on the date of your claim. If you did not fall under the LHA rules when your claim started but you now do because you moved home, the authority uses the LHA figure that applies on the date you move. In both cases, the LHA figure then continues to be used for your award until it has to be changed (paras 8.11-14).

Awards for past periods

8.10 If your HB claim is backdated (para 5.50), the authority uses the LHA figure that applied at the beginning of that backdating period (and this figure is used until it has to be changed: paras 8.11-14).

April changes to LHA

8.11 When the rent officer/NIHE issues new LHA figures for the beginning of April each year (para 8.26) these apply automatically in all LHA cases – from the first Monday in April (or 1st April if your rent is due monthly). These are the same as the HB up-rating dates (table 1.4).

Other changes to LHA

8.12 Your LHA figure is also reviewed, and changed if appropriate, whenever:

(a) there is a change in the size or category of dwelling that applies to your household (typically because someone has moved in or out: table 8.2); or

(b) a member of your family or a relative (para 7.71) with no separate right of occupation dies (referred to in the law as a 'linked person') even if this would not change the size or category of dwelling that applies to you; or

(c) you move home (within the area of the authority or outside it); or

(d) your actual weekly rent changes, and you notify the authority of the change. This rule allows the authority to reconsider how your rent compares with the LHA figure (para 8.6).

8.8   HB 2(1),12D(1),(2),13C(1),(2)(a)-(c),13D(12); HB60+ 2(1),12D(1),(2),13C(1),(2)(a)-(c),13D(12);
        NIHB 2(1),13(1),(2),14C(1),(2)(a)-(c),14D(10); NIHB60+ 2(1),13C(1),(2),14C(1),(2)(a)-(c),14D(10)

8.9   HB 13C(2)(a); HB60+ 13C(2)(a); NIHB 14C(2)(a),114A(10); NIHB60+ 14C(2)(a),95A(10)

8.10   HB 13C(3); HB60+ 13C(3); NIHB 14C(3); NIHB60+ 14C(3); DAR 8(15)

8.11   HB 2(1),12D(1),(2),13C(2)(d),(3),(4),(6); HB60+ 2(1),12D(1),(2),13C(2)(d),(3),(4),(6);
        NIHB 2(1),13C(1),(2),14C(2)(d),(3),(4),(6); NIHB60+ 2(1),13C(1),(2),14C(2)(d),(3),(4),(6)

8.12   DAR 7A,8(15); NIDAR 7A

8.13   In each of the above events (para 8.12), the new LHA figure applies from the same day the change of circumstances applies from (paras 17.18 onwards).

8.14   If event (a) occurs (in para 8.12) that nearly always means your HB changes. If event (b) occurs your HB is unlikely to change (because of the protection for bereavement: para 7.68). If event (c) occurs, your HB changes only if a different LHA figure now applies. Event (d) is uncommon, but if it occurs it can result in either an increase or a decrease in your HB. No other changes in your circumstances trigger a change to your LHA figure.

Examples: Eligible rent and LHA figures

A new claim

A claimant has lived in her home since 2011. She decides to claim HB.

Her date of claim falls on Thursday 2nd July 2015.

So she falls within the LHA scheme from Thursday 2nd July 2015.

(Her HB will probably start the following Monday: para 5.45.)

A move

A claimant has lived in her home since 2006, and has been on HB since 2007.

She moves home on Monday 14th September 2015.

So (unless the UC scheme now applies to her) she falls within the LHA scheme from Monday 14th September 2015.

A change of circumstances

A claimant has been on HB within the LHA scheme since May 2015.

A non-dependant then moves in on Wednesday 9th September 2014 – so she requires an extra bedroom.

So the new LHA applies from Monday 14th September 2015.

Sizes and categories of dwelling

8.15   If your claim falls within the LHA rules, your eligible rent depends on the size and category of dwelling appropriate to your household (para 8.5), with the maximum size being a four-bedroom dwelling. Table 8.2 shows which category applies, depending on your household size (and personal circumstances); and further details follow (paras 8.16-21).

8.14   HB 13D(2)-(3B),(12); HB60+ 13D(2)-(3B),(12); NIHB 14D(2)-(3B),(12); NIHB60+ 14D(2)-(3B),(12)

8.15   HB 13D(2)(c),(12); HB60+ 13D(2)(c),(12); NIHB 14D(2)(c),(10); NIHB60+ 14D(2)(c),(10)

Table 8.2 **Categories of accommodation**

Details of the occupiers	**LHA category**
Single occupier	
(a) You are aged under 35 and do not fall within any of the excepted groups in para 8.17.	One-bedroom shared accommodation
(b) You are aged under 35 and fall within any of the exceptions in para 8.17	One-bedroom self-contained accommodation
(c) You are aged 35 or over and occupy 'shared accommodation'.	One-bedroom shared accommodation
(d) You are aged 35 or over and you occupy 'self-contained accommodation'.	One-bedroom self-contained accommodation
Couple, no other occupiers	
(e) Neither you nor your partner fall within any of the excepted groups in para 8.17 and you occupy 'shared accommodation'.	One-bedroom shared accommodation
(f) You occupy 'self-contained accommodation'.	One-bedroom self-contained accommodation
(g) You or your partner fall within any of the excepted groups in para 8.17.	One-bedroom self-contained accommodation

Any other household

One bedroom is allowed for each of the following, but only up to the maximum:

(a) each couple;

(b) each other person aged 16 or over;

(c) two children under 16 of the same sex;

(d) two children under 10 of the same or opposite sex;

(e) each other child.

Additional bedrooms: One or more additional bedrooms can be allowed up to the maximum if you are a foster parent, require overnight care, and/or if you have a disabled child who needs their own bedroom (paras 7.46-63).

Maximum size: This is four bedrooms including any additional bedrooms you qualify for.

Notes

'Occupier' has the same meaning as in paragraph 8.16.

'Self-contained accommodation' means you have exclusive use (para 8.20) of:

- at least two rooms (counting only bedrooms and living rooms, but regardless of whether you share other facilities); or

- one room and a bathroom, a toilet and a kitchen or cooking facilities.

'Shared accommodation' means any other accommodation which is not self-contained.

Which occupiers are included?

8.16   When the authority decides the size of accommodation you qualify for (table 8.2) it takes into account all of the following occupiers who are part of your household:

(a)   you and any member of your family (partner, children and young persons: para 4.8);

(b)   non-dependants (para 4.39);

(c)   lodgers (para 4.48); and

(d)   any other person who occupies your dwelling 'as their home' (but not any joint tenants who are not a member of your household: para 8.20).

For further details of which occupiers are included, and when an additional bedroom is allowed, see paragraphs 7.39-63. However, under the LHA rules the maximum size category is a four-bedroom dwelling (regardless of the number of occupiers, and even when an additional bedroom is 'allowed').

Examples: What size dwelling?

1. A single claimant

A single claimant aged 37 is renting a bedsit in a house in multiple occupation.

So she qualifies for the LHA for one-bedroom shared accommodation.

2. The claimant moves

The same claimant as above moves to a one-bedroom self-contained flat.

So she qualifies for the LHA for one-bedroom self-contained accommodation.

3. A younger single claimant

A single claimant aged 23 is renting a bedsit in a house in multiple occupation.

He qualifies for the LHA for one-bedroom shared accommodation.

4. A couple with two children

A couple have two children, a boy aged 7 and a girl aged 9.

The children are under 10, so are expected to share a bedroom, so the couple qualify for the LHA for two-bedroom accommodation.

When the daughter reaches 10, because the children are of opposite sexes, they are no longer expected to share a bedroom, so the couple qualify for the LHA for three-bedroom accommodation.

5. A couple with a lodger

A couple without children have a lodger in their home.

They qualify for two-bedroom accommodation.

8.16   HB 2(1),(1A),(1C); HB60+ 2(1); NIHB 2(1),(1A),(1C); NIHB60+ 2(1)

Definition of 'young individual'

8.17   If you are single (para 4.7) and under the age of 35 you are counted as a 'young individual' and you only qualify for the shared accommodation rate (table 8.2) except if you:

(a)   are under the age of 22 and you were previously in social services care under a court order (under section 31(1)(a) of the Children Act 1989 in England and Wales, or equivalent provisions in Scotland and Northern Ireland) that was made or in force at any time after your 16th birthday;

(b)   are under the age of 22 and you were previously provided with accommodation by social services (under section 20 of the Children Act 1989 in England and Wales, or equivalent provisions in Scotland and Northern Ireland) but you no longer live there, or if you do it is no longer provided by social services;

(c)   qualify for a severe disability premium in your HB (para 12.38);

(d)   are aged 25 or over (but under 35) and have been in a homeless hostel for three months (the full details are in para 8.18);

(e)   are aged 25 or over (but under 35) and you are an ex-offender who poses a serious risk of harm to the public and you are managed under a multi-agency ('MAPPA') agreement (e.g. police, social services) at management level 2 or 3 (see circular HB/CTB A14/2011 for details);

(f)   have a non-dependant living with you;

(g)   require overnight care (para 7.50); or

(h)   are a foster parent who is a 'qualifying parent or carer' (para 7.49).

Former residents of homeless hostels

8.18   If you are aged 25 or over but under 35 you do not count as a young individual if you:

(a)   have at some time previously occupied a hostel for homeless people for at least three months. The three month qualifying period does not need to have been continuous, and the law does not require it to have been recent (for example, it could have been when you were under 25); and

(b)   during that time you were offered, and accepted, support with rehabilitation or resettlement within the community.

For these purposes, 'hostel' has its normal HB meaning (para 2.30), and a hostel counts as being for homeless people if its 'main purpose… is to provide accommodation together with care, support or supervision for homeless people with a view to assisting [them] to be rehabilitated or settled within the community'.

Joint tenants

8.19   A joint tenant who is also a member of your household is included as an occupier: [2011] UKUT 156 (AAC) (where the claimant's father was included).

8.17   HB 2(1),(1A),(1B); NIHB 2(1),(1A),(1B)

8.19   HB 13D(12); HB60+ 13D(12); NIHB 14D(10); NIHB60+ 14D(10)

8.20   If you have a joint tenancy and your fellow joint tenants are not members of your household, you are allocated the category that applies to you (and the same applies to each other joint tenant). If you are single this is likely to be one-bedroom shared accommodation because it is unlikely you that will have 'exclusive' use of two rooms (table 8.2). Your 'exclusive use' must be a legal right, not just what happens in practice: [2011] UKUT 156 (AAC) and [2014] UKUT 36 (AAC).

Examples: Joint occupiers

1. Three friends

Three friends jointly rent a three-bedroom house. They maintain separate households.

They each qualify for the LHA for one-bedroom shared accommodation.

2. Two sisters, one with a non-dependant

Two sisters jointly rent a three-bedroom house. They maintain separate households. One has a grown-up son living with her.

The son is the non-dependant of his mother.

So his mother qualifies for the LHA for two-bedroom accommodation – and there is a non-dependant deduction in her case only.

Joint tenants with non-dependants

8.21   If you are a joint tenant and you have a non-dependant who is part of your household but not the other joint tenants (for example three friends live together and the mother of one of them lives with them), you qualify for two-bedroom accommodation (and any non-dependant deduction applies to you alone and not to your fellow joint tenants).

How the LHA figures are set

8.22   It is the rent officer/NIHE (paras 9.33-34) who determines:

(a)   all LHA figures (paras 8.24-32); and

(b)   the 'broad rental market areas' they apply to (paras 8.33-34).

Publicity

8.23   LHA figures and broad rental market areas are public information, and the authority must 'take such steps as appear to it appropriate' to bring them to the attention of people who may be entitled to HB. Most authorities have published them on their websites and elsewhere. They are also available online [www].

Determining the LHA figures

8.24   The following paragraphs describe how the rent officer sets the LHA figures. The rules given below are those applying from 2015 onwards.

8.23   HB 13E; HB60+ 13E; NIHB 14E; NIHB60+ 14E
         Great Britain: https://lha-direct.voa.gov.uk/search.aspx
         Northern Ireland: www.nihe.gov.uk/index/benefits/lha/current_lha_rates.htm

8.25   The rent officer sets LHA figures for the following categories of dwelling:

(a) one-bedroom shared accommodation;

(b) one-bedroom self-contained accommodation;

(c) two-bedroom dwellings;

(d) three-bedroom dwellings; and

(e) four-bedroom dwellings.

In each case the rent officer must give a weekly figure and an approximate monthly equivalent: it is the weekly figure which is used in assessing HB.

8.26   The rent officer determines the LHA figures on the last working day in January each year, to apply from April that year (para 8.11).

8.27   For certain areas and categories of dwelling (listed in the table referred to in the footnote), each year's LHA figure is set at the lowest of:

(a) the previous year's LHA figure increased by 4%; or

(b) the national LHA cap (para 8.30).

8.28   In all other cases, each year's LHA figure is set at the lower of:

(a) the rent at the 30th percentile of the data (para 8.31); or

(b) the previous year's LHA figure increased by 1%.

8.29   If the result of the above calculations results (most unusually) in the LHA figure for a larger category of dwelling being lower than the LHA figure for a smaller category, the figure for the larger is increased to equal that for the smaller.

National LHA caps

8.30   The national LHA caps (para 8.27) are as follows:

(a) £260.64 pw for one-bedroom (shared or self-contained) accommodation;

(b) £302.33 pw for two-bedroom accommodation;

(c) £354.46 pw for three-bedroom accommodation;

(d) £417.02 pw for four-bedroom accommodation.

Data and assumptions

8.31   The 30th percentile rent (para 8.28) is the highest rent paid within the bottom 30% of rents taken from the rent officer's data for each category (para 8.25). In fixing it the rent officer uses data for the year ending on the preceding 30th September. This data takes account of the range of rents which a landlord 'might reasonably have been expected to obtain' on dwellings which:

8.25   ROO 4B(6), sch 3B para 1; NIED 3(6), sch para 1

8.26   ROO 2,4B(2A),(2B),(3A); SI 2014 No 3126; NIHB sch 2 para 15;
         NIHB60+ sch 2 para 15; NIED 3(2),(2A),(3); NISR 2015/2

8.27-28 ROO sch 3B paras 2(2),(3),(8),(10) and 6 (table) as amended by SI 2014 No. 3126; NIED sch paras 2(2),(3),(8),(10) and 6 (table)

8.29   ROO sch 3B para 3; NIED sch para 3

8.30   ROO sch 3B para 2(9) as amended by SI 2014 No. 3126; NIED sch para 2(9) as amended by NISR 2015/2

(a)　are let on assured tenancies;

(b)　have the relevant number of rooms for the category in question;

(c)　are in a reasonable state of repair; and

(d)　are in the relevant broad rental market area (paras 8.33-34).

But if within a broad rental market area, there are insufficient rents to enable the rent officer to provide a representative LHA figure for a particular category of dwelling, the rent officer may add 'rents for dwellings in the same category in other areas in which a comparable market exists.'

8.32　　In using the data, the rent officer must:

(a)　'assume that no-one who would have been entitled to [HB] had sought or is seeking the tenancy': in practice they do this simply by ignoring any rent payable by a person on HB; and

(b)　exclude the value of all ineligible service charges.

Determining broad rental market areas

8.33　　The rent officer determines each broad rental market area in the same way for both LHA cases and rent referral cases (para 9.66) (except that in Northern Ireland it applies to LHA cases only: para 9.67), and this is defined in the law as follows:

(a)　The area must be one where a person 'could reasonably be expected to live having regard to facilities and services for the purposes of health, education, recreation, personal banking and shopping, taking account of the distance of travel, by public and private transport, to and from those facilities and services'.

(b)　It must contain 'residential premises of a variety of types' held on a 'variety of tenancies'.

(c)　It must contain 'sufficient privately rented premises' to ensure that the rent officer's figures 'are representative of the rents that a landlord might reasonably be expected to obtain in that area'.

The areas are then normally defined by reference to postcodes.

8.34　　On average each broad rental market area is roughly twice the size of a local authority and does not follow the boundary of any local authority wholly or partly within it. In practice this means a broad rental market area may completely cover and extend beyond one or more local authority area and (less commonly) some local authority areas may contain more than one broad rental market area. The DWP takes the view that the areas can be fairly large and that the changes it made to the law restored this intention following R (Heffernan) v the Rent Service where the use of large areas for setting the local reference rent (paras 9.58-61) was criticised.

8.31　　ROO sch 3B para 2(1),(4)-(7); NIED sch para 2(1),(4)-(7)

8.32　　ROO sch 3B para 2(5); NIED sch para 2(5)

8.33　　ROO sch 3B paras 4,5; NIED sch paras 4,5

8.34　　ROO sch 3B para 4 substituted by art 2(4)(b) of SI 2008/3156 as from 05/01/2009 following:
R (Heffernan) v the Rent Service 30/07/08 HL [2008] UKHL 58
www.publications.parliament.uk/pa/ld200708/ldjudgmt/jd080730/heffer-1.htm

Amending areas or figures

8.35   Rent officers can amend individual LHA figures. They can also amend broad rental market areas, but only where the Secretary of State agrees this should be done. In either case, they must notify authorities of this.

8.36   The above amendments are taken into account in HB as follows:

(a) if your LHA goes down as a result, this is implemented as a change of circumstances from the Monday following the date the rent officer makes their amendment (so as to avoid you being overpaid);

(b) if your LHA goes up as a result, this is implemented back to the date the LHA in question applied from (so you receive any arrears).

Appeals about the areas or figures

8.37   Unlike the rules if your claim is referred to the rent officer, there is no right of appeal to another rent officer about a broad rental market area or about the amount of an LHA figure. Nor is there a right of appeal to a tribunal (although you can appeal to a tribunal about the number of occupiers in your household and therefore which particular LHA figure is to be applied). This means that any challenge would have to be by judicial review in the High Court (Sheriff Court in Scotland).

8.38   Some judicial reviews were begun (e.g. in relation to the London broad rental market areas) before LHAs came in, but all were settled by negotiation. Those judicial reviews were begun by authorities, but it would seem that an individual claimant might also be able to do this.

Data provided to the rent officer by the authority

8.39   In England, Scotland and Wales each authority sends the rent officer data to assist them in excluding the effect of HB on market rents (para 8.32). This is done between the first and fifth working day of every month, and contains details of rents, facilities, letting dates and dates of HB entitlement for everyone who was receiving HB in the private sector at any time in the previous month.

8.35   ROO 4B(1A); NIED 3(1)

8.36   HB 18A; HB60+ 18A; ROO 7A(4); NIHB 14F; NIHB60+ 14F

8.39   HB 114A(1),(2); HB60+ 95A(1),(2)

Chapter 9 **Eligible rent: special cases**

- Exempt accommodation: see paras 9.2-9.8.
- Eligible rent in exempt accommodation: see paras 9.9-12.
- Rent restrictions in exempt accommodation: see paras 9.13-30.
- Rent referral cases: see paras 9.31-39.
- Eligible rent in rent referral cases: see paras 9.40-44.
- When rent determinations are made: see paras 9.45-49.
- How rent determinations are made: see paras 9.50-72.
- Boarder cases: see paras 9.73-77.
- Protected tenancies and old HB claims: paras 9.78-85.
- Shared ownership: see paras 9.86-87.
- Homeless households in temporary accommodation: see paras 9.88-94.

9.1 This chapter explains when the normal rules for working out your eligible rent (chapters 7 and 8) do not apply, and how it is worked out in these cases. These special rules usually apply if you have an older claim or if you live in specialist accommodation such as a hostel, other supported housing or a mobile home.

Exempt accommodation

9.2 This section gives the rules about when your home qualifies as exempt accommodation. Broadly this means if you rent your home from a not-for-profit landlord who provides you with care, support or supervision (paras 9.4-6). Even if you do not live in exempt accommodation, in certain circumstances if you have a very old HB claim at the same address (see paras 9.80 and 9.84) your eligible rent is worked out as if you were.

Overview of exempt accommodation

9.3 If your home qualifies as exempt accommodation the main features of how your HB is calculated are as follows:

(a) your eligible rent is the actual rent you pay minus amounts for ineligible services and (in Northern Ireland) rates;

(b) your rent (and HB) is not affected by the social sector size criteria ('the bedroom tax');

(c) in certain circumstances if your rent is considered too high for your needs your eligible rent can be lower;

(d) but even if your rent is considered too high, there are protections if you are vulnerable (for example, if you are elderly or disabled) ;

(e) the rent officer/NIHE may set a rent (a 'determination') but your council is not obliged to use their figure when it calculates your eligible rent;

(f) you can continue to get HB even if you are on universal credit (paras 1.17 and 2.38).

Definition of exempt accommodation

9.4 You are treated as living in 'exempt accommodation' if:

(a) your home is 'provided by':

- a housing association, whether registered or unregistered (para 7.10),
- a registered charity (para 2.26),
- a not-for-profit voluntary organisation (para 2.25), or
- an English non-metropolitan county council;

(b) but only if (in each case) 'that body or a person acting on its behalf also provides [you] with care, support or supervision'.

9.5 Both conditions (para 9.4) must be satisfied for your home to qualify as exempt accommodation. If your home is in a group of dwellings (such as sheltered housing) you do not qualify just because other homes in the group do (for example, if support is provided to only some of the residents), the conditions must apply to your home (CH/1289/2007):

(a) Your home must be 'provided by' one of the organisations listed (para 9.4(a)). This means one of these organisations must be your immediate landlord (CH/3900/2005 and [2009] UKUT 12 (AAC)): for example, if your home is rented from a landlord that holds it on a lease, that landlord, rather than the superior landlord. It is your landlord that must be one of these bodies; it is not sufficient if only your landlord's managing agent is.

(b) The care, support or supervision (para 9.4(b)) must be provided either by your landlord directly or by someone else on his or her behalf – and there are many other considerations to take into account, as shown in table 9.1. (For a helpful summary of older cases, see circular HB/CTB A22/2008.)

9.6 In England, Scotland and Wales, your home also qualifies as 'exempt accommodation' if your landlord has received funding for resettlement from the DWP under section 30 of the Jobseekers Act 1995 (this mainly applies to hostels and other similar resettlement places).

9.7 Exempt accommodation is so called because your rent is exempt from a local reference rent and/or single room rent determinations. Your council sometimes also calls exempt accommodation 'old cases' because, regardless of the actual age of your claim, the rules for assessing your eligible rent are based on those in force before January 1996. These rules are in 'old' HB regulations 12, 13 and 13ZA, which are found in the HB Consequential Provisions Regulations (see footnote).

Supported accommodation and exempt accommodation

9.8 Specified 'supported accommodation' is explained in paragraphs 2.37-39 and table 2.1. Not all supported accommodation is exempt accommodation. However, if your home meets one of the other definitions of supported accommodation (table 2.1 (b) to (d)), it is

---

9.4   CPR sch 3 para 4(1)(b),(10); NICPR sch 3 para 4(1)(b),(9)

9.7   CPR sch 3 para 5; NICPR sch 3 para 5

worth checking whether it also meets the definition of exempt accommodation. If it does, the rules in this section apply (as well as the rules in para 2.38).

Eligible rent in exempt accommodation

9.9   If your home qualifies as exempt accommodation your eligible rent is:

(a) the actual rent you pay on your home (but this is subject to limits: paras 9.13-30; and see also para 9.85 for protected tenancies);

(b) minus amounts for service charges which are ineligible for HB. These are worked out in the same way as for social sector rents (paras 7.17 and chapter 10);

(c) minus, in Northern Ireland, the amount in your rent you pay for rates, (except where you are billed for your rates separately).

If you are a joint tenant your eligible rent is adjusted in the same way as it would be if you were a council/NIHE tenant (para 7.21). For other items included in setting your rent that are not services (overheads, management costs, garages, land, business premises and space for a carer) see paragraphs 10.57-62.

Table 9.1 **Care, support or supervision: case law**

1. Meaning of 'care, support or supervision' (CSS)

This part of the table applies to exempt accommodation (paras 9.2-6), and also to other kinds of supported accommodation (paras 2.37-39).

- ■ *Meaning of CSS:* the phrase 'care, support or supervision' has its ordinary English meaning (R(S) v Walsall MBC, confirming R(H) 2/07).

- ■ *Availability of CSS:* The CSS must be available in reality to the tenant, and there must be a real prospect that they will find the service of use (R(H) 4/09 and [2009] UKUT 109 (AAC) para 44).

- ■ *Meaning of 'support':* 'Support' might well be characterised as 'the giving of advice and assistance to a claimant in coping with the practicalities of [their] life, and in particular [their] occupation of the property' ([2010] AACR 2 para 129). It is more than ordinary housing management ([2009] UKUT 107 (AAC) para 71).

- ■ *Continuity of support:* The support provided must be on-going (R(H) 4/09). For example, help with gaining exemption from council tax because the tenant is severely mentally impaired is more like a setting up cost and is not enough ([2010] AACR 2 para 120).

- ■ *Need for and provision of 'support':* 'What matters is simply whether support is provided to more than a minimal extent, and it is… implicit that support is not "provided" unless there is in fact some need for it' ([2009] UKUT 150 (AAC) para 73).

- ■ *Amount of CSS:* To count as CSS what is provided must be more than minimal. On the facts of the cases in question an average of ten minutes per tenant per week

---

9.9   HB 2(4),11(1)(d); HB60+ 2(4),11(1)(d); NIHB 2(4),11(1)(d); NIHB60+ 2(4),11(1)(d); HB old 12(3)-(5) in CPR sch 3 para 5

was not enough (R(H) 7/07), but three hours per tenant per week might be enough (CH/1289/2007). In another case, just helping with HB claims and reviews, and carrying out safety and security inspections, was not enough to be more than minimal; but 'proactively considering what physical improvements or alterations to the properties could usefully be made' in the case of adaptations desirable in the light of the tenant's disability, could be enough ([2010] AACR 2 para 188).

■ *When there is no relevant history:* Where there is no history of the support being provided (because it is a new development), it is necessary to look at what is contemplated ([2009] UKUT 109 (AAC)).

2. Provision of CSS in exempt accommodation

This part of the table applies only to exempt accommodation.

■ *CSS provided by the landlord:* A landlord can provide CSS by making arrangements for it, or by paying for someone to do it ([2009] UKUT 107 (AAC) para 71).

■ *CSS provided on behalf of the landlord:* For CSS to be provided 'on behalf of' the landlord, there must be 'a sense of agency between the [CSS provider and the landlord], or to put it another way, a contract, or something akin to it'. An arrangement that is merely a joint venture is not enough; nor is it enough that there is a contract between the CSS provider and e.g. social services (R(S) v Walsall MBC, confirming R(H) 2/07).

■ *CSS provided by landlord as well as care provider:* The landlord may provide CSS without being the principal provider of it to that particular tenant ([2010] AACR 2 para 188).

■ *Availability of CSS from elsewhere:* 'The likely nature, extent and frequency of [the CSS], and the extent of support available to the claimant from elsewhere' are to be taken into account in considering whether the CSS provided by a landlord is more than minimal ([2009] UKUT 107 (AAC) para 71).

■ *Who pays for the CSS?* It is irrelevant that the landlord is (or is not) paid to provide the CSS by someone else ([2009] UKUT 107 (AAC) para 71).

■ *Support vs housing management:* 'Support' means that the landlord does more than an ordinary landlord would do (R(H) 4/09). It is more than ordinary housing management; and carrying out repairs and maintenance do not generally amount to support. But if the tenancy agreement 'imposes unusually onerous repairing and maintenance obligations on the landlord', this can amount to support; as can the fact that a claimant's disabilities impose a 'materially greater burden on the landlord' ([2009] UKUT 107 (AAC) para 71).

■ *Live-in carers:* While the presence of a live-in carer may or may not amount to CSS (depending on who provides the carer), the case law on carers in exempt accommodation is more relevant to whether the size of the accommodation is reasonable (paras 7.57 and 9.20).

T9.1   R(S) v Walsall MBC 19/12/08 HC (Admin) [2008] EWHC (Admin) 3097 and 03/09/09 HC (Admin) [2009] EWHC (Admin) 2221
         www.bailii.org/ew/cases/EWHC/Admin/2009/3097.html
         www.bailii.org/ew/cases/EWHC/Admin/2009/2221.html

Exempt accommodation and rent determinations

9.10   If you live in exempt accommodation your HB claim may require a rent determination – made by the rent officer (or in Northern Ireland the NIHE) – as follows:

(a) if your home falls within any of the types of accommodation described in paragraph 9.36 (e.g. your landlord is a registered housing association), no rent determination is required (or permitted) unless your rent or the size of your home is unreasonable (para 9.37);

(b) in any other case a rent determination is always required.

9.11   When a rent determination is required for exempt accommodation, the same procedures apply as in rent referral cases (paras 9.45-49) ,except as described in the next paragraph.

9.12   If you live in exempt accommodation where a rent referral is required (para 9.10(b)), unlike in other rent referral cases, the rent determinations are not binding on the authority (though they may affect subsidy: paras 23.29-30): they play an advisory role in the authority's consideration of whether to restrict your eligible rent (paras 9.16 and 9.29).

Rent restrictions in exempt accommodation

9.13   This section explains:

(a) when your eligible rent can be restricted if you live in exempt accommodation;

(b) (and if it can be) when you are protected against those restrictions; and

(c) how much the restriction should be (if you are not protected).

9.14   When the authority makes a decision about all of the above your claim must be considered in its individual circumstances. Your authority must not apply rigid rules that automatically treat every case the same way (GM para A4.962), and it cannot allow subsidy considerations (para 9.30) to override the requirements of the HB regulations and case law. All the matters described in this section may be appealed to a tribunal (chapter 19).

Unreasonableness

9.15   The first question your authority must decide is whether:

(a) your rent is 'unreasonably high' (para 9.19); or

(b) your home is 'larger than is reasonably required' (para 9.20); or

(c) your rent increase is 'unreasonably high' (para 9.21); or

(d) if your rent increase occurs less than 12 months after the previous one whether it is 'unreasonable having regard to the length of time since that previous increase' (para 9.22).

9.16   In deciding (a) to (c) above, the authority must compare your rent with that of suitable alternative accommodation, taking account of all of the other people who live with you (paras 9.17-18). In deciding (a) and (b), your authority may also 'make reference' to any rent officer/NIHE determination made that applies to your home (paras 9.10-12) – and the DWP advises that it 'must' do this (GM A4.1122) – but your authority must not be bound by it.

9.10   HB 14(1)-(2), sch 2; HB60+ 14(1)-(2), sch 2; NIHB 15(1),(3), sch 3; NIHB60+ 15(1),(3), sch 3

9.15   HB old 13(3),13ZA(1) in CPR/NICPR sch 3 para 5

Suitable alternative accommodation

9.17   When your authority considers what 'suitable alternative accommodation' is for your claim (para 9.16) it:

(a) must take account of the nature of any alternative accommodation including any exclusive and shared facilities, having regard to the your age and state of health and of the other occupiers (para 9.18). 'For example, if you are disabled or elderly you might have special needs and require more expensive or larger accommodation' (GM para A4.1171);

(b) must only take into account alternative accommodation with security of tenure which is reasonably equivalent to what you have (GM para A4.1170);

(c) must have 'sufficient information to ensure that like is being compared with like… Unless that can be done, no safe assessment can be made of the reasonableness of the rent in question or the proper level of value' (Malcolm v Tweeddale DC HBRB);

(d) may take account of alternative accommodation outside its own area if there is no comparable accommodation within it. But if this is necessary, it is unreasonable to make 'comparisons with other parts of the country where accommodation costs differ widely from those which apply locally' (GM para A4.1172).

Occupiers

9.18   When deciding what suitable alternative accommodation is, the occupiers the authority must take into account are:

(a) you and your 'family' (partner, children, young persons: para 4.8); and

(b) any 'relative' (para 7.71) of you or your partner (including non-dependants, lodgers and joint tenants) who has no separate right to occupy your home.

Unreasonably high rents

9.19   In deciding whether your rent is unreasonably high, the authority must take account of suitable alternative accommodation (paras 9.17-18). It should do this by working through the following questions (R v Beverley BC ex p Hare):

(a) What is the actual rent (including all eligible and ineligible services) you pay for your home?

(b) What would be suitable alternative accommodation for you (para 9.17)? And, in order to determine this, what services are needed to make it suitable and what other factors need to be taken into account?

(c) What would the rent be (including all eligible and ineligible services) for such accommodation?

(d) Is the rent in (a) unreasonably high by comparison with (c)? 'Unreasonably high' means more than just 'higher' (Malcolm v Tweeddale DC HBRB and CH/4306/2003).

9.17   HB old 13(9)(a) in CPR/NICPR sch 3 para 5; Malcolm v Tweeddale HBRB 06/08/91 CS 1994 SLT 1212

9.18   HB old 13(10),(11) in CPR/NICPR sch 3 para 5

9.19   See 9.17 and R v Beverley DC HBRB ex p Hare 21/02/95 QBD HLR 637

Unreasonably large dwellings

9.20 In deciding whether your home is larger than you reasonably require, the authority must take account of suitable alternative accommodation (paras 9.17-18). The size of your home is judged by reference to you 'and others who also occupy that dwelling'. These include the occupiers described above (para 9.18) and also non-dependants and lodgers who are not relatives. It can also include resident carers (para 7.57). (The specific rules of the social sector and LHA size criteria in chapters 7 and 8 do not apply here.)

Unreasonably high rent increases

9.21 In deciding whether a rent increase is unreasonably high, the authority must take account of suitable alternative accommodation (paras 9.17-18). The comparison should be made with 'more suitable' rather than 'less suitable' accommodation: [2009] UKUT 162 (AAC). When this matter is being considered by a tribunal it should do so as if it was being done at the time when the authority should have been deciding it; and if evidence for that period is unavailable or unclear, it must make findings of fact about what was likely to have been the case: [2009] UKUT 162 (AAC). 'Unreasonably high' means more than just 'higher' (Malcolm v Tweeddale DC HBRB and CH/4306/2003).

Unreasonably prompt rent increases

9.22 Regardless of whether an increase is too high, if an increase occurs unreasonably close to the previous one your eligible rent can be reduced by either the whole or part of the latest increase. But this rule only applies if the latest increase takes place less than 12 months after the previous one – so an annual increase cannot be too soon.

Protected groups

9.23 You are protected against a restriction because your home is considered unreasonably large or your rent unreasonably high if one of the following applies (paras 9.19-20):

(a) you could previously afford the rent without help from HB (the details are in paras 7.66-67); and

(b) there has been a bereavement in your household within the past year (the details are in paras 7.68-69); and

(c) you are considered vulnerable for one of certain specified reasons (such as if you are elderly or disabled). The rules are described paragraphs 9.25-27.

(But the correct law that relates to the first two of these is in the footnote to this paragraph.)

9.24 You are protected against a restriction for an unreasonable rent increase (paras 9.21-22) if you fall within the second category (a recent bereavement: paras 7.68-69).

9.20   HB old 13(3)(b) in CPR/NICPR sch 3 para 5
9.21   HB old 13ZA(1)(a) in CPR/NICPR sch 3 para 5; Malcolm v Tweeddale HBRB 06/08/91 CS 1994 SLT 1212
9.22   HB old 13ZA(1)(b) in CPR/NICPR sch 3 para 5
9.23   HB old 13(5)-(8) in CPR/NICPR sch 3 para 5
9.24   HB old 13ZA(2),(3) in CPR/NICPR sch 3 para 5

Who is considered vulnerable

9.25   You are considered to be vulnerable (para 9.23(c)) and have some protection against a restriction if any of the occupiers in your home (para 9.18):

(a) has reached state pension credit age (para 1.24); or

(b) is responsible for a child or young person in your household (paras 4.3 and 4.23-38); or

(c) has limited capability for work for ESA purposes (para 12.20) (or under the old work fitness test if that still applies). Capability for work is decided by the DWP, not the authority; and under the current rules of assessment (not as they were decided in the past) (CH/4424/2004).

If any of the above applies then the authority must not reduce your eligible rent unless there is cheaper suitable alternative accommodation available (para 9.26) and it is reasonable to expect you to move (para 9.27).

9.26   What counts as suitable alternative accommodation is described in paragraphs 9.17-18. The point here is that it must be available – and available more cheaply. For example, accommodation you have recently left, or an offer of accommodation you have refused, may be available – but only while it actually remains available to you, and not after it has been let to someone else. The DWP advises that 'authorities should regard accommodation as not available if, in practice, there is little or no possibility of [you] being able to obtain it, for example because it could only be obtained on payment of a large deposit which [you do] not have' (GM para A4.1222).

However, that does not mean that the authority is expected to find a home for you, and 'it is… quite sufficient if an active market rent is shown to exist in houses in an appropriate place at the appropriate level [to which the] rent is restricted'. Provided the authority has at least evidence of that, it is sufficient 'to point to a range of properties, or a bloc of property, which is available without specific identification of particular dwelling houses' (R v East Devon DC HBRB ex p Gibson).

9.27   When the authority is considering whether it is reasonable to expect you to move, it must take the following into account:

(a) your prospects of retaining employment; and

(b) the effect on the education of any child or young person mentioned in paragraph 9.18 who would have to change school

and, if you appeal, the authority is expected to provide evidence that it has done this (R v Sefton MBC ex p Cunningham).

Restricting the eligible rent

9.28   If your rent could be restricted for the reasons in paragraph 9.15(a)-(c) and you are not in one of the protected groups (paras 9.23-27), the authority must make a restriction:

9.25   HB old 13(4),(9)(b) in CPR/NICPR sch 3 para 5

9.26   HB old 13(4) in CPR/NICPR sch 3 para 5; R v East Devon DC HBRB ex p Gibson 10/03/93 CA 25 HLR 487

9.27   HB old 13(9)(b) in CPR/NICPR sch 3 para 5; R v Sefton MBC ex p Cunningham 22/05/91 QBD 23 HLR 534

9.28   HB old 13(1),(9)(a), 13ZA(1),(9)(a) in CPR/NICPR sch 3 para 5

(a) if this is because your home is unreasonably large or your rent is unreasonably high (paras 9.19-20), this means the authority must decide how much to reduce your eligible rent; or

(b) if this is because of an unreasonable rent increase (paras 9.21-22), this means the authority must decide how much of the rent increase to disallow.

In either case, the authority must take account of suitable alternative accommodation (paras 9.17-18).

9.29   When it is considering the level of the restriction the authority should work through the following steps (Mehanne v Westminster CC HBRB and R v Beverley BC ex p Hare):

(a) are there any circumstances which may make a small reduction appropriate;

(b) the appropriate level for a reduction; and

(c) how was that figure arrived at?

The level of the restriction does not have to equal the whole element that is considered unreasonable: it could be less, or less for the time being. But the reduction cannot be more than that: the authority must not reduce your eligible rent below the cost of suitable alternative accommodation (R v Brent LBC ex p Connery). And if the rent officer/NIHE has made a determination, the authority must not automatically adopt that figure as the eligible rent (para 9.12).

The impact of subsidy

9.30   When the authority is considering whether your home is unreasonably large or your rent is unreasonably high or in any case where you are in a protected group (paras 9.23-27) it cannot take into account the impact on it of the subsidy rules (paras 23.29-30). However, it may consider the subsidy implications in deciding the amount of the restriction to be applied (paras 9.28-29): R v Brent LBC ex p Connery. In reaching its decision on this, the authority must properly exercise its judgment and discretion (paras 1.52-53) and in doing so the DWP's opinion is that the authority 'cannot restrict on financial grounds alone' (GM para A4.1173).

Rent referral cases

9.31   This section gives the rules by which your eligible rent is calculated if your claim is referred to the rent officer/NIHE for a rent determination. These include certain unreasonably large or expensive social sector lettings (paras 9.35-37), and older or special types of private sector lettings (para 9.38). (But see paragraphs 9.10-12 if you live in exempt accommodation.)

Overview of the rent referral scheme

9.32   If your rent is referred to the rent officer/NIHE for a rent determination the main features of how your HB is calculated are as follows:

(a) your eligible rent is set by reference to various rent determinations (independent valuations);

9.29-30 R v Westminster CC HBRB ex p Mehanne 08/03/01 HL (2001) UKHL 11
www.publications.parliament.uk/pa/ld200001/ldjudgmt/jd01308/mehanne-l.htm
R v Brent LBC ex p Connery 20/10/89 QBD 22 HLR 40

(b) in England, Scotland and Wales rent determinations are by the rent officer and in Northern Ireland by the NIHE;

(c) these rent determinations are binding on your authority and limit the HB it can pay (except in exempt accommodation: paras 9.10-12);

(d) in certain circumstances this limit can be delayed for 13/52 weeks if you could previously afford the rent or had a bereavement.

The rent officer

9.33   Rent officers are independent of the authority. In England, they are employed by the Valuation Office Agency; in Wales by the Rent Officers Wales (part of the Welsh Government); and in Scotland by the Rent Service Scotland (part of the Scottish Government). For how to appeal against rent officer determinations, and how errors in them are dealt with, see paragraphs 19.99-109.

The Northern Ireland Housing Executive

9.34   In Northern Ireland, the NIHE has the same HB functions as the rent officer in Great Britain. For how to appeal against rent determinations, see paragraph 19.110.

Rent referral for social landlords

9.35   If you pay rent to a social landlord your claim is not normally referred to the rent officer/NIHE for a rent determination. The only exception to this rule is if both the conditions in the next two paragraphs are met (but see para 9.39 for protected tenancies and shared ownership).

9.36   The first condition is that your home must be:

(a) rented from a registered housing association (paras 7.8-9 and 7.11); or

(b) except in Northern Ireland, a caravan, mobile home or houseboat on land belonging to the authority itself (see also para 16.15); or

(c) except in Northern Ireland, a caravan or mobile home on a county council site for gypsies or travellers (para 2.29) where you pay rent/site fees to that council.

However, if (a) applies and your original tenancy was with the authority (para 7.6 and table 7.1) no rent determination is required until the first rent increase after the date your tenancy was transferred.

9.37   The second condition is that the authority considers that:

(a) your rent is unreasonably high; or

(b) if you have a pension age claim only (paras 1.23-25), your home is unreasonably large for the occupiers.

Private sector rent referral cases

9.38   If you rent your home from a private landlord your HB claim is referred for a rent determination if (but see para 9.39 for exceptions):

9.35-38 HB 12C(1),13(1),13C(5),(6),14(1)(a)-(h) sch 2 paras 3,11(2)(a); HB60+ 12C(1),13(1),13C(5),(6),14(1)(a)-(h) sch 2 paras 3,11(2)(a); NIHB 13B(1),14(1)14C(5)15(1),(4), sch 3 paras 3,5(2)(a); NIHB60+ 13B(1),14(1)14C(5)15(1),(4), sch 3 paras 3,5(2)(a)

(a) you are a boarder (para 9.73);

(b) your home is a caravan, mobile home or houseboat (para 2.29);

(c) you live in a hostel (para 2.30); and

(d) any other letting where you have received HB at the same address without any break in your claim since before 7th April 2008.

Private landlord means any landlord who is not the authority or a registered housing association which in England includes a profit-making registered housing association if your home is let at a commercial rent (para 7.11(c)).

Exceptions

9.39   If you have a protected tenancy (para 9.79) or a shared ownership (para 9.86) tenancy your claim is never referred for a rent determination. Different rules apply if your claim is referred for a determination but your home qualifies as exempt accommodation (paras 9.10-12).

Eligible rent in rent referral cases

9.40   If your claim is referred to the rent officer/NIHE your eligible rent (also called 'maximum rent' in the law) is set by the rental valuations provided by the rent officer/NIHE. These are called 'rent determinations'. In straightforward cases, your eligible rent simply equals the lowest of these rent determinations.

9.41   If your claim is referred to the rent officer the detailed rules for setting your eligible rent are given in table 9.2, including the adjustments and variations that apply if you are a joint tenant or a boarder, or if you live in a hostel, caravan, mobile home or houseboat. There are also rules about when rent determinations are made, and apply in HB (paras 9.45-49), how the rent officer/NIHE makes those determinations (paras 9.50-72), and the special procedures that apply if you are a boarder in England, Scotland or Wales (paras 9.73-77).

Table 9.2 **Eligible rent in rent referral cases**

Step 1: The referred rent

This equals your actual rent. In England, Scotland and Wales it is the figure the authority refers to the rent officer (RO).

Step 2: Rent determinations

The RO (in Northern Ireland the NIHE) uses the referred rent to consider whichever of the following apply in your case (paras 9.52 and 9.54-64):

(a) a significantly high rent determination;

(b) a size-related rent determination;

9.41   HB 2(1),12B(3)-(6),12C,13,14(1),(2)(a),(3),(7),(8); HB60+ 2(1),12B(3)-(6),12C,13,14(1),(2)(a),(3),(7),(8); ROO 3(1),6(2),(3),7,sch 1 paras 6,7,9, sch 4 paras 1,2

T9.2   HB 2(1),12B(3)-(6),12C,13,14(1),(2)(a),(3),(7),(8); HB60+ 2(1),12B(3)-(6),12C,13,14(1),(2)(a),(3),(7),(8); ROO 3(1),6(2),(3),7,sch 1 paras 6,7,9, sch 4 paras 1,2

(c)   an exceptionally high rent determination;

(d)   a local reference rent determination;

(e)   a single room rent determination;

(f)   a service charge determination.

Step 3: The claim-related rent determination

The RO/NIHE also makes a claim-related rent determination. This is:

(a)   the lowest of any determinations made at (a),(b),(c) above; or

(b)   if none of those was made, the referred rent.

Step 4: Adjustment for ineligible services (other than board)

If the claim-related rent determination is the referred rent (step 3), the authority deducts any service charge determination (step 2(f)) from it.

Step 5: Adjustment for joint tenants

If you are a joint tenant, the authority apportions the claim-related rent determination (steps 3 and 4) and any local reference rent determination (step 2(d)) between your fellow joint tenants (using the rules in para 7.21).

Step 6: Adjustment for boarders

If you are a boarder (para 9.73), the authority deducts the standard amount for meals (table 10.4) from the claim-related rent determination (steps 3 and 4) and any local reference rent determination (step 2(d)) – but only when the RO/NIHE included your board in that determination.

Step 7: Eligible rent

The authority sets your eligible rent. This is the lowest of:

(a)   the claim-related rent determination (steps 3 to 6);

(b)   any local reference determination (steps 2(d), 5 and 6);

(c)   any single room rent determination (step 2(e)).

Variations for hostels

If you live in a hostel (para 2.30), the RO/NIHE does not make determinations (c), (d) and (e) in step 2. References to them should be ignored.

Variations for caravans, mobile homes and houseboats

If you live in caravan, mobile home or houseboat (para 2.29), the RO/NIHE does not make a size-related rent determination (step 2(b)). References to it should be ignored.

Notes

- ■   The table assumes all the figures are weekly (para 6.41).

- ■   A higher eligible rent can apply if your claim is protected (para 9.42).

- ■   Step 4 is based on rent officer guidance (Rent Officers Handbook, Ineligible charges).

Examples: Eligible rent in rent referral cases

1. Sole tenant

A claimant under the age of 35 is a sole tenant of her home. Her actual rent is £80 per week. The rent officer has provided the following figures:

- a claim-related rent determination of £70 per week;
- a local reference rent determination of £65 per week;
- a single room rent determination of £60 per week.

Her eligible rent is simply the lowest figure: £60 per week.

2. Joint tenants

Three claimants in their 40s jointly rent a house for £180 per week. They have identical rooms. The rent officer has provided the following figures:

- a claim-related rent determination of £150 per week;
- a local reference rent determination of £135 per week;
- no single room rent determination (because none of them are under 35).

The two figures given above are divided between the three joint tenants, giving £50 per week and £45 per week.

The eligible rent of each of them is the lower figure: £45 per week.

Protected groups

9.42   You may be protected for a limited period against the effect of a rent referral on your eligible rent if:

(a) you could previously afford your rent (i.e. without HB); or

(b) you or a member of your household has had a bereavement.

The details are in paragraphs 7.64-71 (but references to the law are in the footnotes to this paragraph).

Can the eligible rent be even lower?

9.43   In certain circumstances the authority may decide to use its 'over-riding power to reduce your eligible rent' (described in paragraph 8.7) to a level below the figure calculated in table 9.2.

9.44   Also if, during an award of HB, your actual rent reduces to below the eligible rent calculated in table 9.2 (which would be rare), your eligible rent is also reduced to match your (new) actual rent minus any ineligible service charges included in it. For these purposes ineligible service charges are assessed as in chapter 10.

9.42   HB 13ZA; HB60+ 13ZA; NIHB 14ZA; NIHB60+ 14ZA

9.43   HB 12B(6),12C(2),(3); HB60+ 12B(6),12C(2),(3)

9.44   HB 13ZB; HB60+ 13ZB; NIHB 14B; NIHB60+ 14B

When rent determinations are made

The general rule

9.45 Your claim is referred for rent determination or a fresh rent determination on each occasion when:

- you have made a new claim which relates to the type of case the authority must refer (paras 9.35 and 9.38);

- you have an existing determination and you have notified the authority of a 'relevant change of circumstances'. These are all listed in table 9.4;

- there is an existing determination that relates to your tenancy (even if it was originally made for a previous tenant) and 52 weeks have passed since that determination was made.

Further rules apply if you live in a hostel (para 9.46) or if you have applied for a 'pre-tenancy determination' (para 9.70).

Hostel cases

9.46 If a rent determination has been made for one letting in a hostel (para 2.30), it applies to all similar lettings in that hostel for 12 months.

The rent referral

9.47 In England, Scotland and Wales the authority should refer your claim to the rent officer within three working days. When it makes the referral, it should inform the rent officer of (among other details):

- your actual rent (the referred rent – para 9.51); and

- any service charges included within it (other than meals) which are ineligible for HB (see paras 9.52, 10.8 and table 10.2 for details).

Any matter decided by the authority (such as which services are ineligible, and steps 4 to 7 in table 9.2) are appealable to a tribunal (chapter 19).

How quickly should a determination be made

9.48 In England, Scotland and Wales the rent officer should provide his/her determinations within five working days after receiving the referral or any further information needed (26 working days if he/she intends to visit the home). In Northern Ireland the NIHE should make its determinations within three working days. (For appeals about rent determinations, see paras 19.99-110.)

9.45   HB 14(1)-(3),(6),(8) sch 2 para 2; HB60+14(1)-(3),(6),(9) sch 2 para 2; NIHB 15,16,sch 3 para 2; NIHB60+15,16,sch 3 para 2

9.46   HB 14(2)(a),(7); HB60+ 14(2)(a),(7); NIHB 15; NIHB 60+ 15

9.47   HB 14(5),(6),114A(1),(6)-(9); HB60+ 14(5),(6),95A(1),(6)-(9)

9.48   ROO 2(1),3(1)

When determinations take effect

9.49   Table 9.3 shows what date a rent determination takes effect in relation to your claim.

Table 9.3 **When determinations take effect**

Reason triggering the determination	Date from which rent officer or NIHE determination is implemented
A claim	The start of your HB award
A 'relevant change of circumstances'	The date the change itself takes effect (typically the following Monday: chapter 17)
52 weeks have passed	If the new determination means you qualify for:
	more HB or the same amount, and your rent is payable weekly or in multiples of weeks:
	the day the referral was due, unless that is not a Monday, in which case from the Monday immediately before that day
	more HB or the same amount, and your rent is payable otherwise than above:
	the day the referral was due (which could be any day of the week)
	less HB (regardless of when rent is payable):
	the Monday following the date the rent officer determination 'was received' by the authority

---

How rent determinations are made

9.50   The following paragraphs describe the various determinations that can be made if your rent is referred. In England, Scotland and Wales the rent officer bases his/her determinations on the date the authority made the referral. In Northern Ireland the determinations are based on the date the NIHE is required to make them. In all four countries, if you have moved out, the determinations are based on the circumstances at the end of the letting.

9.49   DAR 7A(3),8(6A),(6B); NIDAR 7A(3),8(6A),(6B)

T9.3   DAR 7A(3),8(6A),(6B); NIDAR 7A(3),8(6A),(6B)

Table 9.4 **'Relevant changes of circumstances'**

(a) Except if you live in a hostel (para 2.30), there has been a change in the number of occupiers (excluding the beginning or end of an absence on operations as described in para 7.45).

(b) Any child or young person in your household has reached the age of 10 or 16 – but only if, at the last referral, the rent officer/NIHE made a size-related rent determination (para 9.56).

(c) You have just become, or ceased to be, eligible for an additional bedroom – as a foster parent, because you require overnight care, or you are responsible for a disabled child who needs their own room (paras 7.46-63).

(d) There has been a change in your household composition – but only if, at the last referral, the rent officer/NIHE made a size-related rent determination (para 9.56). (One example is when two people have ceased to be a couple.)

(e) There has been a substantial change or improvement in the condition of your home – regardless of whether there has been an associated change in the rent. (For example, central heating has been installed.)

(f) You have moved into a new home.

(g) There has been a substantial change in the terms of your letting agreement (excluding a change in a term relating to rent alone) – regardless of whether there has been an associated change in the rent. (For example, the landlord has taken over the responsibility for internal decorations from you or vice versa.)

(h) There has been a rent increase and:

- the rent increase was made under a term of your agreement (which need not be in writing but must be a term of your letting, not merely a provision of law: CH/3590/2007) and that term is the same (or substantially the same) as when the previous rent determination was made; and

- at the previous referral, the rent officer/NIHE did not make any of the following determinations: a significantly high rent determination, a size-related rent determination or an exceptionally high rent determination (paras 9.55-57).

(i) When the previous rent determination was made, you were not a 'young individual' (para 9.62), but you are now a 'young individual' (for example, if you were in social services care and have now reached age 22: para 8.17).

The referred rent

9.51   This is simply your actual rent. In England, Scotland and Wales it is the figure the authority refers to the rent officer (para 9.47). In all four UK countries it is the figure used in making all the following determinations (para 9.52-62).

T9.4   HB 14(1),(8), sch 2 para 2; HB60+14(1),(8), sch 2 para 2; NIHB 15(1), sch 3 para 2; NIHB60+15(1),(8), sch 3 para 2
9.51   HB 114A(3)(d),(8)(a); HB60+ 95A(3)(d),(8)(a)

Service charge determinations

9.52   The rent officer provides a valuation of certain ineligible charges (other than meals) identified by the authority (paras 9.47, 10.8 and table 10.2). This is a service charge determination, and is used to adjust the referred rent when the authority decides your eligible rent (step 4 in table 9.2).

9.53   If the authority has provided evidence of service charge costs, the rent officer normally accepts these unless they are very high or suggest the landlord is delivering the service inefficiently. If the authority has provided no evidence of costs then the rent officer normally uses a standard deduction from their own evidence base as a starting point.

Claim-related rent determinations

9.54   This determination is always made if your rent is referred. It is not a separate valuation in its own right but only:

(a)   the lowest of the following three determinations (paras 9.55-57); or

(b)   if none of those exist, the referred rent (para 9.51).

Note that when the referred rent is used as the claim-related rent, any service charge determination is deducted from it (step 4 in table 9.2).

Significantly high rent determinations

9.55   This determination is only made if your actual rent exceeds a reasonable market rent, and the difference is 'significant' rather than substantial. It is the highest market rent the landlord might reasonably expect to obtain for your home, having regard to similar dwellings in the vicinity (England, Scotland and Wales) or locality (Northern Ireland) (paras 9.66-67). The DWP advises that the rent officer may also make this determination if the landlord or the authority placed an 'unreasonably low value' on ineligible charges other than meals (GM A4.1552).

Size-related rent determinations

9.56   This determination is made if your home exceeds the size criteria (table 9.5). It is the market rent the landlord might reasonably expect to obtain on a hypothetical property that has the number of rooms that match the size criteria (paras 9.68-69) but otherwise resembles your home or corresponds to it as closely as possible. It does not apply to caravans, mobile homes or houseboats (para 2.29). The rental evidence from which this valuation is made is normally drawn from the 'vicinity' (England, Scotland and Wales) or locality (Northern Ireland) (paras 9.66-67). But where there is no evidence of dwellings that are the right size, the rent officer/NIHE must use the nearest vicinity/locality to the dwelling where it does exist.

9.52   ROO sch 1 paras 6(3),7; NIHB sch 2 paras 6(3),7; NIHB60+ sch 2 paras 6(3),7

9.54   ROO sch 1 para 6; NIHB sch 2 para 6; NIHB60+ sch 2 para 6

9.55   ROO sch 1 para 1; NIHB sch 2 para 1; NIHB60+ sch 2 para 1

9.56   ROO 7, sch 1 para 2; NIHB sch 2 para 2; NIHB60+ sch 2 para 2

Exceptionally high rent determinations

9.57 This determination is not specific to your home (it reflects a general level of rents): it is made if either of the above determinations (paras 9.55-56) is 'exceptionally high' compared with other rents in the 'neighbourhood' (England, Scotland or Wales) or locality (Northern Ireland) (paras 9.66-67). It does not apply if you live in a hostel (para 2.30). Because it is set by reference to the neighbourhood (rather than the broad rental market area) it is not necessarily the same rent as the highest rent used to calculate the mid-point in a local reference rent determination (para 9.64).

Local reference rent determinations

9.58 This determination is made if any of the above determinations (paras 9.55-57) exceeds the local reference rent (para 9.59) for a home that is the right size for your household (para 9.61). It does not apply if you live in a hostel (para 2.30).

9.59 The 'local reference rent' is the mid-point between the highest and lowest rents for lettings that are the right size (para 9.61) within your broad rental market area (or, in Northern Ireland, locality).

9.60 When the rent officer/NIHE works out the highest and lowest rent, he/she must exclude any rents that are exceptionally high or low. This is usually done by plotting a graph of all the rents in ascending order. The highest and lowest rents are found at the points on the line at which the curve starts to rise or fall steeply at either end (so that the remaining rents in the middle broadly form a straight line): Heffernan (No 2) v the Rent Service.

9.61 The rental evidence used to calculate the local reference rent must match the size criteria for your claim (paras 9.68-69) – or the size of your home if smaller. And if you live in one room it must match the same category as your home from one of the following:

(a) one-room dwellings if you are a boarder;

(b) other one-room dwellings if you share a kitchen, toilet, bathroom and living room with someone who is not a member of your household (paras 4.3-6);

(c) any other one-room dwellings.

Single room rent determinations

9.62 This determination is made only if you are a 'young individual'. If you are single (para 4.7) and under the age of 35 you are a 'young individual' unless you meet any of exceptions (a) to (h) in paragraph 8.17. This determination does not apply if your landlord is a registered housing association (paras 7.8-10) or if you live in a hostel (para 2.30).

9.63 A single room rent determination is the mid-point between the highest and lowest rents for lettings in the same broad rental market area (or, in Northern Ireland, locality) as your home which have:

(a) exclusive use of (only) one bedroom;

9.57   ROO 6(2), sch 1 para 3; NIHB sch 2 para 3; NIHB60+ sch 2 para 3

9.58   ROO 6(2), sch 1 para 4; NIHB sch 2 para 4; NIHB60+ sch 2 para 4

9.60   Heffernan (No 2) v The Rent Service 01/12/09 HC (Admin) [2009] EWHC (Admin) 3539 www.bailii.org/ew/cases/EWHC/Admin/2009/3539.html

9.62   ROO 6(2),sch 1 para 5; NIHB 15(3)(a), sch 2 para 5; NIHB60+ 15(3)(a), sch 2 para 5

(b)   shared use of a living room;

(c)   shared use of a toilet and bathroom; and

(d)   shared use of a kitchen, and no exclusive use of facilities for cooking or preparing food.

Rent Service guidance states that evidence should be excluded if it relates to a bedroom which does not exactly meet the above conditions (e.g. if there is no shared living room, or more than one shared living room).

9.64   The highest and lowest rent should not include ineligible service charges (apart from meals). The rent officer/NIHE must deduct the ineligible charges at the start of the process, not from the single room rent at the end. Apart from that, when the rent officer/NIHE works out the highest and lowest rent, the same points apply as in paragraph 9.60.

General rules

9.65   All rent determinations (paras 9.55-64) 'assume that no one who would have been entitled to housing benefit had sought or is seeking the tenancy' (this is designed to prevent 'feedback' whereby HB levels start to influence and distort market rents). In practice this works by excluding any lettings where the tenant is on HB from the rent officer's rental evidence. Rents used to make determinations are what 'a landlord might reasonably have been expected to obtain'. Lettings used to make a comparison are assumed to be in a reasonable state of repair and let on an assured tenancy (uncontrolled tenancy in Northern Ireland). Rents paid to housing associations and charities are also excluded from the rent officer's evidence base.

The areas used for comparison

9.66   In England, Scotland, Wales the following geographic terms are used to set rent determinations (paras 9.55-64):

(a)   a 'broad rental market area' means the same as in LHA cases (paras 8.33-34);

(b)   a 'neighbourhood' means 'a distinct area of residential accommodation';

(c)   a 'vicinity' is 'the area immediately surrounding the dwelling' (or, for size-related rent determinations only, if that area does not contain any comparable dwellings, the nearest area which does).

9.67   In Northern Ireland, a single term 'locality' is used in place of all the above. This is not defined, but it seems reasonable that its meaning varies so that where the term 'neighbourhood' is used in Great Britain; 'locality' has an approximately similar meaning to neighbourhood; and so on.

The size criteria

9.68   The size criteria are shown in table 9.5. They are used for size-related, exceptionally high and local reference rent determinations (paras 9.56-61). The size criteria take account of every 'occupier' (para 9.69).

9.65   ROO sch 1 paras 1-5,7,8; NIHB sch 2 paras 1-5,7,8; NIHB60+ sch 2 paras 1-5,7,8

9.66   ROO sch 1 paras 1(4), 3(5), 4(6),(7)

9.67   NIHB sch 2 paras 1-5; NIHB60+ sch 2 paras 1-5

9.68   ROO 2(1), sch 2 paras 1,1A,2,3

9.69   For these purposes an 'occupier' includes all of the following:

(a) you and the members of their family (your partner, children and young persons: para 4.8);

(b) non-dependants (para 4.39);

(c) lodgers (para 4.48);

(d) joint tenants (para 4.52); and

(e) any other person who occupies your home 'as their home'.

The authority, not the rent officer, decides which occupiers are included: R v Swale BC HBRB ex p Marchant. For further details about which occupiers the authority should include, and when an additional bedroom is allowed, see paragraphs 7.39-63.

Table 9.5 **The size criteria for rent referral cases**

The size criteria are used for size-related rent, exceptionally high rent, and local reference rent determinations (paras 9.56-58). For who is counted as an occupier for these purposes, see paragraph 9.69.

Bedrooms

General rules: One room is allowed as a bedroom for each of the following:

(a) each couple;

(b) each other person aged 16 or over;

(c) two children under 16 of the same sex;

(d) two children under 10 of the same or opposite sex;

(e) each other child.

Additional bedrooms: One or more additional bedrooms can be allowed if you are a foster parent, you require overnight care, and/or if you are responsible for a disabled child who needs their own bedroom (paras 7.46-63).

Living rooms

One, two or three living rooms are allowed as follows:

(a) one if there are one to three occupiers;

(b) two if there are four to six occupiers;

(c) three if there are seven or more occupiers.

Total rooms

The size criteria relate to the total number of bedrooms or living rooms allowed (under either of the above headings). It is irrelevant whether you actually use those as bedrooms or living rooms.

9.69   R v Swale BC HBRB ex p Marchant 09/11/99 CA 32 HLR 856 www.casetrack.com case reference QBCOF 1999/0071/C

T 9.5   ROO 2(1),sch 2; NIHB 2(1),sch 2 para 10; NIHB60+ 2(1),sch 2 para 10

Pre-tenancy determinations

9.70 If your claim is one of the kind that the authority must refer to the rent officer (paras 9.35-38) you can request a rent determination before you move into your home – or before you renew your tenancy agreement (so long as it is at least 11 months since their last agreement began). This is called a pre-tenancy determination (PTD). It can help you decide whether you will be able to afford the new agreement. To get a PTD, you must complete and sign an application to the authority, and your landlord must sign to show their consent.

9.71 In England, Scotland and Wales, the authority forwards this to the rent officer within two working days – except where it is incomplete or where a valid determination already exists, in which case the authority must notify you of that. The rent service should provide a rent determination within five working days. In Northern Ireland, the NIHE should make a rent determination within seven working days.

9.72 If the authority receives your HB claim for a home where a PTD exists (whether or not you requested it), it uses the PTD as though it was an ordinary rent determination. This lasts until there is a relevant change of circumstances (table 9.4) or 52 weeks have passed.

Boarder cases

9.73 This section applies in England, Scotland and Wales if your rent includes 'board and attendance'. This means meals plus some further service such as serving the meals. This procedure means that the rent officer (not the authority) decides whether your claim is treated as a boarder and is referred to him or her for a rent determination (para 9.76). It does not apply in Northern Ireland where NIHE decides all matters concerning your rent (see paras 9.47-48 if you are a boarder).

Boarders in Great Britain

9.74 If you pay for meals (board) as part of your rent the following special procedures apply if (apart from the fact you pay board and attendance) you could fall within the LHA scheme (chapter 8). So for example, if you live in a hostel, caravan, mobile home or houseboat (para 9.38) your rent is always referred to the rent officer so the ordinary rent referral procedures apply instead: (paras 9.47-48).

9.75 The authority first applies to the rent officer for a 'board and attendance determination', and supplies only the following information:

(a) the address of your dwelling including the postcode and any room number;

(b) the length of your tenancy and when it began;

(c) whether your rent includes ineligible charges for fuel, meals or water;

(d) whether your rent includes any ineligible charges for cleaning, window cleaning, emergency alarm systems, medical, nursing or personal care, or general counselling and support; and

---

9.70   HB 14(4),(8); HB60+ 14(4),(8); ROO 3(1); NIHB 16; NIHB60+16

9.73   HB 13C(5)(e); HB60+ 13C(5)(e); NIHB 14C(5)(e); NIHB60+ 14C(5)(e)

9.74   HB 13C(5)(e); HB60+ 13C(5)(e)

9.75   HB 13D(10),(11), 114A(3),(4); HB60+ 13D(10),(11), 95A(3),(4); ROO 4C

(e)   the total rent payable, after deducting (only) the authority's valuation of the charges mentioned in (d).

The rent officer then determines whether a 'substantial' amount of your rent is attributable to board and attendance and informs the authority of the outcome. If he/she decides that a substantial part of your rent is for board and attendance you are treated as a boarder and the ordinary rent referral rules apply (and not the LHA rules). Anecdotal evidence consistently suggests that rent officers do not consider breakfast alone to be 'substantial'.

9.76   If the rent officer notifies the authority that you are a boarder, the authority provides all the information it normally provides in a rent officer referral (apart from the information it has already provided) and this counts as the date of the referral. The rent officer then makes a determination on the same basis as any other claim referred to him/her (paras 9.50 onwards), and all the rules about rent referral cases apply.

9.77   If the rent officer notifies the authority that you are not a boarder, the authority simply treats the claim as an ordinary LHA case and all the rules in chapter 8 apply.

Protected tenancies and old HB claims

9.78   This section describes how to calculate your eligible rent if you have a very old HB claim and/or if you have a protected tenancy or some other very old letting agreement. If you have one of these older claims your eligible rent is worked out using the rules that applied when your claim was made ('the old rules': see para 9.7).

9.79   The terms 'protected tenant' and 'protected tenancy' are not terms used in the law or guidance. In ordinary usage they are any tenancy where law that governs your security and rent is regulated by the 'Rent Acts' and which usually only applies if your agreement started before January 1989. In this guide the term includes any pre-January 1989 tenancy in England, Scotland and Wales, and in Northern Ireland some types of older tenancy (para 9.83), whether or not it is protected by the Rent Acts or if the rent has been registered (i.e. fixed) by the rent officer.

9.80   Your eligible rent is worked out using 'the old rules' only if all of the following apply:

(a)   you have been continuously entitled to HB since 1st January 1996 (in Northern Ireland, 1st April 1996);

(b)   you have not moved home since; and

(c)   your landlord is not the council/NIHE or a registered housing association.

In certain circumstances short breaks in your claim can be ignored as can a move if your home was made uninhabitable by fire, flood or a natural disaster (see Guide to Housing Benefit 2012-13 paras 7.18-21 for details).

9.81   In England and Wales your letting is a protected tenancy if:

(a)   (regardless of the agreement) it was entered into before 15th January 1989; or

(b)   it is a housing association secure tenancy; or

9.76   HB 14(4A), 114A(5); HB60+ 14(4A), 95A(5); ROO 4C(2)

9.79   HB sch 2 paras 4-8; HB60+ sch 2 paras 4-8; NIHB sch 3 para 4; NIHB60+ sch 3 para 4

(c) it is any other type of housing association or private sector letting where the rent officer is entitled to register a rent.

9.82 In Scotland your letting is a protected tenancy if:

(a) (regardless of the agreement) it was entered into before 2nd January 1989; or

(b) it is a housing association tenancy or any other kind of private sector letting where the rent officer is entitled to register a rent.

9.83 In Northern Ireland your letting is a protected tenancy if it is one to which article 3 of the Housing (Northern Ireland) Order 1978 applies. Your tenancy falls within article 3 if your rent is controlled (tied to a historic rateable value) or is fixed by a rent officer. In broad terms this applies to your tenancy if:

(a) in certain circumstances, it began before 1st October 1978; or

(b) it began on or after 14th June 2006; and

   ▪ your house or flat was built or converted before 6th November 1956; and

   ▪ it does not meet the fitness standard.

Eligible rent

9.84 If your claim falls under 'the old rules' (para 9.80) your eligible rent is always worked out in the same way as for exempt accommodation (paras 9.9-30) whether or not you also have a protected tenancy.

9.85 If you have a protected tenancy (and do not fall under the old rules: para 9.84), your eligible rent is worked out in the same way as for a social tenant (paras 7.17-22) – except that:

(a) the social sector size criteria apply, except in the rare instance where your landlord is neither the authority itself nor a registered housing association (paras 7.8-10);

(b) if your rent has been registered by the rent officer, the eligible rent cannot exceed this;

(c) if you are an assured tenant and your rent has been fixed by a rent assessment committee, the eligible rent cannot exceed that figure – but this lasts only for one year from the date your rent was fixed (and is rare).

Shared ownership

9.86 This section describes how your eligible rent is calculated if you have a shared ownership tenancy. You have a shared ownership tenancy (also called 'equity sharing') if you are part-buying and part-renting your home from a social or private landlord.

Eligible rent

9.87 If you have a shared ownership tenancy your eligible rent is worked out in the same way as for a council tenant (paras 7.5 and 7.17-22), except that the social sector size criteria (paras 7.23-25) do not apply (para 7.4). Your HB can only cover your rent and not your mortgage payments – but you may get help with your mortgage interest as part of your JSA/ESA/IS or state pension credit (see chapter 25).

9.85   HB 12B(2); A13(2)(a); HB60+12B(2); NIHB 13A(2); NIHB60+ 13A(2); CPR sch 3 para 5(1),(2); NICPR sch 3 para 5(1),(2)

9.86   HB 12B(2); A13(2)(b), 14(2)(b), sch 2 para 12; HB60+ 12B(2) 14(2)(b), sch 2 para 12; NIHB 13A(2); NIHB60+ 13A(2)

Homeless households in temporary accommodation

9.88 This section applies in England, Scotland or Wales if you have been housed in 'temporary accommodation' (paras 9.90-92) by your council because you are homeless. But these rules do not apply if the temporary home you have been housed in belongs to the authority itself (i.e. it is a council house or flat: see para 9.94).

9.89 If you are housed in temporary accommodation (paras 9.90-92) your eligible rent is calculated as described in paragraph 9.93 but the authority may not receive full subsidy to cover the cost (paras 23.332-35 and table 23.2).

What is temporary accommodation?

9.90 Your home only counts as 'temporary accommodation' if it meets both the first and second conditions in paragraphs 9.91-92 below.

9.91 The first condition is that the accommodation must have been made available to you by the authority or a registered housing association (para 7.8) as result of your homelessness application to the authority.

9.92 The second condition is that the accommodation is:

(a) 'board and lodging' (as defined in table 23.2); or

(b) held by the authority or registered housing association on a short-term lease ('licensed accommodation' as defined in table 23.2); or

(c) provided by someone else but which the authority or registered housing association has a right to use under an agreement (other than a leasehold agreement).

Eligible rent in temporary accommodation

9.93 If your home counts as temporary accommodation (paras 9.90-92) your eligible rent is calculated in the same way as for a social sector tenant but the social sector size criteria (paras 7.23-25) do not apply. In theory, how your eligible rent is calculated depends on whether your landlord (para 7.3) is the authority or a registered housing association, but in practice provided the authority considers your rent to be reasonable the outcome is the same (paras 7.7, 7.13).

Eligible rent: households housed in authority's own stock

9.94 If you are temporarily housed by your council as homeless in one of its own homes (i.e. in a council house or flat) then your eligible rent is calculated as for a council tenant in the normal way (chapter 7). But note that properties the council holds on a short-term lease (table 23.2) for this purpose do not count as the council's own homes and so will qualify as 'temporary accommodation'.

9.87   HB A13(2)(b)

9.88   HB A13(2)(e),(3),(4)

9.91   HB A13 (3)

9.92   HB A13(4)

9.93   HB 12B(1)(a),(2), A13(2)(e)

9.94   A13(4)(b)

Chapter 10 **Service charges**

■ General information about service charges (including their definition, distinguishing them from rent, etc): see paras 10.1-25.

■ Eligible services (communal areas, etc): paras 10.26-39.

■ Ineligible services (daily living expenses, leisure items, water, fuel, meals, care and support charges: see paras 10.40-56.

■ Other items included in your rent (garages, land, space for a carer, business premises): see paras 10.57-62.

10.1 This chapter deals with service charges (and related charges) which may be included as part of your actual rent, or payable as well as your rent. It explains which service charges you pay are eligible for HB and which are not. For advice about how to distinguish between service charges and other charges that may be included in your rent, see paragraphs 10.8-12.

10.2 This chapter applies if you are the tenant of, and pay rent to, a social landlord as described in chapter 7. It also applies if your claim is assessed under any of the special cases described in chapter 9 (for example, if you live in 'exempt accommodation', or if you are a private tenant who has been on HB since before April 2008). Except for paragraph 10.3 it does not apply if your HB is assessed under the LHA rules (chapter 8).

LHA cases and service charges

10.3 No assessment of your service charges is made if your claim falls under the LHA rules. Instead the whole of your actual rent (rent and service charges) is eligible for HB up to the value of the LHA figures (paras 8.5-7). No deduction is made for service charges that would apply if you did not fall under the LHA rules (such as if you were the tenant of a social landlord: chapter 7) case because the rent officer has already deducted these when calculating the LHA figures (para 8.32). Broadly the overall result is that if your actual rent is less than the LHA figure you gain, and if it is more then you lose. The remainder of this chapter does not apply if you fall under the LHA rules.

The importance of service charges

10.4 If you are a tenant you may pay for services either as part of your rent (whether or not it is mentioned in the letting agreement) or separately. As illustrated in the examples, there are two main methods of showing service charges in your letting agreement:

10.1   HB 12(1)(e),(8), sch 1; HB60+ 12(1)(e),(8), sch 1; CPR sch 3 para 5(1); NIHB 13(1)(e),(8) sch 1; NIHB60+ 13(1)(e),(8), sch 1;
        NICPR sch 3 para 5(1)

10.3   HB 13D(1),(4),(5),(12); HB60+ 13D(1),(4),(5),(12); NIHB 14D(1),(4),(5),(10); NIHB60+ 14D(1),(4),(5),(10)

(a) your rent may be shown as so much per week (or month, etc) including certain services; or

(b) it may be shown as so much per week (or month, etc) with an amount for service charges being due on top of your rent.

10.5   If you are a tenant of a social landlord (chapter 7) or if your HB is assessed under any of the special cases described in chapter 9, any service charges payable are considered as described below. This is so that they can be correctly included in, or excluded from, your eligible rent (para 7.17), which in turn affects the amount of your HB.

(a) If a charge is 'eligible for HB', this means that it can be included in your eligible rent. It does not need to be valued; and no deduction is made for it at any stage in deciding the amount of your eligible rent unless the charge for it is excessive (para 10.23).

(b) If a charge is 'ineligible for HB', this means that it cannot be included in your eligible rent. With certain exceptions, it needs to be valued and deducted at some point in deciding your eligible rent (para 10.21).

The above points can be particularly significant if your landlord is not a registered housing association (para 7.8) but you live in supported housing that qualifies as 'exempt accommodation' (such as if your landlord is a small charity: para 9.4). If this applies your council is likely to look carefully at each service to distinguish eligible and ineligible elements (such as support) because it has a strong financial incentive to ensure that your eligible rent does not exceed the rent officer's valuation (para 23.28). It is therefore essential for your landlord to provide a detailed breakdown of the charge for each service they provide.

Examples: Service charges

1. A council tenant claimant's weekly rent is expressed as being £100 per week including £20 per week for fuel for their own flat and £10 per week for heating, lighting, cleaning and maintaining communal areas. In this case the eligible rent is £80 per week. The ineligible charge for fuel for the tenant's own flat is deducted.

2. A housing association claimant's weekly rent is expressed as being £70 per week plus £20 per week for fuel for the claimant's own room and £10 per week for heating, lighting, cleaning and maintaining communal areas. In this case the eligible rent is £80 per week. The eligible charge for the communal areas is added.

Notes

■ The facts in the two examples are the same but are expressed differently.

■ Information about the service charges illustrated is given later in this chapter.

■ The terms 'net rent' and 'gross rent' are sometimes used to distinguish between different methods of expressing a rent figure. But they are used in different ways nationally and are best avoided for HB purposes.

Who deals with your service charges for HB?

10.6   If you live in Northern Ireland the NIHE deals with all matters for your HB claim to do with service charges. If you live in England, Scotland or Wales the authority always identifies whether a charge is eligible/ineligible but either the authority or the rent officer is responsible for determining its value as follows:

(a) if you are a council tenant, protected tenant, shared ownership tenant, or live in temporary accommodation (paras 9.78-92) the authority values it;

(b) if (a) does not apply and your landlord is not-for-profit (such as a housing association or a charity) and you live in the kind of supported housing that qualifies as 'exempt accommodation' (para 9.4) the authority values it;

(c) if (b) does not apply and your landlord is a registered housing association (paras 7.8-10) and the authority considers your rent to be reasonable (para 7.7), the authority values it;

(d) if your claim is one to which the rent referral rules apply (for example, your rent is unreasonably high, or you live in a hostel or mobile home and so on: paras 9.35-38), valuation of service charges is carried out as in the next paragraph.

See table 10.1 for further details about how service charges are identified and assessed.

10.7   When a claim is referred to the rent officer (para 10.6(d)) service charge valuation is carried out as follows:

(a) the authority values any ineligible charges that are not valued by the rent officer (table 10.2) and deducts them from the actual rent (except an amount for meals); the result is the 'referred rent' (para 9.47) (and the rent officer is notified of these deductions when the referral is made);

(b) the rent officer takes the referred rent (which includes eligible services), and if he or she has made a significantly high, size-related or exceptionally high rent determination (paras 9.55-57) caps it at whichever of those determinations is the lowest (and in this case this is the 'claim-related rent');

(c) if none of the determinations in (b) apply the rent officer values any ineligible service charges that he/she is responsible for (table 10.2) and deducts them from the referred rent (and in this case this is the 'claim-related rent');

(d) if the rent officer has made a local reference rent or single room rent determination then that figure is passed back to the authority and used instead of the claim-related rent (being the lower of the two); and

(e) where the rent includes meals the authority deducts the appropriate amount (table 10.4) from the rent officer's lowest figure, but if it is a single room rent determination then that figure is the eligible rent unless the claim-related rent less the amount for meals results in a lower figure.

Ineligible charges in (a) above includes any deduction from an eligible charge that is excessive (para 10.23).

10.6   HB 12B(2),(5), B13(2)(a); HB60+ 12B(2),(5); CPR sch 3 para 5(1); NIHB 13A(2),(6), 14(2),(5),(7),(9), 15(1), sch 2 paras 6(2A),(3),7; . NIHB60+ 13A(2),(6), 14(2),(5),(7), 15(1), sch 2 paras 6(2A),(3),7; NICPR sch 3 para 5(1)

10.7   HB 12C(2), 13(2)-(5),(7), 114A(3)(d)-(f),(4)(b),(6),(8)(a); HB60+ 12C(2), 13(2)-(5), 95A(3)(d)-(f),(4)(b),(6),(8)(a); ROO sch 1 paras 6(2A),(3), 7

Table 10.1 **How to assess service charges**

Step 1: Does the charge relate to a service performed or facility provided? (para 10.13)

■ If yes, it is a service charge (and cannot be rent), go to step 2.

■ If no, it is not a service charge but it may (or may not) be 'rent' (para 10.15).

Step 2: Does your right to occupy your home depend on payment of the service charge? (para 10.16)

■ If yes, go to step 3.

■ If no, it is not eligible for HB.

Step 3: Does the charge relate to an ineligible service? (table 10.2 and paras 10.40-56)

■ If no, go to step 4.

■ If yes, it is not eligible for HB.

Step 4: Are you a council/NIHE tenant; or the tenant of any other social landlord where a rent determination is not required? (table 7.1 and paras 9.35-37)

■ If yes, the authority decides all issues including whether the service charge is excessive.

■ If no, got to step 5.

Step 5: Do you live in 'exempt accommodation' (not covered by step 4)? (para 9.4)

■ If yes, the authority decides all issues including whether any eligible service charge is excessive. The authority must refer your rent and service charges to the rent officer but the authority is not required to use the rent officer's valuation (but they should consider it with any other evidence) (paras 9.10-12).

■ If no, your rent and service charges are assessed under rent referral rules. The authority decides whether each service is eligible and the rent officer values it (para 10.7 and table 10.2). The authority must use the rent officer's valuation.

Notes

See paragraph 10.6 for who is responsible for valuing a service charge once the authority has identified it. For how a charge is valued, see paragraph 10.21 if it is ineligible and paragraph 10.22 if it is eligible.

T10.1   HB 12(1)(e),(8), 12B(2), 12C, B13(2), 13(2),(5),(7), sch 1; CPR sch 3 para 5(1); HB60+ 12(1)(e),(8), 12B(2), 12C, 13(2),(5), sch 1; NIHB 13(1)(e),(8), 13A(2), 13B, 14(2),(5),(7), sch 1; NIHB60+ 13(1)(e),(8), 13A(2), 13B, 14(2),(5), sch 1

Distinguishing 'rent' from service charges

10.8   Decision makers (councils/tribunals) pay more attention nowadays to the distinction between services (as described above) and other costs included when your landlord sets the rent. For example, your landlord's overheads such as vacant lettings cannot be a service because they do not provide any benefit to the tenant: CH/3528/2006 and paragraph 10.13. For the same reason, rent collection costs including bad debt provision, and passing on costs like council tax, are usually regarded as rent rather than a service (para 10.15).

10.9   If you incur charges for: renting a garage or land, an additional room for a live-in carer, or additional rent to cover your arrears (all of which are 'rent' within its ordinary meaning) then special rules apply: see paragraphs 10.57-62 for details.

10.10   It is not always easy to distinguish between 'rent' and service charges and it is fairly common for landlords to categorise charges incorrectly. Neither your landlord's classification nor the tenancy agreement determines whether an item is (or is not) rent or a service charge: it is the law which does so: [2009] UKUT 28 (AAC) (para 10.11). But the mere fact that your landlord categorises something incorrectly should not be held against them: CH/3528/2006.

10.11   If a charge relates to an item that falls within the definition of services (para 10.13) then it is a service charge (and it cannot be rent): CH/3528/2006. And if it is, the authority must next decide if it is eligible: CH/3528/2006. So, for example, if your landlord provides you with support or counselling to help you sustain your tenancy (or to every tenant) as part of their general housing management, it is a service and it is ineligible (table 10.2 and para 10.53). The fact that your landlord has classified it as 'housing management' or 'intensive housing management' does not mean that it is somehow eligible as 'rent' just because it has been classified as housing management (para 10.10).

10.12   But just because an item is not a service it does not necessarily follow that the charge made for it must be rent (and therefore eligible for HB). It must still relate to a matter that is properly considered in setting the rent: CH/3528/2006.

Definition of 'services'

10.13   'Services' are defined as 'services performed or facilities… provided for, or rights made available to, the occupier…' and 'service charge' as any periodical charge for any such service. A helpful test is to ask: does the tenant derive any benefit or value from the function, or does the benefit or value wholly lie with the landlord?

10.14   A charge for furniture and/or household equipment is treated as a service charge and is eligible for HB; unless those goods become part of your personal property (para 10.44), e.g. under a hire purchase agreement. It seems likely that 'household equipment' includes computers (and see para 10.32).

10.15   Any item that is not a service may (or may not) be part of the rent – provided it relates to a matter that is properly considered in setting the rent. In most cases provision for vacant tenancies (voids), bad debts and long-term maintenance are allowed as rent provided that the total charge (rent and eligible services) is not excessive: [2010] UKUT 222 (AAC).

10.8   HB 12(1)(e),(8); HB60+ 12(1)(e),(8); CPR sch 3 para 5(1); NIHB 13(1)(e),(8); NIHB60+ 13(1)(e),(8); NICPR sch 3 para 5(1)

10.13   HB 12(8); HB60+ 12(8); CPR sch 3 para 5(1); NIHB 13(8); NIHB60+ 13(8); NICPR sch 3 para 5(1)

10.14   HB 12(8), sch 1 para 1(b); HB60+ 12(8), sch 1 para 1(b); NIHB 13(8), sch 1 para 1(b), NIHB60+ 13(8), sch 1 para 1(b)

Which service charges are eligible?

10.16   A service charge is only eligible for HB if:

(a)   you have to pay it as a condition for the right to occupy your home (whether the condition is part of the original tenancy agreement or a separate contract); and

(b)   it is not listed in the regulations as ineligible (table 10.2, paras 10.40-56); and

(c)   it is not excessive in relation to the service provided (para 10.23).

10.17   The first condition (para 10.16(a)) need not have applied from the start of your tenancy. It is eligible for HB (subject to the other conditions) from whenever you agreed to pay it, if the alternative would have been to lose your home.

10.18   Details of which kinds of service charge are eligible for HB (subject to the above points) follow, and are summarised in table 10.2. Helpful advice on services is given by the DWP (GM A4.700-950).

10.19   Some not-for-profit landlords sometimes provide services 'for free' but this is often because the charge is wholly funded from elsewhere. DWP guidance concerning hostel residents (though the point is relevant to all claims) states that 'HB should be based only on items included in the resident's charge. [Authorities] must confirm which services are included in the hostel charge' (GM A4.1950).

Management and administration costs of eligible services

10.20   If a service is eligible (table 10.2), the costs of any management and administrative support required (e.g. staff time) to provide it are also eligible, so long as the costs are reasonable and not excessive (para 10.24): [2010] UKUT 222 (AAC).

Valuing ineligible service charges

10.21   When the rent officer is responsible for valuing ineligible charges see paragraph 10.7; when the authority is (para 10.6), this is done as follows:

(a)   if the amount can be identified from your letting agreement or in some other way (for example, a detailed breakdown provided by your landlord), the authority uses that value;

(b)   but if the identified amount is unrealistically low for the service provided, or if the amount cannot be identified, the authority must decide what amount is fairly attributable to the value;

(c)   however, different rules apply if the charge is for water, fuel or meals (paras 10.45-52).

In practice separating out charges is not always straightforward, particularly for not-for-profit landlords whose functions are often provided by staff whose duties include a mix of activities that are legitimately part of the rent (paras 10.8-15) and both eligible and ineligible services.

10.16   HB 12(1)(e),(8), sch 1 paras 1-5; HB60+ 12(1)(e),(8), sch 1 paras 1-5; CPR sch 3 para 5(1); NIHB 13(1)(e),(8), sch 1 paras 1-5; NIHB60+ 13(1)(e),(8), sch 1 paras 1-5; NICPR sch 3 para 5(1)

10.21   HB 12B(2), B13(2)(a); HB60+ 12B(2); CPR sch 3 para 5(1); NIHB 13A(2); NIHB60+ 13A(2); NICPR sch 3 para 5(1)

Table 10.2 **Service charges summary**

As described throughout this chapter, further details apply in many of the following cases.

Type of service charge	Eligible for HB?	Valued by rent officer
Provision of a heating system	YES	NO
Fuel for communal areas	YES	NO
Other fuel	NO	NO
Meals	NO	NO
Water charges	NO	YES*
Laundry	NO	YES*
Leisure items	NO	YES*
Other day-to-day living expenses not included above	NO	YES*
Furniture/household equipment if the tenant becomes the owner (for example, under hire purchase)	NO	YES*
Any other furniture and household equipment (i.e. the landlord retains ownership)	NO	NO
Communal window cleaning	YES	NO
Other exterior window cleaning which the occupier(s) cannot do	YES	NO
Other window cleaning	NO	NO
Communal cleaning	YES	NO
Other cleaning	NO	NO
Emergency alarm systems	NO	NO
Counselling and support	NO	NO
Medical/nursing/personal care	NO	NO
Most communal services relating to the provision of 'adequate accommodation'	YES	NO
Any other service that is not related to the provision of adequate accommodation	NO	YES*

* The rent officer only makes a valuation when the authority refers a claim to him/her (paras 9.35-38 and 10.7); in any other case the authority values the charge.

T10.2   HB 114A(3)(d)-(f), sch 1 paras 1,2(1),5; HB60+ 95A(3)(d)-(f), sch 1 paras 1,2(1),5; NIHB 15(1), sch 1 paras 1,2(1),5;
NIHB60+ 15(1), sch 1 paras 1,2(1),5

Valuing eligible service charges

10.22   When the authority is responsible for valuing eligible service charges (para 10.6), it does so as follows:

(a) if the amount can be identified from the letting agreement or in some other way, it uses the amount so identified as the value;

(b) but if this identified amount is excessive, or if the amount cannot be identified, the authority decides what amount is fairly attributable to the value.

Excessive eligible service charges

10.23   The authority must consider the cost of comparable services to decide whether the charge is excessive, and if it is the authority must decide how much would be reasonable and disallow the excess. But even if a service charge is reasonable the authority may still restrict the global rent if the total eligible charge (i.e. rent plus service charges) is unreasonable (paras 7.19-20, 9.13, 9.28).

10.24   The requirement to consider comparable costs does not prevent the authority from concluding that the charge is excessive for other reasons, and in particular it can take account of what is required to provide the service satisfactorily. For example, if the authority considered a concierge service could be adequately provided by using two workers but your landlord employed four, it could still restrict the charge even if your landlord's wage rates were shown to be comparable with others. In such cases the authority is entitled to make a restriction even if it does not have sufficient evidence to put a precise figure on what a proper charge would be: [2010] UKUT 222 (AAC).

10.25   If you are already on HB and you are seeking to get your eligible rent increased (e.g. to reflect a service charge increase or to include a new service), the burden of proof (para 1.45) is on you to show that the increased charge is eligible by providing the necessary evidence. You cannot rely on the fact that the authority has no evidence with which to make a comparison to prevent it from restricting the charge: [2010] UKUT 222 (AAC).

Eligible services

10.26   This section relates to charges that are eligible for HB. Eligible charges often relate to communal areas. As a general rule, a service charge that would be ineligible if provided for your own exclusive use is eligible if it relates to communal areas. (For example, cleaning your own room is ineligible, but cleaning the communal areas is eligible.) In relation to all eligible services in this section see also paragraph 10.20 on the management and administrative costs of providing them.

'Communal areas'

10.27   Certain service charges relating to the cleaning, maintenance and fuel supplied to 'communal areas' are eligible for HB. For these limited purposes (and to determine who is a non-dependant: para 4.44) 'communal areas' means:

10.22   HB 12B(2), B13(2)(a), sch 1 paras 3,4; HB60+ 12B(2), sch 1 paras 3,4; CPR sch 3 para 5(1); NIHB 13A(2), sch 1 paras 3,4; NIHB60+ 13A(2), sch 1 paras 3,4

10.23   HB 12B(6),12C(2), B13(4), sch 1 para 4; HB60+ 12B(6),12C(2), sch 1 para 4; NIHB 13A(7),13B(2), sch 1 para 4; NIHB60+ 13A(7),13B(2), sch 1 para 4

(a) areas of common access in any type of accommodation (halls, corridors and stairways; also probably reception areas that do not count as a 'room'); and

(b) in 'sheltered accommodation' only (para 10.28), common rooms (such as a lounge or dining room).

In all other situations communal areas are not defined and have their ordinary English meaning.

'Sheltered accommodation'

10.28 'Sheltered accommodation' is not defined in the regulations. The term is wide enough to include 'extra care' and 'very sheltered' housing, or indeed any accommodation that is 'more than ordinary accommodation [and is] for people who are in some way (and probably for some defined reason) more vulnerable than most people are, or are vulnerable in a particular kind of way'. If resident staff are at hand, there need not be a warden/manager or an alarm system: [2011] AACR 38, approving [2011] UKUT 136 (AAC).

Cleaning communal areas and other window cleaning

10.29 Except where the cost is met by the local authority as part of its Supporting People (para 10.53) programme the following charges are eligible for HB:

(a) cleaning rooms and windows in 'communal areas' (para 10.27); and

(b) cleaning the outside of windows which no-one in your household can do (for example, your windows if you live in one of the upper floors in a block of flats).

Any other cleaning charges (such as cleaning your own room) are not eligible (paras 10.43 and 10.53).

Fuel and water in communal areas

10.30 A charge for fuel used in communal areas (para 10.27) is eligible for HB, but only if it is separate from the fuel charge for your own accommodation. The law does not say whether water charges for communal areas are eligible (e.g. water used to maintain a communal garden), but case law on other matters suggests that, provided the charge is separately identified, it is eligible for HB (para 10.39).

Provision and maintenance of a heating system

10.31 A charge for providing a heating system (both in the common parts and in your own home) is eligible for HB, but only if it is separate from any charge for fuel.

Communal facilities

10.32 Charges for the following communal services are eligible for HB:

(a) children's play areas;

(b) equipment for receiving radio or 'Freeview' TV channels (e.g. an aerial for a block of flats) and their relay into your home through the communal areas, including any

---

10.27   HB sch 1 para 8; HB60+ sch 1 para 8; NIHB sch 1 para 8; NIHB60+ sch 1 para 8;

10.29   HB sch 1 para 1(a)(iv); HB60+ sch 1 para 1(a)(iv); NIHB sch 1 para 1(a)(iv), NIHB60+ sch 1 para 1(a)(iv)

10.30   HB sch 1 para 5; HB60+ sch 1 para 5; NIHB sch 1 para 5; NIHB60+ sch 1 para 5

10.31   HB sch 1 para 8; HB60+ sch 1 para 8; NIHB sch 1 para 8; NIHB60+ sch 1 para 8

charges for the installation, upgrade and maintenance of that equipment (less any element included for subscription channels: paragraph 10.42). A similar argument seems likely to apply to charges for access to the internet (and see para 10.14);

(c) communal laundry facilities (but not personal laundry service: paragraph 10.42).

10.33   Any other charge for leisure facilities (including sports facilities or television rental, licence and subscription fees) that is not covered above (para 10.32) is not eligible for HB.

All other eligible services (security, grounds maintenance, etc)

10.34   Except for any ineligible item (paras 10.42 and 10.53) any other charge for a service that is 'related to the provision of adequate accommodation' is eligible for HB. Items that fall under this heading are not restricted to services in respect of the common areas (although more often than not they will be).

10.35   The DWP advises (GM A4.730, and A4 Annex D) that this heading includes charges in respect of:

(a) portering and refuse removal;

(b) the security of the dwelling (para 10.38);

(c) lifts, communal telephones and entry phones; and

(d) the time people such as scheme managers or caretakers spend on eligible services (para 10.20).

10.36   What is meant by the 'provision of adequate accommodation' is fairly narrow and is restricted to only those services that are necessary for the enjoyment of your home (for example, a lift in a block of flats and costs associated with maintaining it): R v Swansea HBRB ex p. Littler/R v St Edmundsbury HBRB ex p Sandys.

10.37   In deciding what is necessary for the enjoyment of the dwelling, no account can be taken of your personal needs. It is only the adequacy of the accommodation that counts, not your ability to take advantage of it or any services you may need in order to do so (Littler/Sandys and GM A4 Annex).

10.38   A charge for a concierge service (including the costs of any management and administrative support: paragraph 10.20) is eligible so far as it relates to the safety and security of the dwelling: [2010] UKUT 222 (AAC). Note that while a charge for services that relate to the security of your home itself (such as a door entry system) are eligible, services connected with you or your family's personal safety (such as a call out service for harassment) are not (para 10.56).

10.39   Charges for maintenance of communal areas are also eligible. This includes a charge for maintaining a communal garden provided that your landlord has an obligation to provide it and you merely have a right of access to it (rather than exclusive use): [2011] UKUT 22 (AAC). However, a charge for maintaining your private garden (i.e. where you have exclusive use of it) is not eligible for HB, even where your landlord has agreed to maintain it: CH/755/2008 and [2011] UKUT 22 (AAC).

10.32-33   HB sch 1 para 1(a)(ii),(iii); HB60+ sch 1 para 1(a)(ii),(iii); NIHB sch 1 para 1(a)(ii),(iii); NIHB60+ sch 1 para 1(a)(ii),(iii)

10.34   HB sch 1 para 1(g); HB60+ sch 1 para 1(g); NIHB sch 1 para 1(g); NIHB60+ sch 1 para 1(g)

10.36   R v Swansea HBRB ex parte Littler 15/07/98 CA 48 BMLR 24; R v St Edmondsbury HBRB ex parte Sandys 24/07/97 QBD 30 HLR 800

10.39   HB sch 1 paras 1(g), 8; HB60+ sch 1 paras 1(g), 8; NIHB sch 1 paras 1(g), 8; NIHB60+ sch 1 paras 1(g), 8

Ineligible services

Day-to-day living expenses: the general rule

10.40 Charges for items that relate you or your other household members' general living expenses are not eligible for HB so any charges included in your rent must be deducted from it. Examples of items that count as daily living expenses under this rule are in paragraph 10.42 (but this list is not exhaustive).

10.41 For certain items (e.g. fuel, meals) the law sets out how the ineligible charge should be calculated and these rules are described in the following paragraphs. In any other case the authority or the rent officer (as appropriate: paragraphs 10.6-7 and table 10.2) must decide the value.

10.42 All the following count as daily living expenses, and are ineligible for HB:

(a) fuel;

(b) water;

(c) meals;

(d) laundry (e.g. washing sheets, etc);

(e) medical expenses or other expenses relating to personal hygiene;

(f) cleaning of rooms and window cleaning (but see paragraph 10.29);

(g) transport;

(h) TV (and radio) rental, licence and subscription fees and any other charges for providing equipment to the individual home (e.g. a TV, individual satellite dish, set-top box) or any other leisure items.

10.43 Note that charges in respect of fuel and cleaning for communal areas are eligible for HB (paras 10.29-30), as are charges for cleaning the outside of windows so long as no-one in your household can do them and the cost is not met by your council through its Supporting People programme.

10.44 Note also that charges for renting household furniture and fittings are eligible for HB, but charges for acquiring them are not (para 10.14 and table 10.2).

Water charges

10.45 In Great Britain, water charges (except perhaps water use in communal areas: para 10.30) are not eligible for HB so any charges included in the rent must be deducted. (But no deduction is made if you are billed by the water company and pay the bill yourself, since they are not then part of the rent.) The same applies in Northern Ireland, though for the time being, until a separate system for water charging is in place, water charges remain eligible for HB in respect of rates (although the rates element is deducted from your rent).

10.40   HB sch 1 paras 1(a),(e), 2(1), 5; HB60+ sch 1 para 1(a),(e), 2(1), 5; NIHB sch 1 para 1(a),(e), 2(1), 5; NIHB60+ sch 1 para 1(a),(e), 2(1), 5

10.41   HB sch 1 paras 2,5,6; HB60+ sch 1 paras 2,5,6; NIHB sch 1 paras 2,5,6; NIHB60+ sch 1 paras 2,5,6

10.42   HB sch 1 paras 1(a),(e),2(1),5; HB60+ sch 1 para 1(a),(e),2(1),5; NIHB sch 1 para 1(a),(e),2(1),5; NIHB60+ sch 1 para 1(a),(e),2(1),5

10.45   HB 2(1) – 'water charges', 12B(2),(5), B13(2)(a), 13(2); HB60+ 2(1),12B(2),(5), 13(2); ROO sch 1 paras 6A(2)(d),(3), 7; NIHB 2(1), 13A(2),(6),14(2), sch 2 paras 6(2A)(d),(3),7; NIHB60+ 2(1), 13A(2),(6),14(2), sch 2 paras 6(2A)(d),(3),7

10.46   Except where your claim is referred to the rent officer (para 10.6), the authority decides the value of water charges as follows:

(a)   if the charge is based on your consumption, either the actual amount or an estimate;

(b)   otherwise, if your accommodation is a self-contained unit, the actual amount of the charge;

(c)   otherwise, a proportion of the water charge for the self-contained unit you share equal to the floor area of your accommodation divided by the floor area of the self-contained unit as a whole (but in practice authorities sometimes use simpler methods).

If your claim is referred to the rent officer (para 10.6), he or she values water charges (para 10.7).

Fuel

10.47   Charges for fuel used in your home (such as gas, electricity, etc, and also any standing charges or other supply costs) are not eligible for HB so any charges included in your rent must be deducted. (No deduction is made if you are billed by your energy company and pay the fuel bill yourself, since the fuel charges are not then part of your rent.) For charges for fuel used in the communal areas (e.g. heating and lighting) and providing a heating system, see paragraphs 10.30-31.

10.48   When the authority is responsible for valuing any fuel charges (para 10.6), the rules depend on whether the amount of the charge is known (paras 10.49-50). If your claim is referred to the rent officer he or she is responsible for valuing fuel charges (para 10.7 and table 10.2).

10.49   If the charge is identifiable, the authority uses this figure as the fuel charge. However, if this is unrealistically low or includes an element for communal areas which cannot be separated out, the charge is treated as unidentifiable.

Table 10.3 **Standard weekly fuel deductions**

If the claimant and any family occupy more than one room

Fuel for heating	£28.80
Fuel for hot water	£3.35
Fuel for lighting	£2.30
Fuel for cooking	£3.35
Fuel for any other purpose	NIL
Fuel for all the above	£37.80

10.46   HB 12B(2),(5), B13(2)(a); HB60+ 12B(2),(5); CPR sch 3 para 5(1); NIHB 13A(2),(6); NIHB60+ 13A(2),(6); NICPR sch 3 para 5(1)

10.47   HB sch 1 para 5; HB60+ sch 1 para 5; NIHB sch 1 para 5; NIHB60+ sch 1 para 5

10.48-49 HB sch 1 para 6(1); HB60+ sch 1 para 6(1); NIHB sch 1 para 6(1); NIHB60+ sch 1 para 6(1)

T10.3   HB sch 1 para 6(2)-(4); HB60+ sch 1 para 6(2)-(4); NIHB sch 1 para 6(2)-(4); NIHB60+ sch 1 para 6(2)-(4)

If the claimant and any family occupy one room only	
Fuel for heating and any hot water and/or lighting	£17.23
Fuel for cooking	£3.35
Fuel for any other purpose	NIL
Fuel for all the above	£20.58

10.50 If the charge is not identified, the authority deducts the standard amounts, as shown in table 10.3 (a lower deduction applies if you only occupy one room). If the standard amounts are applied, the authority must invite you to provide evidence from which the 'actual or approximate' charge can be estimated; and, if the evidence is reasonable, the authority must use the estimated amount instead.

Meals

10.51 Charges for meals are not eligible for HB so if they are included in your rent a deduction must be made. For these purposes, 'a meal' includes preparation (e.g. where it is prepared somewhere else and then delivered) and also the provision of unprepared food (e.g. cereal, bread still in its wrappings).

10.52 The authority (not the rent officer) makes the deduction for meals. The standard amounts for meals shown in table 10.4 are always deducted, never the actual amount your landlord charges. A deduction is made for each person in your household whose meals are included in your rent (whether this is for you, a member of your family or some other person in your household such as a non-dependant). No deduction is made for anyone whose meals are not included (for example, a baby). When appropriate, deductions are calculated separately (for example fewer meals may be provided for someone who goes out to work than for someone who does not).

Table 10.4 **Standard weekly meals deductions**

A separate amount is assessed and deducted for each person whose meals are provided.

If at least three meals are provided every day

For the claimant, and each other person from the first Monday in September following his or her 16th birthday	£26.85
For each child	£13.60

If breakfast only is provided

For the claimant, and each other person of any age	£3.30

10.50   HB sch 1 para 6(2)-(4); HB60+ sch 1 para 6(2)-(4); NIHB sch 1 para 6(2)-(4); NIHB60+ sch 1 para 6(2)-(4)

10.51   HB sch 1 para 2; HB60+ sch 1 para 2; NIHB sch 1 para 2; NIHB60+ sch 1 para 2

10.52   HB 12B(2)(b), 12C(2), B13(2)(a), 13(5),(7), sch 1 para 2; HB60+ 12B(2), 12C(2), 13(5), sch 1 para 2;
          NIHB 13A(2)(b), 12B(2) 14(5),(7), sch 1 para 2; NIHB60+ 14(5),(7), sch 1 para 2

All other cases	
For the claimant, and each other person from the first Monday in September following his or her 16th birthday	£17.85
For each child	£9.00

Personal care and support charges

10.53   Support charges are never eligible for HB. This includes charges for:

(a) cleaning and window cleaning over and above that mentioned in paragraphs 10.29 and 10.43;

(b) emergency alarm systems (to summon assistance in the event of a fall, an accident, etc);

(c) counselling and support; and

(d) medical, nursing and personal care.

If you need any of these services you may be able to have the cost met by Supporting People, a government programme for funding support services administered by local authorities (in Northern Ireland by the NIHE) and independent of HB. For a detailed explanation of care, support and supervision in 'exempt accommodation' please see paragraph 9.5 and table 9.1.

10.54   In theory the law is straightforward: support is not eligible for HB. In practice, separating any support charge from other eligible charges your landlord provides is more difficult because the member of staff who provides your support will also provide services that are eligible as part of the same job. The task of separating ineligible services from eligible one is further complicated by the fact that some staff duties are usually eligible as part of the rent (and so are not services at all) and some duties are services but contain both eligible and ineligible elements.

10.55   Whether a particular activity is a landlord function (and so eligible as part of the rent) or whether it constitutes a service is not determined by how the tenancy agreement describes it nor by the landlord's classification – it is the law that does so (para 10.10). The mere fact that the landlord classifies a charge as 'intensive housing management' does not mean a service that the law says is support is somehow eligible for HB (para 10.11).

10.56   In separating rent, eligible and ineligible service charges the two key tests are:

(a) does the activity constitute a service (paras 10.11 and 10.13): in broad terms does it provide something that has value to you (as the tenant) rather than the landlord?; and

(b) if it is a service (and not an excluded item: paras 10.42 and 10.53), is it concerned with the 'provision of adequate accommodation' (paras 10.36-37), or is it provided to help you maintain your tenancy so that you can take advantage of the property's facilities (in which case it is support).

So as a general rule any activity undertaken by your landlord that varies in intensity according to your personal needs is more likely to be considered support (and so not eligible for HB).

T10.4   HB sch 1 para 2; HB60+ sch 1 para 2; NIHB sch 1 para 2; NIHB60+ sch 1 para 2

10.53   HB sch 1 para 1(a),(c)-(f); HB60+ sch 1 para 1(a),(c)-(f); sch 1 para 1(a),(c)-(f); NIHB sch 1 para 1(a),(c)-(f)

10.53   HB sch 1 para 1(f); HB60+ sch 1 para 1(f); sch 1 para 1(f); NIHB sch 1 para 1(f)

Other items included in setting rents

10.57 The distinction between services and other items that should be included as 'rent' are set out in paragraphs 10.8-15. Your landlord's overheads and management costs are usually rent (para 10.8) but whether a charge is 'rent' or a 'service charge' is not determined by your landlord's classification of the charge (para 10.10).

10.58 If an item is 'rent' then it is eligible for HB without the further conditions that apply to services (para 10.16) provided only that the charge is not excessive: paras 7.19-20. In particular, any part of your overall charge that represents your landlord's liability for council tax (e.g. if you are a lodger or live in a house made up of bedsits) is 'rent' (GM A4.160-161). Special rules apply to rent for garages, land and business premises (paras 10.60 and 10.62).

Increases to cover arrears of rent

10.59 If your rent has been increased to recover any arrears you owe, that part of the rent is not eligible for HB. This rule applies only to cover arrears you have personally incurred for rent on your current or former home. It does not apply if your landlord has increased the rent for all of his or her tenants as a result of arrears generally.

Garages, land, etc

10.60 The rent on a garage, mobility scooter shed, or any other buildings, gardens or land included in your letting agreement, is eligible for HB if:

(a) the facility provided is used for occupying the dwelling as your home; and

(b) you acquired them at the same time as the dwelling; and

(c) you had no option but to rent them at the same time.

Alternatively these facilities are also eligible for HB if you have made or are making reasonable efforts to end your liability for them.

Space for a carer

10.61 If you are a council/NIHE tenant, housing association tenant where referral to the rent officer is not required (para 7.11), or if you live in 'exempt accommodation' (para 9.4), a room for a live-in carer is included in your eligible rent in the normal way, even if your carer occupies a room down the corridor from you: [2009] UKUT 28 (AAC) and [2009] UKUT 116 (AAC). If the room is separated from your own (as in the second case) it is still counted as part of your accommodation because 'functionally and purposively, [you need two rooms to live – one for you and one for your] carer. Common sense dictates that it should not matter whether there is a connecting door between the two.' The situation is different if the carer does not live in your home (for example where you have a rota of carers); or if you want your parents to stay and care for you, but they live elsewhere: [2009] UKUT 79 (AAC). See also paragraphs 7.46-63.

10.59   HB 11(3); HB60+ 11(2); NIHB 11(3); NIHB60+ 11(2)

10.60   HB 2(4)(a); HB60+ 2(4)(a); NIHB 2(4)(a); NIHB60+ 2(4)(a)

Business premises

10.62   Rent on any part of your home which is used for business, commercial or other non-residential purposes is not eligible for HB. For example, if you rent both a shop and the flat above it, only the part of the rent relating to the flat is eligible for HB. If the rent on the business premises is not separately identified from the rent on the home, the authority decides how much relates to each. If you are self-employed and work from home, see paragraphs 14.43-44.

10.62   HB 12B(3),12C(2), B13(2)(a); HB60+ 12B(3),12C(2); NIHB 13A(3),13B(2); NIHB60+ 13A(3),13B(2)

Chapter 11 **Eligible rates**

- The future of HB for rates and other schemes in Northern Ireland: see paras 11.1-2.
- An overview of domestic rates in Northern Ireland (including liability and exemptions and so on): see paras 11.3-12.
- Rate rebates and eligible rates for HB: see paras 11.13-19.
- Rate relief (and how to calculate it): see paras 11.20-30.
- Lone pensioner allowance: see paras 11.31-8.

HB for rates, other schemes and their demise in 2016

11.1 This chapter applies only in Northern Ireland for 2014-15. It describes three schemes that provide help with your domestic rates whether the bill is paid by you or your landlord. The three schemes are: HB for rates, rate relief and the lone pensioner allowance.

11.2 The three schemes described were originally expected to end on 31st March 2015 but this has been postponed for one year to provide time for the legislation to pass through the Northern Ireland Assembly. From April 2016 these schemes are expected to be replaced by a new rate rebate scheme administered by Land and Property Services. Like council tax rebates in Great Britain, the new rate rebate scheme is not part of the social security system. The new scheme will be described in *Help with Housing Costs* Volume 1, 2016-17.

Rates overview

11.3 Domestic rates are the form of local taxation in Northern Ireland. Rates are a tax on residential properties known as dwellings (which for convenience we also refer to as 'your home'). Responsibility for paying them normally falls on the occupier: see paragraph 11.7. Land and Property Services (LPS) are responsible for the billing and collection of the tax.

Table 11.1 **Domestic rates: key considerations**

(a) Which dwelling is being considered?

(b) What is the capital value (or social sector value) for that dwelling?

(c) What is the aggregate rate poundage in that district?

(d) Who is liable for the rates?

(e) Is the dwelling exempt from rates altogether?

(f) Do they qualify for a disability reduction?

(g) Do they qualify for full or partial HB on their rates?

(h) Do they qualify for rate relief on any remaining rates?

(i) Do they qualify for lone pensioner allowance on any remaining rates?

Dwellings and annual rates

11.4   The domestic rate is an annual bill. One rates bill is issued per dwelling, unless the dwelling is exempt (para 11.8). A 'dwelling' means any house, flat, houseboat or mobile home, etc, whether lived in or not.

11.5   The amount of your rates bill depends first on the capital value set by LPS, assessed as the open market sale value of your home on 1st January 2005 (capped to a maximum of £400,000). If you are a NIHE or registered housing association tenant the capital value is substituted by a 'social sector value', calculated by the DSD based on the rent you pay for your home.

11.6   The amount of annual rates is calculated by multiplying the capital value (or £400,000 if the cap applies: para 11.5) by the rate in the pound ('rate poundage') for the year. The capital value and aggregate rate poundage for each district is shown on the bill and can be found on the LPS website.

Liability for rates

11.7   The rates bill goes to the owner or occupier of the dwelling. For example:

   (a) if you are a NIHE or housing association tenant the rates bill goes to your landlord, who recovers the cost by increasing the overall amount of rent you pay;

   (b) if you are a private tenant the rates bill may go to you, or your landlord may add it to your rent (para 11.11);

   (c) if you are an owner occupier the rates bill is sent to you.

Note that if you are a tenant and your landlord has paid the rates bill, then they have in effect included the amount in your rent whether or not it was a conscious decision to do so.

Exemptions

11.8   Certain dwellings are exempt from rates. This is not automatic – you must make an application to Land and Property Services. An occupied dwelling is exempt if the landlord is a registered charity. There are very few other exemptions and they mainly relate to unoccupied properties.

Disability reductions

11.9   Your rates bill is reduced by 25% if your home has been adapted or extended because of the disability of anyone who lives there. The reduction is not automatic: you must make an application to Land and Property Services.

Rate rebates, rate relief and lone pensioner allowance

11.10   If you are liable for rates on a dwelling that is your normal home (including, if you are a tenant, where your rent includes an amount towards your rates: para 11.11) then you can get any or all of rate rebate, rate relief or lone pensioner allowance. But you cannot get rate rebate or rate relief (but can get lone pensioner allowance) if you are:

   (a) in certain circumstances, a migrant or recent arrival in the UK (chapter 20); or

   (b) a full-time student (for exceptions see table 22.1).

11.6   www.dfpni.gov.uk/lps/

11.11   A person is eligible for all three of these schemes whether they pay rates direct to Land and Property Services, or via the rent they pay their landlord. If you are a tenant and your landlord pays the rates bill then they have in effect included the amount in your rent whether or not it was a conscious decision to do so. The only time that your rent does not include rates is if you receive the rates bill in your own name.

11.12   However, if you are a tenant, your rate rebate, rate relief or lone pensioner allowance cannot be awarded until a rates bill is issued. Once it has, your rate rebate and rate relief are awarded retrospectively provided you notify the NIHE within one month of receiving it; this time limit can be extended in special circumstances. Otherwise your benefit is awarded according to the usual HB rules (paras 5.45-49). If you are claiming lone pensioner allowance, the award starts from the date your rates liability commenced, or the date you qualify if later.

Rate rebates and eligible rates

What are rate rebates?

11.13   A rate rebate (HB for rates) reduces the amount of rates you pay. It is worked out in a similar way to your HB for rent. It is funded by subsidy payable to Land and Property Services or NIHE. To find out where to apply for a rate rebate, see paragraph 1.28 and table 1.6.

Eligible rates

11.14   Your eligible rates is the figure used in calculating your entitlement to rate rebate (HB for rates). It is calculated by working through the following steps:

1. Start with the annual rates due on your home (paras 11.5-6) after any capping that may apply.

2. If you are entitled to a disability reduction (para 11.9), use the rates figure after that has been made.

3. If you are a joint occupier apportion the result.

4. Convert it to a weekly figure (as described in para 6.41).

Note that unlike HB for rent, there is no power to restrict the eligible rates if your home is too expensive or too large.

Impact of rates changes on eligible rent

11.15   If your rent includes an amount for rates (para 11.11), a change in the rates (such as the new amount applying from each April, or following the award of a disability reduction) means your eligible rent changes too. Since there is no duty on you or your landlord to advise of changes to rates, the NIHE alters your HB for rent and rates automatically when advised by Land and Property Services.

11.10   NICBA 129(1)(a); NIHB 8(1)(a),9(1); 10(1),53(1); NIHB60+ 8(1)(a); 9(1),10(1)

11.11   NIHB 12(2), 13(3)(b),(6); NIHB60+ 12(2), 13(3)(b),(6)

11.14   NIHB 11(1)(a), 12(3), 78(3); NIHB60+ 11(1)(a), 12(3), 59(3)

11.15   NIHB 12(1),(2); 84(2)(a),(b); NIHB60+; 12(1),(2),65(2)(a),(b)

Apportionment of eligible rates

11.16   Your eligible rates figure is apportioned if:

(a) you occupy only part of a rateable unit (for example, if you are a lodger or live with others in a multi-occupied property). In this case only the proportion of the rates payable for your accommodation is eligible for HB;

(b) if you are jointly liable to pay rates with one or more other occupiers – for example if you have a joint tenancy (see para 7.21);

(c) part of the rateable unit is for business use – such as a shop with a flat above. This is done in the same way as for eligible rent (para 10.62).

Calculating rate rebate

11.17   The method of calculating your rate rebate is given in paragraphs 6.2-8 and 6.41-42 and see examples at the end of this chapter. As with your HB for rent, non-dependant charges may apply (table 11.2) and see paragraphs 6.14-27 for details.

Table 11.2 **Non-dependant deductions: 2015-16**	
If non-dependant is on JSA(IB), ESA(IR), IS or state pension credit	£0.00
If non-dependant works 16+ hours/week (paras 6.19-20) and has gross income of:	
▣ £394.00 or more per week	£9.90
▣ £316.00 to £393.99 per week	£8.25
▣ £183.00 to £315.99 per week	£6.25
▣ under £183.00 per week	£3.30
Any other non-dependant:	£3.30

Awarding rate rebate as a credit or as a payment

11.18   A rate rebate is awarded as a credit to your rates account except only that the NIHE may choose (at its discretion) to pay your HB for rates as an allowance (along with any HB for rent) if:

(a) your rent includes an amount for rates (para 11.11); and

(b) you qualify for HB for rent or would do but for any non-dependant deduction or the deduction made because you have excess income (i.e. the 'taper': para 6.8).

11.19   When HB is paid as an allowance, it is paid either to you or your landlord following the same rules as HB for rent (paras 16.20-22 and 16.34-66). But if your total HB (for rent and rates) is £2 per week or less it can be paid four-weekly; and if it is less than £1 per week it can be paid every six months.

11.16   NIHB 12(2),(4)-(6); NIHB60+; 12(2),(4)-(6)

T11.2   NIHB 72(1)(a),(b),(8)(b),(10); NIHB60+ 53(1)(a),(b),(8)(b),(9)

11.18   NIHB 87(2),88,89(5); NIHB60+ 68(2),69,70(5)

> **Example: Calculation of eligible rates**
>
> A dwelling has a capital value of £135,000 in an area where the rate poundage is £0.0057777 per £1 of capital value. Capping does not apply so the annual rates payable are:
>
> | £135,000 x 0.0057777 | = | £780.00 |
> |---|---|---|
>
> The weekly eligible rates (to the nearest 1p) are therefore:
>
> | £780.00 ÷ 365 x 7 | = | £14.96 if paid separately from rent or |
> |---|---|---|
> | £780.00 ÷ 52 | = | £15.00 if paid along with rent. |

Rate relief

What is rate relief?

11.20 The rate relief scheme was introduced in Northern Ireland on 1st April 2007 following changes in the assessment of domestic rates from being based on an outdated historic rental value to a recent open market capital value. Because of the way rate rebates are calculated, you get no financial benefit from a change in your rates. The rate relief scheme gives you an extra reduction to compensate for this.

11.21 Rate relief is not part of the HB scheme, and is funded from the rates themselves rather than from government subsidy. It is possible for you to qualify for rate relief even if you do not for HB and since the same information is required for both a full assessment is always carried out.

Who gets rate relief?

11.22 Your rate relief is considered automatically (so no claim is needed) if you:

(a) qualify for a rate rebate (HB); but

(b) you still have rates to pay – other than any amount arising from a non-dependant deduction or recovery of an overpayment.

So if you already qualify for maximum HB (para 6.2) for rates, including where you are repaying an overpayment, you cannot get rate relief. In any other case where you have made a claim for, and are awarded a rate rebate, you also get rate relief. If you do not qualify for a rate rebate but you still have rates to pay you can claim rate relief separately.

Calculating rate relief

11.23 Rate relief is calculated in the same way as your rate rebate – except that:

(a) your rate relief is worked out on the amount of rates remaining after rate rebate has been granted – ignoring any non-dependant deduction;

(b) if you have a pension age claim and/or if you qualify for a carer premium your applicable amount is higher (para 11.24);

(c) if you have a pension age claim the upper capital limit is £50,000 (tariff income applies as in HB);

11.22   NISR 2007/203; NISR 2007/204; NISR 2007/244; NISR 2011/43

(d) the taper percentage used in the calculation is 12% of your excess income;

(e) the deductions for non-dependants and the income bands that apply to them are different to HB for rent (see table 11.2).

Examples of the calculation are given at the end of this chapter.

11.24 Your applicable amount is calculated the same way as for HB except:

(a) the rate of the carer premium is £41.52;

(b) if you or your partner have attained state pension credit age (para 1.24) but are aged under 65 your personal allowance is: £173.88 if you are single or a lone parent, £253.94 if you are a couple;

(c) if you or your partner are aged 65+ your personal allowance is: £190.96 if you are a single claimant or a lone parent, £273.13 if you are a couple.

Awarding rate relief

11.25 Your rate relief is used to reduce the amount of rates you pay. If you are an owner occupier or a private tenant, it is credited to your rates account by Land and Property Services. If you are a NIHE or housing association tenant, it is paid to your landlord and so reduces the overall rent and rates you pay.

Reconsiderations and appeals

11.26 The rules about how you can get a written statement of reasons, request a reconsideration, and request an appeal, are the same as if you were claiming HB for rent (chapter 19). Although rate relief is not a social security benefit, an appeal tribunal nonetheless deals with your appeal and, whenever practicable, deals with your rate relief appeal at the same time as your HB appeal.

Overpayments of rate relief

11.27 Overpaid rate relief can be recovered in the same circumstances as any overpaid HB for rent (paras 18.11-15).

11.28 Any recoverable overpayment of rate relief can be recovered by any lawful method, but the main methods used are:

(a) charging the amount back to your rates account;

(b) deducting it from any future rate relief award you are entitled to.

11.29 A recoverable overpayment of rate relief can be charged back to your rates account. But this method is not normally used if you are a NIHE or housing association tenant, except where the account is now closed (for example following a death or a move) and there remains sufficient credit on the account to make a recovery from it.

11.24   NISR 2007/203, Reg 17(2)(c); NISR 2007/244; NISR 2011/43

11.25   NISR 2007/203; NISR 2007/204

11.26   NISR 2007/203; NISR 2007/204

11.27   NISR 2007/203; NISR 2007/204

11.30 A recoverable overpayment of rate relief can be deducted from your future rate relief award. If you have an ongoing award the maximum rate of deduction is limited to the amounts in table 18.3. But this limit does not apply to deductions from lump sum arrears of rate relief. Any deductions to recover rate relief overpayments are additional to those to recover HB overpayments.

Lone pensioner allowance

What is lone pensioner allowance?

11.31 Lone pensioner allowance was introduced in Northern Ireland on 1st April 2008 following a review of domestic rating policy by the Northern Ireland Executive, which concluded that single people over 70 required further assistance to help with rates charges. In some respects it is similar to the single person discount within council tax but applies only to people aged 70 or above. You may qualify for lone pensioner allowance whether or not you qualify for HB or rate relief.

11.32 Lone pensioner allowance is not part of either the HB or rate relief schemes and is funded by the Northern Ireland Executive.

Who gets lone pensioner allowance?

11.33 If you are liable for rates on your normal or only home, aged 70 or over, and you live alone (but see para 11.34 for details of limited exceptions) you will receive lone pensioner allowance. The allowance is not means tested; but it is not awarded automatically, you must make a claim for it either alongside your HB and/or rate relief or separately. If you qualify for full HB and/or rate relief you cannot also get lone pensioner allowance since it is based on the rates you still have left to pay.

Living alone

11.34 In limited circumstances, even though someone else lives in your household, you can still be treated as living alone and thus qualify for lone pensioner allowance. This applies if:

(a) the person living with you is a resident carer (conditions apply);

(b) the person living with you is aged less than 18;

(c) you are receiving child benefit for the person who lives with you;

(d) the person living with you is severely mentally impaired (conditions apply).

Calculating lone pensioner allowance

11.35 Since the lone pensioner allowance is not means tested, if you qualify you receive a flat rate 20% reduction on the rates you have to pay. If you also qualify for rate rebate (HB), rate relief or a disability reduction the allowance is applied to the amount of rates left to pay. If you do not qualify for any other kind of reduction the allowance is applied to your full rates charge. Examples of lone pensioner allowance calculations are at the end of this chapter.

11.33   NISR 2008/124

Awarding lone pensioner allowance

11.36 Like rate relief, lone pensioner allowance is used to reduce the amount of rates you pay on your home. If you are an owner occupier or a private tenant, it is credited to your rate account by Land and Property Services. If you are a NIHE or housing association tenant, it is paid to your landlord and so reduces the overall rent and rates you have to pay.

Overpayments of lone pensioner allowance

11.37 An overpayment of lone pensioner allowance is only likely to occur if you no longer live alone (such as if a new partner moves in) or you no longer have rates to pay on your home (for example, if you move). An overpayment of lone pensioner allowance cannot be recovered from any HB or rate relief you are entitled to unless you agree to this but it can be recovered by any other lawful method. If you are an owner occupier or a private tenant the recovery is usually made by charging the amount back to your rates account. If you are a NIHE or housing association tenant, and the account is now closed (for example following a death or a move) there may be sufficient credit on the account or assets in an estate to make a recovery. If you later re-qualify for lone pensioner allowance, recovery can be made by deducting the overpayment from any lump sum arrears of your new award.

Appeals

11.38 If you want to appeal a decision relating to lone pensioner allowance it is considered by the Valuation Tribunal; you must appeal within 28 days of being notified of the decision. Note that this differs from the usual time limit of one month for both HB and rate relief appeals.

Examples: Rate rebate, rate relief and lone pensioner allowance

A claimant without a non-dependant

A couple in their 40s have no non-dependants. They are not on JSA(IB), ESA(IR) or income support. Their income exceeds their applicable amount by £20 per week. Their eligible rates are £15 per week.

Rate rebate (HB for rates)	£
Eligible rates	15.00
minus 20% of excess income (20% of £20.00)	– 4.00
equals weekly rate rebate	11.00
Rate relief	
Rates due after rate rebate	4.00
minus 12% of excess income (12% of £20.00)	– 2.40
equals weekly rate relief	1.60

A claimant with a non-dependant

A single claimant in her 50s has a non-dependant son living with her. The claimant is not on JSA(IB), ESA(IR) or income support. Her income exceeds her applicable amount by £10 per week. Her eligible rates are £18.00 per week. Her son works full-time with gross income of £400 per week.

Rate rebate (HB for rates)	£
Eligible rates	18.00
minus non-dependant deduction	– 9.90
minus 20% of excess income (20% of £10.00)	– 2.00
equals weekly rate rebate	6.10

Rate relief	
Rates due after rate rebate – ignoring non-dependant deduction	2.00
minus 12% of excess income (12% of £10.00)	– 1.20
equals weekly rate relief	0.80

Lone pensioner allowance

A person aged 72 lives alone and has a weekly rates charge of £18. She does not receive either HB or rate relief.

	£
Weekly rates to pay	18.00
Minus lone pensioner allowance (20% of £18)	– 3.60
Net amount to pay	14.40

If the same person receives £10 per week HB and £2 per week rate relief:

	£
Weekly rates to pay	18.00
Minus HB	– 10.00
Minus rate relief	– 2.00
Rates left to pay	6.00
Minus lone pensioner allowance (20% of £6)	– 1.20
Net amount to pay	4.80

Chapter 12 **Applicable amounts**

■ Calculating the applicable amount: basic rules: see paras 12.1-7.

■ Allowances for you and your family: see paras 12.8-14.

■ Working age components and the disability premium: see paras 12.15-32.

■ Other premiums for disability and caring: see paras 12.33-48.

■ Further definitions and special cases: see paras 12.49-54.

Calculating the applicable amount: basic rules

What is the applicable amount?

12.1   The applicable amount represents your family's basic living expenses. It is compared to your income when calculating how much HB you are entitled to (paras 6.6-8). It is also sometimes used for other HB matters (for example, as part of the rules that govern student eligibility: table 22.1).

Definitions

12.2   In this chapter the following terms all have the specific HB meanings given in chapter 4:

(a) 'family', 'single claimant', 'lone parent' and 'couple' (paras 4.7-8);

(b) 'partner' (paras 4.9-22); and

(c) 'child' and 'young person' (paras 4.23-38).

For 'pension age' and 'working age' see paragraph 1.23-25 and table 1.5. Further definitions are found in paragraphs 12.49-52.

How much is your applicable amount?

12.3   Your applicable amount is the total of:

(a) your personal allowance (including any partner);

(b) a personal allowance for each child or young person in the family; and

(c) any additional amounts (known as premiums and components) you qualify for.

The figures for 2015-16 are given in table 12.1. Detailed conditions are in the rest of this chapter. Further definitions and special cases are in paragraphs 12.49-54.

12.2   CBA 137; NICBA 133; HB 2(1) definitions – 'child', 'claimant', 'family', 'partner', 'young person', 22;
HB60+ 2(1), 22; NIHB 2(1), 20, NIHB60+ 2(1), 20

12.3   CBA 135; NICBA 131; HB 22, sch 3; HB60+ 22, sch 3; NIHB 20, sch 4; NIHB60+ 20, sch 4

How many premiums and components at once

12.4   Except as described in the remainder of this chapter, there are no limitations on how many premiums and components can be awarded at a time.

How to be better off if you are a couple on ESA

12.5   If you are a couple and one or both of you or your partner receives ESA (or national insurance credits instead of ESA) your applicable amount can be higher or lower depending on which one of you makes the claim for HB (para 5.4). If this applies to you and you are worse off because the wrong member has claimed HB your council should advise you that you would be better off if you swapped roles (GM BW3.143 and BW3.305). To ensure that you are better off through the right member making the HB claim, see the next two paragraphs.

12.6   If both you and your partner receive ESA (or credits) but you receive different components, you are better off if the member who gets the support component claims HB.

12.7   If only one of you receives ESA the member who claims HB should be as follows:

(a)   if you are both aged under 18, the member who gets ESA;

(b)   if one of you receives the support component, that member;

(c)   if one of you qualifies for a disability premium and the other a work-related activity component, the member who qualifies for the disability premium;

(d)   if neither of you qualify for a disability premium, the member who receives the work-related activity component.

'ESA', 'support component' and 'work-related activity component' means receiving ESA with that component or national insurance credits (para 12.23) instead of ESA.

Example: A 'better off' problem for couples

Information

A working age couple meet the condition for a disability premium which relates to being disabled or long-term sick (e.g. one of them is on DLA or is registered blind), but one partner in the couple is on ESA(C).

Entitlement to additions in the HB applicable amount

This depends on which partner is the HB claimant.

(a)   If the HB claimant is on ESA(C):

their HB applicable amount does not include a disability premium (at any point), but it does include a work-related activity or support component from the claimant's 14th week on ESA(C).

12.4   HB sch 3 paras 4-5, 6(1); HB60+ sch 3 para 4; NIHB sch 4 para 4; NIHB60+ sch 3 para 4

12.6   HB sch 3 paras 23-26; NIHB sch 4 paras 23-26

12.7   HB sch 3 paras 1(3)(a),(c), 13(9), 22-26; NIHB sch 4 paras 1(3)(a),(c), 13(9), 22-26

(b) If the HB partner is on ESA(C):

their HB applicable amount includes a couple-rate disability premium (from the beginning), but it never includes a work-related activity or support component.

Conclusion

So they are better off if (b) applies to them – by about £30 per week HB during the first 13 weeks on ESA(C) (and by a lower amount after that).

Allowances for you and your family

12.8   This section gives the conditions for the basic allowances in your applicable amount that take account of your family size: they comprise 'personal allowances' (para 12.3) and the family premium (para 12.13).

Personal allowances: you and your partner

12.9   A personal allowance is always awarded for you (if you are single or a lone parent), or you and your partner if you are a couple. (For polygamous marriages see para 12.53.)

12.10   If you are aged under 25 (18 if a lone parent/couple) and getting ESA or credits instead of ESA (paras 12.21, 12.23) the start of your main phase results in the higher HB personal allowance (table 12.1).

12.11   If you are a couple both aged under 18 and only one of you is on main phase ESA, see paragraph 12.7 to ensure you are better off.

Personal allowances: children and young persons

12.12   A personal allowance is awarded for each child or young person in your family (paras 4.23-38).

Family premium

12.13   You are awarded this premium if there is at least one child or young person in your family (paras 4.23-38).

12.14   A higher 'protected rate' of the family premium applies in certain circumstances if you are a lone parent who has been on HB since 5th April 1998. The protected rate is £22.20. The conditions are in GM BW3.75-76.

12.9   HB 22(a), sch 3 para 1; HB60+ 22(a), sch 3 para 1; NIHB 20(a), sch 4 para 1; NIHB60+ 20(a), sch 4 para 1

12.10   HB sch 3 paras 1,1A; NIHB sch 4 paras 1,1A

12.12   HB 22(b), sch 3 para 2(1); HB60+ 22(b), sch 3 para 2(1); NIHB 20(b), sch 4 para 2(1); NIHB60+ 20(b), sch 4 para 2(1)

12.13   HB 22(c), sch 3 para 3(1)(b); HB60+ 22(c), sch 3 para 3; NIHB 20(c), sch 4 para 3; NIHB60+ 20(c), sch 4 para 3

12.14   HB sch 3 para 3(1)(a),(3)-(5); NIHB sch 4 para 3(1)(a),(3)-(5)

Table 12.1 **Weekly HB applicable amounts**

Personal allowances

Single claimant	aged under 25 – on main phase ESA	£73.10
	aged under 25 – other	£57.90
	aged 25+ but under pension age	£73.10
	over pension age but under 65	£151.20
	aged 65+	£166.05
Lone parent	aged under 18 – on main phase ESA	£73.10
	aged under 18 – other	£57.90
	aged 18+ but under pension age	£73.10
	over pension age but under 65	£151.20
	aged 65+	£166.05
Couple	both under 18 – claimant on main phase ESA	£114.85
	both under 18 – other	£87.50
	at least one aged 18+ both under pension age	£114.85
	at least one pension age, both under 65	£230.85
	at least one aged 65+	£248.30
Plus for each child/ young person		£66.90

Additional amounts

Family premium	at least one child/young person	£17.45	
Disability premium	single claimant/lone parent	£32.25	*
	couple (one/both qualifying)	£45.95	*
Disabled child premium	each child/young person	£60.06	
Enhanced	single claimant/lone parent	£15.75	*
disability premium	couple (one/both qualifying)	£22.60	*
	each child/young person	£24.43	
Work related activity component	single claimant/lone parent/couple	£29.05	*
Support component	single claimant/lone parent/couple	£36.20	*
Carer premium	claimant or partner or each	£34.60	
Severe	single rate	£61.85	
disability premium	double rate	£123.70	

* Only awarded with working age claims (para 1.24)

Examples: Applicable amounts

Except for the lone parent in the fourth example, none of the following qualifies for any of the premiums for disability or for carers.

Single claimant aged 23

Personal allowance:	Single claimant aged under 25	£57.90
	No additional amounts apply	
	Applicable amount	£57.90

Couple with two children aged 13 and 17

The older child is still at school so still counts as a dependant of the couple.

Personal allowances:	Couple, at least one over 18, both under pension age	£114.85
	Child aged 13	£66.90
	Young person aged 17	£66.90
Additional amount:	family premium	£17.45
	Applicable amount	£266.10

Couple aged 48 and 65

Personal allowance:	Couple at least one aged 65	£248.30
	Applicable amount	£248.30

Disabled lone parent with a child aged 6

The lone parent is in receipt of the enhanced rate of the daily living component of personal independence payment and so qualifies for a disability premium and enhanced disability premium. She has one child aged 6. Her mother (who lives elsewhere) receives carer's allowance to care for her. So she does not qualify for the severe disability premium.

Personal allowances:	Lone parent aged over 18 (and under pension age)	£73.10
	Child	£66.90
Additional amounts:	Family premium	£17.45
	Disability premium (single rate)	£32.25
	Enhanced disability premium (single rate)	£15.75
	Applicable amount	£205.45

Working age components and the disability premium

12.15   The components, disability premium and transitional addition described in this section (paras 12.16-32) can only apply to you if you have a working age claim (paras 1.23-25 and table 1.5).

12.16 If you or your partner have a sickness or disability that affects your fitness to work then you may be entitled to either:

(a) a work-related activity component: see paras 12.18-23;

(b) a support component: see paras 12.18-23; or

(c) a disability premium: see paras 12.24-27 (and for other ways for qualifying for this premium see paras 12.31-32).

You can only receive one of these at any one time. You do not necessarily receive the one that is the highest value – that is determined by the DWP's assessment of your (or your partner's) fitness for work and, if you are a couple, which one of you makes the claim. See paragraphs 12.5-7 to ensure you are better off.

12.17 If you qualify for a component, and your period of sickness or disability began before 27th October 2008, you may also be entitled to a transitional addition: see paras 12.28-30.

The components and the ESA fitness for work

12.18 The general rule is that you are awarded a work-related activity component or support component in your HB if:

(a) you have claimed employment and support allowance (ESA); and

(b) the DWP has decided you qualify for that particular component (see paras 12.20-22), and

- has awarded it in your ESA, or
- would have done so except that you qualify for national insurance credits instead of ESA (see para 12.23).

12.19 The rules are more complex if you are a couple. If only one of you qualifies for an ESA component, or you both qualify for the same ESA component, you get that component in your HB. But if you qualify for one ESA component and your partner qualifies for the other ESA component, you get the component you (the HB claimant) qualify for. This means you can be 'better off' depending on which one of you claims HB (see paras 12.5-7).

12.20 When you claim ESA, you qualify for the work-related activity component if the DWP decides you have 'limited capability for work'. But you qualify for the support component (which is worth more) if the DWP decides your disability is so serious that you have 'limited capability for work-related activity'. In other words, the type of activities the DWP expects you to undertake are more limited than if you were awarded the work-related activity component.

12.21 The DWP's decision about this is called a 'work capability assessment'. The DWP:

(a) makes this decision during the 'assessment phase' of your ESA;

(b) awards your component during the 'main phase' of your ESA.

Your assessment phase runs for the first 13 weeks of your ESA claim, and your main phase runs from week 14 onwards (see also para 12.22).

12.16   HB sch 3 paras 13(9), 22(1); NIHB sch 4 paras 13(9), 22(1)

12.17   HB sch 3 paras 13(9), 22(1); NIHB sch 4 paras 13(9), 22(1

12.18-19 HB sch 3 paras 21,21A,23,24; NIHB sch 4 paras 21,21A,23,24

12.20   HB 2(1) 'limited capability for work', 'limited capability for work-related activity', sch 3 para 21(1)(b); NIHB 2(1), sch 4 para 21(1)(b)

12.22 Your ESA is 'linked' to a previous ESA award if the start of your current period of limited capability for work is within 12 weeks of your previous award ending. 'Linked' ESA awards form a continuous period, so your 'assessment phase' starts from the first day of your previous ESA award, and means some or all of the 13 weeks are already served in your current award.

12.23 The DWP awards you national insurance credits instead of ESA if the only reason you do not qualify for ESA is because:

(a) you do not meet the national insurance contribution conditions for ESA; or

(b) you were receiving ESA(C) but your award has expired because it was paid for the maximum period of one year.

Disability premium and the old fitness for work test

12.24 Paragraphs 12.25-27 explain when you get a disability premium instead of a component. For the general rules about other ways you can get a disability premium, see paragraphs 12.31-32.

12.25 You are awarded a disability premium in your HB if you count as long-term sick under the 'old' fitness for work test. This only applies to you if your period of sickness started before 27th October 2008 and you:

(a) get long-term incapacity benefit (IB);

(b) get severe disablement allowance (SDA); or

(c) are getting national insurance credits (instead of IB or SDA) and you have been incapable of work for one year or more. This one year period need not be continuous: two or more periods of sickness are added together if the gap between them is eight weeks or less.

12.26 The rules are more complex if you are a couple. You get a disability premium at the couple rate in your HB if:

(a) either of you is on long-term IB or SDA, even if the other one is on ESA; or

(b) you (the HB claimant) are getting national insurance credits and have been incapable of work for one year or more (see para 12.25(c)), even if your partner is on ESA.

This means you can be better off depending on which one of you claims HB (see paras 12.5-7).

12.27 You do not count as long-term sick under the old fitness for work test if you have transferred from IB or SDA to ESA, or from receiving national insurance credits under the 'old' test to receiving them under the ESA fitness for work test. Once you have transferred you can't go back, but you may qualify for a transitional addition in your HB (see paras 12.28-30).

12.25-26 HB sch 3 paras 13(1)(a)(i),(b),(6), 21A; HB sch 4 paras 13(1)(a)(i),(b),(6), 21A

12.27 HB sch 3 para 13(9); NIHB sch 3 para 13(9)

Transitional addition after transferring to ESA

12.28 You qualify for a transitional addition in your HB if your disability premium stops because you transfer:

(a) from long-term IB, SDA, or national insurance credits instead of these (see paras 12.25-26);

(b) to contributory ESA, or national insurance credits instead of this (see paras 12.18-23).

The transitional addition prevents you from being worse off as a result of transferring.

12.29 But you do not qualify for a transitional addition if:

(a) you transfer to income-related ESA; or

(b) you are a couple and you qualify for a disability premium under the rules in paragraphs 12.31-32.

In each case, this is because you can't be worse off (but if (b) applies to you, see paragraphs 12.5-7 to ensure this).

12.30 A transitional addition restores your applicable amount to the value it had immediately before you transferred to contributory ESA or national insurance credits. After that:

(a) any subsequent increase in your applicable amount due to a change in your circumstances or the annual up-rating is deducted from your transitional addition until it is eroded to nil;

(b) you transitional addition ends before it is eroded to nil if your contributory ESA ends or your HB ends;

(c) but if you start back on HB within 12 weeks of your previous award, your transitional addition is restored.

Example: Transitional addition

A single man aged 37 transferred from long-term IB to the work-related activity component of ESA(C). Before he transfers, his applicable amount is:

■ personal allowance	£73.10
■ disability premium	£32.25
■ total	£105.35

After he transfers, his HB applicable amount is:

■ personal allowance	£73.10
■ work-related activity component	£29.05
■ total	£102.15
His transitional addition is the difference between the two totals	£3.20
This restores his applicable amount to	£105.35

12.28   HB sch 3 para 27(1); NIHB sch 4 para 27(1)

12.30   HB sch 3 paras 27(2), 30,31; NIHB sch 4 paras 27(2), 30, 31

Disability premium: general rules

12.31   You are awarded a disability premium if you have a working age claim (see paras 1.23-25), and are not on ESA or national insurance credits instead of ESA, and

(a) you are severely sight impaired, blind or have recently regained your sight (paras 12.51-52);

(b) you receive one of the following qualifying disability benefits:

  ■   disability living allowance,

  ■   personal independence payment,

  ■   the disability element or severe disability element of working tax credit,

  ■   any benefit which is treated as attendance allowance (para 12.50),

  ■   an armed forces independence payment, or

  ■   war pensioner's mobility supplement; or

(c) you have an invalid vehicle supplied by the NHS or get DWP payments for car running costs.

12.32   The rules are more complex if you are a couple. You get a disability premium at the couple rate if:

(a) either of you meets the conditions in paragraph 12.31, and neither of you are on ESA or national insurance credits instead of ESA; or

(b) you (the HB claimant) meet the conditions in paragraph 12.31, and your partner is on ESA or national insurance credits instead of ESA.

This means you can be 'better off' depending on which of you claims HB (see paras 12.5-7).

Other premiums for disability and caring

12.33   The premiums described in this section (see paras 12.34-48) can apply to you whether you have a working age or pension age claim (except as described in paragraph 12.36).

Disabled child premium

12.34   You qualify for this premium if there is a child or young person in your family who:

(a) is severely sight impaired, blind or has recently regained their sight (paras 12.51-52); or

(b) receives personal independence payment or disability living allowance (either component at any rate).

The premium is awarded for each child or young person who qualifies. If your child dies the premium continues for eight weeks following their death. If your child loses their qualifying benefit because they are in hospital special rules apply – see paragraph 12.54 and table 12.2 for details.

12.31-32   HB sch 3 paras 12, 13(9); NIHB sch 4 paras 12, 13(9)

12.33   HB sch 3 para 13(1)(a)(i),(9); NIHB sch 4 para 13(1)(a)(i),(9)

12.34   HB sch 3 paras 16(a)-(e), 20(7); HB60+ sch 3 para 8(a)-(e), 12(3);
           NIHB sch 4 paras 16(za),(a)-(c), 20(7); NIHB60+ sch 4 para 8(za),(a)-(c), 12(3)

Enhanced disability premium

12.35   You are awarded the enhanced disability premium:

(a)   if you or your partner qualify (para 12.36); and/or

(b)   for each child or young person in your family who qualifies (para 12.37).

Two or more of these premiums are awarded if appropriate – for example, if you or your partner qualifies and also one or more children qualify. If you lose your qualifying benefit as a result of a stay in hospital special rules apply (para 12.54 and table 12.2).

12.36   An enhanced disability premium for you or your partner is awarded if:

(a)   you have a working age claim (para 1.24);

(b)   you (or if you are a couple either you or your partner) receive the enhanced rate of the daily living component of personal independence payment, the highest rate of the care component of disability living allowance or an armed forces independence payment; or

(c)   you qualify for an ESA(C) support component (but not if your partner only does).

If you are a couple, the couple rate is awarded even if only one of you meets the conditions: so if only one of you qualifies for an ESA support component you are better off if they are the HB claimant (paras 12.5-7).

12.37   An enhanced disability premium is awarded for each child or young person in your family who receives the enhanced rate of the daily living component of personal independence payment, highest rate of the care component of disability living allowance, or (if they are a young person) an armed forces independence payment. If your child dies the premium continues for eight weeks following their death.

Severe disability premium

12.38   There are three conditions for this premium:

(a)   you must be receiving one of the following qualifying benefits:

- the daily living component of personal independence payment,
- attendance allowance,
- the middle or highest rate care component of disability living allowance,
- a benefit which is treated as attendance allowance (para 12.50), or
- an armed forces independence payment; and

(b)   you must have no non-dependants (but see paragraph 12.40 below for exceptions) living with you; and

(c)   no-one must be receiving carer's allowance to care for you (but see paragraph 12.42 for circumstances where a carer's allowance is awarded but treated as not being paid).

12.35   HB sch 3 para 20(9); HB60+ sch 3 para 12(2); NIHB sch 4 para 20(9); NIHB60+ sch 4 para 12(2)

12.36   HB sch 3 para 15(1)(a)-(d); NIHB sch 4 para 15(1)(a),(aa),(b)

12.37   HB sch 3 para 15(1)(b)-(d),(1A); HB60+ sch 3 para 7; NIHB sch 4 para 15(1)(a),(aa),(b),(1A); NIHB60+ sch 4 para 7

12.38   HB sch 3 para 14(2); HB60+ sch 3 para 6(2); NIHB sch 4 para 14(2); NIHB60+ sch 4 para 6(2)

If you are a couple, except where one of you is severely sight impaired or blind (para 12.49), both of you must be receiving a qualifying benefit. Special rules apply if you lose your qualifying benefit during a stay in hospital (paras 12.39, 12.41, 12.54 and table 12.2).

12.39 If you are single or a lone parent and you satisfy all the conditions in paragraph 12.38 you get the single rate of severe disability premium. If you are in a couple a severe disability premium is awarded as follows:

(a) if you both satisfy all three conditions, you get the double rate;

(b) if you both satisfy the first two conditions but only one of you satisfies the third condition, you get the single rate;

(c) if you are the claimant and you satisfy all three conditions, and your partner is severely sight impaired, blind or has recently regained their sight (paras 12.51-52), you get the single rate. In this case, the member who satisfies all the conditions must be the claimant to qualify for the premium. If the 'wrong' partner makes the claim, you should be advised to 'swap the claimant role';

(d) if you have been getting the double rate, but one of you loses your qualifying benefit as a result of being in hospital for four weeks, then you get the single rate from that point;

(e) if you are in a polygamous marriage, you get the double rate if all members of the marriage satisfy all three conditions in paragraph 12.38; the single rate if all members of the marriage satisfy the first two of those conditions but one member has a carer who gets a carer's allowance in respect of caring for one of them; and the single rate if you are the claimant and you satisfy all three conditions and all the other members of the marriage are severely sight impaired, blind or have recently regained their sight (paras 12.51-52).

12.40 When assessing the second condition in para 12.38 (non-dependants that live with you) your council must ignore any person in your household who:

(a) is a member of your family (para 4.7);

(b) is aged under 18 or who is excluded from the definition of a non-dependant (table 4.2);

(c) is severely sight impaired, blind or who has recently regained their sight (paras 12.51-52);

(d) receives any of the qualifying benefits in para 12.38(a) (for example, attendance allowance); or

(e) is jointly liable with you or your partner for rent unless they were a non-dependant in the previous eight weeks or they are a close relative (para 2.58) and your council believes their liability was created to take advantage of the HB scheme.

12.39   HB sch 3 paras 14(3), 20(6); HB60+ sch 3 paras 6(3), 12(1); NIHB sch 4 paras 14(3), 20(6); NIHB60+ sch 4 paras 6(3), 12(1)

12.40   HB sch 3 para 14(4); HB60+ sch 3 para 6(6); NIHB sch 4 para 14(4); NIHB60+ sch 4 para 6(6)

12.41   When assessing the third condition in para 12.38 (whether your carer receives carer's allowance) your council must treat your carer as receiving carer's allowance during any period when:

(a) you are a member of a couple and carer's allowance has stopped as a result of you losing your qualifying benefit because you have been in hospital for four weeks or more. (This ensures that if you receive the premium at the single rate you continue to receive it at that rate while you (or your partner) are in hospital).

(b) your carer has stopped receiving carer's allowance as a penalty for a benefit fraud conviction.

12.42   When assessing the third condition in para 12.38 (you or your partner's carer receives carer's allowance) your council must ignore any period when you (or your partner's) carer:

(a) receives an award of carer's allowance but it is not in payment because it is overlapped by other benefits (para 12.45);

(b) receives arrears of carer's allowance, in other words any backdated part of the carer's allowance award does not cause an overpayment of the severe disability premium.

Example: Severe disability premium, etc

A husband and wife are both under pension age and both receive the standard rate of the daily living component of personal independence payment. Their daughter of 17 is in full-time employment and lives with them. Their son lives elsewhere and receives carer's allowance for caring for the husband. No-one receives carer's allowance for the wife.

Disability premium: Because of receiving personal independence payment, they are awarded the couple rate of disability premium.

Enhanced disability premium: Because they get the standard (not the enhanced) rate of the daily living component of personal independence payment, this cannot be awarded.

Severe disability premium:

■ Both receive the appropriate type of personal independence payment.

■ Although their daughter is a non-dependant, she is under 18.

■ Their son receives carer's allowance for caring for one of them.

So they are awarded the single rate of severe disability premium (for the second reason in para 12.39).

12.41   HB sch 3 para 14(5)(b),(7); HB60+ sch 3 para 6(7)(b),(8)(b); NIHB sch 4 para 14(5)(b),(7); NIHB60+ sch 4 para 6(7)(b),(8)(b)

12.42   HB sch 3 paras 14(6), 19; HB60+ sch 3 paras 6(8)(a), 11; NIHB sch 4 paras 14(6), 19; NIHB60+ sch 4 paras 6(8)(a), 11

Carer premium

12.43   You qualify for this premium if you or your partner are 'entitled to' carer's allowance (para 12.45) or you were 'entitled to' (para 12.45) carer's allowance within the past eight weeks (including if the reason you are no longer entitled to the allowance is that the person you cared for has died).

12.44   If you are a couple you can get one or two carer premiums, one if only one of you satisfies the condition, two if you both do. If you are in a polygamous marriage you get one premium for each partner who satisfies the condition.

12.45   You only have to be 'entitled to' carer's allowance: it does not necessarily have to be in payment. This means that if an award has been made but it cannot be paid because it is overlapped by another benefit (typically: retirement pension, ESA(C), JSA(C) or widowed parent's allowance) then that is sufficient. But if your carer's allowance is overlapped by retirement pension you only receive a carer premium if the person you are caring for continues to receive attendance allowance (or equivalent benefit).

12.46   You cannot be entitled to carer's allowance until you have made a claim for it – but once you have done so and entitlement has been confirmed (with or without payment) it continues indefinitely until such time as you no longer satisfy the conditions for it (e.g. the person being cared for dies). It does not matter that the original claim for carer's allowance was made before the HB claim: the claimant continues to be 'entitled' to carer's allowance without the need to make a further claim for it (CIS/367/2003).

12.47   If you are awarded carer's allowance but later lose it as a result of taking part in a government training scheme you continue to be treated as entitled to it.

Interaction of carer and severe disability premium

12.48   Although carer's allowance qualifies you for a carer premium, the person you care for may lose their severe disability premium (but not during any period your carer's allowance is backdated: para 12.42(a)). However this happens only if your carer's allowance (or part of it) is actually in payment and not if it is overlapped (para 12.45) – see second example. If you are a couple it is therefore possible to qualify for a severe disability premium (at the single or double rate) and two carer premiums if you care for each other.

12.43   HB sch 3 para 17; HB60+ sch 3 para 9; NIHB sch 4 para 17; NIHB60+ sch 4 para 9

12.44   HB sch 3 para 20(8); HB60+ sch 3 para 12(4); NIHB sch 4 para 20(8); NIHB60+ sch 4 para 12(4)

12.45   HB sch 3 paras 7(1)(a),(2), 17(1); HB60+ sch 3 paras 5(2), 9(1); NIHB sch 4 paras 7(1)(a),(2), 17(1); NIHB60+ sch 4 paras 5(2), 9(1)

12.46   AA 1(1); NIAA 1(1)

12.47   HB sch 3 para 7(1)(b); HB60+ sch 3 para 5(1)(b); NIHB sch 4 para 7(1)(b); NIHB60+ sch 4 para 5(1)(b)

12.48   HB sch 3 paras 14(1)(a),(b), 19; HB60+ 6(1)(a),(b), 11; NIHB sch 4 paras 14(1)(a),(b), 19; NIHB60+ sch 4 paras 6(1)(a),(b), 11

Examples: Carer premium and overlapping benefits

Claimant over 65

A claimant and her partner are both aged over 80 and in receipt of retirement pension. She looks after her partner who has been in receipt of attendance allowance since 3rd February 2015. On 6th February 2015 she made a claim for carer's allowance and was notified by the DWP that she was entitled to carer's allowance from 9th February 2015 but it could not be paid because it was overlapped by her retirement pension (in other words, payment of the latter prevents payment of the former).

On 4th May 2015 she makes a claim for HB for the first time and is awarded HB from 9th February 2015 (para 5.52). The award includes the carer premium. If her partner subsequently dies, she would lose the premium after a further eight weeks.

Claimant under 65

A claimant aged 49 is in receipt of bereavement allowance. He cares for his severely disabled sister who receives the daily living component of personal independence payment. He lives alone in his own flat. He claims carer's allowance and is entitled to it but it cannot be paid because it is overlapped by his bereavement allowance. Once having claimed carer's allowance he remains 'entitled' to it indefinitely until such time as he no longer meets the conditions for it (e.g. he starts work, becomes a student or his sister dies or no longer receives the daily living component of personal independence payment). While he remains entitled to carer's allowance he should be awarded the carer premium in his HB without the need for a further claim for carer's allowance even if there are breaks in his HB award. One year after his bereavement, his bereavement allowance ends and his carer's allowance is put into payment. His sister is also entitled to the severe disability premium during the period while his bereavement allowance is in payment (because although he is 'entitled' to carer's allowance it is not in payment: para 12.45). But once his carer's allowance is in payment she will lose her severe disability premium.

Special cases

DWP concessionary payments

12.49   For the purpose of entitlement to any premium, if you receive a DWP concessionary payment compensating for non-payment of any qualifying benefit it is treated as if it were that benefit.

Benefits treated as attendance allowance

12.50   You are treated as being in receipt of attendance allowance (paras 6.16, 12.31, 12.38, 12.40) if you receive any type of increase for attendance paid with an industrial injury benefit or war disablement pension. Qualifying payments include constant attendance allowance, 'old cases' attendance payments, severe disablement occupational allowance and exceptionally severe disablement allowance (GM BW2 annex B para 7).

12.49   HB sch 3 para 18; HB60+ sch 3 para 10; NIHB sch 4 para 18; NIHB60+ sch 4 para 10

12.50   HB 2(1) definition – 'attendance allowance'; HB60+ 2(1); NIHB 2(1); NIHB60+ 2(1)

Meaning of severely sight impaired, blind or recently regained sight

12.51 For the purpose of determining whether a non-dependant deduction applies (para 6.16) or entitlement to certain premiums in this chapter (paras 12.31, 12.34, 12.39-40) you are 'severely sight impaired' or 'blind' if you have been certified as such by a consultant ophthalmologist. You or your family member cannot qualify for any premium as severely sight impaired for any period before 26th November 2014 (the date the law was changed).

12.52 If you were previously certified as 'severely sight impaired' or blind you are treated as still being so for a further 28 weeks from the date you regained your sight (i.e. from the date when your certification was revoked).

Polygamous marriages

12.53 If you are in a polygamous marriage (para 4.20) your personal allowance is the appropriate amount in table 12.1 for a couple according to the age of the oldest member in the marriage plus (during 2015-16) the appropriate amount for each additional spouse as follows:

(a) if you and every partner in the marriage are all under pension age (para 1.24): £41.75;

(b) if at least one of you is pension age but none of you are aged 65 or over: £79.65;

(c) if at least one of you is aged 65 or over: £82.25.

Premiums and components are awarded in a similar way as for a couple – see paragraph 12.39(e) for rules about the severe disability premium.

If you or your family are in hospital

12.54 Certain premiums may be lost if you (or your partner) lose your qualifying benefit as a result of you spending four weeks or more in hospital – see table 12.2 for details. In addition, your right to HB is lost if you are single/a lone parent after you have been in hospital for 52 weeks; or, if it is your partner or child, they are unlikely to be treated as a member of your family: in either case this overrides any special rules in table 12.2 (paras 3.3, 3.32, 4.21, 4.37).

12.51   SI 2014/2888; NISR 2014/275; HB sch 3 para 13(1)(a)(v); HB60+ sch 3 para 6(4); NIHB sch 4 para 13(1)(a)(v); NIHB60+ sch 4 para 6(4)

12.52   HB sch 3 para 13(2); HB60+ sch 3 para 6(5); NIHB sch 4 para 13(2); NIHB60+ sch 4 para 6(5)

12.53   HB 23; HB60+ sch 3 para 1(3),(4); NIHB 21; NIHB60+ sch 4 para 1(3),(4)

Table 12.2 **Loss of certain premiums after a period in hospital**

(a) Disability premium (paras 12.25 and 12.32)

- ▓ If you or your partner lose your personal independence payment, disability living allowance or one of the equivalent benefits in paragraph 12.50 solely because of being in hospital for four weeks* or more the disability premium is still awarded.

(b) Enhanced disability premium (para 12.35)

- ▓ If you, your partner or child lose your personal independence payment or disability living allowance solely because of being in hospital for four weeks* or more (after 12 weeks if it is for your child) the enhanced disability premium is still awarded.

(c) Disabled child premium (para 12.34)

- ▓ If your child loses their personal independence payment or disability living allowance solely because of being in hospital for 12 weeks* or more the enhanced disability premium is still awarded.

(d) Severe disability premium (para 12.38)

- ▓ If you are single or a lone parent and you lose your personal independence payment or disability living allowance because you have been in hospital for four weeks* or more you lose your severe disability premium.

- ▓ If you are a couple and you or your partner lose your personal independence payment or disability living allowance solely because of being in hospital for four weeks* or more the severe disability premium is still awarded.

(e) Carer premium (para 12.43)

- ▓ You or your partner's carer's allowance continues until you have spent over 12 weeks in hospital, and your carer premium continues for a further eight weeks after that (making 20 in total).

- ▓ If the person you or your partner care for is in hospital you will lose your carer's allowance after they have been in hospital for four weeks* (or 12 weeks if you care for a child) and your carer premium continues for a further eight weeks after that (making 12 in total or 20 if you care for a child).

* The four/twelve week period does not have to be continuous but can be made up of two or more separate periods which are less than 29 days apart.

T12.2(a) HB sch 3 para 13(1)(a)(iii),(iiia); NIHB sch 4 para 13(1)(a)(iii)

T12.2(b) HB sch 3 para 15(1)(b),(c); NIHB sch 4; para 15(1)(b)

T12.2(c) HB sch 3 para 16(a),(d); HB60+ sch 3 para 8(a),(d); NIHB sch 4; para 16(a); NIHB60+ sch 4 para 8(a)

T12.2(d) HB sch 3 para 14(2)(a),(b),(5)(a),(c); HB60+ sch 3 para 6(2)(a),(b),(7)(a),(c); NIHB sch 4; para 14(2)(a),(b),(5)(a);
              NIHB60+ sch 4 para 6(2)(a),(b),(7)(a)

T12.2(e) HB sch 3 para 17(2),(4); HB60+ sch 3 para 9(2); NIHB sch 4; para 17(2),(4); NIHB60+ sch 4 para 9(2)

Chapter 13 **Income**

■ General rules about assessing income: see paras 13.1-8.

■ State benefits, pensions and payments: see paras 13.9-22.

■ Council benefits and payments: see paras 13.23-25.

■ Private pensions, maintenance, rent and other income: see paras 13.26-40.

■ Additional rules about income disregards: see paras 13.41-45.

■ Notional income: see paras 13.46-57.

General rules

13.1   This chapter and chapter 14 explain how your income is assessed for HB purposes, including:

  (a) unearned income (see paras 13.9-40);

  (b) earned income (see chapter 14);

  (c) notional income (see paras 13.46-57); and

  (d) assumed income from your capital (see para 15.5).

This section gives rules relating to all types of income.

'Your' income

13.2   If you are single, your own income is taken into account. If you are in a couple, the income of your partner is taken into account as well. If you are in a polygamous marriage, the income of all your partners is included. In this chapter and chapter 14, 'your' income always includes the income of your partner (or partners). But if a child or young person in your family has income of their own, this is never included and nor is the income of a non-dependant (but see para 13.57).

How your income affects your HB

13.3   If you are on a passport benefit (see para 13.5), all your income is disregarded (ignored) and you qualify for maximum HB: see para 6.2.

13.4   If you are not on a passport benefit, some kinds of income are counted and some are wholly or partly disregarded. The details are in this chapter and chapter 14. The more income you have (apart from disregarded income) the less HB you qualify for: see para 6.8. (See also para 13.15 if you are on the savings credit of SPC.)

13.1   HB 27(1)(a),(b),(4); HB60+ 25, 29(1),(2); NIHB 24(1)(a),(b),(4); NIHB60+ 23, 27(1),(2)

13.2   CBA 136(1); HB 25; HB60+ 23; NICBA 132(1); NIHB 22; NIHB60+ 21

13.3   CBA 130(1)(c)(i),(3)(a); HB sch 4 para 12, sch 5 paras 4,5; HB60+ 26; NICBA 129(1)(c)(i),(3)(a); NIHB sch 5 para 12, sch 6 paras 4,5; NIHB60+ 24

13.4   CBA 130(1)(c),(3); HB 36(2), 38(2), 40(2), sch 4, sch 5; HB60+ 33(8),(9), sch 4, sch 5; NICBA 129(1)(c),(3); NIHB 33(2), 35(2), 37(2), sch 5, sch 6; NIHB60+ 31(8),(9), sch 5, sch 6

The passport benefits

13.5   The passport benefits are:

(a) income-based JSA;

(b) income-related ESA;

(c) income support;

(d) the guarantee credit of SPC; and

(e) universal credit if you live in supported accommodation (see para 6.4).

Current income

13.6   Your current income is taken into account for the period it covers (apart from the amounts which are disregarded). In the case of a state benefit this means the period for which it is payable.

Arrears of income

13.7   The rules in para 13.6 also apply to arrears of income. So income paid for a past period counts as income in that period (apart from the amounts which are disregarded).

Para 15.13 explains when arrears of income turn into capital.

Weekly income

13.8   HB is a weekly benefit, so your income is assessed as a weekly figure. The law says this is done by accurately calculating or estimating the likely amount of your average weekly income. In practice this means:

(a) the actual weekly amount if your income is paid weekly; or

(b) the weekly equivalent if your income is paid on a non-weekly basis (see para 6.44).

In working age HB claims, unearned income must not be averaged over a period longer than 52 weeks. In pension age HB claims, it is not in practice averaged over a period longer than one year. For earned income see paras 14.8-10 and 14.29-31.

Examples: Assessing income

1. A working age HB claim

A couple in their 30s have two children at school. One partner works full time. The other receives child maintenance from the children's father, child benefit, and child tax credit. They have £3,000 in a savings account.

When they claim HB, their income is assessed as follows:

■   the child benefit and the child maintenance are disregarded (see tables 13.1 and 13.6)

13.5   HB sch 4 para 12, sch 5 paras 4,5, sch 6 paras 5,6; HB60+ 26; NIHB sch 5 para 12, sch 6 paras 4,5, sch 7 paras 5,6; NIHB60+ 24V

13.6   HB 27(1), 31(1),(2); HB60+ 30(1), 33(1),(6); NIHB 24(1), 28(1),(2); NIHB60+ 28(1), 31(1),(6)

13.7   HB 27(1), 31(1),(2); HB60+ 30(1), 33(1),(6); NIHB 24(1), 28(1),(2); NIHB60+ 28(1), 31(1),(6)

13.8   CBA 136(4); HB 27(1), 29-31; HB60+ 30(1), 33(1); NICBA 132(3); NIHB 24(1), 26-28; NIHB60+ 28(1), 31(1)

■ the child tax credit is counted as income (see para 13.12):
   it works out as   £101.84 pw

■ the earnings are counted as their income, after all the appropriate
   deductions and disregards have been made (see chapter 14):
   they work out as   £285.49 pw

■ they do not have assumed income from their capital (see para 15.5)

This figure is used in calculating their HB. So their total income is   £387.33 pw

2. A pension age HB claim

A single woman in her 70s receives a state pension, a private pension,
and a war widow's pension. She has £12,000 in a savings account.

When she claims HB, her income is assessed as follows:

■ her council runs a local scheme which disregards the whole of the
   war widow's pension (see paras 13.16-18)

■ the state pension and the private pension are counted as her
   income (see paras 13.13 and 13.27): they work out as   £130.95 pw

■ she has assumed income from her capital (see para 15.5) of   £4 pw

This figure is used in calculating her HB. So her total income is   £134.95 pw

State benefits, pensions and payments

13.9   This section gives the rules for state benefits and pensions, tax credits and war
pensions.

13.10   Table 13.1 lists which state benefits, pensions and other payments are disregarded.
Table 13.2 lists the ones which are taken into account, and summarises the other rules which
apply.

Table 13.1 **Disregarded state benefits, pension, etc**

Income from all the following is wholly disregarded. For the first five 'passport benefits'
see also para 13.3.

   (a) income-based JSA (JSA(IB)

   (b) income-related ESA (ESA(IR))

   (c) income support

   (d) the guarantee credit of SPC

   (e) universal credit

   (f) disability living allowance (DLA)

T13.1   HB 40(2), sch 5; HB60+ 29(1), 33(9), sch 5; NIHB 37(2), sch 6; NIHB60+ 27(1), 31(9), sch 6

T13.1(a)-(e) HB sch 5 para 4; HB60+ 26; NIHB sch 6 para 4; NIHB60+ 24

(g) personal independence payment (PIP)

(h) attendance allowance (AA)

(i) benefits equivalent to attendance allowance (see para 13.22)

(j) child tax credit (CTC) in pension age HB claims (see para 13.12)

(k) child benefit

(l) guardian's allowance

(m) Christmas bonus

(n) social fund payments (see also para 15.50)

(o) government and related payments to disabled people to help with obtaining or retaining work (for example by buying special equipment)

(p) payments from government work programme training schemes. There are rare exceptions in working age claims (see GM paras BW 2.597-611), but even in these cases expenses for travel etc are always disregarded

(q) payments compensating for non-payment of:

- ▪ (a) to (i) in working age HB claims
- ▪ all the above in pension age HB claims.

Note: Payments (n) to (p) and in most cases (q) are also disregarded as capital. See paras 15.50-52 for details about this and about arrears of benefits.

Table 13.2 **Counted state benefits, pensions etc**

Income from the following is counted in full.

(a) contribution-based JSA (JSA(C)) (see para 13.11)

(b) contributory ESA (ESA(C)) (see para 13.11)

(c) working tax credit (WTC) (see para 13.12)

(d) child tax credit (CTC) in working age HB claims (see para 13.12)

T13.1(f)-(g)	HB sch 5 para 6; HB60+ 29(1)(j)(i),(ia); NIHB sch 6 para 7; NIHB60+ 27(1)(h)(i)
T13.1(h)-(i)	HB 2(1) definition – 'attendance allowance', sch 5 para 9; HB60+ 2(1), 29(1)(j) (ii)-(v); NIHB 2(1), sch 6 para 10; NIHB60+ 2(1), 27(1)(h) (ii)-(iv)
T13.1(j)	HB60+ 29(1); NIHB60+ 27(1)
T13.1(k)	HB sch 5 para 65; HB60+ 29(1)(j)(vi); NIHB sch 6 para 64; NIHB60+ 27(1)(h)(v)
T13.1(l)	HB sch 5 para 50; HB60+ 29(1)(j)(vii); NIHB sch 6 para 52; NIHB60+ 27(1)(h)(vi)
T13.1(m)	HB sch 5 para 32; HB60+ 29(1)(j)(x); NIHB sch 6 para 33; NIHB60+ 27(1)(h)(ix)
T13.1(n)	HB sch 5 para 31, sch 6 para 20; HB60+ 29(1)(j)(ix); NIHB sch 6 para 32, sch 7 para 21; NIHB60+ 27(1)(h)(viii)
T13.1(o)	HB sch 5 para 49, sch 6 paras 43,44; HB60+ 29(1); NIHB sch 6 para 51, sch 7 para 44; NIHB60+ 27(1)
T13.1(p)	HB 2(1) definitions, sch 5 paras A2,A3,13,15,58,60,61; HB60+ 29(1); NIHB 2(1), sch 6 paras 13,15,60; NIHB60+ 27(1)
T13.1(q)	HB 2(1) definition – 'concessionary payment', sch 5 para 9; HB60+ 2(1), 29(1)(ii)-(v); NIHB 2(1), sch 6 para 10; NIHB60+ 2(1), 27(1)
T13.2(a)-(m)	HB 31(1),(3), 40(1); HB60+ 29(1)(b),(c),(j); NIHB 28(1),(3), 37(1); NIHB60+ 27(1)(b),(c),(h)

(e)   state pension (see para 13.13)

(f)   the savings credit of SPC (see para 13.14)

(g)   carer's allowance

(h)   maternity allowance

(i)   bereavement allowance

(j)   incapacity benefit (IB)

(k)   severe disablement allowance (SDA)

(l)   widow's pension

(m)   industrial death benefit

The following have individual rules.

(n)   widowed mother's allowance and widowed parent's allowance: disregard £15 per week and count the rest as income

(o)   industrial injuries disablement benefit: disregard any increase for attendance (see para 13.22) and count the rest as income

(p)   bereavement payment: this counts as capital (not income)

(q)   war pensions: see paras 13.16-18

(r)   increases in benefits for dependants: see para 13.20

(s)   reductions in benefits: see para 13.21

(t)   statutory sick, maternity, paternity and adoption pay: count as earned income (see table 14.1(c) and paras 14.15-16)

Note: See paras 15.50-52 for arrears of payments (c), (d) and (f).

JSA(C) and ESA(C)

13.11   Contribution-based JSA and contributory ESA are counted in full as your income. In the longer term they will become known as just JSA and ESA once JSA(IB) and ESA(IR) are abolished: see para 1.15.

WTC and CTC

13.12   Working tax credit is counted in full as your income (in working age and pension age HB claims). Child tax credit is counted in full as your income in working age HB claims, but is wholly disregarded in pension age HB claims. Table 17.5 shows what period a payment of WTC or CTC covers. In some uncommon cases, part of the earned income disregards can be deducted from your WTC or CTC: see para 14.61(c) and (d).

T13.2(n)   HB sch 5 para 16; HB60+ sch 5 paras 7,8; NIHB sch 6 para 17; NIHB60+ sch 6 paras 8,9

T13.2(o)   HB 2(1) definition – 'attendance allowance', sch 5 para 9; HB60+ 2(1), 29(1)(j)(iii),(n); NIHB 2(1), sch 6 para 10; NIHB60+ 2(1), 27(1)(h)(iii),(l)

T13.2(p)   HB 44(1); HB60+ 29(1)(j)(xiii); NIHB 41(1); NIHB60+ 27(1)(h)(xi)

13.11   HB 31(1),(2), 40(1); HB60+ 31(1)(a), 33(6); NIHB 28(1),(2), 37(1); NIHB60+ 29(1)(a), 31(6)

13.12   HB 27(1)(c),(2)(b), 31(1), 32, 40(1); HB60+ 30(1)(a),(c),(2)(b), 32; NIHB 24(1)(c),(2)(b), 28(1), 29, 37(1); NIHB60+ 28(1)(a),(c),(2)(b), 30

State pension

13.13   State pension is counted in full as your income. If you defer your state pension:

(a) it is not included as your income until you begin receiving it. Any increase you receive (because you deferred it) is then included;

(b) any lump sum you receive (because you deferred your state pension) is disregarded as your capital until your state pension begins.

Savings credit

13.14   The savings credit of state pension credit (SPC) is counted in full as your income. But if you are also on the guarantee credit of SPC, see para 13.3.

Other rules if you are on savings credit

13.15   The following rules apply if you are on savings credit (but not guarantee credit):

(a) the DWP assesses your income and capital as part of your savings credit claim;

(b) the DWP tells the council these income and capital figures (when you first claim HB or savings credit, and then whenever your circumstances change);

(c) the council adjusts these figures as shown in table 13.3;

(d) the council uses the adjusted figures to calculate your HB.

Table 13.3 **People on savings credit: adjusting the DWP's figures**

If you are on savings credit, the following adjustments are made whenever the DWP tells the council your income and capital (see para 13.5).

Your income

The DWP tells the council:

- the amount of your savings credit; and

- your 'assessed income figure' (AIF). This is the DWP's assessment of your income (apart from savings credit).

The council adds these together, and then deducts the following amounts:

If you receive:	The amount is:
(a) maintenance from a current or former husband, wife or civil partner	the full HB disregard (see table 13.6)
(b) a war disablement or bereavement pension	any amount disregarded under a local scheme (in other words, any amount over £10: see para 13.18)

13.13   HB60+ sch 6 para 26A as implied by CPR 2; SI 2005/2677 regs 11,12; NIHB60+ sch 7 para 28

13.14   HB 31(1),(2), 40(1); HB60+ 31(1)(a), 33(6); NIHB 28(1),(2), 37(1); NIHB60+ 29(1)(a), 31(6)

13.15   HB60+ 27(1)-(3); NIHB60+ 25(1)-(3)

(c)	earned income and you are a lone parent	£5
(d)	earned income from 'permitted work'	£104 or £20 (as shown in table 14.5)
(e)	earned income and you qualify for the HB child care disregard	the full HB disregard (see para 14.63)
(f)	Earned income and you qualify for the HB additional earnings disregard	£17.10 (see para 14.68)

If you have a partner who was excluded from your savings credit claim but is included in your HB claim, the council assesses their income and adds it.

Your capital

The DWP tells the council the amount of your capital. The council changes this only if your capital increases to more than £16,000, in which case your HB stops.

War disablement and bereavement pensions

13.16   Table 13.4 gives the rules for assessing income from:

(a) pensions under the Armed Forces Pensions and Compensation schemes (and similar payments) for:

- war disablement;
- war widows;
- war widowers; and
- war bereaved civil partners;

(b) payments compensating for non-payment of the above;

(c) equivalent payments from governments outside the UK; and

(d) pensions paid to the victims of Nazi persecution by the governments of Germany or Austria, or by the government of the Netherlands: [2014] UKUT 187 (AAC).

The payments in (a) include both 'service attributable pensions' for service before 5th April 2005 and 'guaranteed income payments' for service on or after that date.

13.17   War pensions not included in para 13.16 are assessed in the same way as private pensions: see para 13.27.

Local schemes for war disablement and bereavement pensions

13.18   Councils in Great Britain can run a 'local scheme' to disregard more than £10 per week of the war disablement and bereavement pensions in para 13.16 (apart from those which are always wholly disregarded: see table 13.4).

13.19   Most councils do this, and some disregard the whole amount. The government pays councils up to 75% of the cost of running a local scheme (see para 23.4), but decisions about local schemes are not appealable to a tribunal (see table 19.2).

T13.3   HB60+ 27(3)-(8); NIHB60+ 25(3)-(8)

13.16   HB sch 5 para 15; HB60+ 29(1)(e)-(h)(l)-(m), sch 5 para 1; NIHB sch 6 para 15; NIHB60+ 27(1)(e)-(f),(j)-(k), sch 6 para 1

13.18   AA 134(8)-(10); SI 2007 No. 1619

Table 13.4 **War disablement and bereavement pensions**

This table applies to the pensions etc in para 13.16.

Assessment in Great Britain

(a) Disregard the whole amount of:

- ■ 'pre-1973' special payments to war widows, war widowers and war bereaved civil partners (currently £90.41 per week: circular HB A2/2015);

- ■ a mobility supplement paid with any war disablement or bereavement pension; and

- ■ an increase for attendance paid with any war disablement or bereavement pension (para 13.22) or an Armed Forces independence payment.

(b) Disregard £10 per week from the total of any other war disablement or bereavement pension. A larger amount can be disregarded if your council runs a local scheme (see paras 13.18-19).

Assessment in Northern Ireland

(c) Disregard the whole amount of all war disablement and bereavement pensions.

Increases in benefits for dependants

13.20   The following applies if you receive an increase for a dependant in any of the state benefits which count as income (see table 13.2):

(a) if the increase is for your partner, it is included as your income;

(b) if the increase is for a child or younger person in your family, it is included as your income in working age HB claims, but disregarded in pension age HB claims;

(c) if the increase is for someone not in your family, it is disregarded.

Reductions in benefits

13.21   The following applies if you receive a reduced amount of any of the state benefits which count as income (see table 13.2):

(a) only the reduced amount is counted as your income if the reduction is:

- ■ because of the rules about overlapping state benefits;

- ■ because your WTC or CTC is reduced to recover an earlier year's overpayment;

- ■ because your incapacity benefit is reduced when you have an occupational pension (CH/51/2008); or

- ■ in pension age HB claims, because a state benefit is reduced when you are in hospital;

T13.4   HB 2(1) definitions – 'guaranteed income payment', 'war pension' etc, 31(1), 40(1), sch 5 paras 8,15,53-55; HB60+ 2(1), 29(1)(e)-(h),(l),(m), 30(1)(a), sch 5 paras 1-6; NIHB 2(1), 28(1), 37(1), sch 6 paras 9,15,55-57; NIHB60+ 2(1), 27(1)(f),(j),(k), 28(1)(a), sch 6 paras 1-7

13.20   HB 40(1), sch 5 para 52; HB60+ 29(1)(j)(viii), 30(1)(a), sch 5 para 13; NIHB 37(1), sch 6 para 54; NIHB60+ 27(1)(h)(vii), 28(1)(a), sch 6 para 14

13.21   HB 40(1),(5),(5A),(6); HB60+ 29(3)-(5), 30(1)(a); NIHB 37(1),(3),(3A),(4); NIHB60+ 27(3)-(5), 28(1)(a)

(b) but the gross amount (the amount before the reduction is made) is counted as your income in any other circumstances, for example if a state benefit (but not WTC or CTC) is reduced to:

  ▓ recover an overpayment; or

  ▓ pay your rent, fuel, water or other priority debts.

Benefits equivalent to attendance allowance

13.22   For all HB purpose the following benefits are equivalent to attendance allowance:

  (a) any increase for attendance paid with industrial injuries disablement benefit; and

  (b) any increase for attendance paid with a war disablement pension.

For example, these include constant attendance allowance, 'old cases' attendance payments, severe disablement occupational allowance, and exceptionally severe disablement allowance.

Council benefits and payments

13.23   This section gives the rules for benefits, allowances and other payments from local councils.

13.24   Table 13.5 lists which council allowances and payments are disregarded.

Social services and similar payments for care and support

13.25   The payments in table 13.5 (a)-(h) are disregarded if they are paid by:

  (a) a social services department in Great Britain;

  (b) the Health and Social Services Board, a Health and Social Services Trust or a Juvenile Justice Centre in Northern Ireland;

  (c) a voluntary organisation on behalf of the above; or

  (d) in the case of respite care payments, a Primary Care Trust.

Table 13.5 **Disregarded council payments**

Income from the following is wholly disregarded. For payments (a) to (h) see also para 13.25.

  (a) foster care payments, also called kinship care payments in Scotland;

  (b) adoption allowances;

  (c) special guardianship payments;

  (d) payments to avoid taking children into care;

  (e) payments to care leavers, including payments passed on to you by a care leaver aged 18 or more who lives with you;

13.22   HB 2(1) definition – 'attendance allowance'; HB60+ 2(1); NIHB 2(1); NIHB60+ 2(1)

13.25   HB 2(1), sch 5 paras 25-28A,57; HB60+ 29(1); NIHB 2(1), sch 6 paras 26-29A,59; NIHB60+ 27(1)

T13.5(a)-(f) HB 2(1) definition – 'voluntary organisation', sch 5 paras 25-28A; HB60+ 29(1); NIHB 2(1), sch 6 paras 26-29A; NIHB60+ 27(1)

(f) boarding out and respite care payments, including contributions you receive from the person you are caring for;

(g) community care payments;

(h) direct care payments;

(i) supporting people payments, for housing-related support to help you maintain your tenancy;

(j) 'local welfare provision' or 'occasional assistance', paid to help you meet a crisis and avoid harm, avoid becoming homeless, avoid entering institutional care (for example residential care, hospital or prison) or set up home after leaving institutional care;

(k) discretionary housing payments;

(l) council tax rebates, other council tax reductions, and HB itself.

Note: In some cases these are also disregarded as capital. See paras 15.50-52 for details about this and about arrears of benefits.

Other unearned income

13.26 This section gives the rules for private pensions, maintenance, charitable and voluntary payments, rent, and other kinds of income. For assumed income from capital see para 15.5, and for student income see chapter 22.

Private pensions

13.27 Income from a private pension is counted in full, after any deductions have been made for tax paid on it. This applies to any kind of:

(a) occupational pension;

(b) personal pension; or

(c) pension from the Pension Protection Fund.

But if a court has ordered part of your pension to be paid to someone else (for example your former partner), that part is disregarded (CH/1672/2007). See also paras 13.50-51.

Maintenance

13.28 Table 13.6 gives the rules for assessing maintenance you receive from a former partner or anyone else (other than your current partner).

13.29 If you pay maintenance for a child or anyone else, the amount you pay cannot be deducted when your income is assessed. But if it is for a student son or daughter, see para 13.43.

T13.5(g)-(h) HB sch 5 para 57; HB60+ 29(1); NIHB sch 6 para 59; NIHB60+ 27(1)

T13.5(i) HB sch 5 para 63; HB60+ 29(1); NIHB sch 6 para 63; NIHB60+ 27(1)

T13.5(j) HB 2(1) definition – 'local welfare provision', sch 5 para 31A; HB60+ 29(1)

T13.5(k) HB sch 5 para 62; HB60+ 29(1); NIHB sch 6 para 62; NIHB60+ 27(1)

T13.5(l) HB sch 5 para 41; HB60+ 29(1); NIHB sch 6 para 43; NIHB60+ 27(1)

13.27 HB 2(1), definition – 'occupational pension' 31(1), 35(2), sch 5 para 1; HB60+ 2(1), 29(1)(c),(d),(t),(x), 30(1)(a), 33(12), 35(2); NIHB 2(1), 28(1), 32(2), sch 6 para 1; NIHB60+ 2(1), 27(1)(c),(d),(r),(v), 28(1)(a), 31(12), 33(2)

Table 13.6 **Income from maintenance**

	Assessment
Maintenance for a child or young person	
Working age claims:	
(a) if it is paid by:	
■ a husband, wife or civil partner you or your partner are separated from, or	
■ a parent or step-parent of the child/young person, or	
■ someone whose payments of maintenance mean they can reasonably be treated as the father of the child or young person	Disregard in full
(b) if it is paid by someone else	Count in full
Pension age HB claims	
(c) whoever it is paid by	Disregard in full
Maintenance for you or your partner, if you have a child or young person	
Working age claims:	
(d) if it is paid by you or your partner's former partner	Disregard £15 pw
(e) if it is paid by someone else	Count in full
Pension age HB claims	
(f) if it is paid by you or your partner's current or former husband, wife or civil partner	Disregard £15 pw
(g) if it is paid by someone else	Disregard in full
Maintenance for you or your partner, if you do not have a child or young person	
Working age HB claims	
(h) whoever it is paid by	Count in full
Pension age HB claims	
(i) if it is paid by you or your partner's current or former husband, wife or civil partner	Count in full
(j) if it is paid by someone else	Disregard in full
Maintenance for a non-dependant	
(k) working age HB claims	Same as (d), (e) or (h)
(l) pension age HB claims	Disregard in full

Note: 'Partner', 'child', 'young person', and 'non-dependant' have the same meanings as in chapter 4. But 'husband', 'wife' and 'civil partner' have their ordinary English meanings.

13.29   HB 31(1); HB60+ 30(1); NIHB 28(1); NIHB60+ 28(1)

T13.6   HB 31(1), sch 5 paras 47,47A; HB60+ 29(1)(o), sch 5 para 20; NIHB 28(1), sch 6 para 49,49A; NIHB60+ 27(1)(m), sch 6 para 21

Charitable and voluntary payments

13.30   Payments of income you receive which are charitable and/or voluntary are wholly disregarded. For example, these could be from a charity, family, friends etc (but for maintenance see table 13.6). For payments of capital see para 15.53. If the only money you have is charitable or voluntary income, you qualify for maximum HB (see paras 5.20 and 6.7).

Rent

13.31   Table 13.7 gives the rules for assessing rent you receive from people living in your home. Table 13.8 gives the rules for rent you receive on other property. But if you are self-employed and you receive rent as part of your business, see table 14.2(j).

Examples: Letting out a room

1. A lodger whose rent does not include meals

A couple on HB have a spare room. They let it out to a lodger for £80 per week inclusive of fuel and water, but not meals.

Their income from this lodger (see table 13.7(c)) is £80 minus £20, which is £60 per week.

2. A lodger whose rent includes meals

The couple increase the lodger's rent to £100 per week because they now provide him with meals.

Their income from the lodger (see table 13.7(b)) is now £80 minus £20, which is £60, the result being divided by two, which is £30 per week.

Table 13.7 **Rent from people in your home**

(a) Household members

Rent (or 'keep') you receive from a child, young person or non-dependant in your home is wholly disregarded.

(b) Lodgers whose rent includes meals (boarders)

If you receive rent from one or more lodgers in your home and their rent includes meals (see para 4.49):

■ start with the total amount your lodger(s) pay you each week (for rent, meals and any other services);

■ deduct £20 for each lodger you charge for (counting adults and children);

■ divide the result by two;

■ this gives your weekly income.

13.30   HB sch 5 para 14(1)(a),(b),(2); HB60+ 29(1); NIHB sch 6 para 14(1)(a),(b),(2); NIHB60+ 27(1)

T13.7(a)   HB sch 5 para 21; HB60+ 29(1); NIHB sch 6 para 22; NIHB60+ 27(1)

T13.7(b)   HB sch 5 para 42; HB60+ 29(1)(p), sch 5 para 9; NIHB sch 6 para 44; NIHB60+ 27(1)(n), sch 6 para 10

T13.7(c)   HB sch 5 para 22; HB60+ 29(1)(v), sch 5 para 10; NIHB sch 6 para 23; NIHB60+ 27(1)(t), sch 6 para 11

(c) Lodgers whose rent does not include meals

If you receive rent from one or more lodgers in your home and their rent does not include meals:

- ▓ start with the total amount your lodger(s) pay you each week (for rent and any other services);
- ▓ deduct £20 for each separate letting;
- ▓ this gives your weekly income.

Table 13.8 **Rent from property other than your home**

(a) When the rent counts as income

The rent you receive counts as unearned income:

- ▓ only in working age HB claims; and
- ▓ only if the property's capital value is disregarded for any of the reasons in table 15.1(b) to (g).

In these cases your unearned income equals the rent you receive on the property, minus outgoings you pay on the property (during the period the rent covers) for:

- ▓ mortgage payments (both interest and capital);
- ▓ council tax (rates in Northern Ireland);
- ▓ water charges; and
- ▓ tax paid on the resulting income.

No other outgoings can be deducted.

(b) When the rent counts as capital

The rent you receive counts as capital (not income):

- ▓ in working age HB claims other than those described in (a); and
- ▓ in all pension age HB claims.

In these cases, your capital:

- ▓ increases when you receive the rent;
- ▓ but decreases when you pay for outgoings on the property, for example agent's fees, repairs, cleaning etc, as well as those listed in (a).

Annuities

13.32   If you have an annuity, you get payments from an insurance or similar company in return for investing an initial capital sum with them. Payments from an annuity are counted in full as unearned income (not capital), after any deductions have been made for tax paid on them.

T13.8(a)   HB sch 5 paras 1, 17(2),(3); NIHB sch 6 paras 1, 18(2),(3)

T13.8(b)   HB 46(4), sch 5 paras 1, 17(1); HB60+ 29(1), sch 5 para 22; NIHB 43(4), sch 6 paras 1, 18(1); NIHB60+ 27(1), sch 6 para 23

13.32   HB 41(2), sch 5 para 1; HB60+ 29(1)(d), 33(12); NIHB 38(2), sch 6 para 1; NIHB60+ 27(1)(d), 31(11)

Home income plans

13.33   A home income plan is an annuity in which the invested capital sum is a loan secured against your home. The payments you receive are assessed as unearned income (see para 13.32). But if you were aged 65 or more when you began the home income plan, the following amounts are disregarded from the payments:

- tax paid on them;
- mortgage repayments made using them; and
- repayments on the loan.

Equity release schemes

13.34   If you are in an equity release scheme, the payments you receive are a form of loan secured against your home. In pension age HB claims, payments from an equity release scheme count in full as unearned income. This also seems likely to be the case in working age HB claims (because of the way loans are treated in HB: see para 15.54), but the law does not specifically say so.

Mortgage and loan protection policies

13.35   If you have insurance against being unable to pay your mortgage or another loan (because of unemployment, sickness, etc), payments you receive from that policy are assessed as follows:

(a)   in pension age HB claims, the payments are wholly disregarded;

(b)   in working age HB claims, payments for the following are disregarded:

- the mortgage or loan repayments;
- the payments due on the policy;
- in the case of a mortgage protection policy, the payments due on another policy you were required to have to insure against loss or damage to your home,

and the rest (if any) counts as your income.

Income from trusts

13.36   Income you receive from a trust is counted as your unearned income, with the following exceptions:

(a)   income from some government supported trust funds is wholly disregarded (see para 13.37);

(b)   income from personal injury trusts is wholly disregarded (see para 13.38);

(c)   in pension age HB claims, if you receive discretionary income from a trust:

- £20 per week is disregarded if it is for your rent (other than any part of the rent which is not met by HB because of a non-dependant deduction), mortgage

---

13.33   HB 41(2), sch 5 para 1; HB60+ 29(1)(d), 33(12), sch 5 para 11; NIHB 38(2), sch 6 para 1; NIHB60+ 27(1)(d), 31(11), sch 6 para 12

13.34   HB60+ 29(1)(w),(8); NIHB60+ 27(1)(u),(8)

13.35   HB sch 5 para 29; HB60+ 29(1); NIHB sch 6 para 30; NIHB60+ 27(1)

13.36   HB 31(1), sch 5 para 14(1)(c); HB60+ 29(1)(i), sch 5 para 12; NIHB 28(1), sch 6 para 14(1)(c); NIHB60+ 27(1)(g), sch 6 para 13

interest or other housing costs that could be met by the guarantee credit of SPC, council tax (in Northern Ireland rates), water charges, household fuel, food, or ordinary clothing or footwear;

- the whole amount is disregarded if it is for anything else.

For further details about trusts see paras 15.37-41.

Government supported trust funds

13.37 Income from the Independent Living Fund, the Macfarlane Trust, the London Bombings Charitable Relief Fund and some other government supported trust funds is disregarded. For the details see para 15.42.

Income for a personal injury

13.38 Income you receive for a personal injury is wholly disregarded. For the details see paras 15.43-45.

Other sources of unearned income

13.39 Table 13.9 lists other kinds of unearned income which are disregarded, along with the exceptions which apply in working age HB claims. For grants, loans, EMAs, and other student payments see chapter 22.

13.40 Apart from that, if you have any other source of unearned income it is:

(a) counted as income in working age HB claims, apart from any tax paid on it;

(b) disregarded in pension age HB claims.

Table 13.9 **Other unearned income disregards**

The following kinds of income are wholly disregarded (except as shown in (k) to (n)):

(a) expenses you receive as a volunteer or for charitable or voluntary work;

(b) expenses you receive as a member of a service user group (for example when these are run by local councils, social landlords or health authorities);

(c) expenses you receive from your employer (for exceptions see table 14.1(n));

(d) payments you receive as a teacher under the Student Loans Repayment Scheme;

(e) payments for travel for hospital visits;

13.37 HB 2(1) definition – 'Macfarlane Trust' etc, sch 5 para 35; HB60+ 29(1); NIHB 2(1), sch 6 para 37; NIHB60+ 29(1)

13.38 HB sch 5 para 14; HB60+ sch 5 paras 14,15; NIHB sch 6 para 14; NIHB60+ sch 6 paras 15,16

13.40 HB 31(1), sch 5 para 1; HB60+ 29(1); NIHB 28(1), sch 5 para 1; NIHB60+ 27(1)

T13.9(a) HB sch 5 para 2; HB60+ 29(1); NIHB sch 6 para 2; NIHB60+ 27(1)

T13.9(b) HB 2(1) definition – 'service user group', 35(2)(d), sch 5 para 2A; HB60+ 29(1), 35(2)(f); NIHB 2(1), 32(2)(d), sch 6 para 2A; NIHB60+ 27(1), 33(2)(e)

T13.9(c) HB 35(2)(b), sch 5 para 3; HB60+ 29(1), 35(2)(b); NIHB 32(2)(b), sch 6 para 3; NIHB60+ 27(1), 33(2)(b)

T13.9(d) HB sch 5 para 12; HB60+ 29(1); NIHB60+ 27(1)

T13.9(e),(f) HB sch 5 para 44; HB60+ 29(1); NIHB sch 6 para 46; NIHB60+ 27(1)

(f)   payments for health service supplies;

(g)   payments replacing free milk and vitamins;

(h)   payments replacing healthy start vouchers;

(i)   payments for travel for prison visits;

(j)   payments you receive as a holder of the Victoria Cross or George Cross, and similar payments (see para 15.48);

(k)   payments in kind (in other words, in goods rather than money or vouchers)

■   but in working age HB claims, goods bought for you by someone who receives income an your behalf can count as notional income: see para 13.50;

(l)   concessionary coal

■   but in working age HB claims, cash in lieu of it is counted as unearned income (R v Doncaster MBC and another ex parte Bolton);

(m) juror's allowance

■   but in working age HB claims, compensation for loss of earnings or state benefits is counted as unearned income;

(n)   career development loans paid by banks in Great Britain under arrangements with the Learning and Skills Council

■   but in working age HB claims, loans for living expenses are counted as unearned income until the course you are on ends.

Note: In working age HB claims, payments (e) to (i) are also disregarded as capital for 52 weeks.

Additional rules about income disregards

13.41   The rules about disregards for each kind of unearned income are given earlier in this chapter. Those for earned income are in chapter 14. This section gives further rules about disregards which can apply to more than one kind of unearned or earned income.

Income tax

13.42   Income tax paid on any kind of unearned income is always disregarded in the assessment of that income. For earned income see paras 14.19-21 and 14.53-55.

T13.9(g),(h)   HB sch 5 para 45; HB60+ 29(1); NIHB sch 6 para 47; NIHB60+ 27(1)

T13.9(i)   HB sch 5 para 46; HB60+ 29(1); NIHB sch 6 para 48; NIHB60+ 27(1)

T13.9(j)   HB sch 5 para 10; HB60+ 29(1); NIHB sch 6 para 11; NIHB60+ 27(1)

T13.9(k)   HB 35(2)(a), sch 5 para 23; HB60+ 29(1); NIHB 32(2)(a), sch 6 para 24; NIHB60+ 27(1)

T13.9(l)   HB60+ 29(1); NIHB60+ 27(1); R v Doncaster MBC & Another ex p Boulton 11/12/92 QBD 25 HLR 195

T13.9(m)   HB sch 5 para 39; HB60+ 29(1); NIHB sch 6 para 41; NIHB60+ 27(1)

T13.9(n)   HB 41(4); HB60+ 29(1)

13.42   HB sch 5 para 1; HB60+ 33(12); NIHB sch 6 para 1; NIHB60+ 31(11)

Parental contributions to a student

13.43   If you make a parental contribution to a son or daughter who is a UK student, the following amount is disregarded from the total of your unearned and earned income:

(a) if you were assessed as having to make a contribution towards their student loan or grant, the whole of that contribution;

(b) if (a) does not apply, and they are under 25, any amount you contribute up to:

- ■   £57.90 per week, if they receive no grant; or

- ■   minus the weekly amount of their discretionary grant, if they receive a discretionary grant.

Income outside the UK

13.44   Unearned or earned income you receive outside the UK is assessed in the normal way (as described in this chapter and chapter 14), and any commission for converting it to sterling is then disregarded. But if you are prohibited (by the country you receive the income in) from bringing it to the UK, the whole amount is disregarded.

The over-riding limit on certain disregards

13.45   If you qualify for more than one of the following unearned income disregards, the disregard from all of them is limited to £20 per week:

(a) the £15 disregard from widowed mother's allowance or widowed parent's allowance (see table 13.2(n));

(b) in England, Scotland and Wales, the £10 disregard from war pensions for disablement or bereavement (see table 13.4(b)), but this does not stop your council running a local scheme (see para 13.18);

(c) in pension age HB claims, the £20 disregard from discretionary trust income (see para 13.36(c));

(d) in working age HB claims, the £10 disregard from income from student loans (see table 22.2(d));

(e) in working age HB claims, the £20 disregard from income from student access funds (see para 22.30).

Apart from that, you get the full amount of any disregard you qualify for.

13.43   HB sch 4 para 11, sch 5 paras 19,20; HB60+ sch 4 para 6, sch 5 paras 18,19; NIHB sch 6 paras 20,21; NIHB60+ sch 5 para 6, sch 6 paras 19,20

13.44   HB sch 4 paras 13,14, sch 5 paras 24,33; HB60+ 29(1)(k), 33(7), sch 4 para 10, sch 5 paras 16,17;
NIHB sch 5 paras 13,14, sch 6 paras 25,34; NIHB60+ 27(1)(i), 31(7), sch 5 para 10, sch 6 paras 17,18

13.45   HB sch 5 para 34; HB60+ sch 5 para 12(3)(b),(c); NIHB sch 6 para 35; NIHB60+ sch 6 para 13(3)(b),(c)

Notional income

13.46 This section explains when you are counted as having unearned or earned income you do not in fact have. This is called 'notional' income.

13.47 For working age HB claims, this section also includes rules about notional capital when these are similar. The main rules about notional capital are in paras 15.56-59.

Types of notional income

13.48 You can be counted as having notional income when:

(a) there is income available to you (paras 13.50-52);

(b) in working age HB claims, you are paid income on behalf of someone else (paras 13.53 and 13.55);

(c) someone else is paid income on your behalf (paras 13.54-55);

(d) you have deprived yourself of income (see para 13.56);

(e) a non-dependant has more income and capital than you (para 13.57); or

(f) in working age HB claims, you are paid less than the going rate for a job (see para 14.24).

Assessing notional income

13.49 If you are counted as having notional income, it is assessed in the same way as actual income and all the disregards given earlier in this chapter and in chapter 14 apply. This means this section does not apply if you are on a passport benefit.

Money which is available to you

13.50 If income is available to you and you could get it by applying for it, it is counted as your notional income (but only from when you would get it if you did apply). In working age HB claims, this rule also applies to capital. For further details see paras 13.51-52.

13.51 In pension age HB claims, the rule in para 13.50 applies only to income from:

(a) a private pension (see para 13.27); or

(b) a state pension unless you have deferred it (see para 13.13).

For DWP guidance, see GM paras BP2.680-750.

13.52 In working age HB claims, the rule in para 13.50 applies to any kind of income or capital except for:

(a) income/capital from a private pension (see para 13.27);

(b) income/capital from a personal injury payment (paras 15.43-44);

(c) income/capital from a discretionary trust;

(d) income/capital from WTC or CTC;

13.49   HB 42(11),(12); HB60+ 25; NIHB 39(11),(12); NIHB60+ 23

13.50   HB 42(2), 49(2); HB60+ 41(1),(4); NIHB 39(2), 46(2); NIHB60+ 39(1),(4)

13.51   HB60+ 41(1)-(7); NIHB60+ 39(1)-(7)

13.52   HB 42(2),(12A), 49(2); NIHB 39(2),(12A), 46(2)

(e)   income from expenses or earnings as a service user group member;

(f)   income from a DWP rehabilitation allowance; or

(g)   capital from a loan you could raise against disregarded property or against other disregarded capital.

The DWP says this rule should not be used in the case of any state benefit if there is a doubt about whether you would qualify or how much you would get (see GM para BW2.682). See also paras 13.49 and 15.59.

Payments received by one person on behalf of another

13.53   In working age HB claims, if you receive payments of income on behalf of someone else, they are counted as your notional income if you keep or use them for yourself or your family. This rule also applies to payments of capital. For exceptions see para 13.55.

13.54   If someone else receives payments of income on your behalf, they are counted as your notional income if they are from:

(a)   a private pension (paras 13.27 and 13.55(a)); or

(b)   some other source, but in this case only if the payment is used for your or your family's:

■   rent (other than any part of the rent which is not eligible for HB, or not met by HB because of a non-dependant deduction);

■   council tax (rates in Northern Ireland); or

■   water charges, household fuel, food or ordinary clothing or footwear (apart from school uniform/sportswear).

In working age HB claims, this rule also applies to payments of capital. For exceptions see para 13.55.

13.55   The rules in paras 13.53-54 do not apply to

(a)   income/capital from a private pension (see para 13.27) if:

■   the person whose pension it is, is bankrupt (or sequestered in Scotland) and has no other income; and

■   the person it is paid to is their trustee in bankruptcy or someone else acting on behalf of their creditors;

(b)   income/capital from the government-sponsored trusts and funds in paras 15.42(a) to (d);

(c)   income/capital from government work programme training schemes;

(d)   income from expenses or earnings as a service user group member; or

(e)   income from cash in lieu of concessionary coal.

See also paras 13.49 and 15.59.

13.53   HB 42(6)(c), 49(3)(c); NIHB 39(6)(c), 46(3)(c)

13.54   HB 2(1) definition – 'ordinary clothing and footwear', 42(6)(a),(b),(13), 49(3)(a),(b),(8), sch 5 para 23(2); HB60+ 42(1); NIHB 2(1), 39(6)(a),(b),(14), 46(3)(a),(b),(8), sch 6 para 24(2); NIHB60+ 40(1)

13.55   HB 42(7),(12A), 49(4); HB60+ 29(1), 42(2),(3); NIHB 39(7),(12A), 46(4); NIHB60+ 27(1), 40(2),(3)

Income you have deprived yourself of

13.56   If you have deprived yourself of income, it is counted as your notional income. To 'deprive' yourself of income means:

   (a)   you have disposed of it (for example by stopping it being paid); and

   (b)   your purpose in doing so was to make yourself entitled to HB or to more HB.

This rule is likely to be interpreted in a similar way to the rule about deprivation of capital (see table 15.3(a) to (e)), but in practice it is rare. It does not apply to income from expenses or earnings as a service user group member, or to income from a state pension you have deferred (see para 13.13). See also para 13.49.

If your non-dependant has more income and capital than you

13.57   You are counted as having your non-dependant's income and capital (instead of yours) if:

   (a)   they have more income and capital than you; and

   (b)   you and they arranged to 'take advantage of' (abuse) the HB scheme, for example by deliberately making them your non-dependant rather than making you their non-dependant.

This rule is in practice rare. It does not apply if you are on a passport benefit.

13.56   HB 42(1),(12A); HB60+ 41(8)-(8C),(11),(12); NIHB 39(1),(12A); NIHB60+ 39(8)-(10A),(13),(14)

13.57   HB 26; HB60+ 24, 27(4)(f); NIHB 23; NIHB60+ 22, 25(4)(f)

Chapter 14 **Earned income**

- General rules: see paras 14.1-4.
- Employed earnings and how they are assessed: see paras 14.5-16.
- Calculating net earnings: see paras 14.17-25.
- Self-employed earnings and how they are assessed: see paras 14.26-35.
- Calculating net profit: see paras 14.36-59.
- Earnings disregards: see paras 14.60-73.

General rules

14.1   This chapter explains how your earned income is assessed for HB purposes.

14.2   In this chapter, 'your' earned income always includes the earned income of your partner. See paras 13.1-8 for details about this and for other general rules.

14.3   The rules in this chapter apply to income from employment or self-employment in the UK (England, Wales, Scotland and Northern Ireland). If you are claiming HB in Northern Ireland they also apply to income from employment or self-employment in the Republic of Ireland. For other countries see para 13.44.

The amount of your earned income

14.4   For HB purposes, the amount of your earned income is:

(a) the weekly amount of your (and your partner's):
- net earnings from employment (see para 14.17), and/or
- net profit from self-employment (see para 14.36);

(b) minus the earned income disregards which apply to you (see para 14.60).

It can also include notional earnings (see para 14.24).

> **Example: Earned income**
>
> One partner in a couple is employed and has net earnings of £230 per week. The other is self-employed and has a net profit of £150 per week. They qualify for a standard earned income disregard of £20 per week.
>
> Their combined earned income, after the disregard has been made is £360 per week. This figure is used in calculating their HB.

14.4   HB 2(1) definition – 'earnings', 36(1),(2), 38(1),(2); HB60+ 2(1), 33(8)(a), 36(1), 39(1);
        NIHB 2(1), 33(1),(2), 35(1),(2); NIHB60+ 2(1), 31(8)(a), 34(1), 37(1)

Employed earnings

14.5   This section explains what employed earnings are and the information used to assess them. This information is needed to calculate your 'net earnings', which is the figure used in HB. (The calculation is in paras 14.17-32.)

What are employed earnings

14.6   Your employed earnings are your earnings from employment 'under a contract of service' (an employment contract) or 'in an office'. An 'office' means the kind of job that may not have an employment contract. People employed in an office include directors of limited companies, local authority councillors and clergy.

14.7   Table 14.1 explains which payments count as employed earnings and which do not. Payments which count as employed earnings are usually shown on your pay slip. For arrears of earnings see para 13.7.

Table 14.1 **Employed earnings**

The following count as employed earnings:

(a) Employed earnings generally (see para 14.6).

(b) Employed earnings paid in a lump sum.

(c) Sick, maternity, paternity and adoption pay from your employer.

(d) Statutory sick, maternity, paternity and adoption pay (but see para 14.16).

(e) Holiday pay.

(f) Retainers.

(g) Bonuses and commission.

(h) Tips.

(i) Payments in lieu of notice.

(j) Payments in lieu of earnings (but for redundancy payments see (q) below).

14.6   CBA 2(1)(a); HB 2(1) definition – employed earner; HB60+ 2(1), 29(1)(a); CBA 2(1)(a); NIHB 2(1) ; NIHB60+ 2(1), 27(1)(a)

14.7   HB 35; HB60+ 35; NIHB 32; NIHB60+ 33

T14.1(a)   HB 35(1); HB60+ 35(1); NIHB 32(1); NIHB60+ 33(1)

T14.1(b)   HB 41(3); HB60+ 26; NIHB 38(3); NIHB60+ 24

T14.1(c)   HB 35(1)(j); HB60+ 35(1)(k); NIHB 32(1)(k); NIHB60+ 33(1)(k)

T14.1(d)   HB 35(1)(i); HB60+ 35(1)(h)-(j); NIHB 32(1)(i); NIHB60+ 33(1)(h)-(j)

T14.1(e)   HB 35(1)(d); HB60+ 35(1)(d); NIHB 32(1)(d); NIHB60+ 33(1)(d)

T14.1(f)   HB 35(1)(e); HB60+ 35(1)(e); NIHB 32(1)(e); NIHB60+ 33(1)(e)

T14.1(g)   HB 35(1)(a); HB60+ 35(1)(a); NIHB 32(1)(a); NIHB60+ 33(1)(a)

T14.1(h)   HB 35(1); HB60+ 35(1); NIHB 32(1); NIHB60+ 33(1)

T14.1(i)   HB 35(1)(c); HB60+ 35(1)(c); NIHB 32(1)(c); NIHB60+ 33(1)(c)

T14.1(j)   HB 35(1)(b); HB60+ 35(1)(b); NIHB 32(1)(b); NIHB60+ 33(1)(b)

(k) Non-cash vouchers which are earnings for national insurance purposes.

(l) Councillor's allowances, but for expenses see (n) below (R(IS) 6/92). For detailed guidance see GM paras BW2.83-95.

(m) Company director's income (see para 14.6).

The following have individual rules:

(n) Expenses paid by your employer:

■   these are disregarded if they are 'wholly, exclusively and necessarily incurred' in carrying out your employment. For example, for travel between workplaces (R(IS) 16/93, CIS 507/94), or all travel if you don't have a fixed workplace and can be asked to work anywhere in your area (CH/1330/2008, in which the claimant was a care worker);

■   apart from that, they count as your employed earnings. For example, for travel between your home and workplace, or for caring for a member of your family.

(o) Expenses you receive as a member of a service user group are disregarded (for example when these are run by councils, social landlords or health authorities).

(p) Compensation payments for unfair dismissal or under laws about equal pay etc, whether made by an employment tribunal or in an out of court settlement:

■   count as your employed earnings in working age HB claims;

■   do not count as your employed earnings in pension age HB claims (but are likely to be included as your capital).

(q) Redundancy payments count as your capital, not earnings (but for payments in lieu of notice see (j) above).

(r) Payments in kind (in other words, in goods rather than money or vouchers) are disregarded (see also table 13.9(k)). But payments in private currencies count as your employed earnings, for example in local exchange trading schemes (see GM paras BW2.99-101) or in internet currencies.

(s) Bounty payments you receive as:

■   a part-time firefighter;

■   a part-time lifeboat worker;

■   an auxiliary coastguard; or

■   a member of the Territorial Army or similar reserve forces

---

T14.1(k)   HB 35(1)(k); HB60+ 35(1)(g); NIHB 32(1)(l); NIHB60+ 33(1)(g)

T14.1(l)   HB 35(1); HB60+ 35(1); NIHB 32(1); NIHB60+ 33(1)

T14.1(m) HB 35(1); HB60+ 35(1); NIHB 32(1); NIHB60+ 33(1)

T14.1(n)   HB 35(1)(f),(2)(b); HB60+ 35(1)(f),(2)(b); NIHB 32(1)(f),(2)(b); NIHB60+ 33(1)(f),(2)(b)

T14.1(o)   HB 2(5), 35(2)(d); HB60+ 2(6) 35(2)(f); NIHB 2(4A), 32(2)(d); NIHB60+ 2(5A), 33(2)(e)

T14.1(p)   HB 35(1)(g),(gg),(h), 41(3); HB60+ 35(2)(e); NIHB 32(1)(g),(gg),(h), 38(3); NIHB60+ 33(2)(d)

T14.1(q)   HB 35(1)(b), 44(1); HB60+ 35(1)(b), 44(1); NIHB 32(1)(b), 41(1); NIHB60+ 33(1)(b), 44(1)

T14.1(r)   HB 35(2)(a),(3); HB60+ 35(2)(a),(3); NIHB 32(2)(a),(3); NIHB60+ 33(2)(a),(3)

T14.1(s)   HB 46(1); NIHB 43(1)

count as your capital, not earnings, if they are paid to you annually or at longer intervals (see also table 14.5(f)).

(t)   Advances of earnings and loans from your employer count as your capital, not earnings.

(u)   Tax refunds on your earnings count as your capital, not earnings.

(v)   Occupational pensions count as your unearned income (see para 13.27).

(w)   Strike pay counts as your unearned income in working age HB claims, but is disregarded in pension age HB claims.

(x)   Self-employed earnings are assessed separately (see paras 14.26-35, and for royalties and similar payments see paras 14.58-59).

Notes

▨   The rules in (b), (s), (t) and (u) are given in the law for working age HB claims. They are also likely to apply for pension age HB claims.

▨   See also paras 14.13-16 if you are absent from work or your job ends.

Assessing employed earnings

14.8   When your employed earnings are assessed, the overall aim is 'estimating the amount which is likely to be' your average weekly net earnings (for net earnings see para 14.17). This is done using information from an assessment period or employer's estimate (see paras 14.9-11), but other relevant information should also be taken into account in order to obtain a fair and accurate result. For these purposes, your earnings count as belonging to the period they cover, whether they are paid at the beginning or end of that period or part way through it. (Before 9th February 2015, when the law changed, earnings paid at the end of a period counted for the following period: [2014] UKUT 369 (AAC).)

Assessment periods

14.9   In working age HB claims, when you make your claim your assessment period is usually:

(a)   the two months before you claimed if you are paid monthly; or

(b)   the five weeks before you claimed if you are paid weekly; or

(c)   if you have not been working long enough for the above to apply:

▨   the period you have been working if what you have been paid is representative;

▨   if what you have been paid is not representative, or you haven't yet been paid, an employer's estimate is used (see para 14.11);

(d)   but if your earnings vary, whatever period gives a more accurate result.

T14.1(t)   HB 46(5); NIHB 43(5)

T14.1(u)   HB 46(2); NIHB 43(2)

T14.1(v)   HB 35(2)(c); HB60+ 35(2)(c); NIHB 32(2)(c); NIHB60+ 33(2)(c)

T14.1(w)   HB 35(1); HB60+ 29(1); NIHB 32(1); NIHB60+ 27(1)

14.8   HB 27(1)(a), 29(1)-(3), 29A; HB60+ 30(1)(a), 33(2),(2A),(3),(3A); NIHB 24(1)(a), 26(1)-(3), 26A; NIHB60+ 28(1)(a), 31(2),(2A),(3),(3A)

14.9   HB 2(1) definition – 'assessment period', 29(1)-(3); NIHB 2(1), 26(1)-(3);

If your earnings change while you are on HB, your assessment period is whatever period gives an accurate result, but it must not be longer than 52 weeks.

14.10 In pension age HB claims, when you make your claim your assessment period usually uses the following information:

(a) your most recent two payments if they are one month or more apart; or

(b) your most recent four payments in other cases; or

(c) whatever payments give a more accurate result;

(d) but if your hours vary over a recognisable cycle (for example you work a regular pattern of shifts, or you work in term-times but not school holidays), information about the whole of that cycle.

If your earnings change while you are on HB, the rules in (c) or (d) usually apply.

Employer's estimates

14.11 Your council can ask your employer to provide information about your earnings (see also para 5.13), or can ask you to obtain this information from your employer. Many councils have a 'certificate of earnings' form which can be used for this.

Examples: Assessing employed earnings

1. A claimant's weekly earnings have been the same over the five weeks before she claimed HB.

   ■ Her weekly net earnings (see para 14.17) are calculated from this weekly amount.

2. A claimant's monthly earnings have varied over the two months before he claimed HB. Evidence about his earlier earnings shows that an average can fairly be taken over the past six months.

   ■ His weekly net earnings are calculated from the past six months' figures.

3. A claimant has moved to the area for a new job. She claims HB a few days after starting work.

   ■ She is asked to provide an employer's estimate, and her weekly net earnings are calculated from that.

Starting a job

14.12 When you start a job, your earnings can be estimated to begin with (see paras 14.9(c) and 14.11). They are taken into account from the Monday following the first day you are paid for (see para 17.21), even if your first pay day is later on. But if you have been out of work for 26 weeks or more, you may qualify for an 'extended payment' of HB (see para 17.46).

Leaving a job

14.13 When you leave a job, your earnings are taken into account until the Sunday following the last day you are paid for (see para 17.21). But in working age HB claims, holiday pay counts as your capital, not earnings, if it is payable more than four weeks after you left.

14.12   HB 29A(b); HB60+ 33 (2A)(b),(3A)(b); NIHB 26A(b); NIHB60+ 31(2A)(b),(3A)(b)

14.13   HB 35(1)(d), 46(3); NIHB 32(1)(d), 43(3)

14.14   And if your job ended before your first day of entitlement to HB:

(a) in working age HB claims, all your earnings from that job are disregarded except for compensation (see table 14.1(p)) and retainers;

(b) in pension age HB claims, all your earnings from that job are disregarded.

Absences from work

14.15   When you are absent from work, your earnings are reassessed if they change (see para 17.21). This applies to all absences, whether they are:

(a) due to sickness (with or without leave);

(b) due to maternity, paternity or adoption leave;

(c) 'with good cause' (for example you are laid off);

(d) on holiday;

(e) on strike; or

(f) for any other reason (including absences 'without good cause').

But in working age HB claims, holiday pay counts as your capital, not earnings, if it is payable more than four weeks after your absence began.

14.16   And in working age HB claims, if your absence:

(a) began before your first day of entitlement to HB; and

(b) is for one of the reasons in para 14.15(a), (b) or (c), all your earnings from that job are disregarded except for employer's and statutory sick, maternity, paternity or adoption pay, compensation (see table 14.1(p)) and retainers.

Calculating net earnings

14.17   It is your 'net earnings' which are used in assessing your HB. They are calculated as follows, using the information described in paras 14.8-16:

(a) start with your gross earnings: see para 14.18;

(b) deduct amounts for tax and national insurance: see paras 14.19-21;

(c) deduct half of your pension contributions: see para 14.22;

(d) convert the result to a weekly figure: see para 6.44;

(e) this gives your weekly net earnings: see para 14.23.

See also paras 14.60-73 for the earned income disregards.

Gross earnings

14.18   Your 'gross earnings' are the total of your employed earnings: see paras 14.5-16 and table 14.1.

14.14   HB sch 4 paras 1(a),(b), 2(a),(b),(i), 16; HB60+ sch 4 para 8; NIHB sch 5 paras 1(a),(b), 2(a),(b),(i), 16; NIHB60+ sch 4 para 8

14.15   HB 35(1)(d), 46(3); NIHB 32(1)(d), 43(3)

14.16   HB sch 4 paras 1(c), 2(a),(b),(ii), 16; ; NIHB sch 5 paras 1(c), 2(a),(b),(ii), 16;

14.17   HB 2(1) definition – 'net earnings', 29(4), 36; HB60+ 2(1), 28, 36; NIHB 2(1), 26(4), 33; NIHB60+ 2(1), 26, 34

14.18   HB 35; HB60+ 35; NIHB 32; NIHB60+ 33

Example: Calculation of net earnings

A single claimant is employed and her gross earnings are £1,450 per month. From this, her employer deducts £100 each month for tax, £30 each month for class 1 national insurance contributions (NICs), and £40 each month towards a pension scheme. Her net earnings are calculated as follows.

From her gross earnings	£1,450 pcm
deduct:	
■ tax	£100 pcm
■ NICs	£30 pcm
■ half her pension contributions	£20 pcm
This gives her net earnings	£1,300 pcm

They are converted to a weekly figure:

■ £1,300 x 12 ÷ 52	£300 pw

The earned income disregards which apply to her are then deducted (see para 14.60).

Deductions for tax and national insurance

14.19   Deductions are made from your gross earnings for:

■ income tax; and

■ class 1 national insurance contributions (NICs).

The deductions equal the amounts deducted by your employer for these. The amounts should be shown on your pay slip. The exceptions to this are in paras 14.20-21.

14.20   If your gross earnings were assessed using an employer's estimate (see para 14.11) or you have notional earnings (see para 14.24), the deductions are calculated by the council. They equal what would be deducted (if they were actual earnings) for:

■ income tax, using only the personal allowance for someone under 65 (even if you are over 65), and only the basic rate of tax; and

■ class 1 NICs.

14.21   If you are claiming HB in Northern Ireland and work in the Republic of Ireland, the deductions are calculated by the NIHE. They equal what would be deducted for tax and class 1 NICs if you worked in Northern Ireland.

Deductions for pension contributions

14.22   If you make contributions towards an occupational or personal pension, one half of the amount you contribute is deducted from your gross earnings. If your gross earnings were assessed using an employer's estimate (see para 14.11) or you have notional earnings (see para 14.24), the deduction is calculated by the council. It equals one half of what you would contribute (if they were actual earnings).

14.19   HB 36(3),(a),(d); HB60+ 36(2),(a),(d); NIHB 33(3),(a),(d); NIHB60+ 34(2),(a),(d)

14.20-21   HB 36(6),(a),(b), 42(12)(a),(b); HB60+ 36(5),(a),(b); NIHB 33(6),(a),(b),(7),39(12)(a),(b); NIHB60+ 34(5),(a),(b),(6)

14.22   HB 36(3)(b),(c),(4),(5),(6)(c), 42(12)(c); HB60+ 36(2)(b),(c),(3),(4),(5)(c);
        NIHB 33(3)(b),(c),(4),(5),(6)(c), 39(12)(c); NIHB60+ 34(2)(b),(c),(3),(4),(5)(c)

Net earnings

14.23   The above calculation (see paras 14.18-22) gives your net earnings. They are converted to a weekly figure (see para 6.44). No other amounts can be deducted from them, even if you have to pay work expenses which are not met by your employer. Your weekly net earnings are used in calculating your HB (but only after the earned income disregards have been made: see paras 14.60-73).

Notional earnings

14.24   In working age HB claims, you are counted as having 'notional' earnings (see para 13.48(f)) if:

(a) you work or provide a service for someone;

(b) they pay you less than the rate for comparable employment in the area, or do not pay you; and

(c) none of the exceptions in para 14.25 apply.

Your notional earnings equal the amount (if any) which would be reasonable for the comparable employment. Apart from that, notional earnings are assessed in the same way as actual earnings (but see para 14.20 and 14.22).

14.25   The rule in para 14.24 does not apply to work you do or a service you provide:

(a) for someone whose means are insufficient to pay you, or to pay you more; or

(b) for a charitable or voluntary organisation or as a volunteer, if it is reasonable for you to work without being paid; or

(c) in a government work programme training scheme or work placement.

Self-employed earnings

14.26   This section explains what self-employed earnings are; and the information used to assess them. This information is needed to calculate your 'net profit', which is the figure used in HB. (The calculation is in paras 14.36-57.)

What are self-employed earnings

14.27   Your self-employed earnings are your earnings which:

(a) are from 'gainful employment'; but

(b) are not employed earnings (see para 14.6).

This applies whether you are a sole trader or in a partnership. Royalties and similar payments also usually count as self-employed earnings (see paras 14.58-59).

14.23   HB 2(1) definition – net earnings, 29(4), 36; HB60+ 2(1), 28, 36; NIHB 2(1), 26(4), 33; NIHB60+ 2(1), 26, 34

14.24   HB 27(4), 42(9),(12); NIHB 24(4), 39(9),(12)

14.25   HB 42(9),(10),(10A),(12A); NIHB 39(9),(10),(10A),(12A)

14.27   HB 2(1) definition – 'self-employed earner', 37(1); HB60+ 2(1), 38(1); NIHB 2(1), 34(1); NIHB60+ 2(1), 36(1)

14.28   Your self-employed earnings only include payments which:

(a) are income (not capital); and

(b) are 'derived from' your self-employment.

Table 14.2 lists payments which (for those reasons) do not count as self-employed earnings. Apart from that, self-employed earnings include payments in money, in kind (in other words, in goods) and in any other form (for example barter).

Table 14.2 **Self-employed earnings: exclusions**

The following do not count as self-employed earnings:

(a) Your business assets. These are capital (not income) and are disregarded (see para 15.33).

(b) Grants and loans to your business. These are usually capital and (if so) are disregarded as part of your business assets.

(c) New enterprise allowance. This can help you start up in business if you are on JSA, ESA or IS [www]. It can pay you:

- a weekly allowance for up to 26 weeks: this is unearned income and is disregarded (circular A11/2011);

- a low cost loan: this is disregarded as part of your business assets (circular A8/2011).

(d) Access to work. This can help you start up in business if you have a disability [www]. It is unearned income and is disregarded (see table 13.1(p)).

(e) Other government work programme training schemes. Payments from these are usually disregarded (see table 13.1(p)).

(f) Sports Council awards. These are usually disregarded (see para 22.32).

(g) Foster care and kinship care payments. These are disregarded (see table 13.5(a)).

(h) Boarding out and respite care payments. These are disregarded (see table 13.5(f)).

(i) Rent you receive on your home (see table 13.7).

(j) Rent you receive on other property: R(FC) 2/92 (see table 13.8). But if you rent out properties as a business this may count as 'gainful employment', and (if so) your income from it is counted as self-employed earnings.

(k) Employed earnings are assessed separately (see paras 14.5-16).

(l) Income you receive as a director of a limited company counts as employed earnings (not self-employed earnings).

14.28   HB 37(1); HB60+ 38(1); NIHB 34(1); NIHB60+ 36(1)

T14.2   HB 37(2); HB60+ 38(2); NIHB 34(2); NIHB60+ 36(2)
www.gov.uk/new-enterprise-allowance
www.gov.uk/access-to-work

Assessing self-employed earnings

14.29   When your self-employed earnings are assessed, the overall aim is 'estimating the amount which is likely to be' your average weekly net profit (for net profit see para 14.36). This is done using information from an assessment period (see paras 14.30-32), but other information should be taken into account to obtain a fair and accurate result.

Assessment periods

14.30   Your assessment period is whatever period is appropriate to enable the most accurate estimation of your weekly net profit (CH/329/2003, [2003] UKUT 104 (AAC)). In working age HB claims it must not be longer than one year, and in pension age HB claims it is a year unless this would not be appropriate.

14.31   When you make your claim for HB your assessment period is usually:

(a) the most recent full year for which you have accounts or other records; or

(b) the period you have been self employed if this is less than a year; or

(c) in either case, a shorter or different period if this would be more representative;

(d) but if you are just starting self-employment, an estimated future period (see para 14.33).

If your self-employed earnings change while you are on HB (see para 14.35), your assessment period should usually be from the date the change occurred to the most recent date you have figures for (CH/329/2003, [2003] UKUT 104 (AAC)). For DWP guidance on assessment periods see GM paras BW2.330, BW2.333.

Providing accounts or other records

14.32   You are expected to provide information about your income and expenses in your assessment period. You can draw up accounts or other records yourself, or get an accountant or someone else to do this for you. They can be drawn up on:

(a) a cash flow basis, counting income when it comes in, and expenses when you pay them; or

(b) a more formal accounting basis, counting income when you issue a bill, and expenses when you receive a bill,

so long as you are reasonable, consistent, and fairly reflect your income and expenses.

Example: Self-employed earnings and net profit

Dennie Wroclaw is a self-employed window-cleaner. The records of his most recent year's trading show he had gross income of £10,268, and spent £354 on telephone, postage and stationery, £3,534 on petrol and other costs for his van, £187 on overalls and disposable equipment, £507 on advertising, and £613 to pay someone to cover his round while he was on holiday. His mileage records show that two-thirds of his use of the van is for his business (see para 14.41).

14.29   HB 27(1)(a), 30(1); HB60+ 30(1)(a), 37; NIHB 24(1)(a), 27(1); NIHB60+ 28(1)(a), 35

14.30   HB 2(1) definition – 'assessment period', 30(1); HB60+ 2(1), 37; NIHB 2(1), 27(1); NIHB60+ 2(1), 35

The council decides that year is appropriate as his assessment period (see para 14.31), as the figures are likely to represent his current income and expenses. His pre-tax profit (see para 14.36) is calculated as follows.

From his gross income	£10,268 pa
Deduct his allowable expenses (see table 14.3):	
telephone, postage and stationery	£354 pa
business use of van (2/3 of £3,534)	£2,356 pa
overalls and disposable equipment	£187 pa
advertising	£507 pa
holiday cover payments	£613 pa
This gives his pre-tax profit	£6,251 pa

This is used to calculate his weekly net profit (see para 14.36). The earned income disregards which apply to him are then deducted (see para 14.60).

Starting self-employment

14.33   When you start self-employment, your self-employment earnings can be estimated to begin with (see para 14.31(d)). The estimate usually covers the first 13 weeks you will be self-employed. Most councils have a form you can use to give your estimated income and expenses for this period, and expect you to provide records of your actual income and expenses after that. If you have been out of work for 26 weeks or more, you may qualify for an 'extended payment' of HB: see para 17.46.

Leaving self-employment

14.34   When you leave self-employment, all your self-employed earnings are disregarded from the date you stopped being self-employed, except for royalties etc (see para 14.58-59).

Changes in your self-employed earnings

14.35   Your self-employed earnings can change in different ways. Generally speaking:

(a)   short-term variations in your cash flow (for example from week to week) are a normal part of being self employed, and do not mean your HB should be reassessed; but

(b)   significant changes in your trading pattern mean your HB should be reassessed. For example, this could be because you change from full-time to part-time or from part-time to full-time, or gain or lose a major customer, or have a break from trading because you are sick or are caring for someone.

14.34   HB sch 4 para 4A; HB60+ sch 4 para 8; NIHB sch 5 para 4A; NIHB60+ sch 5 para 8

Calculating net profit

14.36   It is your 'net profit' which is used in calculating your HB. This is calculated as follows using the information described in paras 14.29-35:

(a) start with your gross income: see para 14.37;

(b) deduct your allowable expenses: see paras 14.38-45 (or if you are a childminder see para 14.52);

(c) this gives your pre-tax profit (or if you are in a partnership your share is your pre-tax profit): see paras 14.46-52;

(d) deduct amounts for tax and national insurance: see paras 14.53-55;

(e) deduct half your pension contributions: see para 14.56;

(f) convert the result to a weekly figure: see para 6.44;

(g) this gives your weekly net profit: see para 14.57.

See also paras 14.60-73 for the earned income disregards.

Gross income

14.37   Your gross income is the total of your self-employed earnings before any deductions have been made from them: see paras 14.26-35.

Allowable expenses

14.38   Your allowable expenses are deducted from your gross income. There are two main conditions about this:

(a) expenses are only allowable if they are 'wholly and exclusively incurred' for the purposes of the business: see paras 14.40-44;

(b) but expenses are not allowable if they are not 'reasonably incurred': see para 14.45.

Some types of expenses also have special rules, and these are all included in table 14.3.

14.39   Table 14.3 summarises which expenses are allowable and which are not, and further details are in paras 14.40-45. Different rules apply if you are a childminder: see para 14.52.

'Wholly and exclusively incurred' expenses

14.40   An expense is wholly and exclusively incurred for your business if all of it is for your business and no part of it is for anything else. For example, if you use a van only for your business (and do not use it for domestic, private or other purposes), your vehicle costs for the van are allowable expenses. See also paras 14.41-44.

14.36   HB 2(1) definition – "net profit", 30(2), 38; HB60+ 2(1), 28,39; NIHB 2(1), 27(2), 32; NIHB60+ 2(1), 26,37

14.37   HB 37(1); HB60+ 38(1); NIHB 34(1); NIHB60+ 36(1)

14.38   HB 38(3)(a),(4),(7); HB60+ 39(2)(a),(3),(6); NIHB 35(3)(a),(4),(7); NIHB60+ 37(2)(a),(3),(6)

14.40   HB 38(3)(a),(4); HB60+ 39(2)(a),(3); NIHB 35(3)(a),(4); NIHB60+ 37(2)(a),(3)

T14.3(a)-(e)   HB 38(6),(8)(b); HB60+ 39(5),(7)(b); NIHB 35(6),(8)(b); NIHB60+ 37(5),(7)(b)

T14.3(f)   HB 38(3)(a),(4),(7); HB60+ 39(2)(a),(3),(6); NIHB 35(3)(a),(4),(7); NIHB60+ 37(2)(a),(3),(6)

T14.3(g)-(n)   HB 38(5),(8)(a); HB60+ 39(2)(a),(3),(6); NIHB 35(5),(8)(a); NIHB60+ 37(2)(a),(3),(6)

Table 14.3 **Self-employed expenses**

This table is about which expenses are allowable if you are self-employed (see paras 14.38-39).

Allowable expenses

(a) Expenditure (from your income) on repairing an existing business asset, apart from costs covered by an insurance policy.

(b) Capital repayments on a loan used for repairing an existing business asset, apart from costs covered by an insurance policy.

(c) Capital repayments on a loan used for replacing business equipment or machinery (this includes a loan for replacing a car: R(H) 5/07).

(d) Interest payments on any business loan.

(e) Any VAT you pay (minus any VAT you receive).

(f) Any other expenditure which meets the conditions in para 14.38. For example, the following expenses are likely to meet those conditions:

- telephone, postage, stationery and delivery costs,
- transport and vehicle costs,
- materials, supplies, stock and protective clothing,
- advertising and subscriptions to trade and professional bodies,
- bank charges, insurance costs, and accountancy and legal fees,
- hire and leasing charges,
- staff costs and payments to subcontractors,
- premises costs such as rent, rates, cleaning and fuel.

Non-allowable expenses

(g) Capital expenditure, such as buying a vehicle, equipment of a lasting nature, or business premises.

(h) Capital repayments on a loan, unless (b) or (c) above applies.

(i) Depreciation of capital assets (even if you claim a capital allowance in your tax return).

(j) Expenditure on setting up or expanding your business (but interest on loans for this is allowable: see (d) above).

(k) Losses you have incurred before your assessment period (see paras 14.30-31).

(l) Expenditure on business entertainment.

(m) Debts you are owed, but proven bad debts are allowable and so are costs you incur in recovering debts. (This rule is given in the law for working age HB claims. It is also likely to apply for pension age HB claims.)

(n) Expenditure for domestic or private purposes (see also paras 14.41-44).

(o) Any other expenditure which does not meet the conditions in para 14.38.

Expenses for mixed purposes

14.41   If an expense is partly for your business and partly for another purpose, you can separate it out to find the business part. This is also called 'apportioning' expenses. For example, if you use a car for both business and personal purposes, you can keep records of your mileage and then separate the costs on that basis. The business part is then allowable. But the calculation does not have to be that detailed, so long as the method you use is fair and reasonable.

14.42   Even expenses you would incur anyway can be apportioned. For example you would have to pay for insurance and a vehicle licence on a car (and perhaps repay a car loan) even if you did not use it for your business, but you can apportion these expenses in the same way as the petrol you use (R(H) 5/07, which followed R(FC) 1/91).

Expenses if you work from home

14.43   If you work from home, part of your accommodation costs are an allowable expense. For example, this can include part of your fuel for heating and lighting, standing charges, and rent (see also para 14.44). The business part of these should be calculated in a fair and reasonable way, taking into account the size of your working area compared with the size of the rest of your home, and the amount of time you use it for business rather than domestic purposes. In one case a self-employed claimant used the second bedroom in their home only for business purposes. The difference between the total rent on their home and the rent officer's valuation of the rent for a one-bedroom flat was accepted as an appropriate allowable expense (para 12 of R(H) 5/07).

14.44   But when part of your rent is allowed as a business expense, that part cannot be included in your eligible rent: see para 10.62. This affects you if your eligible rent is based on your actual rent (see chapters 7 and 9), but not if it is based on a local housing allowance (see chapter 8).

'Reasonably incurred' expenses

14.45   Whether an expense is reasonably incurred depends on the circumstances of the individual case (R (P) 2/54), including how much you earn from your business (R (G) 1/56). If an expense is appropriate and necessary, it should always be considered reasonably incurred unless it is excessive (R (G) 7/62). If an expense is excessive only the part which is reasonable is allowable.

Pre-tax profit (chargeable income)

14.46   Deducting your allowable expenses from your gross income gives your pre-tax profit. In the law it is called your 'chargeable income'. Further rules about pre-tax profit are in paras 14.47-52. See also paras 14.53-56 for deductions for tax etc.

Pre-tax profit for business partnerships

14.47   If you are self-employed in a partnership, your pre-tax profit is worked out for your business and then divided between you. The same applies if you are a share fisherman.

14.45   HB 38(7); HB60+ 39(6); NIHB 35(7); NIHB60+ 37(6)

14.46   HB 38(3)(a); HB60+ 39(3)(a); NIHB 35(3)(a); NIHB60+ 37(3)(a)

The division is made in the same way as you actually share your income and expenses. For example if there are two of you and you share your income and expenses equally, the pre-tax profit of each of you is half the pre-tax profit of the business.

Pre-tax profit and couples

14.48   If you are a couple and are also business partners, your pre-tax profit is divided between you (see para 14.47). If one of you is self-employed and employs the other one, the wages or salary are:

(a) allowable expenses for the self-employed one; and

(b) employed earnings for the other one.

If you make a loss

14.49   If your allowable expenses are greater than (or equal to) your gross income, your pre-tax profit is nil, so your self-employed earnings are nil (R(H) 5/08).

14.50   Your losses cannot be deducted from any other employed or self-employed earnings you have, or your partner or any other family member has (R(H) 5/08).

Pre-tax profit and drawings

14.51   If you take drawings from your business (for example as a kind of wage or salary you pay yourself), this has no effect on the calculation of your pre-tax profit. Drawings are not part of your gross income (R(H) 6/09) and are not an allowable business expense (GM paras BW2.390-396).

Pre-tax profit if you are a childminder

14.52   If you are a self-employed childminder:

(a) your expenses are not deducted from your gross income;

(b) instead, your pre-tax profit always equals one-third of your gross income.

This is intended to make the calculation easier and fairer.

Example: A self-employed childminder

Hendl Drimic is a self-employed childminder. She receives gross income from her childminding which averages £240 per week. She works from her home and it would be difficult to assess her expenses, but she does not have to do this because her pre-tax profit is calculated as follows (see para 14.52).

Her gross income is	£240
Of this only one-third is counted as her pre-tax profit	£80
This is too low for deductions for tax and national insurance (see table 14.4).	
So her net profit (see para 14.36) is also	£80

The earned income disregards which apply to her are then deducted (see para 14.60).

14.47   HB 38(1)(b); HB60+ 39(1)(b); NIHB 35(1)(b); NIHB60+ 37(1)(b)

14.50   HB 38(10); HB60+ 39(10); NIHB 35(10); NIHB60+ 37(10)

14.52   HB 39(3)(b); HB60+ 40(3)(b); NIHB 36(3)(b); NIHB60+ 38(3)(b)

Deductions for tax and national insurance

14.53 Deductions are made from your pre-tax profit for:

(a) income tax; and

(b) classes 2 and 4 national insurance contributions (NICs).

The deductions are calculated by the council and are called 'notional tax' and 'notional NICs'. They are unlikely to be the same as the amounts you actually pay HMRC, because the expenses which are allowable in HB are different from the expenses and allowances you can claim in your tax return.

14.54 Table 14.4 shows how the deductions are calculated. It gives the figures for the tax year from 6th April 2015 to 5th April 2016 (this tax year contains 366 days). The calculation:

(a) uses annual figures. So if your pre-tax profit is not an annual amount it is converted to an annual figure;

(b) uses the tax and NICs figures for the tax year which is 'applicable to' your assessment period (see paras 14.30-31). If your assessment period spanned two tax years, councils interpret this in different ways. Many use the most straightforward method of using the figures for the tax year containing your date of claim for HB (or the date your HB is reassessed).

When making the calculation, councils can ignore national changes in the tax and NICs rates and allowances for up to 30 weeks.

14.55 The calculations in table 14.4 apply in Northern Ireland even if your self-employment is based in the Republic of Ireland.

Table 14.4 **Notional tax and NICs: 2015-16 tax year**

This table shows how your notional tax and national insurance contributions (NICs) are calculated if you are self-employed (see paras 14.53-55). All three calculations are made (though one or more of them may give a figure of nil).

(a) Income tax

- start with your annual pre-tax profit
- subtract the personal allowance which applies to you. If you were born after 5th April 1948, this is £10,600
- if there is a remainder, multiply it by 20%
- the result is the annual amount of your notional tax.

(b) Class 2 NICs

- if your annual pre-tax profit is £5,965 or more, the annual amount of your notional class 2 NICs is £145.60.

14.53   HB 38(1)(b)(i),(3)(b),(9)(a), 39; HB60+ 39(1)(b)(i),(2)(b),(8)(a), 40; NIHB 35(1)(b)(i),(3)(b),(9)(a), 36; NIHB60+ 37(1)(b)(i),(2)(b),(8)(a), 38

14.54   HB 2(1) definition – 'basic rate', 'tax year', 34, 39(1),(2); HB60+ 2(1), 34, 40(1),(2); NIHB 2(1), 31, 36(1),(2); NIHB60+ 2(1), 32, 38(1),(2)

14.55   NIHB 35(12); NIHB60+ 37(11)

T14.4   HB 2(1) definition – 'basic rate', 'tax year', 39; HB60+ 2(1), 40; NIHB 2(1), 36; NIHB60+ 2(1), 38

(c) Class 4 NICs

- start with your annual pre-tax profit (but if it is greater than £42,385, start with £42,385)

- subtract £8,060

- if there is a remainder, multiply it by 9%

- the result is the annual amount of your notional class 4 NICs.

Notes

(a) If you were born before 6th April 1948, use the personal allowance that applies to you [www]. No other allowances are taken into account apart from the personal allowance. The 40% tax rate is never used.

(b) £145.60 is 52 times the weekly class 2 NICs of £2.80, there being 52 Sundays in the 2015-16 tax year. If your pre-tax profit is below £5,965, your notional class 2 NICs are nil (even if you have not applied to HMRC for exemption).

(c) The 2% class 4 NICs rate for income over £42,385 is not used. (This appears to be the intention of HB law, even though it has not been amended to keep it up to date with NICs law.)

Example: Notional tax and NICs

A self-employed book-keeper claims HB in December 2015 and provides her most recent accounts, which are for the year to 31st October 2015. The council decides that year is appropriate as her assessment period (see para 14.31). In that year she had gross income of £14,000 and allowable expenses of £1,400, so her pre-tax profit is £12,600. She doesn't contribute to a pension scheme. Her notional tax and national insurance contributions (NICs) are calculated as follows (see table 14.4).

(a) Notional tax

from her pre-tax profit	£12,600.00 pa
subtract the personal allowance	£10,600.00 pa
	= £2,000.00 pa
and multiply this by 20% to give her notional tax	£400.00 pa

(b) Notional class 2 NICs

her pre-tax profit is greater than £5,965 so her notional class 2 NICs are	£145.60 pa

(c) Notional class 4 NICs

from her pre-tax profit	£12,600.00 pa
subtract the lower earnings threshold	£8,060.00 pa
	= £4,540.00 pa
and multiply this by 9% to give her notional class 4 NICs	£408.60 pa

(d) Net profit

■ from her pre-tax profit deduct: £12,600.00 pa

■ her notional tax £400.00 pa

■ her notional class 2 NICs £145.60 pa

■ her notional class 4 NICs £408.60 pa

■ this gives her annual net profit £11,645.80 pa

■ it is converted to a weekly figure:

■ £11,645.80 ÷ 366 x 7 £222.73 pw

The earned income disregards which apply to her are then deducted (see para 14.60).

Deductions for pension contributions

14.56 If you make contributions towards:

(a) a personal pension scheme; or

(b) an annuity for a retirement pension for yourself or a dependant,

half of the amount you contribute is deducted from your pre-tax profit. If your contributions change (or you start or stop making contributions) your HB is reassessed.

Example: Pension contributions

The self-employed book-keeper in the previous example begins making pension contributions of £40 per month in February 2016. Her HB is reassessed to take account of this as follows. (Her trading pattern has not changed so her income and expenses do not need to be reassessed: see para 14.35.)

Her weekly net profit was £223.34 pw

From this, deduct the weekly equivalent of her
pension contributions (see para 6.44):

■ £40 x 12 ÷ 366 x 7 £9.21 pw

This gives her new weekly net profit £214.13 pw

The earned income disregards which apply to her are then deducted (see para 14.60).

Net profit

14.57 The above calculation (see paras 14.37-56) gives your net profit. This is converted to a weekly figure (see para 6.44). Your weekly net profit is used in calculating your HB (but only after the earned income disregards have been made: see paras 14.60-73).

14.56 HB 38(1)(b)(ii),(3)(c),(9)(b),(11),(12); HB60+ 39(1)(b)(ii),(2)(c),(8)(b),(10),(11);
NIHB 35(1)(b)(ii),(3)(c),(9)(b),(11),(13); NIHB60+ 37(1)(b)(ii),(2)(c),(8)(b),(10),(12)

14.57 HB 2(1) definition – 'net profit', 30(2), 38; HB60+ 2(1), 28,39; NIHB 2(1), 27(2), 35; NIHB60+ 2(1), 26,37

Royalties and similar payments

14.58 The following payments count as earned income. In working age HB claims they are assessed as self-employed earnings (see para 14.36), and in practice this is also done in pension age HB claims:

(a) royalties or other payments you receive for the use of, or right to use, a copyright, design, patent or trademark;

(b) payments you receive as an author under the Public Lending Right scheme or a similar international scheme; and

(c) in pension age HB claims, any other 'occasional' payment you earn.

The rules in (a) and (b) only apply if you are the first owner of the copyright etc or an original contributor to the book etc. If you have inherited the right to receive royalties etc, this is unearned income (see para 13.40).

14.59 Because these payments are often annual, six monthly or irregular, there are special rules saying what period they cover:

(a) in pension age HB claims, they are averaged over the year beginning with the date of payment. For example, a payment of £364 is gross income of £7 per week over that year (see para 6.44);

(b) in working age HB claims, work through the following steps:

- start with the weekly amount of your HB (calculated as though you did not receive the royalties etc);

- add to that all the earned income disregards which apply to you (see para 14.60);

- the result is your gross income for each week until payment is used up. For example, if your HB is £90 per week and you qualify for only the £10 per week earned income disregard, a payment of £364 is gross income of £100 per week for three weeks, then £64 in the fourth week.

Earned income disregards

14.60 This section describes the amounts which are disregarded from your earned income. You may qualify for one, two, or all three of the following:

(a) a standard earned income disregard (see para 14.62);

(b) a child care disregard (see paras 14.63-67);

(c) an additional earned income disregard (see para 14.68).

They can be described as the amounts you are allowed to 'keep' before your earned income affects the amount of your HB.

14.58   HB 37(3); HB60+ 33(5),(8)(b),(8A); NIHB 34(3); NIHB60+ 31(5),(8)(b),(8A)

14.59   HB 37(4); HB60+ 33(4); NIHB 34(4); NIHB60+ 31(4)

How the disregards work

14.61   The earned income disregards work as follows:

(a) first add together all your (and your partner's):

- ▪ weekly net earnings from employment (see para 14.17), and

- ▪ weekly net profit from self-employment (see para 14.36);

(b) then (from that total) deduct the standard earned income disregard;

(c) then deduct the child care disregard if you qualify for it. But if:

- ▪ the result of (b) is not enough to deduct the whole of the child care disregard, and

- ▪ you are on working tax credit or child tax credit,

the balance of the child care disregard is deducted from your WTC and/or CTC;

(d) then deduct the additional earned income disregard if you qualify for it. But if:

- ▪ the result of (c) is not enough to deduct the whole of the additional earned income disregard, and

- ▪ you are on working tax credit,

the whole of the additional earned income disregard (not just the balance) is instead deducted from your WTC.

Except as described in (c) and (d), no part of the earned income disregards can be deducted from your unearned income. (See para 13.43 if you make parental contributions to a student.)

Examples: Earned income disregards

1. A couple without children

A couple in their 40s are both employed for 35 hours a week. Their combined net earnings are £500 per week. They do not have children.

From their weekly net earnings deduct:	£500.00
▪ the standard earned income disregard for a couple (see table 14.5 (g))	£10.00
▪ the additional earned income disregard (see para 14.68 and table 14.7(b))	£17.10
This gives the figure used in calculating their HB	£472.90

2. A lone parent with child care costs

A lone parent aged 30 is self-employed for 20 hours a week, and his net earnings are £250 per week. He pays child care charges of £70 per week for his daughter aged 9.

14.61   HB 2(1) definition – 'earnings' 27(1)(c),(2), 36(2), 38(2), sch 4 paras 3-10A, sch 5 para 56;
HB60+ 2(1), 30(1)(c),(2), 33(8), sch 4 paras 1-5A, 7, 9(1),(3), sch 5 para 21;
NIHB 2(1), 24(1)(c),(2), 33(2), 35(2), sch 5 paras 3-10A, sch 6 para 58;
NIHB60+ 2(1), 28(1)(c),(2), 31(8), sch 5 paras 1-5A, 7, 9(1),(3), sch 6 para 22

From his weekly earnings deduct:	£250.00
■ the standard earned income disregard for a lone parent (see table 14.5(b))	£25.00
■ the child care disregard (see paras 14.63-64)	£70.00
■ the additional earned income disregard (see para 14.68 and table 14.7(c))	£17.10
This gives the figure used in calculating his HB	£137.90

The standard earned income disregard

14.62 Everyone who has earned income qualifies for a standard earned income disregard. The disregard has different amounts, but whether you are a single claimant, a lone parent, or a couple, you qualify for only one amount. Table 14.5 explains the conditions for each amount, and which one you qualify for.

Table 14.5 **The standard earned income disregard**

The standard earned income disregard has different amounts (see para 14.62), all given in this table. You qualify for the first amount you meet the conditions for.

(a) 'Permitted work' approved by the DWP: £104 per week

The disregard is £104 per week if you are in 'permitted work'. This means work the DWP has agreed you can do while you are receiving:

■ ESA(C);

■ incapacity benefit;

■ severe disablement allowance; or

■ national insurance credits instead of those benefits

If you are a couple and only one of you is in permitted work, it is disregarded from that one's earned income. But if that is less than £104 per week, the balance up to £20 per week is disregarded from the other one's earned income.

The disregard is set at 16 times the national minimum wage, so when that goes up the £104 per week increases.

(b) Lone parents: £25 per week

Unless (a) applies to you, the disregard is £25 per week if you are a lone parent.

(c) Sickness or disability: £20 per week: working age HB claims

In working age HB claims, unless (a) or (b) apply to you, the disregard is £20 per week if your applicable amount includes:

14.62   HB sch 4 paras 3-10A; HB60+ sch 4 paras 1-5A, 7; NIHB sch 5 paras 3-10A; NIHB60+ sch 5 paras 1-5A, 7

T14.5(a) HB sch 4 para 10A; HB60+ sch 4 para 5A; NIHB sch 5 para 10A; NIHB60+ sch 5 para 5A

T14.5(b) HB sch 4 para 4; HB60+ sch 4 paras 1(a),2; NIHB sch 5 para 4; NIHB60+ sch 5 paras 1(a),2

T14.5(c) HB sch 4 para 3; ; NIHB sch 5 para 3;

■ a work-related activity component (see para 12.20);

■ a support component (see para 12.20);

■ a disability premium (see paras 12.25 and 12.31); or

■ a severe disability premium (see para 12.38).

(d) Sickness or disability: £20 per week: pension age HB claims

In pension age HB claims, unless (a) or (b) apply to you, the disregard is £20 per week if you or your partner:

■ receive attendance allowance;

■ receive any of the qualifying benefits listed in paragraph 12.31(b);

■ receive main phase ESA, or national insurance contributions instead of it (see para 12.23);

■ meet the old work fitness test in paragraph 12.25. But in the case of national insurance credits (paragraph 12.27) the qualifying period is 28 weeks (not one year). And unlike the rules for the disability premium it can be you or your partner who meets this condition; or

■ qualified for the £20 per week disregard (as described in (c) above) at any time in the eight weeks before you reached pension age (see paras 1.23-25), and there have been no breaks in either your entitlement to HB or your employment since you reached that age.

(e) Carers: £20 per week

Unless (a) to (d) apply to you, the disregard is £20 per week if your applicable amount includes a carer premium (see para 12.43)

If you are a couple and only one of you is a carer, it is disregarded from the carer's earned income. But if that is less than £20 per week, the balance up to £10 per week is disregarded from the other one's earned income.

(f) Special occupations: £20 per week

Unless (a) to (e) apply to you, the disregard is £20 per week if you or your partner are:

■ a part-time fire-fighter;

■ a part-time lifeboat worker;

■ an auxiliary coastguard; or

■ a member of the Territorial Army or similar reserve forces.

(See also table 14.1(s).)

T14.5(d)   HB60+ 2(1) definition – 'attendance allowance', sch 4 para 5; NIHB60+ 2(1), sch 5 para 5

T14.5(e)   HB sch 4 paras 5,6; HB60+ sch 4 paras 1(b),4; NIHB sch 5 paras 5,6; NIHB60+ sch 5 paras 1(b),4

T14.5(f)   HB sch 4 paras 8,9; HB60+ sch 4 paras 1(b),3; NIHB sch 5 paras 8,9; NIHB60+ sch 5 paras 1(b),3

(g) **Couples: £10 per week**

For all other couples, the disregard is £10 per week.

(h) **Single claimants: £5 per week**

For all other single claimants, the disregard is £5 per week.

The child care disregard

14.63   You qualify for the child care disregard if:

(a) you pay child care charges to one or more of the providers in table 14.6;

(b) you pay them for one or more children who meet the age condition (see para 14.66); and

(c) you are:

- a lone parent and you work at least 16 hours per week, or
- a couple and you both work at least 16 hours per week, or
- a couple and one of you works at least 16 hours per week and the other one meets one or more of the conditions in para 14.67.

Paragraphs 14.69-72 explain when you count as working at least 16 hours per week.

14.64   The disregard equals the weekly amount of child care charges you pay (see para 14.65), up to:

(a) £175 per week if the charges are for one child;

(b) £350 per week if the charges are for two or more children.

See para 14.61(c) for further information about how the disregard works.

14.65   Table 14.6 explains which child care charges are taken into account. The weekly amount is found by averaging them over whatever period, up to one year, gives an accurate figure. The council can ask the person providing the care for the information about this.

14.66   A child meets the age condition for the child care disregard from birth until:

(a) the first Monday in September following their 15th birthday; or

(b) if they meet the conditions for a disabled child premium (see para 12.34), the first Monday in September following their 16th birthday.

T14.5(g)   HB sch 4 para 7; HB60+ sch 4 para 7(b); NIHB sch 5 para 7; NIHB60+ sch 5 para 7(b)

T14.5(h)   HB sch 4 para 10; HB60+ sch 4 para 7(a); NIHB sch 5 para 10; NIHB60+ sch 5 para 7(a)

14.63   HB 28(1) ; HB60+ 31(1); NIHB 25(1) ; NIHB60+ 29(1)

14.64   HB 27(3); HB60+ 30(3); NIHB 24(3); NIHB60+ 28(3)

14.65   HB 28(5),(10); HB60+ 31(5),(10); NIHB 25(5),(10); NIHB60+ 29(5),(10)

14.66   HB 28(6),(9),(13); HB60+ 31(6),(9),(13); NIHB 25(6),(9),(13); NIHB60+ 29(6),(9),(13)

14.67   The conditions listed in this paragraph are about the child care disregard for couples: see para 14.63(c). If you are a couple and one of you works at least 16 hours per week, the other one does not have to do so if they:

(a)   meet the conditions for:

■   a work-related activity component (see para 12.20),

■   a support component (see paras 12.20-21), or

■   a disability premium;

(b)   are receiving:

■   disability living allowance (DLA),

■   personal independence payment (PIP),

■   attendance allowance, or

■   a benefit equivalent to attendance allowance (see para 12.50),

or would do so except that they are in hospital (see para 12.54 and table 12.2);

(c)   are receiving:

■   main phase ESA (see para 12.21),

■   incapacity benefit at the short-term higher rate or the long-term rate, or

■   severe disablement allowance;

(d)   have been accepted by the DWP as having limited capability for work (see para 12.20) or as being incapable of work (see para 12.25) for a continuous period of 28 weeks (ignoring breaks of up to 12 or 8 weeks respectively);

(e)   have an invalid carriage or similar vehicle;

(f)   are aged 80 or more;

(g)   are in hospital; or

(h)   are in prison (serving a sentence or on remand).

But condition (d) only applies to the HB claimant. (See para 5.4 for how to change which partner in a couple is the claimant.)

14.67   HB 28(1)(c),(11); HB60+ 31(1)(c),(11) ; NIHB 25(1)(c),(11); NIHB60+ 29(1)(c),(11)

14.67(a)   HB 28(11)(a),(b),(ba); HB60+ 31(11),(b),(ba); NIHB 25(11)(a),(b),(ba); NIHB60+ 29(11),(b),(ba)

14.67(b),(c) HB 28(11)(d)-(f); HB60+ 31(11),(d)-(f); NIHB 25(11)(d)-(f); NIHB60+ 29(11),(d)-(f)

14.67(d)   HB 28(11)(c),(ca),(12),(12A); HB60+ 31(11)(c),(ca),(12),(12A); NIHB 25(11)(c),(ca),(12),(12A); NIHB60+ 29(11)(c),(ca),(12),(12A)

14.67(e)   HB 2(1) definition – 'invalid carriage', 28(11)(g); HB60+ 2(1), 31(11)(g) ; NIHB 2(1), 25(11)(g); NIHB60+ 2(1), 29(11)(g)

14.67(f)   HB60+ 31(11)(a); ; NIHB60+ 29(11)(a)

14.67(g),(h) HB 28(1)(c); HB60+ 31(1)(c); NIHB 25(1)(c); NIHB60+ 29(1)(c)

Table 14.6 **Child care providers**

Charges you pay to the following are taken into account for the child care disregard (see paras 14.63-66):

(a) A registered child minder, nursery or play scheme.

(b) A child minding scheme that does not have to be registered, for example, one run by a school or local authority or in Northern Ireland on Crown property.

(c) Any child care provider if the child care has been approved for working tax credit purposes.

(d) An out-of-school-hours scheme provided by a school on school premises, by a local authority, or in Northern Ireland by an education and library board or HSS trust. But in this case only, the child must be aged 8 or more.

(e) A foster parent or kinship carer (apart from the child's own foster parent or kinship carer) under the Fostering Services Regulations 2002, or equivalent provisions in Wales, or the Looked After Children (Scotland) Regulations 2009.

(f) A domiciliary care worker under the Domiciliary Care Agencies Regulations 2002, or equivalent provisions in Wales.

(g) Anyone else who provides care wholly or mainly in the child's home, for example, a friend who comes in to provide care for the child. But this does not apply if they are your partner or a relative of the child. See para 7.71 for who counts as a 'relative'.

But payments you make in respect of compulsory education do not count towards the child care disregard.

The additional earned income disregard

14.68   You qualify for the additional earned income disregard if you meet one or more of the conditions in table 14.7. The amount of the disregard is £17.10 per week. See para 14.61(d) for further information about how the disregard works.

T14.6   HB 28(5),(7)-(9); HB60+ 31(5),(7)-(9); NIHB 25(5),(7)-(9); NIHB60+ 29(5),(7)-(9)

14.68   HB sch 4 para 17; HB60+ sch 4 para 9; NIHB sch 5 para 17; NIHB60+ sch 5 para 9

Table 14.7 **The additional earned income disregard**

You qualify for the additional earned income disregard (see para 14.68) if you meet one or more of the conditions (a) to (e). Paras 14.69-73 explain when you count as working at least 16 or 30 hours per week. The examples illustrate how the conditions work for couples.

(a) You receive working tax credit and it includes the WTC '30 hour element'.

If you are a couple, at least one of you has to qualify for the WTC 30 hour element. See example 1.

(b) You:

- are aged 25 or more; and

- work at least 30 hours per week.

If you are a couple, at least one of you has to meet both halves of this condition. See example 2.

(c) You:

- are responsible for one or more children or young persons; and

- work at least 16 hours per week.

If you are a couple, only one of you has to work at least 16 hours per week. See example 3.

(d) In working age HB claims, you:

- qualify for a work-related activity component, a support component, or a disability premium (see paras 12.18-2 and 12.31); and

- work at least 16 hours per week.

If you are a couple, at least one of you has to meet each half of this condition (but it need not be the same one who meets both halves). See example 4.

(e) In pension age HB claims, you:

- qualify for the £20 disregard for sickness or disability (see table 14.5(d)); and

- work at least 16 hours per week

If you are a couple, at least one of you has to meet both halves of this condition. See example 5.

Note:

For condition (a) you have to be on WTC (and getting the WTC 30 hour element). For conditions (b) to (e) you don't have to be on WTC (but they are the same as the conditions used in WTC for getting the 30 hour element).

T14.7   HB sch 4 para 17(2); HB60+ sch 4 para 9(2); NIHB sch 5 para 17(2); NIHB60+ sch 5 para 9(2)

Examples: The additional earned income disregard for couples

1. A couple on working tax credit

A couple are on WTC. One of them has been awarded the WTC '30 hour element'.

■ They qualify for the additional earned income disregard: see table 14.7(a).

2. A couple without children

A couple are aged 22 and 27. The 22-year-old works for 35 hours a week. The 27-year-old does not work.

■ They do not qualify for the additional earned income disregard: see table 14.7(b). (They would qualify if the 27-year-old worked at least 30 hours a week.)

3. A couple with a child

A couple with a baby. One of them works for 20 hours a week. The other one does not work.

■ They qualify for the additional earned income disregard: see table 14.7(c).

4. A working age couple, one with a disability

A couple are in their 50s. One of them receives personal independence payment (PIP) and does not work. The other one works for 20 hours a week.

■ They qualify for the additional earned income disregard: see table 14.7(d). (They would also qualify if the one on PIP worked at least 16 hours a week, or they both did.)

5. A pension age couple, one with a disability

A couple are in their 70s. One of them receives attendance allowance and does not work. The other one works for 20 hours a week.

■ They do not qualify for the additional earned income disregard: see table 14.7(e). (They would qualify if the one on attendance allowance worked at least 16 hours a week, or they both did.)

Working at least 16 hours per week

14.69 You count as working at least 16 hours per week if:

(a) you are employed or self-employed in work for which payment is made or expected; and

(b) you work at least 16 hours per week every week, or on average (see para 14.70).

The law calls this 'remunerative work'.

14.70 If your hours vary, they are averaged as follows:

(a) if there is no recognisable cycle to your work, over five weeks or whatever period would give a more accurate figure;

(b) if your work has a recognisable cycle (for example you work a regular pattern of shifts), over the whole of that cycle. In this case, the averaging includes periods you don't work;

14.69   HB 6(1); HB60+ 6(1); NIHB 6(1); NIHB60+ 6(1)

14.70   HB 6(2)-(4); HB60+ 6(2)-(4); NIHB 6(2)-(4); NIHB60+ 6(2)-(4)

(c) but if your work has a recognisable cycle of a year (for example you work in term-times but not school holidays) over the whole year, the averaging excludes periods you don't work but the result applies throughout the year. (So if you work at least 16 hours every week in term-times, you count as working at least 16 hours per week throughout the year.)

14.71 Once you count as working at least 16 hours per week:

(a) you continue to do so during the following absences from work:

■ while you are on holiday, or

■ while you are absent from work 'without good cause';

(b) for the purposes of the child care disregard (only), you also continue to do so:

■ while you are on maternity, paternity or adoption leave. This only applies while you are getting statutory maternity, paternity or adoption pay, or maternity allowance, or income support because of paternity leave (these can be paid for up to 39 weeks. And if you are getting the child element of WTC when they stop, it continues to apply until the WTC child element stops), or

■ while you are on sick leave. This is limited to 28 weeks. And it only applies while you are getting statutory sick pay, incapacity benefit at the short-term lower rate, ESA, income support because of incapacity for work, or national insurance credits instead of these.

14.72 You do not count as working at least 16 hours per week:

(a) while you are absent from work 'with good cause' (for example you are laid off);

(b) while you are doing unpaid work;

(c) while your only income is from a Sports Council award;

(d) in any benefit week in which you are on JSA(IB), ESA(IR) or income support for more than three days;

(e) while you are on maternity, paternity or adoption leave, with the right to return to work under your contract or under employment law; or

(f) while you are absent from work due to illness, whether or not you are being paid.

There are exceptions to (e) and (f) in relation to the child care disregard: see para 14.71(b).

Working at least 30 hours per week

14.73 The rules about whether you count as working at least 30 hours per week are the same as in paras 14.69-72, apart from the different number of hours.

14.71-72   HB 2(1) definition – 'adoption leave', 'maternity leave', 'paternity leave', 'sports award', 6(1),(5)-(8), 28(2)-(4),(14),(15);
          HB 2(1), 6(1),(5)-(8), 31(2)-(4),(14)-(16); NIHB 2(1), 6(1),(5)-(8), 25(2)-(4),(14),(15); NIHB60+ 2(1), 6(1),(5)-(8), 29(2)-(4),(14)-(16)

14.73   HB sch 4 para 17(4); HB60+ sch 4 para 9(4); NIHB sch 5 para 17(4); NIHB60+ sch 5 para 9(4)

Chapter 15 **Capital**

- General rules about assessing capital: see paras 15.1-13.
- How capital is valued: see paras 15.14-20.
- Savings and investments: see paras 15.21-27.
- Property and possessions: see paras 15.28-35.
- Trust funds, compensation payments and other capital: see paras 15.36-55.
- Notional capital: see paras 15.56-69.

General rules

15.1 This chapter explains how your capital is assessed for HB purposes, including actual capital (see paras 15.21-55) and notional capital (see paras 15.56-69). This section gives rules relating to all types of capital.

Your capital

15.2 If you are single, your own capital is taken into account. If you are in a couple, the capital of your partner is taken into account as well as yours. If you are in a polygamous marriage, the capital of all your partners is included. In this chapter, 'your' capital always includes the capital of your partner (or partners). But if a child or young person has capital of their own, this is never included.

How your capital affects your HB

15.3 If you are on a passport benefit (see para 13.5), all your capital is disregarded (ignored) and you qualify for maximum HB: see para 6.2.

15.4 If you are not on a passport benefit, some kinds of capital are counted and some are disregarded. The details are in this chapter. Once the amount of your capital is valued (see paras 15.21-27), it is taken into account as follows:

(a) if it is more than £16,000 you are not entitled to HB; otherwise

(b) the first £6,000 is ignored in working age HB claims;

(c) the first £10,000 is ignored in pension age HB claims;

(d) the remainder up to £16,000 is counted as providing you with an assumed amount of income (see para 15.5).

(See also para 13.15 if you are on the savings credit of SPC.)

15.1   HB 44(1); HB60+ 44(1); NIHB 41(1); NIHB60+ 42(1)

15.2   CBA 136(1); HB 25, 45; HB60+ 23; NICBA 132(1); NIHB 22, 42; NIHB60+ 21

15.3   HB sch 6 paras 5,6; HB60+ 26; NIHB sch 7 paras 5, 6; NIHB60+ 24

15.4   CBA 134(1); HB 43, 44(2), 52(1), sch 6; HB60+ 28, 29(2), 43, 44(2); NICBA 130(1), NIHB 40, 41(2), 49(1), sch 7; NIHB60+ 26, 27(2), 41, 42(2)

Assumed income from capital (tariff income)

15.5   The assumed income from your capital (apart from disregarded capital) is calculated as follows (in the law it is also called 'tariff income'):

(a)   in working age HB claims, deduct £6,000 from your capital and divide the remainder by 250;

(b)   in pension age HB claims, deduct £10,000 from your capital and divide the remainder by 500;

(c)   if the result of (a) or (b) is not an exact multiple of £1, round the result up to the next £1.

This gives the weekly amount of your assumed income from capital. It is added to your other income: see para 13.1. (For interest and other kinds of actual income from capital see para 15.26.)

Examples: Assessing capital and assumed income from capital

1. A working age HB claim

A single man in his 40s has £14,085 in his bank account when he claims HB. Of this, £2,000 is an insurance payment he received three weeks ago to replace his motorbike after an accident. He has no other capital.

Assessment:

■   The £2,000 is disregarded (see table 15.1(j))

■   So his capital for HB purposes is   £12,085

Assumed income from capital (tariff income):

■   From the £12,085, £6,000 is deducted leaving   £6,085

■   Dividing this by 250 gives   £24.34

■   Rounding up to the next whole pound gives   £25

■   So he has £25 per week of assumed income from capital

2. A pension age HB claim

A couple in their 80s have £15,085 in their bank account when they claim HB. Of this, £3,000 is arrears of disability living allowance they received three months ago after winning an appeal. They have no other capital.

Assessment:

■   The £3,000 is disregarded (see table 15.2)

■   So their capital for HB purposes is   £12,085

Assumed income from capital (tariff income):

■   From the £12,085, £10,000 is deducted leaving   £2,085

■   Dividing this by 500 gives   £4.17

■   Rounding up to the next whole pound gives   £5

■   So they have £5 per week of assumed income from capital

15.5   CBA 136(2); HB 27(1)(b), 52; HB60+ 30(2)(b); NICBA 132(2); NIHB 24(1)(b), 49; NIHB60+ 28(2)(b)

Distinguishing capital from income

15.6   HB law does not give a definition of capital or income. Instead the rules 'operate at a stage after the money has been classified' (CH/1561/2005). But the distinction is usually straightforward: see paras 15.7-13.

Capital you hold

15.7   DWP guidance says 'As a general rule, capital includes all categories of holdings which have a clear monetary value' (GM para BW1.70). The rules for savings, investments, property and other items are given later in this chapter, including when they count as your capital and when they are disregarded.

Capital someone else holds for you

15.8   If someone else holds your capital for you, it counts as yours. For example, this includes money held for you by the Court of Protection ([2011] UKUT 157 (AAC)) or by someone who has power of attorney for you.

Capital you hold for someone else

15.9   If you hold someone else's capital for them, it does not count as yours. For example, you might be looking after your child's savings for them, or someone you are caring for may have put your name on a joint bank account with them so you can deal with their money for them. It is up to you to provide evidence that the money is not yours, but you do not need to be a formally documented trustee for them ([2010] UKUT 437 (AAC)). (If you are a trustee, see para 15.41.)

Payments of income and capital

15.10   A payment you receive can be income (for example earnings or benefits) or capital (for example an inheritance). This is decided by looking at 'the true characteristics of the payment in the hands of the recipient' (in other words, what it is to you), rather than whether the person pays it you periodically or in a lump sum or whether they (or you) call it 'income' or 'capital' (Minter vs Hull City Council). DWP guidance says it is more likely to be capital if it is '(i) made without being tied to a period, (ii) made without being tied to any past payment, and (iii) not intended to form part of a series of payments' (GM para BW1.71).

Payments of arrears of income

15.11   A payment of arrears of income is assessed in both the following ways:

(a)   it is income for a past period, except when that kind of income is disregarded. This may mean you have been overpaid HB (see chapter 18);

(b)   it is capital from when you receive it until when you spend it. But arrears of some benefits are disregarded as capital for 52 weeks or longer (see para 15.52).

The fact that arrears of income can affect your capital does not stop them being income for a past period. For example a large lump sum settlement of an equal pay claim can be income for a past period if it is 'properly characterised as wages' (Minter vs Hull City Council).

15.10-11   Minter v Hull CC 13/10/11 CA [2011] EWCA Vic 1155 www.bailii.org/ew/cases/EWCA/Civ/2011/1155.html

15.11   HB 27(1), 31(1),(2), 44(1); HB60+ 30, 33(1),(6), 44(1); NIHB 24(1), 28(1),(2), 41(1); NIHB60+ 28, 31(1),(6), 42(1)

Payments of capital in instalments

15.12   If capital is payable to you in instalments, outstanding instalments are assessed as follows:

   (a)   in pension age HB claims, they do not count as your capital until you receive them;

   (b)   in working age HB claims, they count as your capital straight away (in other words even before you receive them). But if they would take your capital over £16,000, they count instead as your income.

When payments of income become capital

15.13   Income you do not spend becomes capital. 'A payment of income… remains income for the period in which it is paid. Any surplus at the end of that period metamorphoses into capital' (CH/1561/2005). This applies to counted income (for example earnings) and also to disregarded income (for example fostering allowances: CIS/3101/2007). So if your income is paid monthly, only what is left at the end of the month is capital. Different rules apply to arrears of income (see para 15.11).

Valuing capital

15.14   The value of each item of capital you have (apart from disregarded capital) is assessed by working through the following steps:

   (a)   start with its current market or surrender value (see para 15.15);

   (b)   then deduct 10% if selling it would involve costs (see para 15.16);

   (c)   then deduct any debt or charge secured against it (see para 15.17).

Further rules are in paras 15.18-20. See para 13.15 if you are on the savings credit of state pension credit.

Market or surrender value

15.15   Dwellings, non-residential property, and some other items have a market value. It is what they would fetch if you sold them on the open market. Your council can ask the Valuation Office Agency to assist them in valuing these (forms for this are in GM BW1 annexes D and E, and further DWP guidance is in circular A25/2009). Insurance policies and some other investments have a surrender value. It is what you would be paid if you cashed them in now. For cash in a bank account see para 15.22.

Sales costs

15.16   If selling a capital item would mean you had to pay a fee or other costs, 10% is deducted from its value. For example this applies to property and shares. You do not have to work out what the actual sales costs would be. Instead, the 10% deduction always applies.

15.12   HB 41(1), 44(1), sch 6 para 18; HB60+ 44(1); NIHB 38(1), 41(1), sch 7 para 19; NIHB60+ 42(1)

15.14   HB 47; HB60+ 45; NIHB 44; NIHB60+ 43

15.15   HB 47; HB60+ 45; NIHB 44; NIHB60+ 43

15.16   HB 47(a); HB60+ 45(a); NIHB 44(a); NIHB60+ 43(a)

Secured debts or charges

15.17   Any debt or charge secured against a capital item is deducted from its value. For example this includes the outstanding mortgage on a property. Only secured debts and charges can be deducted (the law calls them 'encumbrances'). Other debts (such as rent arrears) cannot be deducted from your capital (CH/3729/2007).

Jointly owned capital

15.18   If you own a capital item jointly with one or more other people (other than just your partner), only your share of its capital value is taken into account. This means:

(a) your actual share if you own it in known shares (for example if you own a one-third share and another person owns a two-thirds share): R(IS) 4/03;

(b) an equal share in other cases (for example one-half if there are two of you).

Your share is valued as described in paras 15.14-16. The reason your share is valued rather than the whole item, is that the value of a half-share (for example) can be less than half the value of the whole item. In some cases the value of a share of capital can be minimal (CH/1953/2003).

Examples: Valuing capital

1. Shares in a company

A woman owns 1000 shares. Their sell price is currently £0.78 each.

■ Their market value is 1,000 x £0.78	£780
■ Deduct 10% for sales costs	£78
■ Their value for HB purposes is	£702

2. Jointly owned land

Three brothers jointly own some land in equal shares. It is worth £35,000, but the value of a one-third share is £10,500. One brother claims HB. He took out a loan using his share of the land as security and £5,400 of the loan remains to be paid.

■ The market value of his share is	£10,500
■ Deduct 10% for sales costs	£1,050
■ Deduct the loan	£5,400
■ The value of his share for HB purposes is	£4,050

Capital outside the UK

15.19   If you own capital in a country outside the UK:

(a) its market or surrender value in that country is taken into account (see also para 15.20);

(b) but if you are prohibited (by that country) from bringing the money to the UK, it is valued at what a willing buyer in the UK would give for it.

In each case steps (b) and (c) in para 15.14 then apply.

15.17   HB 47(b); HB60+ 45(b); NIHB 44(b); NIHB60+ 43(b)

15.18   HB 51; HB60+ 49; NIHB 48; NIHB60+ 47

15.19   HB 48; HB60+ 46; NIHB 45; NIHB60+ 44

Capital not in sterling

15.20   If you have capital in a currency other than sterling, any commission for converting it to sterling is disregarded.

Savings and investments

15.21   This section gives the rules for savings and various kinds of investment. (For property and possessions, see paras 15.28-35.)

Savings and cash

15.22   Your savings are counted in full as your capital whether you keep them as cash or in a bank, and interest is included as capital from when it is due. But if you have more than one bank account, and the bank has the power to use money in one to pay an overdraft on another, it is the net amount (across those accounts) which is counted: [2011] UKUT 63 (AAC). See also para 15.13 if your income is paid into an account.

Savings certificates

15.23   National Savings and Ulster Savings certificates count in full as your capital. You can find out their current value using an online calculator, and the DWP says your council should use this to value them (GM BW1.440-451).

Shares and similar investments

15.24   Shares, unit trusts, income bonds and similar investments count in full as your capital. Shares and unit trusts are valued at their current 'sell' price. Then 10% is deducted for sales costs in the case of shares (see para 15.16), but not normally unit trusts because their sell price usually already allows for this.

Pension schemes, annuities, life insurance and funeral plans

15.25   Capital held in the following is wholly disregarded:

   (a)   an occupational or personal pension scheme (see para 13.27);

   (b)   an annuity (see paras 13.32-33);

   (c)   a life insurance policy, including a bond or similar investment which has a life insurance element (R(IS) 7/98), including compensation paid by the UK government (£5,000) to holders of Equitable Life pre-1992 policies (HB G10/2013);

   (d)   in pension age HB claims, a funeral plan contract if its sole purpose is to provide a funeral in the UK for you and/or your partner.

15.20   HB sch 6 para 23; HB60+ sch 6 para 23; NIHB sch 7 para 24; NIHB60+ sch 7 para 23

15.22   HB 44(1); HB60+ 44(1); NIHB 41(1); NIHB60+ 42(1)

15.23   HB 44(1); HB60+ 44(1); NIHB 41(1); NIHB60+ 42(1)

15.24   HB 44(1), 47(a); HB60+ 44(1), 45(a); NIHB 41(1), 44(a); NIHB60+ 42(1), 43(a)

15.25   SI 2013 No 2980 reg 5; HB 2(1) definition – 'policy of life insurance', sch 6 paras 13,17,32; HB60+ 2(1), sch 6 paras 11,12,24,29; NIHB 2(1), sch 7 paras 13,18,31A,33; NIHB60+ 2(1), sch 7 paras 11,12,24,31,31A

Their surrender value is also disregarded (this means what you would get if you cashed them in), but capital you actually receive from them (if you do cash in part or all) is counted in full.

Interest and other actual income from capital

15.26   Interest you receive on a bank account, and other kinds of actual income you receive on capital, are counted as increasing your capital from when they are due. (They are not counted as income, because instead there are rules about assumed income from capital: see para 15.5.) But see tables 13.7 and 13.8 if you receive rent on property you have let out, and para 15.33 for income you receive on business assets.

The value of your right to receive an asset in the future or future income

15.27   Your right to receive an asset in the future or the income from some investments can be sold (the purchaser would receive the income in the future instead of you), so it has a capital value. But this capital value is disregarded in the case of reversionary interest, occupational and personal pensions, annuities, rent, a life interest or life rent (see table 15.1(g)) for a reversionary interest and para 15.31 for life interest/life rent, and any kind of income you cannot bring to the UK (see para 13.44).

Property and possessions

15.28   This section gives the rules for property, money relating to property, personal possessions, and business assets. (For property held in a trust see paras 15.37-40.)

Property

15.29   The rules about property apply to dwellings and non-residential premises. Your home and some other property is disregarded: see the first part of table 15.1. Property which is not disregarded is counted as your capital. Its value is assessed as described in paras 15.14-20. If you have rented it out, this is taken into account in valuing it. For example the presence of a sitting tenant can reduce the value of a dwelling (CH/1953/2003). If ownership of a property is in dispute, it may have no value until the dispute is settled.

Money relating to property

15.30   Money for buying, repairing or improving a home can be disregarded: see the second part of table 15.1. If you receive rent on a property you have let out, see table 13.8.

15.26   HB 46(4); HB60+ 29(1)(i), sch 5 paras 22,24; NIHB 43(4); NIHB60+ 27(1)(g), sch 6 paras 23,25

15.27   HB sch 6 paras 7,13,15,16,31,33; HB60+ sch 6 paras 5,24,27-29; NIHB sch 7 paras 7,13,16,17,32,34; NIHB60+ sch 7 paras 5,24,29-31

15.29   HB 44, sch 6; HB60+ 44(1),(2), sch 6; NIHB 41, sch 7; NIHB60+ 42(1),(2), sch 7

15.30   HB sch 6; HB60+ sch 6; NIHB sch 7; NIHB60+ sch 7

Table 15.1 **Capital disregards relating to property**

Your home and other property

Working age and pension age HB claims: disregards (a) to (g)

In (a) to (e) only one dwelling can be a person's home at any one time. In (a) to (c) there is no time limit.

(a) Your home, and any land or buildings (including croft land in Scotland) which are part of it or are impracticable to sell separately. For example, your home is disregarded if you are a shared owner, or an owner claiming HB for rates in Northern Ireland, or are claiming HB temporarily on other accommodation (see paras 3.12, 3.23).

(b) The home of a partner or 'relative' (see para 7.71) of yours or of anyone in your family, if that partner/relative:

■   has reached state pension credit age (see para 1.24); or

■   is 'incapacitated'. This word has its ordinary English meaning. For example it is not limited to people on ESA or similar benefits.

(c) The home of your partner if:

■   you have not divorced, dissolved your civil partnership or become estranged (in other words your relationship has not ended: CH/3777/2007); but

■   you no longer count as a couple (or polygamous marriage) for HB purposes (see para 4.10).

(d) A home you intend to occupy if:

■   you acquired it within the past 26 weeks*; or

■   you are taking steps to obtain possession of it, and first sought legal advice about this or began legal proceedings within the past 26 weeks*; or

■   you are carrying out essential repairs or alterations to make it fit for occupation or re-occupation, and began doing so within the past 26 weeks*.

(e) Your former home, and any land or buildings (including croft land in Scotland) which are part of it or are impracticable to sell separately, if:

■   you ceased to occupy it because you have divorced, dissolved your civil partnership or become estranged from your partner (in other words your relationship has ended: CH/117/2005 and CH/3777/2007); and either

---

T15.1   HB 44(2), sch 6; HB60+ 44(2), sch 6; NIHB 41(2), sch 7; NIHB60+ 42(2), sch 7

T15.1(a)   HB sch 6 para 1; HB60+ sch 6 para 26; NIHB sch 7 para 1; NIHB60+ sch 7 para 26

T15.1(b)   HB sch 6 para 4(a); HB60+ sch 6 para 4(a); NIHB sch 7 para 4(a); NIHB60+ sch 7 para 4(a)

T15.1(c)   HB sch 6 para 4(b); HB60+ sch 6 para 4(b); NIHB sch 7 para 4(b); NIHB60+ sch 7 para 4(b)

T15.1(d)   HB sch 6 paras 2, 27, 28; HB60+ sch 6 paras 1-3; NIHB sch 7 paras 2, 28,29; NIHB60+ sch 7 paras 1-3

T15.1(e)   HB sch 6 para 25; HB60+ sch 6 para 6; NIHB sch 7 para 26; NIHB60+ sch 7 para 6

■ you are a lone parent and live in it as your home (in this case there is no time limit); or

■ you ceased to occupy it within the past 26 weeks (this time limit cannot be extended).

(f) A home and any other premises you are taking reasonable steps to dispose of, and began doing so within the past 26 weeks*.

(g) Any property you will not own until a future event occurs (for example you reach a particular age). This is called a 'reversionary interest'. (But for a life interest/life rent see para 15.31.)

Money relating to property

Working age HB claims: disregards (h) to (m)

(h) Money which:

■ is from the sale of your former home (including compensation for compulsory purchase – but excluding any home loss payment – as well as money from the sale itself); or

■ was deposited with a housing association as a condition of occupying your home, and which you intend to use for buying a house within the next 26 weeks*. This disregard does not apply if you haven't yet decided what to do with the money (CH/2255/2006).

(i) A local authority grant you received as a council tenant within the past 26 weeks*, for:

■ buying a home; or

■ carrying out repairs or alterations to make a future home fit for occupation.

(j) Insurance or compensation payments you received within the past 26 weeks* for repairs or replacements following loss or damage to your home or personal possessions.

(k) Any other payments received within the past 26 weeks* solely for essential repairs or improvements to your home.

(l) Money deposited with a housing association as a condition of occupying your home.

(m) Tax refunds for interest on a mortgage, or on a loan for home repairs or improvements.

T15.1(f)   HB sch 6 para 26; HB60+ sch 6 para 7; NIHB sch 7 para 27; NIHB60+ sch 7 para 7

T15.1(g)   HB sch 6 para 7; NIHB sch 7 para 7

T15.1(h)   HB sch 6 paras 3,11(b); NIHB sch 7 paras 3,11(b)

T15.1(i)   HB sch 6 para 38; NIHB sch 7 para 39

T15.1(j)   HB sch 6 para 10(a); NIHB sch 7 para 10(a)

T15.1(k)   HB sch 6 para 10(b);;NIHB sch 7 para 10(b);

T15.1(l)   HB sch 6 para 11(a); NIHB sch 7 para 11(a)

T15.1(m) HB sch 6 para 21; NIHB sch 7 para 22

Pension age HB claims: disregards (n) to (p)

(n)   Any money paid to you (or deposited in your name) within the past year for the sole purpose of buying a home. For example this can include money from the sale of your former home, compensation for compulsory purchase, local authority grants, and gifts or loans from relatives or friends.

(o)   Insurance or compensation payments you received within the past year for repairs or replacements following loss or damage to your home or personal possessions.

(p)   Any other payments you received within the past year solely for essential repairs or improvements to your home or a future home.

Extending the 26-week time limits

*   The time limits marked with an asterisk can be extended if it is reasonable to do so in the circumstances. But the time limit in (h) is not extended if your only reason for needing longer is that you are taking a hard line in negotiations about your share of the money from the sale of your home (CH/2255/2006).

Examples: Property

1. The home of a relative

A man owns a house where his mother lives. She is aged 87. He claims HB on the flat he is renting.

■   The value of the house is disregarded: see table 15.1(b).

2. A couple end their relationship

A couple jointly own a house where they live with their school-age children. They decide to end their relationship. The man moves out and rents a flat. He claims HB there. The woman remains in the home with the children.

■   His share of the value of the house is disregarded: see table 15.1(e).

3. A new partner moves in

Nine months after the man moved out (see example 2) the woman's new partner moves in with her and the children.

■   The man's share of the value of the house is no longer disregarded, because the woman is no longer a lone parent and because more than 26 weeks have passed since he moved out: see table 15.1(e).

4. The house is put up for sale

The former partners (see examples 2 and 3) decide to sell the house. They put it on the market.

■   The man's share of the value of the house is disregarded for 26 weeks, or longer if this is reasonable to allow a sale to take place: see table 15.1(f)

T15.1(n) HB60+ sch 6 paras 18,20(a); NIHB60+ sch 7 paras 18,20(a)

T15.1(o)   HB60+ sch 6 paras 18,19; NIHB60+ sch 7 paras 18,19

T15.1(p)   HB60+ sch 6 paras 18,20(b); NIHB60+ sch 7 paras 18,20(b)

5. Money for buying a home

A woman sells her home and moves to a rented flat in a new area while she looks for a new property to buy. She claims HB on the flat. She has £240,000 from the sale, and a further £50,000 which her brother gave her towards a new home.

■ If she is over state pension credit age, both these amounts are disregarded for one year, but no longer: see table 15.1(n).

■ If she is under state pension credit age, only the money from the sale is disregarded, and only for 26 weeks or longer if reasonable: see table 15.1(h).

6. A property which is rented out

A couple own a house which is rented out to tenants through an agency. The house has a market value of £200,000 and there is an outstanding mortgage on it of £175,000. They claim HB on a flat they are renting.

■ The market value of the house is £200,000.

■ Deduct 10% for sales costs, leaving £180,000.

■ Deduct the outstanding mortgage, leaving £5,000.

■ This £5,000 is their capital for HB purposes.

■ The rent they receive on the house also counts as their capital (not income), after allowing for the mortgage interest, agency fees, and other outgoings they pay on it: see table 13.8(b).

Life interest and life rent

15.31 If you have a life interest (or in Scotland a life rent) in property or any other asset, this means you have the right to use it until you die, or someone else dies. Unless the property or other asset is disregarded (see for example table 15.1), the value of the life interest or life rent (if it has a value) is counted as your capital.

Personal possessions

15.32 The value of your personal possessions is disregarded. This means any physical assets apart from land, property and business assets (R(H)7/08). Payments for loss or damage to your personal possessions are also disregarded (see table 15.1(j) and (o)). But in working age claims, personal possessions you bought with the purpose of gaining HB are counted as your capital (see para 15.63).

Self-employed business assets

15.33 If you are self-employed (see para 14.27) your business assets are disregarded:

(a) while you are self-employed;

15.31   HB 44(1); HB60+ 44(1); NIHB 42(1); NIHB60+ 42(1)

15.32   HB sch 6 para 12; HB60+ sch 6 para 8; NIHB sch 7 para 12; NIHB60+ sch 7 para 8

15.33   HB sch 6 para 8(1),(2); HB60+ sch 6 paras 9,10; NIHB sch 7 para 8(1),(2); NIHB60+ sch 7 paras 9,10

(b) if you are not self-employed because of sickness or disability but intend to return to the self-employment, for 26 weeks, or longer if you reasonably need longer to return;

(c) if you have ceased to be self-employed, for as long as you reasonably need to dispose of the assets.

'Business assets' means assets held in the course of your self-employment (CH/4258/2004). Business capital is disregarded (as a business asset) if it is 'part of the fund employed and risked in the business' (R (SB) 4/85 para 11), which is unlikely to be the case unless you keep it separate from your personal savings. But income you receive on your business assets counts as part of your self-employed earnings (see para 14.28).

Company ownership

15.34   If you are a company owner the full value of the company is counted as your capital. If you are in a partnership, this means your share of the full value. The value of a company is always at least equal to the value of all its assets minus the sum of all its liabilities. (Your income counts as your employed earnings: see para 14.6.)

15.35   You are counted as having notional capital (see paras 15.56-58) if:

(a) you are not the owner of a company or a partner in it; and

(b) you are not engaged in activities in the course of the company's business; but

(c) your involvement in the company is equivalent to ownership or partnership.

Your notional capital is assessed as in para 15.34, and the value of your actual interest in the company is disregarded.

Trusts and compensation

15.36   This section gives the rules for trusts, personal injury payments, and other compensation and gallantry payments. (For compensation relating to property and possessions see table 15.1.)

Trusts

15.37   Assets held in a trust, such as cash, investments or property are:

(a) legally owned by the trustees (or trustee) of the trust; and

(b) beneficially owned by the beneficiary (or beneficiaries) of the trust.

The trustees have a duty to use the assets under the terms of the trust for the benefit of the beneficiary, for example by making payments to them. Paras 15.38-41 explain how this is assessed.

If you are a beneficiary of a trust

15.38   Capital held in a trust for you counts in full as your capital, but see para 15.39 for exceptions. If you are not the only beneficiary of the trust, it is your share of the capital which is taken into account (see para 15.18).

15.34   HB 44(1); HB60+ 44(1); NIHB 41(1); NIHB60+ 42(1)

15.35   HB 49(5),(6);HB60+ 47(3),(4);NIHB 46(5),(6);NIHB60+ 45(3),(4)

15.38   HB 44(1); HB60+ 44(1); NIHB 41(1); NIHB60+ 42(1)

15.39   Capital held in a trust for you is disregarded:

(a) if you cannot obtain it until a particular event occurs, for example when you reach a certain age (this is called a 'reversionary' trust); or

(b) if it relates to a personal injury (see para 15.43); or

(c) in pension age HB claims if:

■   it is property, and

■   the trustees make payments to you, or could do so.

15.40   If you receive a payment of capital from a trust (whether the capital in the trust itself is counted or disregarded):

(a) it is disregarded if any of the disregards in this chapter apply to it (see for example table 15.1(k), (n) and (p));

(b) otherwise it counts in full as your capital.

For payments of income from a trust see para 13.36.

If you are a trustee of a trust

15.41   Capital you hold as a trustee is wholly disregarded. But to count as a trustee it is not enough just to say that you are holding money (or other assets) for someone else, or plan to give it to them. You must have received it on clearly stated terms requiring you to hold it for them, or you must have clearly and consistently expressed that you hold it for them and have given up all intentions of using it for yourself (R(IS)1/90). If you meet these conditions it is not necessary for the trust to be legally documented ([2012] UKUT 115 (AAC)).

Government sponsored trust funds

15.42   Any payment of capital or income you receive from the following is disregarded:

(a) the Independent Living Funds (which help severely disabled people live independently);

(b) the Macfarlane Trusts, the Eileen Trust, 'the Fund', and MFET Ltd (for people with HIV from blood and other NHS products);

(c) the Skipton Fund and the Caxton Fund (for people with hepatitis C from blood products);

(d) the Variant Creutzfeldt-Jacob Disease Trust (for people with vCJD and their families); and

(e) the London Bombings Relief Charitable Fund (for victims of the bombings on 7th July 2005 and their families).

The disregards in (a), (b), (c) and (e) have no time limit. The disregard in (d) has no time limit if the payment is to the person with vCJD or their partner or surviving partner, but is limited to two years if it is to a parent or guardian of a child with vCJD. The disregards in (b) to (e) can continue if the payment is passed on to a relative as a gift or inheritance (but the usual HB definition of 'relative' does not always apply here). For further details see GM para BW2.620.

15.39   HB sch 6 paras 7,14; HB60+ sch 6 para 30; NIHB sch 7 paras 7,14; NIHB60+ sch 7 para 32

15.40   HB 44; HB60+ 44(1),(2); NIHB 41; NIHB60+ 42(1),(2)

15.42   HB 2(1) definitions – 'Independent Living Fund' etc, sch 5 para 35, sch 6 paras 24, 34, 55; HB60+ 2(1), 29(1), sch 6 paras 14,16,30; NIHB 2(1), sch 6 para 37, sch 7 paras 25,35,52; NIHB60+ 2(1), 27(1), sch 7 paras 14,16,32

Personal injury payments

15.43   The following payments of capital are disregarded if they relate to a personal injury you or your partner have had:

   (a) damages for personal injury which are:

   ■ held by a court and administered by it, or

   ■ held by someone else and can only be used under a court order or direction;

   (b) any payment for personal injury which is held in a trust; and

   (c) any other payment for personal injury except for capital paid to you by a trust (but see para 15.40(a)).

The disregards in (a) and (b) have no time limit. The disregard in (c) has no time limit in pension age HB claims, but in working age HB claims it is limited to 52 weeks from the day you receive the first or only payment. (It does not start again if you receive a further payment for that injury.) The 52 weeks is called a 'grace period' because it should give you time to form a trust to hold the money (see (b) above) or invest it in an annuity (see para 15.25(b)).

15.44   Payments of income you receive for a personal injury to you or your partner are wholly disregarded. For example this includes income paid to you by a trust or from an annuity in which a personal injury payment was invested. In pension age HB claims, payments of income are also disregarded if they are paid to you by order of a court for a personal injury to your child.

Payments compensating for death of a parent

15.45   If you are under 18, compensation you receive for the death of a parent is wholly disregarded if it is held by a court and administered by it, or held by someone else and can only be used under a court order or direction.

Examples: Personal injury payments

1. A working age HB claim

A woman in her 20s is awarded £500,000 for a personal injury. It is paid into her bank account.

   ■ This is disregarded for 52 weeks (see para 15.43(c)).

Five months later a trust is formed, with her parents and solicitor as the trustees and her as the beneficiary. The whole of the personal injury payment is paid into the trust.

   ■ This is now disregarded without time limit (see para 15.43(b)).

The trust pays her an income of £70 per week.

   ■ This is disregarded in the assessment of her income (see para 15.44).

15.43   HB sch 6 paras 14, 14A, 45, 46; HB60+ sch 6 para 17; NIHB sch 7 paras 14,15,45; NIHB60+ sch 7 para 17

15.44   HB sch 5 para 14(1)(c)-(e); HB60+ sch 5 paras 14,15; NIHB sch 6 para 14(1)(c)-(e); NIHB60+ sch 6 paras 15,16

15.45   HB sch 6 para 45, 46; NIHB sch 7 para 45

The trust later pays her a lump sum of £15,000 for the cost of adapting her home to improve wheelchair access.

- ■ This is disregarded for 26 weeks, or longer if this is reasonable, to allow the work to take place (see para 15.40(a) and table 15.1(k)).

2. A pension age HB claim

A man in his 70s is awarded £500,000 for a personal injury. It is paid into his bank account.

- ■ This is disregarded without time limit (see para 15.43(c)).

Second World War payments

15.46   Payments of compensation are wholly disregarded if they were paid because you, your partner, or your or your partner's deceased husband, wife or civil partner:

(a) were a slave labourer or forced labourer; or

(b) suffered property loss or personal injury; or

(c) were a parent of a child who died; or

(d) were imprisoned or interned by the Japanese

during the Second World War. There is no time limit. The disregard in (d) is always £10,000 (which is the standard amount paid in these cases), and £10,000 is disregarded from the total of your capital without any time limit (so you do not need to keep track of the money).

The families of the disappeared

15.47   In Northern Ireland, compensation paid to the families of the disappeared is disregarded for 52 weeks from the date of payment.

Gallantry payments

15.48   Payments you receive as a holder of the Victoria Cross or George Cross, and similar payments, are wholly disregarded:

(a) in working age HB claims in the assessment of both your income and your capital;

(b) in pension age HB claims in the assessment of your income.

Other capital

15.49   This section gives the rules for benefits which are paid as a lump sum, arrears of benefits, charitable and voluntary payments, loans, and other kinds of capital.

Benefits paid as a lump sum

15.50   Lump sum payments of the following are wholly disregarded:

(a) social fund payments (winter fuel payments, cold weather payments, Sure Start maternity grant and funeral expenses payment);

15.46   HB sch 6 paras 54, 56; HB60+ sch 6 paras 13,15; NIHB sch 7 paras 51,53; NIHB60+ sch 7 paras 13,15

15.47   NIHB sch 7 para 58; NIHB60+ sch 7 para 27

15.48   HB sch 5 para 10, sch 6 para 47; HB60+ 29(1); NIHB sch 6 para 11, sch 7 para 46; NIHB60+ 27(1)

(b) government and related payments to disabled people to help with obtaining or retaining employment;

(c) payments from government work programme training schemes;

(d) in working age HB claims

- adoption payments,

- special guardianship payments,

- payments to avoid taking children into care, and

- payments to care leavers;

(e) community care payments;

(f) direct care payments;

(g) supporting people payments;

(h) 'local welfare provision'; and

(i) discretionary housing payments.

All are also disregarded as income.

15.51   Bereavement payment is paid as a lump sum. It counts in full as capital.

Arrears of benefits and compensation relating to benefits

15.52   Table 15.2 explains when the capital value of arrears of benefits is disregarded. The same rules apply to payments compensating for non-payment of the benefits. Arrears of benefits not included in the table are taken into account as described in para 15.11.

Table 15.2 **Capital disregards: arrears of benefits**

(a) Disregarded arrears

Arrears of all the following are disregarded when your capital is assessed:

- income-based JSA

- income-related ESA

- income support

- state pension credit (both guarantee credit and savings credit)

- universal credit

- WTC and CTC

15.50(a)	HB sch 6 para 20; HB60+ sch 6 paras 18, 21(1),(2)(n); NIHB sch 7 para 21; NIHB60+ sch 7 paras 18, 21(1),(2)(m)
15.50(b)	HB sch 6 paras 43, 44; NIHB sch 7 para 44
15.50(c)	HB 46(7),(8), sch 6 paras A2,A3, 8(3),(4), 35,49,52,55; NIHB 43(7),(8), sch 7 paras 8(3),(4), 36,48,52
15.50(d)	HB sch 6 paras 19,19A,59,60; NIHB sch 7 paras 20,20A,56,57
15.50(e),(f)	HB sch 6 para 58; HB60+ sch 6 para 26D; NIHB sch 7 para 55; NIHB60+ sch 7 para 28C
15.50(g)	HB sch 6 para 57; HB60+ sch 6 paras 18,21(1)(e); NIHB sch 7 para 54; NIHB60+ sch 7 paras 18,21(1)(e)
15.50(h)	HB sch 6 para 20A; HB60+ sch 6 paras 18,21(1)(f)
15.50(i)	HB sch 6 para 9(1)(d); HB60+ sch 6 paras 18,21(1),(2)(k); NIHB sch 7 para 9(1)(d); NIHB60+ sch 7 paras 18,21(1),(2)(j)
15.51	HB 44(1); HB60+ 29(1)(j)(xiii), 44(1); NIHB 41(1); NIHB60+ 27(1)(h)(xi), 42(1)

- disability living allowance (DLA)
- personal independence payment (PIP)
- attendance allowance (AA)
- benefits equivalent to attendance allowance (see para 13.22)
- HB and the former council tax benefit (but not council tax rebates)
- discretionary housing payments (see table 13.5(k))

(b) Standard time limit

The disregard lasts for 52 weeks in working age HB claims, and one year in pension age HB claims, in each case beginning with the day you received the arrears.

(c) Extended time limit

If the arrears:

- are £5,000 or more;
- are paid while you are on HB; and
- are because you were underpaid due to official error (see para 17.63),

the disregard continues for as long as you or your partner remain continuously on HB (including periods one of you remains continuously on HB after the other one's death).

(d) Arrears of war disablement and bereavement pensions

Arrears of the war disablement and bereavement pensions in table 13.4(a) are disregarded:

- for 52 weeks in working age HB claims (the extended time limit does not apply);
- without time limit in pension age HB claims.

Note: The rules in (a) to (c) above also apply to payments compensating for non-payment of the benefits.

Charitable and voluntary payments

15.53   Payments of capital you receive which are charitable and/or voluntary are counted as your capital. But in working age HB claims, payments in kind (in other words in goods not money) are disregarded. For payments of income see para 13.30.

Loans

15.54   Money which was loaned to you (and which you still have) is counted as your capital. But in pension age HB claims, loans for buying a home are disregarded (see table 15.1(n)). And the following count as income, not capital:

(a)   student loans (see para 22.23);

(b)   in working age HB claims, career development loans (see table 13.9(n));

(c)   in pension age HB claims, payments from an equity release scheme (see para 13.34).

T15.2   CBA 123 definition – 'income related benefit'; HB 46(9), sch 6 paras 9,-37,39; HB60+ 44(3), sch 6 paras 18, 21(1)(a)-(d),(2), 22, 26B; NICBA 122; NIHB 43(8); sch 7 paras 9,38,40; NIHB60+ 42(3), sch 7 paras 18, 21(1)(a)-(d),(2), 22,28A

15.53   HB 44(1), 46(6), sch 6 para 34; HB60+ 44(1); NIHB 41(1), 43(6), sch 7 para 35; NIHB60+ 42(1)

Other loans can be counted as income if the council has clear evidence that they should be (R(IS) 6/03, CH/2675/2007). This is likely to mean that (c) above also applies in working age HB claims.

Other kinds of capital

15.55   If you have any other kind of capital, it is counted in full. But for payments you receive as an earner see chapter 14, and for payments you receive as a student see chapter 22.

Notional capital

15.56   This section explains when you are counted as having capital you do not in fact have. This is called 'notional capital'.

Types of notional capital

15.57   In working age HB claims, you can be counted as having notional capital when:

   (a) you have deprived yourself of capital (see paras 15.60-62);

   (b) there is capital available to you (see paras 13.50 and 13.52);

   (c) you are paid capital on behalf of someone else (see paras 13.53 and 13.55);

   (d) someone else is paid capital on your behalf (see paras 13.54-55);

   (e) a non-dependant has more income and capital than you (see para 13.57); or

   (f) you are counted as a company owner or partner (see para 15.35).

15.58   In pension age HB claims, you can be counted as having notional capital when:

   (a) you have deprived yourself of capital (see paras 15.60-62);

   (b) a non-dependant has more income and capital than you (see para 13.57);

   (c) you are counted as a company owner or partner (see para 15.35).

Assessing notional capital

15.59   If you are counted as having notional capital, it is assessed in the same way as actual capital. All the rules and disregards given earlier in this chapter apply. This means this section does not apply if you are on a passport benefit (except as described in table 15.3(e)).

Capital you have deprived yourself of

15.60   If you have deprived yourself of capital, it is counted as your notional capital. To 'deprive' yourself of capital means:

   (a) you have disposed of it (for example by spending it or giving or lending it to someone); and

   (b) your purpose in doing so was to make yourself entitled to HB, or to more HB (we use 'gain HB' to cover both these).

This is called the 'deprivation of capital rule'.

15.55   HB 44(1); HB60+ 44(1); NIHB 41(1); NIHB60+ 42(1)

15.59   HB 49(7); HB60+ 47(5); NIHB 46(7); NIHB60+ 45(5)

15.60   HB 49(1); HB60+ 47(1); NIHB 46(1); NIHB60+ 45(1)

15.61   Table 15.3 explains how the rule works. See paras 15.62-64 for exceptions and further details. See paras 15.59 and 15.65-69 for how notional capital is assessed and how it gradually reduces.

Exceptions

15.62   In pension age HB claims, the deprivation of capital rule does not apply to capital you have used to:

(a) buy goods or services which are reasonable in your circumstances; or

(b) repay or reduce a debt you owe.

In working age and pension age HB claims, the rule does not apply if you are on a passport benefit, except as described in table 15.3(e).

Table 15.3 **Deprivation of capital: case law**

This table is about the deprivation of capital rule (see paras 15.60-62).

(a) *The test of purpose:* To count as depriving yourself of capital, 'the test is one of purpose'. Gaining HB must have formed 'a positive part of your planning'. [2011] UKUT 500 (AAC).

(b) *Thinking about the consequences:* You can only count as depriving yourself if you knew what you were doing. If you did not think about the consequences, you cannot have acted with the purpose of gaining HB. [2011] UKUT 500 (AAC).

(c) *Your personal circumstances:* Your mental state and capabilities are taken into account. A schizophrenic man without an appointee, who lived in 'an intolerable level of chaos', spent almost all of a big windfall on 'alcohol and high living'. He did not count as depriving himself, because it was not shown that he appreciated what he was doing or what the consequences would be. R(H)1/06.

(d) *Mixed motives:* If you had some other reason for disposing of capital (which is 'almost always' the case), you count as depriving yourself of it if gaining HB was 'a significant operative purpose' of doing so. This includes looking at 'whether, given [your] knowledge, it was reasonable in all the circumstances' to act as you did, bearing in mind your obligations (for example, to support yourself, and to other people). [2009] UKUT 145 (AAC) para 9, which cited CJSA/1425/2005 para 40.

(e) *Passport benefits and HB:* If you deprived yourself of capital to gain a passport benefit, you also count as depriving yourself to gain HB if you plainly expected that getting the passport benefit would lead to getting HB. [2009] UKUT 145 (AAC) para 3.

(f) *Buying an asset whose capital value is disregarded:* Even if what you bought is disregarded, you count as depriving yourself if your purpose was gaining HB (see para 15.63). [2009] UKUT 145 (AAC) para 16, which cited R(SB) 40/85 and R(IS) 8/04.

15.62   HB60+ 47(2); NIHB60+ 45(2)

(g) *Buying personal possessions:* In working age HB claims, if you bought a personal possession with the purpose of gaining HB (in this case, a caravan) its value counts as actual (not notional) capital (see para 15.63). [2009] UKUT 145 (AAC) para 16.

(h) *Providing receipts:* If you are asked to provide receipts for capital you have spent, this 'is primarily to enable [the council] to be satisfied the money has not been retained' (see para 15.63). But it 'can also form the basis as to the reasonableness of the expenditure'. [2009] UKUT 145 (AAC) para 12.

(i) *Seeking to recover the money:* It is irrelevant whether you seek to recover money you deprived yourself of. (In this case, a bankrupt claimant's receiver did not do so.) [2009] UKUT 96 (AAC).

Distinguishing notional capital from actual capital

15.63   In general terms, capital you have is your actual capital, and capital you disposed of to gain HB is your notional capital. The Upper Tribunal has summarised the following possibilities ([2009] UKUT 145 (AAC) paras 16, 19):

(a) if you have spent capital on an item which counts as capital (for example shares), the item is your actual capital;

(b) if you have spent capital with the purpose of gaining HB (and (a) does not apply), this is your notional capital;

(c) the exception to (b) is that in working age HB claims, if you bought personal possessions with the purpose of gaining HB, they are counted as your actual capital;

(d) if you spent capital without the purpose of gaining HB (and (a) does not apply), this is neither actual nor notional capital;

(e) if you say you have spent capital but in fact you still have it (for example in an undisclosed bank account), this is your actual capital.

For pension age HB claims, see also para 15.62.

15.64   There are also differences in other situations. For example:

(a) if one person holds capital on behalf of another, there are rules about whether it is your actual capital (see paras 15.8-9);

(b) the exception is that in working age HB claims, if one person is paid capital on behalf of another, there are rules about whether it is your notional capital (see paras 13.53-55).

15.63   HB 44, 49(1), sch 6 para 12; HB60+ 44(1),(2), 47(1),(2); NIHB 41, 46(1), sch 7 para 12; NIHB60+ 42(1),(2), 45(1),(2)

How notional capital reduces

15.65 If you have notional capital because of the deprivation of capital rule (see paras 15.60-62), your notional capital reduces each week: see paras 15.66-69. This is called the 'diminishing notional capital rule'. It is illustrated in the example.

The amount of the reduction

15.66 The reduction equals the amount of HB and other benefits you have lost as a result of having notional capital: see paras 15.67-69. But the only benefits taken into account are HB, JSA(IB), ESA(IR), IS, SPC and (for periods before 1st April 2013) council tax benefit. If the figures for these (apart from HB) relate to a part-week, they are converted to a weekly equivalent.

15.67 In weeks in which you qualify for HB, the reduction equals the amount you have lost in that particular week.

15.68 In weeks in which you do not qualify for HB, the reduction is made at a fixed rate. This equals the amount you lost in the most recent of the following weeks:

(a) the week your notional capital was first taken into account; or

(b) the first week you did not qualify for HB; or

(c) any week in which the fixed rate is recalculated (see para 15.69).

15.69 The fixed rate is recalculated only if you make a new unsuccessful claim for HB (in other words you claim but do not qualify for HB) at least 26 weeks after the fixed rate was:

(a) first calculated (see para 15.68(a) or (b)); or

(b) most recently recalculated (as described in this paragraph).

The new fixed rate is then used if it is higher than (or equal to) the old fixed rate. If it is lower, the old fixed rate continues (but this still counts as a recalculation for (b) above). The fixed rate is not recalculated if you make an unsuccessful claim for HB within the 26 weeks (but the old fixed rate continues). If you make a successful claim for HB (at any time) see para 15.67.

15.65   HB 49(1), 50; HB60+ 47(1), 48; NIHB 46(1), 47; NIHB60+ 45(1), 46

15.66   HB 50(1)-(4),(8); HB60+ 48(1)-(4),(8); NIHB 47(1)-(4),(8); NIHB60+ 46(1)-(4),(8)

15.67   HB 50(1)(a),(2),(3),(8); HB60+ 48(1)(a),(2),(3),(8); NIHB 47(1)(a),(2),(3),(8); NIHB60+ 46(1)(a),(2),(3),(8)

15.68   HB 50(1)(b),(4),(8); HB60+ 48(1)(b),(4),(8); NIHB 47(1)(b),(4),(8); NIHB60+ 46(1)(b),(4),(8)

15.69   HB 50(1)(b),(5)-(8); HB60+ 48(1)(b),(5)-(8); NIHB 47(1)(b),(5)-(8); NIHB60+ 46(1)(b),(5)-(8)

Example: Diminishing notional capital

Catalina Pontilo claims HB

Based on her circumstances, including her actual capital of £15,000, she would qualify for HB of £50 pw (but no other benefits). However, she has deprived herself of capital of £5,000.

■ Notional capital	£5,000
■ Actual capital	£15,000
■ Total capital	£20,000

She does not qualify for HB. The notional capital means she has lost £50 per week. This is the fixed rate reduction.

Catalina P. claims HB 20 weeks later

■ Notional capital (reduced by 20 x £50 = £1,000)	£4,000
■ Actual capital (has reduced to)	£13,000
■ Total capital	£17,000

She does not qualify for HB. The fixed rate of reduction is not recalculated (less than 26 weeks have passed).

Catalina claims HB 10 further weeks later

■ Notional capital (further reduced by 10 x £50 = £500)	£3,500
■ Actual capital (has not changed)	£13,000
■ Total capital	£16,500

She does not qualify for HB. The fixed rate of reduction is recalculated (at least 26 weeks have passed). But the new figure turns out to be £40 per week, so the existing £50 per week fixed rate continues.

Cat claims HB 20 further weeks later

■ Notional capital (further reduced by 20 x £50 = £1,000)	£2,500
■ Actual capital (has reduced to)	£12,000
■ Total capital	£14,500

She qualifies for and is awarded HB. Actual rates of reduction are used while she is on HB.

Chapter 16 **Decisions, notices and payments**

■ HB decisions and notices: see paras 16.1-12.

■ HB payments: rebates, allowances and payments on account: see paras 16.13-28.

■ Paying HB to someone on your behalf: see paras 16.29-33.

■ Paying HB to your landlord or agent: see paras 16.34-66.

Decisions and decision notices

16.1   This section explains how soon the council makes a decision about your claim for HB and about changes to your HB, who decision notices are issued to, and what information the notices should contain.

Decisions about claims

16.2   The council must:

(a) decide your claim for HB within 14 days of receiving the information and evidence it requires, or as soon as reasonably practicable after that; and

(b) issue a decision notice on the day it makes this decision, or as soon as reasonably practicable after that.

The council must decide your claim and issue a decision notice even if you do not provide the information and evidence (see para 5.26), but does not have to decide a claim you have withdrawn.

Other decisions

16.3   The council must also:

(a) decide about changes to your HB, and about any overpayments that occur; and

(b) issue a decision notice within 14 days of making these decisions, or as soon as reasonably practicable after that.

Decision notices

16.4   Decision notices must:

(a) be in writing;

(b) be issued to you and other 'persons affected' by the decision: see paras 16.5-6; and

(c) contain the information described in paras 16.7-9.

16.2   HB 89, 90(1)(a); HB60+ 70, 71(1)(a); NIHB 85, 86(1)(a); NIHB60+ 66, 67(1)(a)

16.3   HB 89(1), 90(1)(b); HB60+ 70(1), 71(1)(b); NIHB 85(1), 86(1)(b); NIHB60+ 66(1), 67(1)(b)

16.4   HB 90(1); HB60+ 71(1); NIHB 86(1); NIHB60+ 67(1)

Persons affected

16.5   The law uses the term 'persons affected' to mean everyone who:

(a) must be sent a decision notice; and

(b) has the right to obtain a statement of reasons, to ask for a reconsideration, and to appeal (see para 16.9).

16.6   All the following (and only the following) are persons affected:

(a) you (the HB claimant);

(b) someone acting for you if you are unable to act on your own behalf (for example an attorney or appointee: see paras 5.5-7);

(c) your landlord or agent if the decision is about whether to pay your HB to them rather than you (see paras 16.34-64);

(d) your landlord or agent or anyone else if the decision is about whether an overpayment is recoverable from them (see paras 18.29-37).

The above are persons affected when their rights, duties or obligations are affected by the decision. So in the situations described in (c) and (d), both you and the landlord, agent or other person are persons affected. A person affected can be either an individual (for example a private landlord) or a corporate body (for example a housing association or a firm of letting agents).

Information in decision notices

16.7   A decision notice issued to you (or to someone acting for you: see paras 5.5-7) must contain the following:

(a) if the decision is about your claim for HB, the notices must contain the information in table 16.1;

(b) if the decision notice is about a change to your HB , the notice must say what the change is (and may also contain the information in table 16.1);

(c) if the decision is about an overpayment of HB, the notice must contain the information in paras 18.68-69.

16.8   There are also rules for decision notices issued to:

(a) landlords and agents about paying HB to them: see paras 16.59-60;

(b) landlords, agents and others when the council decides an overpayment is recoverable from them: see paras 18.68-69.

16.9   Every decision notice (whoever it is issued to) must also contain information about the right to:

(a) obtain a statement of reasons (see para 19.8);

(b) ask for a reconsideration (see para 19.10);

(c) appeal, if the right to appeal applies to the decision (see para 19.24);

and how to do these things.

16.6   HB 2(1) definition – 'person affected'; HB60+ 2(1); DAR 3; NIHB 2(1); NIHB60+ 2(1); NIDAR 3

16.7   HB 90(1), sch 9 paras 1,7,8; HB60+ 71(1), sch 8 paras 1,7,8; NIHB 86(1), sch 10 paras 1,7,8; NIHB60+ 67(1), sch 9 paras 1,7,8

Table 16.1 **Decision notices about claims**

When the council decides your claim for HB, it must issue a decision notice to you
containing the following information.

If you are entitled to HB

(a) Your first day of entitlement.

(b) The normal weekly amount of your HB.

(c) If your HB is a rent allowance, when and how often it will be paid (and if it will be
paid to your landlord/agent, see paras 16.59-60).

(d) Your duty to notify changes of circumstances, and examples of what these might
be (see para 17.3).

If you are not entitled to HB

(e) The reason why you are not entitled.

(f) If your HB is less than 50p a week, the amount and an explanation that this is
below the minimum award (see para 6.9).

All cases whether or not you are entitled

(g) Your weekly eligible rent, and in Northern Ireland rates.

(h) If standard deductions were made for fuel, how you can get these changed (see
para 10.50).

(i) The amount and category of non-dependant deductions.

(j) Your applicable amount and how it was worked out (unless you are on a passport
benefit or universal credit).

(k) Your weekly earned income and weekly unearned income (unless you are on a
passport benefit, universal credit or savings credit).

(l) If you are on savings credit, the DWP's figures for your income and capital, any
adjustments made to them, and the amount of your savings credit (see para 13.15).

(m) Your rights in relation to the decision (see para 16.9).

(n) Any other information the council considers relevant.

Delays in getting a decision or getting a payment

16.10   The DWP expects councils to make decisions about HB claims and changes within
time limits (see paras 16.2-3). It collects information about this (see para 1.34) which is
available online [www]. Delays are usually only acceptable when councils' workloads are at
their heaviest, for example when benefits are uprated in April. The fact that other councils
also have delays is not itself sufficient excuse: R v Liverpool CC ex parte Johnson No 1.

16.9   HB sch 9 paras 2-5; HB60+ sch 8 paras 2-5; NIHB sch 10 paras 2-5; NIHB60+ sch 9 paras 2-5

T16.1   HB sch 9 paras 1-10, 13,14; HB60+ sch 8 paras 1-10, 13,14; NIHB sch 10 paras 1-10, 13,14; NIHB60+ sch 9 paras 1-10, 13,14

16.10   www.gov.uk/government/statistics/housing-benefit-statistics-on-speed-of-processing-2014-to-2015
        R v Liverpool ex p Johnson (No 1) 23/06/94 QBD unreported

16.11   If the council delays making a decision about your HB, you may be able to complain to the Ombudsman (see para 1.35) or apply for judicial review (see para 1.54). If the council has decided you are entitled to HB but delays paying you, you may be able to take action in the county court or sheriff court to enforce payment: Waveney DC v Jones.

Delays and rent arears

16.12   In England and Wales, the following protections apply if you are a tenant of a council or registered housing association, and have got into rent arrears while waiting for a decision about your HB claim. These are in the civil procedure rules which are available online [www].

(a) Your landlord should not begin possession proceedings against you if:

- ■ you have provided all the information and evidence needed to decide your claim,
- ■ there is a reasonable expectation that you will qualify for HB, and
- ■ you have paid any rent which will not be met by HB.

(b) If possession proceedings are begun against you, the court can order the council dealing with your HB claim:

- ■ to explain delays and problems with your HB, and
- ■ to pay costs if these are shown to have caused the proceedings.

Payments of HB

16.13   This section explains how and when your HB is paid, how soon the first payment should be made, and who your HB is paid to. You can ask the council to reconsider a decision it makes about any of these things (see para 19.10), but only some of them can be appealed to a tribunal (see para 19.24 and table 19.2).

How HB is paid

16.14   Your HB is paid:

(a) as a rent rebate if you are a council or NIHE tenant: see paras 16.16-17;

(b) as a rent allowance in all other cases: see paras 16.18-66.

But in Northern Ireland, HB for rates is usually paid as a rate rebate: see para 11.18. And if your liability for rates is to Land and Property Services your HB can be paid to them if the circumstances in paragraphs 16.50-53 apply.

16.15   In England, Scotland and Wales there are two exceptions:

(a) if you are renting a houseboat, mobile home or caravan (see para 2.29) and you pay:

- ■ your mooring charges or site charges to the council, but
- ■ your rent to someone else (for example a private landlord)

your HB for each of these is paid as a rent allowance;

16.11   Waveney DC v Jones 01/12/99 CA 33 HLR 3 www.casetrack.com subscriber site case reference CCRTF/1988/1488/B2

16.12   https://www.justice.gov.uk/courts/procedure-rules/civil/protocol/prot_rent

16.14   AA 134(1A),(1B),(2); NIAA 126(1),(2); NIHB 88,93(5); NIHB60+ 69,74(5)

16.15   AA 134(1A); HB 91A; HB60+ 72A

(b) if you pay your rent to the council because your home is subject to a management order or empty dwelling order, your HB is paid as a rent allowance.

Rent rebates

16.16   If your HB is paid as rent rebate (see paras 16.14-15), this means it is paid straight into your rent account. You do not receive a payment yourself, but you have less rent to pay (and in some cases no rent to pay).

When rent rebates are paid

16.17   The first payment into your rent account should be within 14 days of your HB claim, or as soon as reasonably practicable after that. Payments are then usually made into your rent account on the days your rent is due.

Rent allowances

16.18   If your HB is paid as a rent allowance (see paras 16.14-15), this means it is paid:

(a) to you (the HB claimant);

(b) to someone on your behalf (see paras 16.29-33); or

(c) to your landlord or agent (see paras 16.34-66)

The council decides how to make payments, and should take into account your (or the payee's) reasonable needs and convenience. In most cases the payments are made by credit transfer straight into a bank account or (increasingly rare) by cheque.

16.19   The council should not insist on paying you by credit transfer if:

(a) you do not have a bank account: R (Spiropoulos) v Brighton and Hove CC (see also GM para A6.120 and GLHA para 5.87). But the council may be able to tell you which banks in your area offer basic accounts, and may give you a letter confirming your identity to help you open an account; or

(b) your bank is unlikely to let you take the money out because you have an overdraft. Although the 'right of first appropriation' in banking law says you have the right to instruct your bank that the money will be used to pay your rent rather than reduce your overdraft, this right can be difficult to insist upon (for example, sometimes banks insist on a fresh instruction for each payment).

When rent allowances are paid

16.20   The first payment of your rent allowance should be within 14 days of your HB claim, or as soon as reasonably practicable after that. If the council cannot do this, it should make a payment on account: see paras 16.23-28.

16.16   AA 134(1A); NIAA 126(1)(b),(c)

16.17   HB 91(3); HB60+ 72(3); NIHB 87(3); NIHB60+ 68(3)

16.18   AA 134(1A),(1B); HB 91(1),94; HB60+ 72(1),75; NIAA 126(1); NIHB 87(1),91; NIHB60+ 68(1),72
         R (Spiropoulos) v Brighton and Hove CC 06/02/07 QBD [2007] EWHC 342 (Admin) www.bailii.org/ew/cases/EWHC/Admin/2007/342.html

16.20   HB 91(3); HB60+ 72(3); NIHB 87(3); NIHB60+ 68(3)

16.21   HB 92; HB60+ 73; NIHB 89; NIHB60+ 70

16.21   The council decides how often payments are made after that, and should take into account how often and what dates your rent is due. It can make:

(a)   payments to you (or someone on your behalf):

- every two weeks. You can insist on this if your HB is more than £2 a week,
- every four weeks,
- every calendar month, or
- every week: see para 16.22;

(b)   payments to your landlord or agent:

- every four weeks,
- every calendar month (but only if your rent is due calendar monthly).

The first payment to a landlord or agent can be for a shorter period if they have other tenants on HB. This is to allow all of the HB payments to them to be made on the same dates.

16.22   The council can only pay you weekly if:

(a)   paying you over a longer period is likely to lead to an overpayment; or

(b)   your rent is due weekly and it is in your interests to be paid weekly.

For example, (b) could apply if you have difficulty budgeting. The council is not expected to check whether this is the case, but should take account of information provided by you or by someone on your behalf, including a social worker or key worker (GM para A6.143).

Payments on account

16.23   A 'payment on account' is an estimated amount of HB. The council must make a payment on account if:

(a)   your HB will be paid as a rent allowance (see paras 16.14-15);

(b)   the council is unable to decide your claim within 14 days of receiving it; and

(c)   this is not because you have failed to provide information and evidence: see paras 16.24-25.

The rules about who it is paid to, and how it is paid, are the same as for rent allowances (see paras 16.18-19).

16.24   The council does not have to make a payment on account if:

(a)   it or the DWP has asked you to provide information or evidence reasonably required to decide your HB claim (see paras 5.13-21; and

(b)   you have failed without good cause to provide it.

16.25   But the council does have to make a payment on account if:

(a)   it has asked someone other than you for the information and evidence (GM para A6.161). For example it has asked:

- your landlord or agent for confirmation of your rent,
- the rent officer for a determination about your rent,

16.22   HB 92(6); HB60+ 73(6); NIHB 89(6); NIHB60+ 70(6)

16.23   HB 93(1); HB60+ 74(1); NIHB 90(1); NIHB60+ 71(1)

■ the DWP for confirmation of your benefit entitlement, or

■ the Home Office for confirmation of your conditions of entry or stay; or

(b) you have not provided information or evidence because :

■ you have not been asked for it, or

■ you have good cause , for example it does not exist or you cannot obtain it.

16.26 Payments on account are not discretionary. If you meet the conditions (see paras 16.23 and 16.25), the council:

(a) must make a payment on account within 14 days of receiving your claim, and should not wait to be asked: R v Haringey LBC ex parte Ayub (see also GM para A6.158); and

(b) should continue making payments on account until your HB is decided.

In practice you may need to remind the council to make a payment on account, or your landlord or agent can do this if your HB is likely to be paid to them.

Payments on account amounts and adjustments

16.27 The amount of your payment on account is whatever the council decides is reasonable, based on the information available to it about your individual circumstances. It must notify you (or the payee) that if this turns out to be greater than your entitlement to HB, the overpayment will be recovered (para 18.12).

16.28 When the council decides your claim, the following rules apply. If your entitlement to HB is:

(a) greater than your payments on account, the council must pay the balance;

(b) less than your payments on account, the council must recover the overpayment by making deductions from your future payments of HB (see para 18.41).

If you are not entitled to HB, the council recovers the overpayment from the person it was paid to (see para 18.37).

Paying HB to someone on your behalf

16.29 This section explains when your HB is paid to someone on your behalf. It only applies if your HB is paid as a rent allowance (see paras 16.14-15).

Attorneys, appointees, etc

16.30 If you are unable to act for yourself, the council can pay your HB to an attorney, appointee etc, who claimed HB on your behalf (see paras 5.5-7).

16.26   R v Haringey LBC ex p Ayub 13/04/92 QBD 25 HLR 566

16.27   HB 93(1),(2); HB60+ 74(1),(2); NIHB 90(1),(2); NIHB60+ 71(1),(2)

16.28   HB 93(3); HB60+ 74(3); NIHB 90(3); NIHB60+ 71(3)

16.30   HB 94(2); HB60+ 75(2); NIHB 91(2); NIHB60+ 68(2)

Nominees

16.31 If you want your council to pay your HB to someone else, the council can do this (but if you are unable to act, see instead para 16.30). They are usually called your nominee. You have to write to the council requesting this, and your nominee must either be:

(a) an individual aged 18 or more (for example an adult relative or friend); or

(b) a corporate body (for example a firm of solicitors).

16.32 The law does not stop your landlord or agent being your nominee. But:

(a) if you fall within the LHA scheme in England Scotland or Wales, the DWP suggests (GLHA paras 5.100-101) that the council should not agree to this if it would undermine the main rules about paying HB to your landlord/agent (see paras 16.36-49);

(b) in all other rent allowance cases, it may be simpler to request payment to your landlord/agent using the main rule about this (see para 16.50).

Executors and next of kin

16.33 If HB is due to you when you die, the council must pay it to your executor, or (if you do not have an executor) your next of kin. Your next of kin is the first person in the following list who is aged 16 or more:

(a) your husband, wife or civil partner;

(b) your children or grandchildren;

(c) your parents, brothers or sisters, or their children.

This rule only applies if the executor or next of kin writes to the council requesting payment within one year of your death, or longer if the council agrees. But it does not apply to HB the council has to pay your landlord/agent: see para 16.41.

Paying HB to your landlord or agent

16.34 This section explains when your HB is paid to your landlord or agent. It only applies if your HB is paid as a rent allowance (see paras 16.14-15).

(a) The council must pay your HB to your landlord/agent when the rules in paras 16.36-41 apply to you.

(b) Otherwise, it may pay your HB to your landlord/agent when the rules in paras 16.42-53 apply to you.

(c) Otherwise, it must pay your HB to you, or to someone on your behalf (see paras 16.29-33).

Table 16.2 summarises these rules. See paras 16.54-56 for exceptions if your landlord/agent is not a 'fit and proper person', and paras 16.57-66 for further general rules.

16.31   HB 94(3); HB60+ 75(3); NIHB 91(3); NIHB60+ 68(3)

16.33   HB 97(1)-(4); HB60+ 78(1)-(4); NIHB 94(1)-(4); NIHB60+ 75(1)-(4)

16.34   HB 94(1),95,96; HB60+ 75(1),76,77; NIHB 91(1),92,93; NIHB60+ 68(1),73,74

Table 16.2 **Paying HB to your landlord/agent**

This table summarises when your HB is paid to your landlord or agent (see paras 16.34-35).

When the council must pay your landlord/agent

All rent allowance cases

In all rent allowance cases (see paras 16.14-15), the council must pay your landlord/agent if:

(a) you have eight weeks or more rent arrears, unless it is in your overriding interests not to pay your landlord/agent: see paras 16.37-39

(b) part of your JSA, ESA, income support or state pension credit is being paid to your landlord/agent: see para 16.40; or

(c) rent remains due to your landlord/agent when you die: see para 16.41.

When the council may pay your landlord/agent

LHA cases in England, Scotland or Wales

In LHA cases (see para 8.3) in England, Scotland or Wales, the council may pay your landlord/agent if:

(d) your HB has previously been paid to your landlord/agent under the rules in (a) or (b) above: see para 16.45;

(e) paying your landlord/agent would help you secure or retain your tenancy: see para 16.46;

(f) you are likely to have difficulty managing your finances: see para 16.47;

(g) it is improbable that you will pay your rent: see para 16.48; or

(h) the council is considering whether the rules in (f) or (g) apply to you, but in this case only for up to eight weeks: see para 16.49.

See also (k) and (l) below.

Other rent allowance cases

In other rent allowance cases in England, Scotland and Wales which are not LHA cases, and in all rent allowance cases (including LHA cases) in Northern Ireland, the council/ NIHE may pay your landlord/agent if:

(i) you have requested this or consented to it: see para 16.50; or

(j) it is in your and your family's interest: see para 16.51.

See also (k) and (l) below.

All rent allowance cases

In all rent allowance cases, the council may pay your landlord/agent if:

(k) you have not paid part or all of your rent, but this only applies to your first payment of HB (or first payment following a change to your HB): see para 16.52; or

(l) you have left your home and rent remains due to your landlord/agent: see para 16.53.

When the council must not pay your landlord/agent

All rent allowance cases

In all rent allowance cases, the council must not pay your landlord/agent if:

   (m) your landlord/agent is not a 'fit and proper person', unless paying them is nonetheless in your and your family's best interests: see paras 16.54-56.

Landlord or agent

16.35 When your HB is payable to your landlord or agent, it is payable to:

(a) your landlord if your landlord collects your rent; but

(b) your agent if your agent collects your rent.

In the following paras, we use 'landlord/agent' to mean whichever of these applies.

When HB must be paid to a landlord/agent

16.36 Paras 16.37-41 explain when your HB must be paid to your landlord/agent. The rules about this apply in all rent allowance cases (see paras 16.14-15). See also paras 16.54-66.

HB must be paid to landlord: eight weeks rent arrears

16.37 In all rent allowance cases, the council must pay your HB to your landlord/agent:

(a) if you have eight weeks or more rent arrears, counting arrears of eligible and ineligible service charges as well as arrears of rent: see para 16.38;

(b) unless it is in your overriding interests not to: see para 16.39.

This continues to apply until your rent arrears reduce below eight weeks (but see para 16.45).

16.38 Whether you have rent arrears (including arrears of service charges), and how much they are, are questions of fact (see paras 1.43-46). The council is not expected to check this, but must consider information you or your landlord/agent provide: R v Haringey LBC ex parte Ayub. And it is usually accepted that 'Rent is in arrears once the contractual date for payment has passed irrespective of whether the rent is due in advance or in arrear': Doncaster v Coventry CC. Although this First-tier Tribunal decision is not binding, the DWP considers it correct (HB/CTB A26·2009 and GLHA 4·061).

Example: Eight weeks rent arrears

A private landlord lets a calendar-monthly tenancy from 1st July 2015. She charges rent in advance on the 1st of each month. The tenant does not pay any rent.

So by 2nd August 2015, there are two calendar months of rent arrears. This is more than eight weeks of arrears, so the landlord is entitled to require the council to pay the tenant's HB to her.

16.35   HB 95(1),96(4); HB60+ 76(1),77(4); NIHB 92(1),93(5); NIHB60+ 73(1),74(5)

T16.2   HB 95,96,97(5); HB60+ 76,77,78(5); NIHB 92,93,94(5); NIHB60+ 73,74,75(5)

16.37   HB 95(1)(b); HB60+ 76(1)(b); NIHB 92(1)(b); NIHB60+ 73(1)(b)
           R v Haringey ex p Ayub: see footnote to para 16.26; Doncaster v Coventry CC 05/10/09 032/09/00932

16.39   If you have eight weeks or more rent arrears, it is up to you (or someone on your behalf) to give specific reasons why it is in your 'overriding interests' that your HB should not be paid to your landlord/agent: CH/3244/2007. If this is because your landlord/agent has not done essential repairs, you may be expected to have sent them a solicitor's letter with a schedule of disrepair prepared by a builder or surveyor: CH/3244/2007.

HB must be paid to landlord: deductions from DWP benefits

16.40   In all rent allowance cases, the council must pay your HB to your landlord/agent if the DWP:

(a) is making deductions from your or your partner's:

- JSA (income-based or contribution-based),
- ESA (income-related or contributory),
- income support, or
- state pension credit (guarantee or savings credit);

(b) in order to make direct payments (see 24.19) to your landlord/agent towards your:

- rent arrears, or
- ineligible service charges if you live in a hostel.

This continues to apply until the DWP stops making direct payments (but see para 16.45). The DWP should inform the council when this rule applies to you (GM para A6.188).

HB must be paid to landlord: rent due following death

16.41   In all rent allowance cases, the council must pay your HB to your landlord/agent if:

(b) HB remains due to you when you die, and rent remains due to your landlord/agent; and

(b) the council has already decided (before your death) to pay your landlord/agent.

The amount the council pays your landlord/agent must not be greater than the amount of rent remaining due at the date of your death. Any other HB due to you can be paid to your executor or next of kin (see para 16.33).

When HB may be paid to a landlord/agent

16.42   Paragraphs 16.45-53 explain when your HB may be paid to your landlord/agent.

(a) The rules in paragraphs 16.45-49 and 16.52-53 apply if you fall within the LHA scheme (see para 8.3) in England, Scotland or Wales.

(b) The rules in paragraphs 16.50-53 apply in:

- all other rent allowance cases in England, Scotland and Wales (for example housing association, exempt accommodation, rent referral and boarder cases), and
- all rent allowance cases in Northern Ireland.

See also paragraphs 16.54-66. In England, Scotland and Wales, the overall effect of the rules is that HB is more likely to be paid to the landlord/agent in non-LHA cases than in LHA cases.

16.40   HB 95(1)(a); HB60+ 76(1)(a); NIHB 92(1)(a); NIHB60+ 73(1)(a)

16.41   HB 97(5); HB60+ 78(5); NIHB 94(5); NIHB60+ 75(5)

16.43   The rules in paragraphs 16.45-53 are discretionary. If their conditions are met, the council may (but does not have to) pay your landlord/agent. The DWP has given councils extensive guidance about applying these rules in LHA cases (GLHA 4.00-6.102). But as with all discretions (see para 1.53), the council must make its own decision. It should not have fixed rules or follow guidance without question: CH/2986/2005.

16.44   Some of the rules require the council to consider quite personal things about you, for example, your ability to manage your finances, the likelihood that you will pay your rent, and what your and your family's interests are (see paras 16.47-48 and 16.51). In these cases, the DWP advises (GLHA 5.40-42, 6.40-41 and HB/CTB A26/2009) that the council:

(a)   can take account of information it already has, or obtains from a home visit; and

(b)   should also take account of information provided by you or by someone on your behalf. For example, a relative or friend, a social worker or leaving care worker, or your landlord/agent.

Although this guidance is about LHA cases in England, Scotland and Wales, it is equally reasonable in other rent allowance cases.

HB may be paid to landlord: following a period when it must be

16.45   In LHA cases in England, Scotland and Wales, the council may pay your HB to your landlord/agent if it has previously done so under the rules in paragraphs 16.37-40. It can do this as soon as your rent arrears reduce below eight weeks, or as soon as the DWP stops making direct payments, or (in either case) at a later date.

HB may be paid to landlord: to secure or retain your tenancy

16.46   In LHA cases in England, Scotland and Wales, the council may pay your HB to your landlord/agent if this will assist you to secure or retain your tenancy (or other form of letting). This could encourage your landlord/agent to let to you (or continue to do so) while you are on HB. Some councils use this power to encourage the landlord to let at a lower rent (for example, a rent within the LHA figure) than they would have asked for.

HB may be paid to landlord: difficulty managing your finances

16.47   In LHA cases in England, Scotland and Wales, the council may pay your HB to your landlord/agent if you are likely to have difficulty managing your finances. For example, the DWP says (GLHA 5.61-71) this could be because you:

(a)   have difficulty budgeting, debt problems, or an undischarged bankruptcy;

(b)   are illiterate or unable to speak English;

(c)   are fleeing domestic violence;

(d)   are leaving care or prison; or

(e)   are receiving Supporting People payments, or help from a charity.

See also paragraphs 16.44 and 16.49.

16.45   HB 96(3A)(b)(iii); HB60+ 77(3A)(b)(iii)

16.46   HB 96(3A)(b)(iv),(4); HB60+ 77(3A)(b)(iv),(4)

16.47   HB 96(3A)(b)(i); HB60+ 77(3A)(b)(i)

HB may be paid to landlord: improbable you will pay rent

16.48   In LHA cases in England, Scotland and Wales, the council may pay your HB to your landlord/agent if it is improbable that you will pay your rent. This rule is about whether it is improbable you will pay rent in the future: CH/2986/2005. The DWP says this might be the case if you have regularly failed to pay rent (with no good reason) in the past (GLHA 4.10), for example if the council helped you get your tenancy for this reason (HB/CTB A26/2009). See also paragraphs 16.44 and 16.49.

HB may be paid to landlord: while considering who to pay

16.49   In LHA cases in England, Scotland and Wales, the council may pay your HB to your landlord/agent while it is considering whether the rules in paragraphs 16.47-48 apply to you. The council can do this for up to eight weeks. Alternatively, it can pay you during this time (GLHA 5.71). See also paragraph 16.58.

HB may be paid to landlord: at your request or with your consent

16.50   In rent allowance cases in England, Scotland and Wales which are not LHA cases, and in all rent allowance cases in Northern Ireland, the council/NIHE may pay your HB to your landlord/agent if you request this or consent to it. The law does not require you to give a reason, but you can if you wish.

HB may be paid to landlord: your and your family's interests

16.51   In rent allowance cases in England, Scotland and Wales which are not LHA cases, and in all rent allowance cases in Northern Ireland, the council/NIHE may pay your HB to your landlord/agent if doing so would be in your and your family's interests. Although the rules in paragraphs 16.45-49 do not apply in these cases, the council is in practice likely to take similar considerations into account. See also paragraph 16.44.

HB may be paid to landlord: first payment after a claim or change

16.52   In all rent allowance cases, the council may pay your HB to your landlord/agent if you have not yet paid part or all of your rent for the period HB covers. But this is limited to the first payment following your claim for HB, or following a move or other change affecting your HB. And it only applies when paying your landlord/agent is 'in the interests of the efficient administration' of HB.

HB may be paid to your landlord: when you leave your home

16.53   In all rent allowance cases, the council may pay your HB to your landlord/agent if:

  (a)   you have left the accommodation the HB is paid for; and

  (b)   rent remains due to your landlord/agent there.

16.48   HB 96(3A)(b)(ii); HB60+ 77(3A)(b)(ii)

16.49   HB 96(3B); HB60+ 77(3B)

16.50   HB 96(1)(a),(3A)(a); HB60+ 77(1)(a),(3A)(a)

16.51   HB 96(1)(b),(3A)(a); HB60+ 77(1)(b),(3A)(a)

16.52   HB 96(2); HB60+ 77(2); NIHB 93(2); NIHB60+ 74(2)

16.53   HB 96(1)(c); HB60+ 77(1)(c); NIHB 93(1)(c); NIHB60+ 74(1)(c)

If your landlord/agent is not a fit and proper person

16.54   In all rent allowance cases, the council must not pay your HB to your landlord/agent:

(a)   if your landlord/agent is not a 'fit and proper person' (see paras 16.55-56);

(b)   unless paying them is nonetheless in your and your family's 'best interests'.

This rule overrides the rules in paragraphs 16.37-41 and 16.45-53. DWP guidance (GM A6.204) does not say what your and your family's best interests are, but see paragraph 16.44 for information the council could reasonably take into account.

16.55   DWP guidance (GM A6.198) says the council should only consider whether the landlord/agent is or is not a fit and proper person if it is doubtful about [their] honesty in connection with HB. This could be because they are involved in fraudulent acts relating to HB. The DWP also suggests (GM A6.200) it could be because they have regularly failed to report changes they have a duty to report (see paras 17.3-5), or to repay overpayments which are recoverable from them (see paras 18.34-36).

16.56   The following do not mean a landlord/agent is not a fit and proper person:

(a)   their undesirable activity in non-HB matters, for example contravention of the Housing Acts (GM A6.197);

(b)   using their right to request a reconsideration, or to appeal, before repaying an overpayment; or

(c)   making complaints about maladministration, for example to the Ombudsman.

Decisions about paying a landlord/agent

16.57   The council can make a decision about paying your HB to your landlord/agent:

(a)   when you claim HB; and/or

(b)   when there is a change in your or your landlord/agent's circumstances which affects this.

See paragraphs 16.20-21 for when payments to a landlord/agent are made, and paragraphs 16.23 and 16.26-28 about payments on account.

16.58   The council can suspend payments of HB (see para 17.72) while it is deciding who to pay: CH/1821/2006. But the DWP has encouraged councils not to delay payments in this way (GLHA 5.81).

Decision notices about paying a landlord/agent

16.59   The council must issue two decision notices, one to your landlord/agent and one to you, when:

(a)   it decides to pay your HB to them, or changes the amount of the payment (see para 16.60); or

(b)   they have asked the council to pay your HB to them, but the council has refused: CH/180/2006.

16.54   HB 95(3), 96(3),(4); HB60+ 76(3), 77(3),(4); NIHB 92(3), 93(3),(4); NIHB60+ 73(3), 74(3),(4)

16.57   HB 89(1), 95,96,97(5); HB60+ 70(1), 76,77,78(5); NIHB 85(1), 92,93,94(5); NIHB60+ 66(1), 73,74,75(5)

These must be in writing, and must be issued within 14 days of when the council makes the decision, or as soon as reasonably practicable after that.

16.60 When the council decides to pay your landlord/agent (or change the amount), the decision notice issued to them must contain:

(a) the amount of HB they will receive for you, and when the payments start (or change);

(b) their duty to notify changes of circumstances, and examples of what they might be (see para 17.3);

(c) an explanation about recovering overpaid HB from a blameless tenant (see para 18.46); and

(d) their rights in relation to the decision (see para 16.61);

but it must not contain other information about your HB (for example personal or financial information about you or your household). The decision notice to you must contain the information in (a) to (c), and your rights in relation to the decision. In practice, this is sometimes instead included in the main decision notice about your HB (see para 16.7).

Reconsiderations and appeals about paying a landlord/agent

16.61 When the council decides to pay, or not pay, your landlord/agent, both you and they are a 'person affected' (see para 16.6). So both you and they have the right to obtain a statement of reasons (see para 19.8), and to appeal if the right of appeal applies to the decision (see para 19.24): CH/180/2006.

If the council pays the wrong person

16.62 If the council decided it had a duty to pay your landlord/agent (see para 16.34(a)) but paid you instead, the council must pay your landlord/agent: [2008] UKUT 31 (AAC). What it paid you is an overpayment which is likely to be recoverable from you (see para 18.31).

16.63 If the council decided it had a discretion to pay your landlord/agent (see 16.34(b)) but paid you instead, the council cannot pay your landlord/agent but they can seek compensation from the council: R(H) 2/08, [2010] UKUT 254 (AAC).

16.64 It seems reasonable (following the reasoning in [2008] UKUT 31 (AAC)) that if the council decided it had a duty to pay you (see para 16.34(c)) but paid your landlord/agent instead, the council must pay you. What it paid your landlord/agent is an overpayment which is likely to be recoverable from them (see para 18.34).

How paying your landlord/agent affects your rent

16.65 When the council pays your HB to your landlord/agent, this discharges your liability to pay that amount of rent unless the council recovers it as an overpayment from your landlord/agent: see table 18.4.

16.59   HB sch 9 paras 11,12; HB60+ sch 8 paras 11,12; NIHB sch 10 paras 11,12; NIHB60+ sch 9 paras 11,12

16.60   HB sch 9 paras 11,12; HB60+ sch 8 paras 11,12; NIHB sch 10 paras 11,12; NIHB60+ sch 9 paras 11,12

16.65   HB 95(2), 96(4); HB60+ 76(2), 77(4); NIHB 92(2), 93(5); NIHB60+ 73(2), 74(5)

If your landlord/agent refuses to accept your HB

16.66 A landlord/agent has the right to refuse payments of rent from someone who is not a party to the tenancy agreement: Bessa Plus Plc v Lancaster. Although this is uncommon, it could affect you if:

(a) you are the HB claimant; but

(b) your partner is the sole tenant of your home; and

(c) your landlord/agent refuses to accept payment of your HB (because you are not on the tenancy agreement).

If this happens, you should be able to get the council to pay your HB to you (rather than your landlord/agent), or to your partner as your nominee (see paras 16.31-32).

16.66   Bessa Plus plc v Lancaster 17/03/97 CA 30 HLR 48 www.casetrack.com subscriber site case reference CCRTF 97/0057/H

Chapter 17 **Changes**

17.1 This chapter explains how your entitlement to HB can change or end. This could be because:

(a) there is a change in your circumstances, or in the circumstances of someone relevant to your claim (for example a member of your household or your landlord), or in the law: see paras 17.2-55; or

(b) the council reviews and corrects your entitlement: see paras 17.58-70; or

(c) you request a reconsideration or appeal: see chapter 19.

In the law, changes to your HB are also called 'revisions' or 'supersessions': see paras 17.56-57.

Changes of circumstance

17.2 This section describes the duty to tell the council about changes affecting HB and how the council deals with these.

Telling the council about changes

17.3 You have a duty to tell the council about any 'relevant' change of circumstances. The same duty applies to anyone acting for you (paras 5.5-7), and anyone who receives payments (such as a landlord: para 16.34). This means any change which you (or the other person) could reasonably be expected to know might affect:

(a) your entitlement to HB; or

(b) the amount of your HB; or

(c) how your HB is paid or who it is paid to.

17.4 This duty begins on the date your claim is made, and continues for as long as you are receiving HB.

17.3   HB 88(1),(6); HB60+ 69(1),(9); NIHB 84(1); NIHB60+ 65(1)

17.5   The law lists changes that must be notified to the council and changes that need not be notified (summarised in tables 17.1 and 17.2). These are not exhaustive. For example, you should also notify the council of changes in:

(a)   personal details (name, address, etc);

(b)   rent (unless you are a council or NIHE tenant) and in Northern Ireland rates (unless collected by Land and Property Services);

(c)   family and household details (which could affect your applicable amount or non-dependant deductions);

(d)   capital and income; and

(e)   any matter which affects whether HB is payable to your landlord.

Table 17.1 **Changes you must notify**

The following is a list of the items specifically mentioned in the law. Your duty is wider (paras 17.3-5).

Working age claims (para 1.24)

- The end of your (or your partner's) entitlement to JSA(IB), ESA(IR) or IS.
- Changes where a child or young person ceases to be a member of your family: e.g. when child benefit stops or they leave your household.

Pension age claims (para 1.24)

- Changes in the details of your letting (rent allowances only).
- Changes affecting the residence or income of any non-dependant.
- Absences exceeding or likely to exceed 13 weeks.

Additional matters for claimants on savings credit

- Changes affecting any child living with you (other than age) which might affect the amount of HB.
- Changes to capital which take it (or may take it) above £16,000.
- Changes to a partner who was ignored in assessing savings credit but is taken into account for HB (table 13.3).
- Changes to a non-dependant if the non-dependant's income and capital was treated as being yours (para 13.57).

T17.1   HB 88; HB60+ 69; NIHB 84; NIHB60+ 65

Table 17.2 **Changes you need not notify**

- Beginnings or ends of awards of pension credit (either kind) or changes in the amount – because it is the DWP's duty to notify the council.
- Changes which affect your JSA(IB), ESA(IR) or IS but do not affect your HB.
- Changes in rent if you are a council or NIHE tenant.
- Changes in rates in Northern Ireland if collected by the Rating Service.
- Changes in the age of any member of your family or non-dependant.
- Changes in the HB regulations.

How to notify changes

17.6   You must notify changes to the council. Some councils accept notification by telephone or online, though they can require written rather than telephone notifications, or require written or electronic records to be kept by those making online notifications.

17.7   In all other cases, you must notify changes to the council's 'designated office' (para 5.8). However, the council may accept notification by any other method it agrees to in a particular case.

17.8   If you or your partner are on JSA or IS and are starting work, and this will mean that your JSA/IS will stop (or JSA(C) will change), you may notify this by telephone to the DWP. This is part of the DWP's 'in and out of work' process.

Time limits, etc

17.9   There is a one month time limit for notifying changes, which can be extended to 13 months in special circumstances (para 17.14). Rather than placing a duty on you to meet these time limits, HB law spells out the consequences of not doing so (paras 17.10-15) – which in practice amounts to the same thing.

17.10   If you fail to notify a relevant change, or exceed the above time limits, and the change would:

- reduce or end entitlement to HB – an overpayment has occurred: this may or may not be recoverable (chapter 18);
- increase entitlement to HB – special rules apply (paras 17.11-15).

T17.2   HB 88(3)(4); HB60+ 69(3),(4); NIHB 84(2),(3); NIHB60+ 65(2),(3)

17.6   HB 88(1),(4),(6), 88A, sch 11; HB60+ 69(1),(4),(9), 69A, sch 10; NIHB 84(1),(3), 84A, sch 11; NIHB60+ 65(1),(2), 65A, sch 10

17.10   DAR 8(2); NIDAR 8(2)

Late notification of beneficial changes

17.11   The following rule (para 17.12) applies when:

(a)   you have a duty to notify a relevant change (para 17.3), and the change would increase entitlement to HB (a 'beneficial change'); but

(b)   you take longer than one month to do so (or longer in special circumstances: paras 17.14-15).

17.12   In such cases the change is treated (for HB purposes) as occurring on the date the council received the notification. In other words you lose money, as illustrated in the example.

17.13   The rule does not apply to changes in pension credit or in social security benefits (in such cases the rules in paras 17.32 and 17.34-37 apply instead).

Extending the time limit for notifying a beneficial change

17.14   In the case of a change of circumstances which increases entitlement to HB, the one month time limit for notifying it is extended (and you do not lose money) if:

(a)   the notification is received by the council within 13 months of the date on which the change occurred; and

(b)   you also notify the council of your reasons for failing to notify the change earlier; and

(c)   the council is satisfied that there are or were 'special circumstances' as a result of which it was not practicable to notify the change within the one month time limit. The longer the delay (beyond the normal one month), the more compelling those special circumstances need to be; and

(d)   the council is satisfied that it is reasonable to allow your late notification of the change. In determining this, the council may not take account of ignorance of the law (not even ignorance of the time limits) nor of the fact that an Upper Tribunal or court has taken a different view of the law from that previously understood and applied.

17.15   If the authority refuses your late notification, you have the right to ask the authority to reconsider or to appeal (chapter 19).

Example: Late notified beneficial change

A claimant's wages went down four months ago, but the claimant did not inform the council until today. The council asks why she delayed, but she has no special circumstances.

The change is implemented from the Monday following the day the claimant's written notification of the change was received by the council. The claimant does not get her arrears. (However, if the claimant has 'special circumstances', she may get her arrears: para 17.14.)

17.11   DAR 7(2)(a),(3), 8(3),(5); NIDAR 7(2)(a), 8(3),(5)

17.14   DAR 9; NIDAR 9

Dealing with changes

How the council deals with changes

17.16 The council must make a decision about any change which could affect your HB. For example whether to change the amount, end your award, or change who it is paid to. Paragraphs 17.18-55 give the rules about when changes take effect.

Information, evidence and decision notices

17.17 The council can ask you for information and evidence it reasonably requires in order to make a decision about a change. You are responsible for providing this in the same way as when you made your claim (see para 5.13) and the council must take it into account if you provide it within one month, or longer if reasonable. The council must issue a decision about any change it makes to your HB: see paras 16.3-9.

When changes take effect

17.18 This section describes when a change takes effect in your entitlement to HB. There are two steps involved:

(a) determining the date the change actually occurred; and

(b) working out (from that) what date it takes effect in HB.

The date a change occurs: the general rule

17.19 The starting point is that the date a change actually occurs is the date something new happens (for example, a new baby, a birthday, a change in pay, a rent increase). This is a question of fact (paras 1.43-47).

17.20 Late-notified beneficial changes can be treated as occurring on the date the notification was received (paras 17.11-12). Other special cases are described below (paras 17.22-55).

The date a change takes effect: the general rule

17.21 The date a change takes effect is the Monday after the date the change occurs. Even if the change occurs on a Monday, HB changes on the following Monday. However, there are different rules for moves, changes in rent, and changes in social security benefits and credits. These and other special cases are described below (paras 17.22-55).

17.16   HB 89(1); HB60+ 70(1); NIHB 85(1); NIHB60+ 66(1)

17.17   AA 5(1)(hh); NIAA 5(1)(hh); HB 86(1),90(1)(b), sch 9; HB60+ 67(1),71(1)(b), sch 8;
         NIHB 82(1),86(1)(b), sch 10; NIHB60+ 63(1),67(1)(b), sch 9; DAR 4(5), 7(5); NIDAR 4(4), 7(5)

17.21   HB 79(1); HB60+ 59(1); NIHB 77(1); NIHB60+ 57(1); DAR 7(2)(a)(i), 8(2); NIDAR 7(2)(a)(i), 8(2)

Moves

17.22   There are three rules about moves:

(a) If you move out of a council's area, HB ends. Unless an agency agreement exists (para 1.31), you should claim in your new area if you want HB there.

(b) If your move means you now fall within the UC scheme (paras 2.7-9), HB must end (and can never again be awarded, except in supported accommodation: paras 17.30-31).

(c) Otherwise, if you move within the council's area, this is a change which does not end HB. HB continues at the new amount (so long as you remain entitled).

In each of these cases, table 17.3 gives the date the change or end in entitlement takes effect.

17.23   The date a move occurs may not be straightforward. However, it is the date you change your normal home, rather than a date on your letting agreement, etc (R(H) 9/05 para 3.4).

Table 17.3 **Moves and changes in rent or rates**

What the change is	When it takes effect in HB
HB for hostels with a daily rent liability (para 5.48)	
All moves and all changes in rent liability	HB changes on the exact day
HB in all other cases	
If HB continues after the move or change in rent/rates	HB changes on the exact day
If HB ends as a result of the move or change in rent/rates	HB continues until the end of the benefit week containing the move or change in rent/rates

---

Changes in rent and rates

17.24   If your liability for rent or (in Northern Ireland) rates changes, this takes effect in HB from the date shown in table 17.3. For rent- (and rate-) free periods, see paras 6.42-43.

HB on two homes, etc

17.25   The following changes take effect on the exact day: starting or stopping being eligible for HB on a former home, or on two homes, including stopping being eligible because the (four weeks or 52 weeks) time limit runs out (paras 3.7 and 3.12).

17.22   HB 79(2),(2A)(a),(8), 80(4)(b),(c),(10); HB60+ 59(2),(2A)(a),(8), 61(4)(b),(c),(11); and NIHB 77(2),(3)(a),(10), 78(4)(b),(c),(9);

T17.3   As para 17.22

17.24   NIHB60+ 57(2),(3)(a),(14), 59(4)(b),(c),(9)

17.25   HB 79(2A)(b),(2B), 80(11); HB60+ 59(2A)(b),(2B), 61(12); NIHB 77(3),(4),(11), 78(10); NIHB60+ 57(3),(4),(15), 59(10)

17.26   Whenever you are eligible for HB on two homes, eligible rent in each benefit week is calculated by adding together the daily eligible rent for the two addresses for the appropriate number of days.

Examples: Moves and changes in liability

Moving within a council's area

A woman moves from one address to another within a council's area on Friday 1st May 2015. She is liable for rent at her old address up to and including Thursday 30th April and at her new address from Friday 1st May.

■   Her HB changes on and from Friday 1st May (on a daily basis) to take account of her new eligible rent.

Moving out of a council's area

A man moves out of a council's area on Saturday 18th July 2015. He is liable for rent at his old address (which is not a hostel) up to and including Friday 17th July.

■   His HB ends at the end of the benefit week containing his last day of liability for rent, in other words his last day of HB is Sunday 19th July.

A rent increase

A woman's rent goes up on Saturday 15th August 2015.

■   If her entitlement to HB changes as a result, it changes on and from Saturday 15th August (on a daily basis).

Changes relating to universal credit

17.27   Only people in supported accommodation can get HB while they are on UC (paras 2.7-8 and 2.37-39). If this applies to you and your entitlement to UC starts or ends, the general rules apply (paras 17.19-21):

(a)   the date such a change occurs is the first day of your new or nil entitlement to UC; and

(b)   the change takes effect in HB on the following Monday.

17.28   UC is a monthly benefit. Generally speaking, your first UC assessment month begins on the day your entitlement starts (whichever day of the month this is), and following assessment months begin on the same day of each month. Your entitlement for each assessment month is based on your circumstances at the end of that month, and is paid in arrears.

Ending HB when your new partner is on UC

17.29   If you are on HB (but not UC) and you acquire a partner who is on UC, the UC claim then covers you both. So except in supported accommodation your HB ends. The last day of HB is the day before your first day of entitlement to UC as a couple. Since UC is assessed in arrears (para 17.28) this can be up to (nearly) one month before you actually became a couple. If this results in an overpayment of HB it may or may not be recoverable (paras 18.11-15).

17.27   HB 79(1); HB60+ 59(1); DAR 7(2)(a)(i),(2)

17.29   UCTP 5(2)(b)(ii), 7(2)(a)

Ending HB when you are on UC and move out of supported accommodation

17.30   If your are on UC and HB and you move out of supported accommodation, your HB ends at the end of the HB benefit week containing the move (table 17.3). If you are entitled to UC for housing costs at your new address, then (because UC is assessed in arrears: para 17.28) you get both UC for housing costs and HB for a period. The nearer the date of your move is to the end of a UC assessment month, the longer this dual entitlement lasts. For DWP guidance see circular HB A19/2013 paras 15-17. The guidance does not suggest this dual entitlement involves an overpayment of either benefit.

Starting HB when you are on UC and move into supported accommodation

17.31   If you are on UC and you move into supported accommodation, you need to claim HB (paras 5.10 and 5.41-42). If you were getting UC for housing costs at your old address, then (because UC is assessed in arrears: para 17.28) there may be a gap between the end of those and the beginning of your HB. The nearer the date of your move is to the beginning of a UC assessment month, the shorter the gap is. For DWP guidance see circular HB A19/2013 paras 15-17. See also para 24.9 for discretionary housing payments in such cases.

Examples: Universal credit changes

A claimant's UC assessment months begin on the 5th of each month. So her entitlement to UC for each month is based on her circumstances on the last day of the assessment month (the 4th):

■   If her earnings go down on the 26th July, her UC goes up on 5th July.

■   If she moves into supported accommodation (with a daily rent liability) on 21st September, her UC for housing costs ends on 4th September. But her HB (if she claims on time) does not start till 21st September.

■   If she moves out of supported accommodation (to a private tenancy) on 31st October, her UC for housing costs starts on 5th October. But her HB continues until 31st October.

Changes to pension credit

17.32   If a change in either guarantee credit or savings credit, whether due to a change in your circumstances or due to official error (para 17.61), affects your entitlement to HB, this takes effect from the date shown in table 17.4.

17.30   UCTP 5(2)(a) and as para 17.22

17.31   UCTP 5(2)(a), 6(8)

17.32   HB60+ 41(9), 60; NIHB60+ 39(11), 58; DAR 8(2),(3); NIDAR 8(2),(3)

Table 17.4 **When pension credit starts, changes or ends**

What the change is	When it takes effect in HB
Pension credit starts, increasing entitlement to HB	The Monday following the first day of entitlement to pension credit
Pension credit starts, reducing entitlement to HB	The Monday following the date the authority receives notification from the DWP about this (or, if later, the Monday following the first day of entitlement to pension credit)
Pension credit changes or ends, increasing entitlement to HB	The Monday of the benefit week in which pension credit changes or ends
Pension credit changes or ends, reducing entitlement to HB:	
■ if this is because you delayed notifying a change in circumstances to the DWP	The Monday of the benefit week in which pension credit changes or ends
■ in any other case	The Monday following the date the authority received notification from the DWP about this (or, if later, the Monday following the pension credit change or end)

Note:
If any of the above changes would take effect during your 'continuing payment' period (para 17.54), the change is instead deferred until afterwards.

Changes to tax credits

17.33   When your entitlement to working tax credit or child tax credit starts, changes or ends, the general rule applies (paras 17.19-21). But because of the way tax credits are paid, it can involve counting backwards or forwards from the pay date to work out when the change actually occurs. Table 17.5 explains this and includes examples.

T17.4   As para 17.32

Table 17.5 **When a tax credit starts, changes or ends**

Four-weekly instalments

The pay date is the last day of the 28 days covered by the tax credit instalment.

So if a four-weekly instalment is due on the 30th of the month, it covers the period from 3rd to 30th of that month (both dates included).

For example:

- if that is the first instalment ever of your tax credit, your HB changes on the Monday following the 3rd of the month;
- if that is the first instalment of a new rate of your tax credit, your HB changes on the Monday following the 3rd of the month;
- if that is the last instalment of your tax credit, the date the change occurs is the 31st of the month, and your HB changes on the Monday following the 31st of the month.

Weekly instalments

The pay date is the last day of the 7 days covered by the tax credit instalment.

So if a weekly instalment is due on the 15th of the month, it covers the period from 9th to 15th of that month (both dates included).

For example:

- if that is the first instalment ever of your tax credit, your HB changes on the Monday following the 9th of the month;
- if that is the first instalment of a new rate of your tax credit, your HB changes on the Monday following the 9th of the month;
- if that is the last instalment of your tax credit, the date the change occurs is the 16th of the month, and your HB changes on the Monday following the 16th of the month.

Changes relating to social security benefits (the relevant benefit rule)

17.34   The following rule applies when entitlement to a social security benefit starts, changes, ends or is reinstated. It is sometimes called the 'relevant benefit rule'. It applies to all social security benefits (apart UC or tax credits) received by you, your partner, or a child or young person.

17.35   The date such a change actually occurs is the first day of that new, different, nil or re-instated entitlement. The date the change takes effect in HB is shown in table 17.6.

17.36   However, if you are on HB and begin receiving JSA, ESA or IS towards your housing costs for the first time (e.g. because you have bought your home: paras 25.32-34), HB continues for a further four weeks.

17.34   HB 79(1); HB60+ 59(1); NIHB 77(1); NIHB60+ 57(1); DAR 4(7B),(7C), 7(2)(i),(p),(q),(s), 8(14), (14D),(14E),(14G); NIDAR 4(6B),(6C), 7(2)(h), 8(11)

17.36   HB 11(2),(4); NNIHB 11(2),(4)

Table 17.6 **Changes in social security benefits**

What the change is	When it takes effect in HB
A social security benefit reduces or ends:	
All cases (whether HB increases, reduces or ends as a result)	HB changes on the Monday following the change (see also paras 17.46 and 17.54)
A social security benefit starts, increases or is re-instated:	
If HB increases as a result	HB increases on the exact day (or from the start of the HB award if later)
If HB reduces or ends as a result	HB reduces or ends on the Monday following the change
If HB ended as above, but the social security benefit is then reinstated	HB is reinstated on the exact day
Exception for ESA and PIP:	
If you or your partner convert onto ESA (para 12.28) or convert from one ESA component to another or convert from DLA to PIP	HB changes on the exact day (see also para 17.45)
(This table does not apply to UC or tax credits: paras 17.27-33.)	

17.37   When a social security benefit is found to have been awarded from a date in the past, any resulting increase in HB is awarded for the past period (so you get your arrears: see the second example). This is because the 'relevant benefit rule' over-rides the rule about late notification of beneficial changes (para 17.13).

Changes in income, capital, household membership, etc

17.38   The general rules (paras 17.19-21) apply to all other changes – including changes in income, capital, membership of the family or household, and so on. But see also para 6.27 for when non-dependant deductions are delayed, paras 13.7 and 15.11 for when arrears of income are (or are not) taken into account, and para 17.29 for certain UC cases.

17.39   The council also has a discretion to disregard, for up to 30 weeks, changes in tax, national insurance and the maximum rate of tax credits when these result from a change in the law (e.g. the Budget). This discretion is rarely used.

T17.6   As para 17.34

17.39   HB 34; HB60+ 34; NIHB 31; NIHB60+ 32

Examples: Changes to social security benefits

Going on to disability living allowance (DLA)

A claimant on HB is awarded DLA from Thursday 16th July 2015. The date of change is Thursday 16th July. So her entitlement to HB goes up on Thursday 16th July.

A claimant is found to have been awarded DLA from a date in the past.

No matter how far the DLA goes back, the council must award the claimant any as-yet-unawarded premium that flows from being on DLA (and remove any non-dependant deductions if appropriate) all the way back to the start of his award of DLA (or the start of his award of HB if later).

Starting work

17.40　The general rules (paras 17.19-21) apply when someone starts work. Their effect is that if you start work on a Monday, you get a whole week of HB as though you had not started work. You may – after that – also qualify for an extended payment (para 17.46).

Changes ending HB

17.41　The general rules (paras 17.19-21) apply to any change of circumstances which means that you no longer satisfy all the basic conditions for HB (para 2.2) – for example if your capital now exceeds the upper limit or income is now too high to qualify. The only exception is certain UC cases (para 17.29).

Changes in the law: case law (the anti-test-case rule)

17.42　The 'anti-test-case rule' applies in HB when an Upper Tribunal or court decides a case (a 'lead case') by interpreting the law in a new way. It requires all similar cases ('look-alike cases') to be amended to follow the new interpretation from the date of the decision on the lead case (not earlier). This does not apply to cases the council should have decided before the decision on the lead case; nor to appeals which a First-tier Tribunal 'stayed' to await the decision on the lead case; nor to decisions by Upper Tribunals: CH/532/2006.

Changes in the law: regulations

17.43　When regulations relevant to HB are amended, the council alters your entitlement to HB from the date on which the amendment takes effect (unless entitlement reduces to nil, in which case para 17.41 applies).

Changes in the law: up-ratings, etc

17.44　If the April up-rating for social security benefits or tax credits is different from that for HB (table 1.4), they are treated as up-rated on the same day as HB. The same applies if the DWP's 'assessed income figure' (table 13.3) changes at that time, when you convert onto ESA (para 12.28) between 1st and 16th April (both dates included), and when you convert from DLA to PIP in the same benefit week as the up-rating.

17.42　CPSA sch 7 paras 4(5),(6),18; NICPSA sch 7 paras 4(4),(5); DAR 7(2)(b); NIDAR 7(2)(b)

17.43-44　HB 79(3); HB60+ 60(3); NIHB 77(3); NIHB60+ 58(3); DAR 7(2)(q),(s),8(10),(14E),(14G); NIDAR 8(12)

More than one change

17.45   If your have more than one change, each is dealt with in turn. But the following rules apply when changes which actually occur in the same benefit week would have an effect (under the earlier rules in this chapter) in different benefit weeks:

(a) If one of the changes is in:

- the annual up-rating (but only in cases when this takes effect on the first Monday in April rather than 1st April);

- the amount of liability for rent on a dwelling;

- moving into a new dwelling; or

- starting or stopping being eligible for HB on a former home or on two homes, including when the (4 weeks or 52 weeks) time limit runs out,

the other changes in entitlement instead apply when that applies. And for this rule, the first item in the above list takes priority over the other three.

(b) In all other cases, all the changes take effect from the Monday of the benefit week in which the changes actually occur.

Extended payments

17.46   Extended payments (EPs) help long-term unemployed people who find work, by giving them four weeks extra HB. They also help people who increase their hours or earnings. They are also known as HB 'run-on'. They are like the extended payments some people get in JSA or ESA (and people often get both HB and JSA/ESA EPs at the same time).

Entitlement

17.47   You are entitled to an EP if you meet the conditions in table 17.7. As that table shows, there are two routes to qualifying for an EP; either of these is sufficient.

17.48   No claim is required for an EP. All the matters referred to in table 17.7 are for the council to determine (not the DWP), and the council is entitled to information and evidence in the normal way (paras 17.3-8). You must be notified about your entitlement to an EP.

Period and amount

17.49   An EP is awarded from the date the change (getting a job, etc) takes effect, and it lasts for four weeks (as illustrated in the example). In each of those four weeks, the amount of your EP is the greater of:

(a) the amount awarded in your last full benefit week before the EP started. This means the amount that would have been awarded if there was no benefit cap (para 6.28);

(b) the amount which would be your entitlement in that particular week if there were no such thing as EPs.

17.45   HB 42(8),79(4),(5); HB60+ 41(9),(10),59(4),(5); NIHB 39(8),77(6),(7); NIHB60+ 39(11),(12),57(6),(7); DAR 7(2)(q), 8(14E); NIDAR 7(2)(h), 8(11)

17.47   HB 2(1),72,73; HB60+ 2(1),53; NIHB 2(1),70,71; NIHB60+ 2(1),51

17.49   HB 72A,72B,72E,73A,73B,73E; HB60+ 53A,53B; NIHB 70A,70B,71A,71B; NIHB60+51A,51B

17.50 Throughout the EP, all changes in your circumstances are ignored. But if your entitlement to HB on two homes ceases during the EP, the amount of EP is reduced by the amount of the eligible rent on the home on which you no longer qualify for HB. And no EP is awarded for rent/rates during any period during which you are not liable for rent/rates.

17.51 If you or your partner reach pension credit age during the EP, the figure used for (b) throughout the EP is whichever would be higher using your entitlement before and after that age.

Table 17.7 **Entitlement to an extended payment**

If you have been on a 'qualifying income-related benefit'

You are entitled to an extended payment if:

- you or your partner start employment or self-employment, or increase your hours or earnings;
- this is expected to last for at least five weeks;
- you or your partner have been entitled to ESA(IR), JSA(IB), JSA(C) or IS continuously for at least 26 weeks (or any combination of those benefits in that period);
- immediately before starting the job, etc, you or your partner were on ESA(IR), JSA(IB) or IS. At this point being on JSA(C) is not enough; and
- entitlement to ESA(IR), JSA(IB) or IS ceases as a result of starting the job, etc.

If you have been on a 'qualifying contributory benefit'

You are entitled to extended payment if:

- you or your partner start employment or self-employment, or increase your hours or earnings;
- this is expected to last for at least five weeks;
- you or your partner have been entitled to ESA(C), IB or SDA continuously for at least 26 weeks (or any combination of those benefits in that period);
- immediately before starting the job, etc, you or your partner were on ESA(C), IB or SDA. And neither of you must be on ESA(IR), JSA(IB) or IS; and
- entitlement to ESA(C), IB or SDA ceases as a result of starting the job, etc.

17.51   HB60+ 52; NIHB60+ 50

T17.7   As para 17.46

Example: Extended payments

A claimant who meets all the conditions for an extended payment starts work on Monday 8th June 2015.

His award of HB continues up to and including Sunday 14th June 2015. His extended payment covers the period from Monday 15th June 2015 to Sunday 12th July 2015. If he then continues to qualify for HB after that, the new amount of HB is awarded from Monday 13th July 2015.

HB after an extended payment

17.52 If you qualify for HB based on your new income (and other circumstances) after the end of the EP, this is awarded in the normal way – and there is no requirement for you to make a fresh claim for this.

Variations for movers

17.53 If you are entitled to an EP, you are entitled to it even if you move home during the EP. In Great Britain, if the move is to another council's area, the determination, notification and award of the EP is done by the council whose area you are moving out of. That council may liaise with the council whose area you are moving into; and may pay the EP to it or to you.

Continuing payments

Entitlement

17.54 Continuing payments are awarded in HB whenever the DWP informs the council that someone on JSA(IB), ESA(IR) or income support has reached pension credit age (para 1.23) (or 65 if they stayed on JSA(IB) beyond that age), or has a partner and the partner has claimed pension credit. Continuing payments enable your award of HB to continue without a break while your entitlement to pension credit (if any) is determined.

Period and amount

17.55 The continuing payment starts immediately after the last day of your entitlement to JSA(IB)/ESA(IR)/IS, and lasts for four weeks plus any extra days to make it end on a Sunday. The amount during that period is calculated by treating you as having no income or capital. And if you move home, your eligible rent or rates are the higher of the amounts at the old and new addresses; and any non-dependant deductions are based on the circumstances at the new address.

17.52   HB 72D,73D; HB60+ 53D; NIHB 70C,71C; NIHB60+ 51C

17.53   HB 72C,73C,115,116; HB60+ 53C,96,97

17.54   HB60+ 54; NIHB60+ 52

Example: Continuing payments

A man is on HB and JSA(IB) when he reaches 65, on Thursday 12th November 2015. The DWP informs the council that his entitlement to pension credit is being considered.

His continuing payment of HB is awarded from Thursday 12th November 2015 to Sunday 13th December 2015 – a total of four weeks and four days.

By then the council knows the claimant's entitlement to HB based on his new circumstances, and awards this from Monday 14th December 2015.

Terminology

Revisions and supersessions

17.56   In HB law, a changed decision is also known as a revision or a supersession:

(a) a 'revision' is required when a decision was wrong from the outset. When a decision is revised, the revision goes back to the beginning (to the date of the decision in question);

(b) a 'supersession' is required when there has been a change of circumstances. When a decision is superseded, the supersession does not go right back: there is always a 'before' and an 'after'.

Some examples are given in table 17.8. Each of the above results in a new decision, which can itself be revised or superseded or appealed.

Closed period supersessions

17.57   A 'closed period supersession' is done when someone's entitlement to HB is discovered to have reduced to nil for a fixed period in the past (and recommenced at the same or a different rate after that). For example, a claimant has been on JSA(IB) (and HB) for many years but worked last Christmas for a fixed contract of three weeks for a very high income. He did not declare that fact then, but it is discovered now. A 'closed period supersession' means that the council (now) reduces his entitlement to nil for that past period (and recovers the overpayment: chapter 18). The advantage (administratively and to the claimant) is that the claimant remains currently entitled to HB (based on his original claim) without needing to reclaim. There have been doubts about this rule, but it is correct in income support (CIS/2595/2003), and the DWP considers it to be correct in HB (circular HB/CTB A6/2009).

17.56   CPSA sch 7; NICPSA sch 7; DAR 4,7,8; NIDAR 4,7,8

Table 17.8 **Revisions and supersessions: examples**

Situation	How it is dealt with in HB
Changes of circumstances	
A change notified more than one month after it occurred (this time limit can be extended) if you qualify for more HB	**Supersession:** Typically, from the Monday following the day the council receives the notification (paras 17.11-13)
Any other change of circumstances	**Supersession:** Typically, from the Monday following the day the change occurs (para 17.21)
Overpayments and official errors	
Overpayments, whatever the cause; and underpayments caused by official error	**Revision or supersession:** From when the overpayment or underpayment began
Successful requests for a reconsideration, etc	
Reconsiderations requested within one month (which can be extended)	**Revision:** From the date the decision took effect or should have
Reconsiderations requested outside that time limit (paras 17.68-69 and 19.15)	**Supersession:** From the Monday of the week in which the council received the request
Appeals if the council is able to revise in your favour (para 19.21)	**Revision:** From the date the decision took effect or should have

Reviewing and correcting HB

Reviewing decisions

17.58   The council can reconsider any decision it has made about your HB. This is often called 'reviewing' a decision. A review may show that:

(a) there has been a change of circumstances the council did not know about. In this case the rules in paras 17.9-55 apply;

(b) a decision was wrong from the outset. In this case the rules in paras 17.60-70 apply.

Information, evidence and decision notices

17.59   The council can ask you for information and evidence it reasonably requires in order to review and correct a decision. You are responsible for providing this in the same way as when you made your claim (para 5.13) and the council must take it into account if you

17.58   HB 89(1); HB60+ 70(1); NIHB 85(1); NIHB60+ 66(1)

17.59   AA 5(1); NIAA 5(1); HB 86(1),(3); HB60+ 67(1),(3); NIHB 82(1),(3); NIHB60+ 63(1),(3); DAR 4(5), 7(5); NIDAR 4(5), 7(5)

provide it within one month, or longer if reasonable. The council must issue a decision notice about any change it makes to your HB: see paras 16.3-9.

Correcting decisions

17.60　　The council can correct mistakes in any HB decision it has made. This applies to mistakes found by the council itself, or which you (or the person your HB is paid to) have brought to its attention. The detailed rules are in paragraphs 17.62-70.

17.61　　The law about correcting decisions uses four different terms:

(a) a 'mistake of fact' means that the decision was based on an incorrect fact (without at this stage saying that it was necessarily anybody's fault);

(b) an 'error of law' means that the decision was based on an incorrect understanding of the law;

(c) an 'accidental error' is something on the lines of a slip of the pen – a failure by the authority to put into action (or to record) its true intentions;

(d) an 'official error' is defined independently (para17.63) and can include one or a combination of the above (CH/943/2003).

'Revisions' and 'supersessions' are explained in paras 17.56-57.

Example: 'Mistake of fact' and 'error of law'

In deciding a claim for HB, the council determined that two unmarried people were not a couple.

This would be a mistake of fact if the council made its decision not knowing that they were actually married (e.g. because the claimant had lied or the council misread the application form).

It would be an error of law if the council wrongly believed that two unmarried people could never be a couple for HB purposes.

Correcting accidental errors

17.62　　The council may correct an accidental error in any decision (including a revised or superseding decision), or the record of any decision, at any time. The correction is deemed to be part of the decision or record, and the council must give written notice of the correction as soon as practicable to you and any other person affected.

Correcting other official errors

17.63　　The council may revise (or supersede if it cannot revise) a decision at any time if the decision arose from an 'official error'. An 'official error' means an error by the council, the DWP or HM Revenue and Customs – or someone acting on their behalf (such as a contractor or a housing association which verifies HB claims). However, something does not count as an

---

17.62　　DAR 10A(1),(2); NIDAR 10A(1),(2)

17.63　　DAR 1(2),4(2); NIDAR 1(2),4(2)

'official error' if it was caused wholly or partly by any person or body other than the above, nor if it is an error of law which is shown to have been an error only by a subsequent decision of the Upper Tribunal, the NI Commissioners or a court.

17.64 The effect may be that there has been an underpayment of HB (in which case the arrears must be awarded – no matter how far back they go) or an overpayment (which may or may not be recoverable: chapter 18).

When an appeal decision applies to a case

17.65 The council may revise a decision at any time to take account of an appeal decision in the same case (made by a tribunal, the Upper Tribunal, the NI Commissioners or a court) which the council was not aware of at the time it made the decision. See chapter 19 for the other rules about taking appeal decisions into account.

Mistakes of fact resulting in an overpayment

17.66 The council may revise or supersede a decision at any time if the decision was made in ignorance of, or was based on a mistake as to, some material fact – and the decision was, as a result, more favourable than it would otherwise have been. This creates an overpayment (which may or may not be recoverable: chapter 18).

Mistakes of fact discovered within one month

17.67 The council may revise a decision if, within one month of the date of notifying it, or longer if reasonable, the council has sufficient information to show that it was made in ignorance of, or was based on a mistake as to, some material fact. This can arise only in the case of increases to entitlement (for decreases see para 17.66).

Other mistakes of fact

17.68 If none of the previous rules in this section apply, the council may supersede a decision at any time if the decision was made in ignorance of, or was based on a mistake as to, some material fact. This can arise only in the case of increases to entitlement (for decreases see para 17.66). For example this rule can be used when you request a reconsideration but are out of time, which is sometimes called an 'any time review' (see para 19.15 and the example there).

17.69 The supersession in such a case takes effect from the Monday at the beginning of the benefit week in which:

(a) the request was received from you or another person affected (if a request was indeed made); or

(b) the council first had information to show that the original decision was made in ignorance or mistake of fact (in any other case).

17.65   DAR 4(7); NIDAR 4(6)

17.66   DAR 4(2); NIDAR 4(2)

17.67   DAR 4(1),8(4),(5); NIDAR 4(1),8(4),(5)

17.68   CPSA sch 7 para 4(5),(6); NICPSA sch 7 para 4(4),(5); DAR 7(2)(b),8(4)(5); NIDAR 7(2)(b),8(4),(5)

17.69   DAR 8(4)-(5); NIDAR 8(4)-5)

Other errors of law

17.70   A final rule applies if a decision was based on an error of law but was not due to 'official error' (para 17.63). (This could arise if the Upper Tribunal, NI Commissioners or a court interpret the law in an unexpected way: para 17.42.) The council may supersede the decision at any time. The supersession takes effect from the date on which it is made (or, if earlier, from the date the person's request was received).

Suspending, restoring and terminating HB

17.71   This section describes how the council can suspend, restore and terminate HB. To suspend means stopping making payments for the time being, usually in order to avoid an overpayment or to seek information or evidence. To restore means starting payments again – either at the same amount as before or at a different amount, depending on the circumstances. To terminate means ending an award of HB altogether.

Suspending HB

17.72   The council may suspend HB if any of the following circumstances apply:

(a)   the council doubts whether the conditions of entitlement to HB are fulfilled;

(b)   the council is considering whether to change a decision about HB;

(c)   the council considers there may be a recoverable overpayment of HB;

(d)   a First-tier or Upper Tribunal has made a decision (in this or another case) and the council is awaiting the decision or a statement of reasons, or is considering making a further appeal;

(e)   an appeal has been made, or leave to appeal has been sought, against a decision of a First-tier or Upper Tribunal or court in the case to be suspended;

(f)   an appeal has been made, or leave to appeal has been sought, against a decision of an Upper Tribunal or court in a different HB case, and this may affect the case to be suspended;

(g)   you (or another person affected) have failed to provide information or evidence needed by the council to consider changing a decision about HB.

In such cases, HB is usually suspended in full (though the law permits the council to suspend only part).

Restoring HB

17.73   When payments of HB have been suspended, the council must restore them (to the extent that you are still entitled) within 14 days of the following or as soon as reasonably practicable:

17.70   CPSA sch 7 para 4(5),(6); NICPSA sch 7 para 4(4),(5); DAR 7(2)(b); NIDAR 7(2)(b)

17.71   DAR 4(5), 7(5); NIDAR 4(4)

17.72   DAR 10; NIDAR 10; HB sch 9; HB60+ sch 8; NIHB sch 10; NIHB60+ sch 9

- in cases (a) to (c) (para 17.72), the council is satisfied that HB is properly payable and no outstanding matters remain to be resolved;
- in case (d), the council decides not to make the further appeal (if it decides to make the further appeal case (e) or (f) then applies);
- in cases (e) and (f), the appeal or request for leave has been determined;
- in case (g), the claimant has responded as required (para 17.74).

Information and evidence

17.74 When payments of HB have been suspended for failure to provide information or evidence (para 17.72(g)), the council must notify you of the suspension and of what information and evidence is required. You must then, within one month or such longer period as the council considers necessary:

(a) provide the information or evidence required; or

(b) satisfy the council that the information or evidence does not exist, or is impossible for you to obtain.

Terminating HB

17.75 When payments of HB have been suspended for failure to provide information or evidence (para 17.72(g)) and you have failed to respond as required (para 17.74) your HB entitlement is terminated from the date on which the payments were suspended (i.e. no further payments are made). In some cases, termination should not be done unless a reminder request has been sent: [2008] UKUT 13 (ACC). Terminating benefit under this rule is a kind of supersession: CH/2555/2007. The rule cannot be used to end HB from an earlier date: CH/3736/2006, so if entitlement did end earlier, this is done as an (ordinary) supersession from that earlier date. The second of the examples illustrates this. As may be observed, the two concepts (termination as a type of supersession, and ordinary supersession at nil) each have the same effect of stopping someone's HB (though the case law generally disapproves of this being described as 'cancelling' HB, because that word does not appear in the law: CH/2555/2007). If in the above or other circumstances HB was wrongly terminated, it must be reinstated: CH/2995/2006.

17.76 A decision to terminate HB must be notified to you and any other person affected.

Appeals

17.77 You have a right of appeal to a First-tier Tribunal (table 19.2) about a decision to terminate HB (CH/402/2007), or to restore HB at a different amount or for a different reason; but not about a determination to suspend HB, or to restore HB at the same amount for the same reasons. A decision to suspend HB may, however, be challenged by judicial review if it is irrational: R (Sanneh) v SSWP.

17.74   DAR 11,13(1),(2); NIDAR 11,13(1),(2)

17.75   DAR 13(3),(4); NIDAR 13(3),(4)

17.76   CPSA sch 7 para 15; NICPSA sch 7 para 15; DAR 14; NIDAR 14

17.77   R (Sanneh) v SSWP 30/04/12 QBD [2013] EWHC 1840 (Admin)
         www.bailii.org/ew/cases/EWHC/Admin/2012/1840.html

Examples: Suspending, restoring and terminating HB

A change of circumstances

The council obtains information that a claimant on HB has changed jobs. It suspends his award immediately, and writes to him allowing him one month to respond.

After two weeks, he sends in the necessary information and evidence, and he remains entitled to HB.

The council restores his HB from the date payments were suspended, making any change in his entitlement from the Monday after the day he got the new job.

Another change of circumstances

A claimant has been on HB for some years. On Wednesday 19th August 2015 the council obtains information that he has been doing undeclared work. It suspends his award from the earliest possible date so that the last payment of HB is for week ending Sunday 23rd August 2015, and writes to him allowing him one month to respond.

Shortly afterwards he writes in to admit that he has been working since Monday 8th June 2015 and knows that he does not qualify for HB based on those earnings.

The council terminates his HB on Sunday 23rd August 2015. It also supersedes his HB (at nil) from Monday 15th June 2015. This creates an overpayment of HB from Monday 15th June to Sunday 23rd August inclusive. The overpayment is not due to official error and so is recoverable.

A review

The council decides to review a claimant's award of HB and sends her a short form asking her to confirm her circumstances, allowing her one month to reply. Because the claimant does not reply within the month, the council suspends her HB and writes to her requesting her to say what her circumstances are, allowing her one further month to respond.

Because the claimant again does not reply within a month, the council terminates her award of HB and notifies her of this.

Two weeks later she returns the original short form, declaring that her circumstances have not changed. The council is satisfied with this and restores her HB from the date payments were suspended.

Chapter 18 **Overpayments**

- What is an overpayment: see paras 18.1-6.
- Identifying the cause of an overpayment: see paras 18.7-10.
- Which overpayments are recoverable: see paras 18.11-15.
- Calculating the amount of the overpayment: see paras 18.16-26.
- The discretion to recover and who the authority may recover from: see paras 18.27-39.
- The authority's powers to enforce recovery: see paras 18.61-67.
- Overpayment decision notices: see paras 18.68-71.
- Overpayment, fraud and penalties: see paras 18.72-77.

What is an overpayment?

18.1   An HB 'overpayment' is an amount of HB which has been 'paid' that you had no entitlement to under the HB regulations. The authority may have paid it directly to you or to your landlord or your landlord's agent. If you are a council tenant HB is usually paid as a rebate to your local authority rent account. In Northern Ireland an HB overpayment may take the form of a rebate on your rate account.

18.2   Overpayments can occur when the authority first decides your entitlement or following a change in your entitlement (technically after the authority has revised or superseded an earlier decision). An overpayment can also arise in relation to a payment on account if the authority later decides that it was greater than your entitlement to HB for the relevant period.

18.3   Tribunals dealing with overpayment appeals (except in relation to payments on account) expect the authority to be able to show which revisions or supersessions relate to the overpayment (CH/3439/2004, C3/07-08(IS), C2/10-11(HB)). While a tribunal is able to remedy defective decision-making by the authority (R(IB)2/04), if the authority hasn't made a revision or supersession or if such changes to entitlement have no legal foundation then there is no overpayment.

> **Example: A late reported change in circumstance leading to an overpayment**
>
> Rebecca is 46 and on HB. On 2nd May 2015 her adult son Gabriel returned to live with her. Rebecca should have told her council about this but she didn't. It wasn't until 1st August 2014 that the council found out. It decided that a non-dependant deduction should have been made from Rebecca's HB for Gabriel from Monday 4th May 2015. But Rebecca had

---

18.1   AA 75(1), 134(2); NIAA 73(1), 126(1)-(2); HB 99; HB60+ 80; NIHB 96; NIHB60+ 77

18.2   HB 99; HB60+ 80; NIHB 96; NIHB60+ 77

been paid HB up to and including Sunday 2nd August 2015 on the basis that she had no non-dependants. The authority changed (superseded) Rebecca's HB entitlement from Monday 4th May 2015. It also identified that because of that late change in entitlement an overpayment of HB had arisen.

18.4 The overpayment and recovery of HB creates major difficulties for claimants, landlords and authorities. Many authorities fail to:

(a) follow the correct decision-making process;

(b) notify claimants and landlords correctly;

(c) keep adequate records; or

(d) account for overpayments properly.

As a result they create rent arrears for themselves, debts for claimants and landlords and make inaccurate subsidy claims (DWP S4/2014 para 4(a)).

The authority's duties

18.5 When the authority identifies an HB overpayment it should:

(a) establish the cause;

(b) determine whether or not it is recoverable;

(c) identify the period of the overpayment and calculate the amount;

(d) consider whether or not to recover it;

(e) determine who to recover it from; and

(f) notify you and any other person affected such as your landlord (normally within 14 days or as soon as reasonably practicable after that).

18.6 The DWP provides authorities with detailed guidance on these matters and more in its HB Overpayments Guide (2015) (OG) [www].

The cause of an overpayment

18.7 The authority must establish the cause of the overpayment to:

(a) decide whether it is recoverable;

(b) provide you (and anyone else it should or may recover the overpayment from) with required information;

(c) claim the correct amount of subsidy from central government; and

(d) decide the method of recovery in certain cases.

18.6   www.gov.uk/government/publications/housing-benefit-overpayments-guide

18.8   To establish the cause of the overpayment the authority needs to consider what is the substantial cause of the overpayment viewed in a commonsense way (R (Sier) v Cambridge CC HB Review Board [2001]; [2010] UKUT 57 (AAC) para 19); or who really caused the overpayment ([2011] UKUT 266 (AAC) para 68).

How an overpayment is 'caused'

18.9   The main causes of overpayments are:

(a) claimant error, e.g. you fail to tell the authority about a change of circumstances which you have a duty to report (but if the authority disputes you reported it then it is a question of fact the tribunal is entitled to decide: no authority's procedures are infallible: [2014] UKUT 2013 (AAC)); or

(b) local authority error, e.g. you tell the authority about a change in your circumstances but it fails to act on this information;

(c) DWP error, e.g. the jobcentre plus, pension service, or disability and carers service makes a mistaken award of JSA(IB)/ESA(IR), pension credit or income support;

(d) third party error, e.g. your landlord in receipt of HB gives the authority incorrect information about a rent increase;

(e) no-one's fault, e.g. you get a backdated pay award and this affects your entitlement to HB in the past;

(f) a payment on account turns out to be too great;

(g) HB payment technicalities, e.g. you get a rebate for a future period, but your entitlement is changed before that period; or

(h) other reasons.

More than one cause of an overpayment

18.10   If there is more than one cause of an overpayment, the authority must separate these out (CH/858/2006). This is the case, for example, where you delay telling the authority that your earnings have increased and it then delays acting on that information. The authority should identify the two causes, periods and amounts of the overpayment and make separate decisions about whether the two amounts are recoverable.

Which overpayments are recoverable

Non-recoverable overpayments

18.11   An HB overpayment is not recoverable if:

(a) it arose because of 'official error' by a relevant authority (para 18.13); and

(b) you, someone acting on your behalf, or the person paid the benefit (if different), could not reasonably have been expected to realise it was an overpayment either at the time of receipt of the payment or of any notice relating to that payment (para 18.14).

18.8   R (Sier) v Cambridge CC HBRB 08/10/01 CA [2001] EWCA Civ 1523 www.bailii.org/ew/cases/EWCA/Civ/2001/1523.html

18.11   HB 100(2); HB60+ 81(2); NIHB 97(2); NIHB60+ 78(2)

18.12   All other overpayments are recoverable. This includes:

(a)   an overpayment of a payment on account of HB (para 16.22) which is being recovered by deductions from ongoing HB;

(b)   an overpayment of HB to a council or NIHE tenant, which was caused by an 'official error' (para 18.13) but which relates to a period in the future;

(c)   an overpayment of HB for rates in Northern Ireland caused by a retrospective reduction in regional rates.

Meaning of 'official error'

18.13   An official error is a mistake, whether in the form of an act or omission, made by the authority, the DWP or HMRC (and in Northern Ireland DSD and DEL) or someone on their behalf (such as a contractor or a housing association which verifies HB claims). It does not include cases where you, someone acting on your behalf, or the payee, caused or materially contributed to that error. The test is whether you contributed towards the error, not whether you contributed towards the overpayment (CH/215/2008 at para 28). Overpayment appeals often require consideration of what is and is not an 'official error'. Significant cases are summarised in table 18.1.

Table 18.1 **Overpayments case law: meaning of 'official error'**

- *Terminology:* In this context, a 'mistake' is not different from an 'official error' and it is artificial to try and read different meanings into these two terms (CH/943/2003).

- *Previous tribunal decisions:* Official error includes where an earlier tribunal has decided that a DWP/HMRC decision is wrong (CH/943/2003).

- *Overpayment caused by DWP benefit being reinstated on appeal:* Where the overpayment is caused by the reinstatement of a DWP benefit following an appeal this does not amount to an official error (CH/38/2008).

- *The authority:* In this context includes any part of the authority and is not confined to any department within it (CH/3586/2007).

- *Designated office:* The claimant's circumstances had been repeatedly notified to the housing department. Not to pass the information on to the benefits service or advise the claimant to do so was an official error to which the claimant had not contributed (CH/2567/2007).

- *Whether official bodies talk to each other:* Just because one department of the DWP holds the information it cannot be presumed that another DWP department is also aware of it: 'The claimant's duty is to tell whom she is told to tell' (Hinchy v Secretary of State for Work and Pensions, reported as R(IS)7/05).

18.12   HB 100(1); HB60+ 81(1); NIHB 97(1); NIHB60+ 78(1); HB 93(3), 100(4); HB60+ 74(3), 81(4); NIHB 90(3), 97(4); NIHB60+ 71(3), 78(4)

18.13   HB 100(3); HB60+ 81(3); NIHB 97(3); NIHB60+ 78(3)

- *Failure by DWP to pass on information:* The failure of the DWP to notify the authority that JSA(IB) or income support has ceased is not an official error because the claimant has a duty to notify the authority of this (R (Sier) v Cambridge CC). But this does not apply to pension credit (and some other) cases in which it is the pension, disability and carers service's duty to notify the authority of changes (table 17.2).

- *Failure by DWP to act on a promise:* If the DWP undertook to forward a notice of a change to the authority and then failed to do so, that might amount to official error (CH/939/2004, CH/3761/2005).

- *Failure by the authority to cross-check:* The fact that the claimant disclosed income (etc) in a previous claim (but not in their current claim) does not mean that the authority's failure to cross-check is official error (R(H) 1/04, CH/2794/2004).

- *Failure by the authority to ask a fundamental question about eligibility:* (here, whether the child mainly lived with her mother, the claimant, which it did not) amounted to official error, as can a failure to amend forms CH/4228/2006 and [2014] UKUT 201 (AAC).

- *Failure to recognise relevant information on document provided for a different purpose:* There is no general rule that the failure by the authority to recognise information as relevant which was provided for a different purpose cannot be official error: it depends on the particular circumstances (CH/3925/2006).

- *Failure by authority to check potential changes:* Failure by the authority to check up on potential changes in entitlement to a tax credit is not official error (R(H) 2/04), nor is failure to check up on a potential increase in incapacity benefit (CH/687/2006) or earnings (CH/3/2008).

- *Delay by authority in dealing with a notified change:* In a case in which the claimant notified her increased earnings on 19th April, but her council did not take them into account until 13th May (24 days later), this was quick enough not to constitute official error. In reaching this decision, the commissioner compared the council's duty to act on a change of circumstances with its duty to act on a claim, where there is a time limit of 14 days (para 16.2). The 24 days the commissioner allowed in this case was based on its individual circumstances (CH/858/2006).

- *Delay in applying to the rent officer:* A delay in applying to the rent officer can be an official error (CH/361/2006).

- *Claimant reports wrong amount of benefit due to overpayment deductions:* If the claimant reports the incorrect amount of benefit because the DWP is making deductions, the fact that the authority does not realise the mistake does not amount to an official error (CH/56/08).

- *Claimant's method of notifying changes:* Where a claimant had notified a change by telephone only, and the council had failed to act on it, this did not necessarily mean that the claimant had materially contributed to the error (CH/2409/2005).

T18.1   R (Sier) v Cambridge HBRB see footnote to para 18.8

Awareness of being overpaid

18.14   An overpayment which arises due to official error is recoverable only if you, someone acting on your behalf, or the person paid (if different), could reasonably have been expected to realise that it was an overpayment – either at the time the payment is received, or at the time of any decision notice relating to it is issued. This test is often considered on appeal. Significant cases are summarised in table 18.2.

Table 18.2 **Overpayments case law: awareness of being overpaid in official error cases**

- *Purpose of the rule:* The purpose of the rule is to protect a claimant who has relied on being entitled to the payment so that, having innocently spent it, they do not have to repay money they cannot afford (CH/1176/2003).

- *'Was' or 'might be' an overpayment?* The test is whether there was a reasonable expectation that there was an overpayment not whether there might be one (R v Liverpool CC ex parte Griffiths, CH/2935/2005, CH/858/2006).

- *Burden of proof:* The burden of proof (paras 1.45-46) is on the person stating that they could not reasonably have been expected to realise – not on the council stating that they could (CH/4918/2003).

- *What can a person reasonably be expected to realise?* What a particular claimant could have been expected to realise varies according to their knowledge, experience and capacity (R v Liverpool CC ex parte Griffiths). For example, someone who had needed the council's help to fill in his application form may be less likely to realise he was overpaid (CH/2935/2005); someone from a country where (the equivalent of) tax credits are taken into account in a different way (in the assessment of the equivalent of HB) might not realise that they are taken into account as income in the UK (CH/858/2006).

- *An ordinary reasonable claimant:* An 'ordinary reasonable claimant' cannot be expected to go and find out more about the HB scheme than they are informed of by their council in the notice of their award (CH/2554/2002).

- *Receipt of a notice:* Whether a person could reasonably have been expected to realise at the time of any notice, refers to a notice about the award of HB, not the overpayment notice – otherwise the rule would be meaningless (CH/1176/2003).

- *Comprehensible notice:* If a notice of an award contains the basis of the calculation in a reasonably clear manner, and it is clear that there has been a mistake in the claimant's favour, then the overpayment is recoverable – because the claimant could reasonably have been expected to realise (CH/2409/2005).

- *Claimant queries notice but authority continues to pay wrong amount:* Where the claimant queries the decision notice but the council continues to pay, there comes

---

a point where the claimant is entitled to rely on the notice and accept that the council knows best (CH/3240/2007).

- *Reference to wages omitted in the decision notice:* If there was no reference at all to the claimant's wages in the notice, whereas their other income was listed, a 'claimant of normal intelligence' could reasonably be expected to deduce that there had been a mistake and that they were overpaid (CH/2554/2002).

- *Reference to state retirement pension omitted in the decision notice:* If there was no reference at all to the claimant's state retirement pension in the notice, the claimant might have concluded that the pension was being ignored (perhaps because it was disregarded or because everybody of his age received one); and 'a typical claimant cannot reasonably be expected to read or understand the calculations' so they could not reasonably be expected to deduce that they were overpaid (CH/2554/2002).

- *A disparity between the claimant's declared earnings and the amount on the decision notice:* If this is large (in this case earnings of £210 assessed and notified as less than £50) then it would be reasonable to expect the claimant to realise that they must be being overpaid (CH/2943/2007). For a similar case relating to an incorrect eligible rent, see [2008] UKUT 6 AAC.

- *The claimant must have some reason to believe the council's figures are wrong:* A claimant cannot be expected to seek advice unless they have some reason to believe the figures are wrong. A tribunal should ask the claimant how they reconciled their own knowledge of their earnings with the figures in the notice, to give them the opportunity to explain why they could not be expected to realise there was an overpayment (CH/2943/2007).

- *Claimant telephoned to say they thought there was a mistake:* If there has been an official error, and the claimant alleges they telephoned to say they thought there had been, then the council should determine whether they in fact did so before going on to consider if this affects whether the overpayment is recoverable (CH/4065/2001).

- *Claimant's other actions in relation to the award:* The authority in this case had asked for evidence of earnings for the wrong period. The claimant provided what they asked for, but not other evidence that would have shown his income was higher. His other actions (including telephoning to check things) suggested he was not trying to mislead and there was no reason to suppose he could reasonably have been expected to realise there was an overpayment (CH/1780/2005).

- *Time of receipt of a payment:* The 'time' of a payment by cheque is fairly narrow, but a telephone call from the council a couple of hours after the claimant received a large HB cheque, advising her it was incorrect, may be soon enough to mean that the claimant was aware at the 'time of receipt' that it was an overpayment (CH/1176/2003).

> ■ *When the overpayment is a rebate:* If the overpayment is of a rebate, the council may need to consider whether the claimant could reasonably have been expected to realise that there was an overpayment 'at the times when credits were applied to his rent account' (CH/1675/2005).
>
> ■ *What a landlord could have realised:* It is not always the case that a landlord knows when a claimant has left their accommodation ([2013] UKUT 232 (AAC)). And in the case of a landlord company or housing association, it is what the whole organisation might reasonably have been expected to have realised that is relevant (CH/4918/2003).

Meaning of 'claimant or third party error'

18.15 You or a third party can only 'cause' an overpayment if you intentionally or unintentionally misrepresent, or fail to disclose, a material fact. However, you may not be expected to disclose a fact if you were given clear advice to the contrary by an official of the authority or the DWP (R(SB) 3/89).

The amount of a recoverable overpayment

18.16 The amount of a recoverable overpayment is the difference between what was paid and what you were entitled to under the regulations. The following rules can reduce the amount of the overpayment.

Underlying entitlement

18.17 When the authority calculates the amount of a recoverable overpayment, it should deduct any amount 'which should have been determined to be payable' in respect of the whole or part of the overpayment period:

(a) on the basis of the claim as presented to the authority;

(b) on the basis of the claim as it would have appeared had any misrepresentation or non-disclosure been remedied before the decision; or

(c) on the basis of the claim as it would have appeared if any change of circumstances (except a change of the dwelling which you occupied) had been notified at the time that change occurred.

This means whatever would have been awarded (to you, or to any partner had they claimed) if the authority had known the facts of the case throughout, and all changes of circumstances had been notified on time.

18.16   HB 99; HB60+ 80; NIHB 96; NIHB60+ 77

18.17   HB 104(1); HB60+ 85(1); NIHB 101(1); NIHB60+ 82(1)

18.18   HB not recovered under this rule is called 'underlying entitlement' to distinguish it from any actual entitlement to HB. The application of the underlying entitlement rule is mandatory but the DWP has expressed concern that some authorities are not considering it when calculating recoverable overpayments (DWP G2/2013, para 16).

Why underlying entitlement can occur

18.19   Underlying entitlement overrides the rules about:

(a)   which partner in a couple (or polygamous marriage) is the claimant;

(b)   late notice of beneficial changes (para 17.11): see example 1; and

(c)   late requests for a reconsideration (paras 17.68 and 19.15).

The stage at which the authority considers underlying entitlement

18.20   When a recoverable overpayment arises, the authority may already have information enabling it to allow underlying entitlement (as in example 1). And in all cases, unless there is no possibility of underlying entitlement (e.g. you had more than £16,000 throughout the overpayment period), the authority should invite you to provide information and evidence to establish underlying entitlement (OG paras 3.32-3.34) (using the usual rules about obtaining information and evidence: para 5.13) and the onus is on you to do this (R(H) 1/05).

18.21   If underlying entitlement has not been identified when the authority determines and notifies the overpayment, you (or other overpaid person) may ask the authority to reconsider or appeal to a tribunal (chapter 19) – and in doing so may include information which establishes underlying entitlement. Once the time limit for appeal has expired (one month which can be increased to 13 months in special circumstances), it is not possible to allow underlying entitlement (OG para 3.37) – unless there has been an official error (para 17.63).

Calculation rules for underlying entitlement

18.22   There are two calculation rules:

(a)   only underlying entitlement falling within the overpayment period is used to reduce the amount of the overpayment; and

(b)   underlying entitlement may reduce an overpayment to nil, but it can never be used to actually pay money out to you or anyone else.

If you still paid rent to the authority or rates in Northern Ireland

18.23   If you are a council/NIHE tenant and during the period of the overpayment you paid rent above your erroneous liability then the authority may deduct these payments from the recoverable overpayment. The rule applies equally to payments of rates in Northern Ireland.

18.22   HB 104(1); HB60+ 85(1); NIHB 101(1); NIHB60+ 82(1)

18.23   HB 104(2); HB60+ 85(2); NIHB 101(2); NIHB60+ 82(2)

Examples: Underlying entitlement

1. When there has been late notice of a change

Information: Blythe's non-dependant Gwenyth moved out six months ago, but Blythe did not tell her council until three months ago (and had no special circumstances for the late reporting of this change) so her council removed the non-dependant deduction from three months ago. Today the council discovered that Blythe has undeclared earnings from work over the previous nine months.

Assessment: The underlying entitlement rule means that the council must reduce the amount of the overpayment (due to Blythe's undeclared earnings from work) by the amount it could not award in relation to Gwenyth moving out. This results in a lower recoverable overpayment; it may even reduce the overpayment to nil; but in no circumstances can it result in Blythe getting more benefit.

2. Calculation rules

Information: In William's case, there is a recoverable overpayment of £5 per week for weeks 1 to 20 inclusive (20 x £5 = £100), and underlying entitlement (because William did not tell the council about a beneficial change on time) in weeks 11 to 20 inclusive of £15 per week.

Assessment: The authority uses William's underlying entitlement in weeks 11 to 20 inclusive (10 x £15 = £150) to reduce the overpayment (£100). It is enough to reduce the recoverable overpayment to nil but it can't award the remainder of the underlying entitlement to William.

Deductions if you move home within the same authority

18.24 When the authority calculates a recoverable overpayment caused by you moving home within its area, it has the discretion to offset your HB entitlement at the new address against the HB overpayment on your previous property. However, the authority can only use this rule where:

(a) you were awarded a rent allowance on the old address that you were not entitled to because you had moved; and

(b) the HB on the old and new home is paid to the same person (e.g. you or the same landlord) by the same authority.

Where the authority deducts this amount it should treat an equivalent amount as having been paid in respect of your new home.

18.24   HB 104A; HB60+ 85A; NIHB 101A; NIHB60+ 82A

Example: Calculating an overpayment when you move home

Bob gets a rent allowance of £100 a week. He moves to a new home where he gets HB of £110 a week. Bob doesn't tell the authority about the move for three weeks after leaving the earlier address. This results in an overpayment of £300 on the old address.

Bob is entitled to £330 a week on the new address for the same period. The authority may reduce the amount of the recoverable overpayment on Bob's old home by £300, reducing it to nil, and paying Bob the remaining £30 in relation to his new home.

The diminishing capital rule

18.25 The authority should use this overpayment calculation rule if your recoverable overpayment:

(a) arose due to capital being wrongly taken into account (for any reason); and

(b) was in respect of a period of more than 13 weeks.

Example: The diminishing capital rule

Thomas failed to declare capital of £16,033. When his council discovers this, there has been a recoverable overpayment for 30 weeks. Throughout that time Thomas got HB of £9 per week, he had no other capital at all, and the figure of £16,033 remained the same.

■ In the first 13 weeks, he is not entitled to HB:
Overpayment: 13 x £9   =   £117

■ His capital is then treated as reduced by this amount:
£16,033 – £117   =   £15,916

■ In the second 13 weeks, based on this reduced capital, he is entitled to HB of £5 per week, so the overpayment is £4 per week. Overpayment: 13 x £4   =   £52

■ His capital is then treated as further reduced by this amount:
£15,916 – £52   =   £15,864

■ In the remaining 4 weeks, based on this further reduced capital, he is still entitled to HB of £5 per week, so the overpayment is still £4 per week. Overpayment: 4 x £4   =   £16

■ So the total overpayment of HB for the 30 weeks is   £185

18.26 In such cases, the authority should take the following steps:

(a) at the end of the first 13 weeks of the overpayment period, the authority should treat the capital as reduced by the amount overpaid during those 13 weeks. This gives it an imaginary capital figure which it should use to calculate the overpayment after that;

18.25   HB 103; HB60+ 84; NIHB 100; NIHB60+ 81

(b) the authority should do the same again at the end of each 13 weeks until the end of the overpayment period;

(c) but when the authority calculates your HB after the end of the overpayment period, it should use the actual capital (not the imaginary amount).

This rule reflects the fact that if the authority had awarded you less HB due to the capital being taken into account, you might have used some of the capital to pay the rent or, in Northern Ireland, rates.

The discretion to recover

18.27   If an overpayment is 'recoverable' (paras 18.11-12), this means the authority has the discretion to recover it or not recover it (para 1.53). The question of whether an overpayment is recoverable is therefore separate from the question of whether to recover it. The DWP advises the authority that it should have 'due regard' for individual circumstances (OG paras 2.145-147). The authority should look at your case on its individual merits.

18.28   You can ask the authority to use this discretion but you have no right of appeal to a tribunal about this ([2011] UKUT 266 (AAC) para 71). If the authority exercises its discretion unreasonably or irrationally you could instead seek a judicial review – but should obtain advice about this. This was done in a case where an authority sought to recover an overpayment caused by a war pension awarded for a past period – though the outcome was that the court required the authority to think again taking into account relevant considerations and did not ban recovery (R v South Hams District Council ex p Ash).

Who to recover from

18.29   The authority may recover a recoverable overpayment as follows:

(a) if the overpayment was caused by you or the payee, or someone on their behalf (para 18.15), it is recoverable only from the person who caused the overpayment (and if there is more than one such person, it is recoverable from any of them);

(b) if the overpayment was due to official error, and you or the payee, or someone on their behalf, could reasonably have been expected to realise it was an overpayment (para 18.14), it is recoverable only from the person who could reasonably have been expected to realise (and if there is more than one such person, it is recoverable from any of them);

(c) in any other case (e.g. if the overpayment was no-one's fault) it is recoverable from you and (if different) the payee (in other words from either).

18.30   If, for any of the above reasons, the overpayment is recoverable from you, it may also be recoverable from your partner (para 18.32). In some cases, the effect of the above rules is that the authority has a choice about who to recover the overpayment from (para 18.37).

18.28   R v South Hams DC ex p Ash 10/05/99 QBD [1999] EWHC Admin 418 32 HLR 405

18.29   AA 75(3); NIAA 73(3); HB 101(2), (3A); HB60+ 82(2), (3A); NIHB 98(2),(3A); NIHB60+ 79(2), (2A)

Recovery from you

18.31   The effect of the above rules (para 18.29) is that the authority can recover most overpayments from you. If you die it can recover the overpaid amount from your estate. In fact, the only cases in which the authority cannot recover a recoverable overpayment from you (and can only recover from the payee, typically a landlord or agent) are:

(a) when the payee was the cause of the overpayment (and you played no part in causing it); or

(b) when the payee could reasonably have been expected to realise there was an official error overpayment (and you could not have done so).

Recovery from your partner

18.32   Whenever the authority can recover an overpayment from you (for any of the reasons in para 18.29), it can also recover it from your partner – but only if you were a couple when the overpayment was made and at the time of recovery. A former partner (following the end of a relationship or death), or a new partner after the period of the overpayment, does not meet these conditions so the authority can't recover the overpayment from them. The authority should separately notify your partner when it is going to recover the overpayment from your partner. In these circumstances your partner has the same rights you do: CH/3622/2006 (para 18.38).

18.33   The rules limit the methods of recovery from your partner to:

(a) making deductions from your partner's future HB (para 18.41); or

(b) making deductions from your partner's future DWP benefits (para 18.45).

Recovery from your landlord or their agent

18.34   The effect of the above rules (para 18.29) is that the authority can only recover the overpayment from your landlord or their agent (the 'landlord') if it was the landlord (rather than you) who was paid the HB; and one of the following also applies:

(a) the landlord caused the overpayment; or

(b) the landlord could reasonably have been expected to realise there was an overpayment (in the case of an official error overpayment); or

(c) the overpayment was no-one's fault – in which case it is recoverable from either you or the landlord; and the mere fact that the landlord knew nothing of the overpayment does not prevent recovery from them: Warwick DC v Freeman.

18.35   In such cases, the authority may recover overpaid HB from the landlord if the landlord was paid the HB, but from the agent if the agent was paid the HB (even if the agent has paid it to the landlord: R(H)10/07 and CH/761/2007). When the authority decides to recover from your landlord or their agent they must be separately notified and have the same rights of appeal as you: CH/3622/2006 (para 18.38).

18.31   HB 101(2),(3A); HB60+ 82(2),(3A); NIHB 98(2),(3A); NIHB60+ 79(2),(3A)

18.32   HB 102(1ZA); HB60+ 83(1ZA); NIHB 99(1A); NIHB60+ 80(1A)

18.34   AA 75(3); NIAA 73(3); HB 101(2),(3A); HB60+ 82(2),(3A); NIHB 98(2),(3A); NIHB60+ 79(2),(3A);
         Warwick DC v Freeman 31/10/94 CA 27 HLR 616

18.36   However, an authority must not recover HB from your landlord or their agent if:

(a) the landlord/agent tells the authority or the DWP in writing that they suspect there has been an overpayment; and

(b) it appears to the authority that there are grounds for instituting proceedings for an offence in relation to the overpayment, or that a deliberate failure to report a relevant change of circumstances (other than moving home) caused the overpayment; and

(c) the authority is satisfied that your landlord or their agent did not collude with you in the overpayment, nor contribute (through action or inaction) to its period or amount.

This rule supplements the earlier rule (para 18.34) but does not override it: [2013] UKUT 232 (AAC). For example, if your landlord or their agent gets your HB and notifies the authority that you are doing undeclared work, and does so promptly, this rule prevents the authority from recovering the resulting overpaid HB from your landlord or their agent provided that the landlord's warning notice reaches the authority before it discovers the overpayment (CH/2411/2006).

A choice about who to recover HB from

18.37   When the above rules (para 18.29) allow an authority to recover an HB overpayment from more than one person (e.g. you and your landlord or their agent), you have a joint and several liability to repay the overpayment (R(H) 6/06). The authority may choose which of you to recover from. In one case an authority billed two people at the same time, and a commissioner said this was 'unfortunate' but had no lasting effect on the appeal CH/2583/2007).

Appeals about who the authority can recover HB from

18.38   Once the authority has identified who it may recover the overpayment from, and notified them (all) of this, each of the possible targets is a 'person affected' (para 16.10) and may ask the authority to reconsider the decision or appeal to a tribunal (chapter 19).

18.39   A tribunal's jurisdiction is limited to deciding first, the true entitlement for the period in question and second, whether the resultant overpayment is legally recoverable from you and/or someone else. But it does not have the power to decide the third and final stage: how the authority should effect recovery (CH/2298/2007). A tribunal has a duty to decide whether the authority's selection of possible targets for recovery is correctly drawn up – but not whether it is fair or appropriate to recover from you or someone else (R(H) 6/06 and CH/4213/2007). This applies whether the appellant is you or your landlord or their agent (CH/1129/2004). In unreasonable or irrational cases you could instead seek judicial review but you should obtain advice about this.

Methods of recovery

18.40   The authority may recover a recoverable overpayment of HB by any lawful method. This section describes the methods set out in the law, along with other relevant considerations.

Deducting overpaid HB from future awards of HB

18.41   The authority may deduct a recoverable overpayment of HB from your, or your partner's, future award of HB. This deduction is limited in three ways:

(a) the award of HB must not be reduced below 50p a week;

(b) the amount of the deduction must not be greater than shown in table 18.3; and

(c) the authority should consider deducting a lower amount where hardship might otherwise arise.

The first two limits do not apply to deductions from lump sum arrears of HB.

Table 18.3 **Maximum weekly deductions from HB (2015-16)**

(a) If you have been found guilty of fraud, or admitted fraud after caution, or agreed to pay an administrative penalty (para 18.73)   £18.50

(b) In any other case   £11.10

Plus, in each of the above cases, 50% of:

(c) any £5, £10, £20 or £25 earned income disregard (table 14.5)

(d) any disregard of regular charitable or voluntary payments (para 13.30)

(e) the £10 disregard of war pensions for bereavement or disablement (table 13.4).

18.42   The deductions from your on-going HB entitlement may leave you with more rent to pay – or rent arrears if you don't pay (table 18.4). Your landlord doesn't have to identify these rent arrears separately from other rent arrears – and they can, for example, lead to your eviction.

18.43   The deductions count as recovery from you, not the landlord. This is true even when the authority pays the HB to your landlord/agent. In such cases the landlord/agent has no right to appeal to a tribunal about the deductions (R(H) 7/04).

Overpayments and rent accounts

18.44   If you are a council or NIHE tenant your rent account can include a record of overpaid HB, but the recovered overpayments do not normally constitute rent arrears – and should not, for example, lead to your eviction (unlike the arrears in para 18.42). Table 18.4 identifies when overpaid HB recovered through the rent account results in rent arrears for you.

18.41   AA 75(4),(5); NIAA 73(4),(5); HB 102; HB60+ 83; NIHB 99; NIHB60+ 80

T18.3   AA 75(4),(5); NIAA 73(4),(5); HB 102; HB60+ 83; NIHB 99; NIHB60+ 80

Table 18.4 **When recovered HB overpayments create rent arrears**

Rent rebate (local authority/NIHE tenants)

■ Recovery by deductions from ongoing HB or arrears of HB (para 18.41): Assuming you do not pay any shortfall then this always creates rent arrears (because at no point has the rent due been paid).

■ Recovery by charging your rent account or by sending you a bill (paras 18.44 and 18.51): Recovery by this method does not create rent arrears (R v Haringey ex p Ayub) except if:

(a) the tenancy agreement expressly allows for recovered overpayments of HB to be charged as additional rent; or

(b) following the recovery you fail to say which debt (rent or overpayment) any payments should be attributed to – in which case any payment goes against the earliest debt first.

Rent allowance

■ Recovery by deductions from ongoing HB or arrears of HB (para 18.41): As for rent rebates above.

■ Recovery from a blameless tenant's HB (paras 18.46-47): This never results in rent arrears for the blameless tenant; and does not result in rent arrears for the tenant to whom the overpayment relates except in the same circumstances as in (a) and (b) above.

■ Recovery from the landlord by deductions from the landlord's own benefits or by sending the landlord a bill (paras 18.50-51): The tenant to whom the overpayment relates is treated as not having paid the amount of rent which has been repaid (as a recoverable overpayment) so this creates rent arrears.

■ Recovery by deductions from a guilty landlord's payments (paras 18.48-49): The tenant to whom the overpayment relates is treated as having paid the rent to the value of the deduction.

Recovering overpaid HB from your DWP benefits

18.45   The authority may recover a recoverable HB overpayment by requesting DWP Debt Management to make deductions from your or your partner's DWP benefits. The details of the arrangement are set out in a model service level agreement between authorities and DWP Debt Management (DWP HB G7/2014 Annex). Recovery using this method is only possible if the HB overpayment was due to misrepresentation of, or failure to disclose, a

---

T 18.4   AA 75(5),(6); NIAA 73(5),(6); HB 95(2),107(1),(2); HB60+ 76(2),88(1),(2); NIHB 92(2),104(1),(2); NIHB60+ 73(2),85(1),(2)
          R v Haringey LBC ex p Ayub 13/04/92 QBD 25 HLR 566

18.45   HB 102(1), 105, 106; HB60+ 83(1), 86, 87; NIHB 99(1), 102, 103; NIHB60+ 80(1), 83, 84

material fact (para 18.15); and only if the authority is unable to recover it from future awards of HB. The DWP benefits from which deduction may be made are set out in table 18.5. Recovery from your partner's DWP benefits may only be made by deductions from: IS, JSA(IB), PC, ESA(IR), PIP and UC.

Table 18.5 **Recovering HB overpayments from your DWP benefits**

A recoverable overpayment of HB may be deducted from:

- income support
- jobseeker's allowance
- employment and support allowance
- personal independence payment
- maternity allowance
- industrial injuries benefits
- widow(er)'s benefits
- bereavement benefits

- retirement pension
- incapacity benefit
- state pension credit
- universal credit
- carer's allowance
- disability living allowance
- attendance allowance
- equivalent EU and Swiss benefits

but not from:

- child benefit
- guardian's allowance
- war pensions

- working tax credit
- child tax credit
- statutory sick, maternity, paternity or adoption pay

Deducting overpaid HB from a blameless tenant's HB

18.46   If your HB was overpaid to your landlord or their agent (the 'landlord'), the authority may deduct it from any other tenant's HB that is paid to your landlord. This is often called 'recovery by schedule' (because it is usually only done in the case of landlords with several tenants on HB) or recovery from a 'blameless tenant' (because the other tenant had nothing to do with the overpayment).

18.47   The authority must notify your landlord that your HB was overpaid and who the blameless tenant is. The blameless tenant is not notified, and your landlord must treat them as having paid rent equal to the amount deducted.

Deducting overpaid HB from a guilty landlord/agent's payments

18.48   Special rules apply to the recovery of rent by a landlord or their agent ('the landlord') and to the information on the authority's decision notice where:

18.46   AA 75(5), (6); NIAA 73(5),(6); HB sch 9 para 15(2); HB60+ sch 8 para 15(2); NIHB sch 10 para 15(2); NIHB60+ sch 9 para 15(2)

18.47   AA 75(5), (6); NIAA 73(5), (6); HB 106(2); HB60+ 87(2); NIHB 103(2); NIHB60+ 84(2)

(a)   the overpayment is one for which your landlord has agreed to pay a penalty (para 18.73) or been convicted of fraud; and

(b)   recovery is to be from your landlord; and

(c)   recovery is by deduction from the HB paid by the authority to the landlord for you and you are the tenant to whom the overpayment relates.

18.49   In these circumstances the landlord has no right in relation to the recovered amount against you and must treat your rent as paid by the same amount. The authority must notify you and the landlord of these matters.

Deducting overpaid HB from your landlord's own benefits

18.50   If a recoverable overpayment of HB was paid to your landlord or their agent, the authority may (though this is rare) recover it from your landlord's personal entitlement to:

(a)   HB (in which case the limits in table 18.3 do not apply); or

(b)   DWP benefits (table 18.5) – but only if the overpayment was due to misrepresentation of, or failure to disclose, a material fact.

Recovering HB by sending a bill

18.51   The authority may recover any recoverable overpayment of HB by sending a bill to anyone it can be recovered from (paras 18.29-36). If not paid, the authority can enforce recovery through court action (paras 18.61-67).

Recovering HB by direct earnings attachment (DEA)

18.52   The authority may recover recoverable overpayments of HB by requiring your employer to make deductions from your earnings (or the earnings of any other 'liable person' (someone from whom HB may be recovered: paras 18.29-36) without the need for court action. But this requirement can't be placed on new businesses (which started between 8th April 2013 and 31st March 2014) or micro-businesses (those with less than ten employees immediately before 8th April 2013). DWP's Impact Assessment (2011) [www] suggests that this method of recovery is useful if you are no longer in receipt of benefit and refuse to come to a voluntary agreement to repay the debt. The DWP has made available to authorities an information pack on using DEA (HB G2/2014) [www].

18.53   If the authority decides to use this method of recovery it must send a notice to both you and your employer before your employer can make deductions. The employer should tell the authority if they are not your employer or if they think the new business or micro-business exemption applies. They should do this within ten days of the day after the notice was sent.

18.48   AA 75(5)(b); NIAA 73(5)(b); HB 107; HB60+ 88; NIHB 104; NIHB60+ 85

18.50   AA 75(5); NIAA 73(5); HB 106(2); HB60+ 87(2); NIHB 103(2); NIHB60+ 84(2)

18.51   HB 102(1); HB60+ 83(1); NIHB 99(1); NIHB60+ 80(1)

18.52   HB 106A; HB60+ 87A, Reg 18 and sch 1 of SI 2013 No 384
          www.legislation.gov.uk/uksi/2013/384/pdfs/uksifia_20130384_en.pdf
          www.whatdotheyknow.com/request/hbctb_direct_earnings_attachment

18.53   Regs 19, 24 of SI 2013 No 384

18.54   The authority may vary the notice to decrease or increase amounts or to substitute a new employer for a previous one. Where your employer has to make deductions under more than one notice they should deal with them in date order.

18.55   The DEA notice has effect from the next pay-day which falls at least 22 days after the date on which it is given or sent. The amounts to be deducted are set out in legislation (schedule 2 of SI 2013 No 384). Your employer may deduct up to £1 for administrative costs. Your net earnings should not be reduced below 60% of protected net earnings.

18.56   Your employer must notify you of the amount of the deductions and pay the amount deducted (excluding that for administrative costs) to the authority. Your employer must also keep records of the people in respect of whom such deductions have been made and the amounts deducted.

18.57   You must tell the authority within seven days if you leave the employment or when you become employed or re-employed. The employer should also tell the authority if you are no longer employed by them. It is a criminal offence to fail to make or pay deductions or to provide information.

The effect of insolvency on recovery

18.58   The DWP's Overpayments Guide (OG paras 7.110-188) provides detailed information on the recovery of overpayments where your insolvency has led to formal measures such as bankruptcy, the making of a debt relief order (DRO) (in England and Wales) or sequestration (in Scotland) [www].

18.59   The DWP's Overpayments Guide (OG paras 7.188) draws particular attention to the implications of the recent Supreme Court's judgments in SSWP v Payne & Cooper (England and Wales) and Re Nortel Companies. The current situation is as follows. If bankruptcy has started or an overpayment has been included in a DRO, the authority cannot recover an overpayment that was decided before the order was granted. The Supreme Court confirmed that the authority cannot recover such overpayments even by making deductions from ongoing HB entitlement. Authorities are told in DWP circular HB/CTB U6/2011 that they should stop such recoveries if they are making them. Once the bankruptcy or DRO is discharged the liability to repay is also discharged except for fraudulent overpayments (HB/CTB U1/2012 para 8).

18.60   The DWP (G10/2013, para 35) (following Nortel) advises authorities that when a debtor is discharged from bankruptcy (or sequestration in Scotland) then any non-fraud debts, where the end date of the overpayment is before the date of the bankruptcy or sequestration order, must be written off and that this must take effect immediately. Its previous advice (following R (on the application of Steele) v Birmingham CC and Secretary

---

18.54   Regs 25-26, 29 of SI 2013 No 384

18.55   Regs 17, 19, 20(9) of SI 2013 No 384

18.56   Reg 21-22 of SI 2013 No 384

18.57   Regs 23, 30 of SI 2013 No 384

18.58   www.gov.uk/government/publications/housing-benefit-overpayments-guide

18.59   SSWP v Payne & Cooper 14/12/11 UKSC [2011] UKSC 60 www.bailii.org/uk/cases/UKSC/2011/60.html
Re Nortel Companies 24/07/13 UKSC [2013] UKSC 52 www.bailii.org/uk/cases/UKSC/2013/52.html

18.60   R (on the application of Steele) v Birmingham City Council [2005] EWCA Civ 1824; [2006] 1 W.L.R. 2380

of State for Work and Pensions) had been that a benefit overpayment (including an HB overpayment) did not become a fixed liability until such time as the decision maker had made a determination that the overpayment, or part of it, was recoverable under social security legislation.

Court action

18.61   The DWP advises authorities that legal proceedings should only be considered after attempts to recover by other means have failed and there is good reason to believe you can afford to make repayments (OG paras 7.23). Authorities are told that before pursuing recovery through the courts they should allow your appeal period to run out, allow any outstanding appeal to be decided, send at least two letters requesting repayment and make sure that procedures are in place to check that you are getting all the HB and other benefits you may be entitled to (OG paras 7.20-22). You may find that not all authorities follow this guidance. Court action may take the form of civil proceedings for debt, but the following procedure is simpler for the authority.

The simplified debt recovery procedure

18.62   Authorities have the power to recover HB overpayments by execution in the County Court in England and Wales as if under a court order; and in Scotland as if it were an extract registered decree arbitral (OG paras 7.24-38).

England and Wales

18.63   In England and Wales, this procedure allows a council to register an HB overpayment determination directly as an order of the County Court without the need to bring a separate action. The DWP has provided some much needed guidance on this procedure (OG paras 7.24-38). The authority applies to the court on a standard form (form N 322A) [www], enclosing a copy of the overpayment notice and the relevant fee. The notice must include all the matters in paragraph 18.69 (OG para 5.07). An officer of the court then makes an order and a copy is sent to the authority and to you. Once the order has been made, the normal methods of enforcement are available to the authority – a garnishee order allowing it to obtain money owed to you by a third party; a warrant of execution against goods executed by the county court bailiff; or a charging order, normally against land.

18.64   There is no appeal against the above order, but you or your landlord/agent may apply to the court to set it aside if the overpayment notice was defective or the authority has ignored your HB appeal rights. In the case of other disputes, you should ask the authority to reconsider or appeal to a tribunal (chapter 19) (Ghassemian v Borough of Kensington and Chelsea).

18.62   AA 75(7), 76(6); NIAA 73(7)

18.63   www.gov.uk/government/uploads/system/uploads/attachment_data/file/233076/hbopg-courts.pdf
hmctsformfinder.justice.gov.uk/courtfinder/forms/n322a-eng.pdf

18.64   Ghassemain v Kensington and Chelsea LBC 09/06/09 CA [2009] EWCA Civ 743 www.bailii.org/ew/cases/EWCA/Civ/2009/743.html

Scotland

18.65 In Scotland, an HB overpayment determination is immediately enforceable by the authority as if it were an extract registered decree arbitral (OG paras 7.24). The authority doesn't need to register it with the Sheriff Court. The usual methods of enforcement are available – arrestment of earnings; poinding and warrant sale; arrestment of moveable property and inhibition of heritable property.

Time limits

18.66 The authority must start the above procedures within six years in England and Wales (s9 The Limitation Act 1980). This limitation does not apply to any other method of recovery – such as by deductions from future HB (OG paras 7.00-05). In Scotland your council cannot recover overpayments by any method after 20 years (OG paras 7.05).

18.67 This time limit does not affect how far back an overpayment can go. For example, the authority may discover today that it has overpaid you from the beginning of the HB scheme, and may make a determination to recover it. But the further the overpayment goes back, the more difficult it may be for the authority to obtain the evidence needed to prove the overpayment to the court (OG para 7.00). Also, overpayments from before 6th April 2009 fall within the rules which applied before that date: CH/4213/2007.

Overpayment decision notices

18.68 For every recoverable overpayment, the authority should send a decision notice to you and everyone it can be recovered from (paras 18.29-36), because each of these is a 'person affected' (para 16.6) – regardless of who the authority will actually recover it from (R(H) 6/06). The authority should do this within 14 days of the date it made the decision or as soon as reasonably practicable afterwards.

18.69 The authority's notice about the overpayment should contain the following information:

(a) the fact that there is a recoverable overpayment;

(b) the reason why there is a recoverable overpayment;

(c) the amount of the recoverable overpayment;

(d) how that amount was calculated;

(e) the benefit weeks to which the recoverable overpayment relates;

(f) if overpaid HB is to be deducted from future HB, the amount of the deduction;

(g) any other relevant matters;

(h) your right to request a written statement, to request the authority to reconsider, and to appeal to a tribunal, and the manner and time in which to do these things.

18.66   s38(1),(11) Limitation Act 1980 as amended by s108 Welfare Reform Act 2012, s7 of The Prescription and Limitation (Scotland) Act 1973

18.68   HB 90(1)(b); HB60+ 71(1)(b); NIHB 86(1)(b); NIHB60+ 67(1)(b)

18.69   HB sch 9 para 15; HB60+ sch 8 para 15; NIHB sch 10 para 15; NIHB60+ sch 9 para 15

18.70   A notice must also be issued about your new (lower or nil) entitlement to HB. Both this and the overpayment notice are often inadequate. The main cases about this are summarised in table 18.6.

18.71   The DWP advises authorities that recovery of HB overpayments by deduction from future HB should not begin until one month after notice (unless the overpayment is small) to allow time for an appeal to be made (but advises that it may issue an invoice) (OG paras 4.240 and 4.250).

Table 18.6 Overpayments case law: notices and effect on recovery

- *Failure to give a reason why there is a recoverable overpayment:* To say it was due to a 'change of circumstances' is not itself an adequate explanation as it covers a multitude of possibilities and so does not give the person affected sufficient information to be able to judge whether they have grounds for an appeal (R v Thanet DC ex parte Warren Court Hotels Ltd).

- *Failure to identify the parties the overpayment is recoverable from:* A notice naming only a landlord as the person from whom the overpayment could be recovered was quashed (and so had no effect), because it should have named both the claimant and the landlord (CH/3622/2005, in which the commissioner followed R(H) 6/06).

- *The notices which must be issued and the impact on recoverability:* For an over-payment to be recoverable, notices must be issued about both the new (lower or nil) award of HB and the resulting overpayment. If one (or both) of these is omitted, the overpayment is not recoverable: [2013] 208 (AAC) and R (Godwin) v Rossendale BC.

- *Clarity and completeness of notices:* Decisions must be clear and unambiguous with proper use of statutory language and dates (C3/07-08 (IS)). An authority that issues an incomplete notice may undermine the legal basis of its debt recovery action (Warwick DC v Freeman). But if the defect in the notice is only trivial and no substantial harm has been caused as a result, the authority may be entitled to recover the overpaid benefit (Haringey LBC v Awaritefe).

- *Recovery taken before notice issued:* If, in a 'blameless tenant' case, a council recovers HB before issuing a valid notice, the landlord/agent can apply to the court for repayment of the recovered HB (Waveney DC v Jones).

- *Recovery volunteered before notice issued:* If a landlord/agent voluntarily pays a bill for overpaid HB before the authority has issued a valid notice, they cannot obtain repayment because (unlike in Jones, above) they could have resisted recovery by requesting the authority to reconsider or appealing to a tribunal (Norwich CC v Stringer).

T18.6   R v Thanet ex p Warren Court Hotels 06/04/00 QBD 33 HLR 32 www.casetrack.com case reference CO/523/1999
R (Godwin) v Rossendale BC 03/05/02 CA [2002] EWCA Civ 726 www.bailii.ord/ew/cases/EWCA/Civ/2002/726.html
Haringey LBC v Awaritefe 26/05/99 CA [1999] EWCA Civ 1491 32 HLR 517
Waveney v Jones 01/12/99 CA 33 HLR 3 www.casetrack.com case reference CCRTF 1998/1488/B2
Norwich CC v Stringer 03/05/00 CA 33 HLR 15 www.casetrack.com case reference FC2/7400/B2

Overpayments and fraud

18.72   The Social Security Administration Act 1992 creates several offences related to HB fraud. It allows English and Welsh authorities to investigate and prosecute for these offences. These powers are however being restricted following the introduction of the Single Fraud Investigation Service (SFIS) [www]. This is a single service with powers to investigate and sanction all benefit and tax credit offences. It combines resources across authorities, HMRC, and DWP. Officers working for authorities should see the DWP's Fraud Circulars and the SFIS knowledge hub [www]. SFIS however has no powers in relation to CTR fraud.

Administrative penalties

18.73   An authority may offer you the chance to pay an 'administrative penalty' rather than face prosecution, if:

(a) a recoverable HB overpayment was caused by an 'act or omission' on your part; and

(b) there are grounds for bringing a prosecution against you for an offence relating to that HB overpayment.

You do not have to agree to a penalty. You can opt for the possibility of prosecution instead.

18.74   The authority's offer of a penalty must be in writing, explain that it is a way of avoiding prosecution, and give other information – including the fact that you can change your mind within 14 days (including the date of the agreement), and that the penalty will be repaid if you successfully challenge it by asking for a reconsideration or appeal (OG para 4.330). Authorities do not normally offer a penalty (but prosecute instead) if an overpayment is substantial or there are other aggravating factors (such as being in a position of trust).

18.75   The amount of the penalty is 50% of the recoverable HB overpayment (subject to a minimum of £350 and a maximum of £5,000). For offences that were committed before 8th May 2012 or span that date the penalty is 30% of the recoverable HB overpayment (DWP F6/2012, para 4.2) and the maximum penalty before 1st April 2015 was £2,000.

18.76   The authority may also make an offer of a penalty where an act or omission could have resulted in a recoverable HB overpayment and there are grounds for bringing a prosecution for a related offence. In these cases the penalty is the fixed amount of £350.

Civil penalties

18.77   An authority may impose a civil penalty of £50 on you if you:

(a) make incorrect statements in an HB claim without taking reasonable steps to correct them, or

(b) have been awarded HB but fail to disclose information or report changes in your circumstances without reasonable excuse.

18.72   AA Part VI
         www.gov.uk/government/collections/single-fraud-investigation-service
         https://knowledgehub.local.gov.uk/web/singlefraudinvestigationservicesfiscommunicationshub
         LGFA ss 14A-14C,

18.73   AA 115A; NIAA 109A; SI 1997/2813; NISR 1997/514 LGFA s14C, SI 2013/501

18.77   AA 115C-115D; 121DA(7), SI 2012 No 1990

In each case, the action or inaction has to result in an overpayment wholly after 1st October 2012 before the authority can consider a civil penalty. If you are successfully prosecuted for a fraud or offered an administrative penalty or caution, the authority cannot also issue a civil penalty for the same offence. The authority adds the amount of the civil penalty to the amount of the overpayment. If you want to appeal against a civil penalty you should appeal against the amount of the HB overpayment.

Chapter 19 **Disputes and appeals**

- An overview of the disputes and appeal procedure: see paras 19.1-9.
- Asking the authority to reconsider its decision: see paras 19.10-17.
- Appealing to a tribunal: see paras 19.18-26.
- The process of making an appeal: see paras 18.27-46.
- Members of the appeal tribunal and where it meets: see paras 47-49.
- The tribunal hearing: see paras 19.50-65.
- The tribunal's decision: see paras 19.66-79.
- If a tribunal's decision is wrong, further appeals: see paras 19.80-89.
- Appeals to the Upper Tribunal: see paras 19.90-98.
- Appealing against a rent officer's decision: see paras 19.99-110.

19.1   The first stages of the HB disputes and appeals process are different from those which apply to DWP administered benefits. With these other benefits you are required to give the DWP the opportunity to reconsider disputed decisions formally before you can appeal (a process termed mandatory reconsideration). With these other benefits you also send your appeal directly to Her Majesty's Courts and Tribunal Service (HMCTS). These rules do not apply to disputed HB decisions.

19.2   Also note that the dispute and appeal process in relation to an authority's decisions on CTR is entirely separate and subject to different arrangements from those described in this chapter for HB.

HB disputes and appeals

19.3   An outline of the HB dispute and appeal procedure and the related time limits are set out in table 19.1. This chapter describes the rules in Great Britain and the main variations in Northern Ireland (NI). Please refer to the legislation in the footnotes for further NI details.

19.4   In Great Britain HB appeals are considered by the First-tier Tribunal [www]. Further appeals (on a point of law and if given permission) then go to the Upper Tribunal [www]. Administrative arrangements are the responsibility of HMCTS.

19.5   In Northern Ireland HB appeals are considered by an independent Appeal Tribunal. Further appeals (on a point of law and if given permission) then go to the NI Social Security Commissioners [www]. Administrative arrangements are the responsibility of the Appeals Service (NI) and the NI Court Service [www].

19.4   www.justice.gov.uk/tribunals/sscs
        www.gov.uk/administrative-appeals-tribunal

19.5   www.courtsni.gov.uk/en-GB/Tribunals/OSSC/Pages/OSSC.aspx
        www.dsdni.gov.uk/index/taser-appeals_service.htm

Table 19.1 **The HB disputes and appeals procedure**

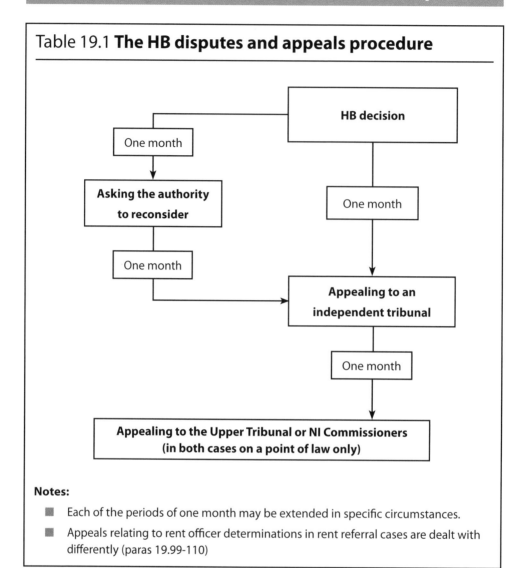

Notes:

- ■ Each of the periods of one month may be extended in specific circumstances.
- ■ Appeals relating to rent officer determinations in rent referral cases are dealt with differently (paras 19.99-110)

Your rights and the rights of other 'persons affected'

19.6   The rights described in this chapter belong to you and any other 'person affected' by an HB decision. The legislation defines who counts as a 'person affected' (para 16.6). It includes:

(a) you (the claimant);

(b) an appointee acting for you;

19.6   CPSA sch 7 paras 3,4,6(3),7,8,23(2); NICPSA sch 7 paras 3,4,6(3),7,8,23(2); DAR 3; NIDAR 3
         Wirral MBC v Salisbury Independent Living Ltd [2012] EWCA Civ 84; [2012] H.L.R. 25;
         www.bailii.org/ew/cases/EWCA/Civ/2012/84.html

(c) your landlord or their agent – but only in relation to a decision about who should be paid an HB rent allowance; and

(d) anyone (e.g. a landlord/agent or a partner) from whom the authority seeks to recover an overpayment (para 19.25).

Only those defined in legislation are persons affected. So, for example, a landlord providing you with supported accommodation may be very concerned about the authority's decision regarding your eligible rent for HB purposes but they are not a person affected in relation to this decision: Wirral MBC v Salisbury Independent Living Ltd reversing [2011] UKUT 44 (AAC).

19.7 Whenever the authority makes a decision about your HB it must notify you (and any other person affected) of:

(a) the right to a written statement of the reasons for that decision;

(b) the right to ask the authority to reconsider; and

(c) the right to appeal to a tribunal (unless the decision is one which cannot be appealed: para 19.26).

Getting a written statement of reasons from the authority

19.8 You can request a statement of reasons about anything that the authority didn't explain in its HB decision notice. Your request should be in writing and signed. You should make the request within one month of the decision's notification date. Other persons affected can also request a statement of reasons. If the person affected is a corporate body the request must be signed by someone aged 18 or over on its behalf. The authority should provide the statement within 14 days so far as this is practicable.

Reconsideration or appeal?

19.9 If you disagree with the authority's HB decision you have two options. You can:

(a) ask the authority to reconsider the decision: this applies to all HB decisions; or

(b) appeal against the decision to an independent tribunal: this applies only to appealable HB decisions (paras. 19.24-25).

If you choose the first option, you can go on to the second option next. If you choose the second option, the authority can treat it as a request for a reconsideration (para 19.21).

Asking the authority to reconsider

19.10 You (and any other person affected) can ask the authority to reconsider any HB decision it has made. For an appealable decision you can do this either instead of or before making an appeal to an independent tribunal. Your request should be in writing and the normal time limit is one month (para 19.11). The law calls this requesting a revision or supersession, but you do not have to use these terms, and it is normally called requesting a reconsideration. If the authority needs information or evidence related to your request, see paragraph 19.16.

19.7   DAR 10; NIDAR 10

19.8   HB 90(2),(4); HB60+ 71(2),(4); NIHB 86(2),(4); NIHB60+ 67(2),(4); DAR 10(2); NIDAR 10(2)

19.10   CPSA sch 7 para 3(1)(b),4(1); NICPSA sch 7 para 3(1)(b),4(1); DAR 4(1),(8),(9),7(2),(6),(7); NIDAR 4(1),(8),(9),7(2),(6),(7)

Time limit for requesting a reconsideration

19.11 Your request for a reconsideration is within the time limit if the authority gets it within one calendar month of the date it notified you of the decision. In calculating this time limit:

(a) any time is ignored from the date the authority gets a request for a statement of reasons (para 19.8) to the date the authority provided the statement (both dates inclusive); and

(b) any time is ignored before the date on which the authority gave notice of the correction of an accidental error (para 17.62); and

(c) the time limit may be extended by the authority as described below (para 19.14).

19.12 If your request for a reconsideration gets to the authority:

(a) within the time limit, the authority must consider revising its decision (para 19.13);

(b) outside the time limit, the authority must consider superseding its decision (para 19.15) and may consider revising it under its own powers, for example where there has been an official error (para 17.63).

19.13 If your request for reconsideration gets to the authority within the time limit, and it alters your entitlement to HB, this takes effect from the date of the original decision. The one exception to this rule is where the authority determines that the original decision took effect from a wrong date, in which case it takes effect from the correct date. In either case, this is a revision. Whether or not the authority alters entitlement, it must notify you of the outcome (para 19.17).

Getting an extension of the time limit for a reconsideration

19.14 The authority should extend the one-month time limit if:

(a) you make the request in writing and it gets to the authority within 13 months of the date on which the decision was notified to you; and

(b) the request says that you are asking for it to be accepted late, and you give the reasons for your failure to request a reconsideration earlier; and

(c) sufficient details are given to identify the disputed decision; and

(d) the request for revision 'has merit'; and

(e) the authority is satisfied that there are or were 'special circumstances' as a result of which it was not practicable for you to request a reconsideration within the one month time limit. The longer the delay (beyond the normal one month), the more compelling those special circumstances need to be; and

(f) the authority is satisfied that it is reasonable to grant the extension. In determining this, the authority may not take account of ignorance of the law or of the time limits, nor of the fact that the Upper Tribunal (in Northern Ireland, the Commissioners) or a court has taken a different view of the law from that previously understood and applied.

19.11 DAR 4(1),(4),10A(3); NIDAR 4(1),(4),10A(3)

19.13 CPSA sch 7 para 3(3); NICPSA sch 7 para 3(3); DAR 6; NIDAR 6

19.14 DAR 4(8),5(1)-(6); NIDAR 4(7),5(1)-(6)

Reconsideration requests received outside the time limit

19.15   If your request for a reconsideration gets to the authority outside the one month time limit, and it refuses to extend this limit, you have no right to ask it to accept a further late request to reconsider the same matter. However, the authority may nonetheless reconsider its decision and should consider making a superseding decision instead (the details are in paras 17.68-69).

Example: Late request for the authority to reconsider its decision

In May 2015 the authority notified Lukasz of its decision on his claim.

Among other things, the decision depended upon an assessment of his self-employed income.

In September 2015, Lukasz asks the authority to reconsider its decision, as he forgot to tell them about part of his expenditure. He has no special circumstances for his delay. However, the authority accepts that (if it had known) it would have allowed that additional expenditure (and he would therefore have got more HB).

The change is implemented from the Monday of the benefit week in which Lukasz's request for a reconsideration gets to the authority. Lukasz does not get his arrears. This is a supersession. (However, if Lukasz has 'special circumstances' for the late reconsideration request, he may get his arrears: para 19.14.)

Information and evidence

19.16   When the authority reconsiders a decision it may ask you to provide any further information and evidence it requires – and must take it into account if you provide it within one month, or longer if reasonable.

Telling you about the outcome of the authority's reconsideration

19.17   In all the circumstances described in this section, the authority must notify you of the outcome of your request for a reconsideration. The authority's decision notice must include the following matters:

(a) whether the authority has changed its decision and, if it has, a statement of what it has altered;

(b) your rights to request a written statement of reasons, to request a reconsideration, and to appeal to a tribunal, and how and when to do these things.

19.15   DAR 5(7),7(2)(b); NIDAR 5(7),7(2)(b)

19.16   DAR 4(5), 7(5); NIDAR 4(4), 7(5)

19.17   DAR 10; NIDAR 10; HB sch 9; HB60+ sch 8; NIHB sch 10; NIHB60+ sch 10; FTPR sch 1(c)

Appealing to a tribunal

19.18 You and any other person affected (para 16.6) can appeal an HB decision to an independent tribunal – but only if it is an appealable decision (para 19.24). You can do this either instead of or after asking the authority to reconsider its decision. If you make an appeal you may see or hear yourself referred to as the 'appellant'. You may also come across the term 'respondent' – this is a reference to the authority (i.e. the maker of the decision you have appealed) and also a reference to anyone else who has a right of appeal (for example the landlord in some overpayment cases). Each of you is a 'party' in the proceedings.

The First-tier Tribunal (GB)

19.19 The First-tier Tribunal is an independent tribunal established under the Tribunals, Courts and Enforcement Act 2007. It is divided into a number of chambers. The Social Entitlement Chamber considers HB appeals as well as appeals on other social security benefits and certain other matters. The procedural rules of the Social Entitlement Chamber are set out in The Tribunal Procedure (First-tier Tribunal) (Social Entitlement Chamber) Rules SI 2008 No 2685. You can find the current rules on the Ministry of Justice website [www].

The Appeal Tribunal (NI)

19.20 In Northern Ireland the composition of the tribunal which decides HB appeals is provided for in regulation 22 of the HB (Decisions and Appeals) Regulations (NI) SR 2001 No 213. The procedural rules are set out in Chapters II to V of Part V of the Social Security and Child Support (Decisions and Appeals) Regulations (NI) SR 1999 No 162 (subject to reg 23 of SR 2001 No 213). You can find the current rules on the Department for Social Development's website [www].

Revisions prompted by an appeal and lapsed appeals

19.21 When the authority gets your appeal it considers whether the decision can be revised. If the authority can revise it to your advantage the decision should be revised and the appeal lapses (does not go ahead). This applies even when you do not get everything that you asked for in the appeal. If the authority revises the decision to your advantage there is then a fresh decision with a fresh dispute period, and fresh rights for you to apply for a reconsideration or appeal.

19.22 Your appeal should automatically go ahead to a tribunal if:

   (a) the decision is not revised by the authority; or

   (b) the decision is revised, but not in your favour; or

   (c) the decision is superseded by the authority.

19.19   Part 1 of the Tribunals, Courts & Enforcement Act 2007; art 6(c) of SI 2010 No 2655; FTPR; www.justice.gov.uk/tribunals/rules

19.20   www.dsdni.gov.uk/index/law_and_legislation/law_relating_to_social_security.htm

19.21   CPSA sch 7 para 3(6); NICPSA sch 7 para 3(6); DAR 4(1),(6); NIDAR 4(1),(6)

19.23   If the authority revises the decision, but not in your favour, the appeal is treated as against the revised decision and you are given an additional month in which to make further representations.

Which decisions can be appealed

19.24   Table 19.2 shows which HB decisions are appealable to a tribunal and which are not. The exclusions are listed in legislation. With the exceptions shown in the table, you and any other 'person affected' has a right of appeal against any decision affecting HB, including:

(a)   a decision on a claim;

(b)   a revised decision (or 'revision': para 17.56);

(c)   a superseding decision (or 'supersession': para 17.56);

(d)   a refusal to make a superseding decision (R(DLA) 1/03 para 51); and

(e)   a determination about an overpayment.

Appeals about overpayments

19.25   In relation to an overpayment appeal you are always a 'person affected'. If the authority decides that the overpayment is recoverable from someone else (e.g. your landlord, their agent or your partner) or both of you, that other person is also always a 'person affected'. So there may be more than one person affected (para 19.18). Each of you has a right of appeal against:

(a)   the existence of the overpayment – i.e. the revised or superseding decision that causes it (R(H) 3/04 para 50); and

(b)   the overpayment determination (Wirral MBC v Salisbury Independent Living Ltd para 13). This includes whether it is recoverable, how much it is, and who it is recoverable from (para 18.39).

Appeals against non-appealable decisions

19.26   If you make an appeal against a non-appealable decision (table 19.2), the authority should identify it as 'out of jurisdiction' when forwarding it to the tribunal. If the tribunal agrees, it should then be struck out by the tribunal so that the appeal does not go ahead. You should have the opportunity to make representations on the matter. Note, though, that non-appealable matters can be the subject of a request for a reconsideration (para 19.10) or judicial review (para 1.54).

19.23   DAR 17(3),(4); NIDAR 17(3),(4)

19.24   CPSA sch 7 paras 1, 6(1),(6); NICPSA sch 7 para 1,6(1),(6)

19.25   Wirral MBC v Salisbury Independent Living Ltd [2012] EWCA Civ 84; [2012] H.L.R. 25; www.bailii.org/ew/cases/EWCA/Civ/2012/84.html

19.26   FTPR 8(2),(4); NIDAR99 46(1)(a),47

Making an appeal

How to appeal

19.27   Your appeal must:

(a) be in writing;

(b) be delivered, by whatever means (e.g. post, fax, email, in person) to the authority;

(c) be signed by you ('the appellant') or your solicitor or a representative authorised by you: [2015] UKUT 28 (AAC);

(d) include your name and address;

(e) provide the name and address of your representative (if you have one);

(f) state which address documents for you should be sent to;

(g) say what is being appealed;

(h) give your grounds of appeal; and

(i) be made within one month or 13 months of the date the disputed decision was sent out by the authority (paras 19.30-35).

19.28   Your appeal does not have to be on a form, though many authorities do have forms for this purpose. If your appeal is set out in a letter, make it clear that it is an appeal to a tribunal (not a request for a reconsideration: para 19.10). Keep a copy of the appeal and all appeal related correspondence.

Table 19.2 **Appealable and non-appealable HB decisions**

Decisions about claims

Non-appealable

- ▣ Which partner in a couple is to be the claimant (para 5.3)
- ▣ Who may claim when someone is unable to act (para 5.5)

Appealable

- ▣ When and how a claim is made (paras 5.8-12)
- ▣ Whether a claim is incomplete (para 5.22)
- ▣ The date of claim and first day of entitlement (paras 5.28-49)
- ▣ Backdating (paras 5.50-58)

Decisions about payments

Non-appealable

- ▣ When and how HB is paid (paras 16.14-20)
- ▣ Making a payment on account (para 16.23)

19.27   DAR 20(1); NIDAR 20(1); FTPR 23, sch 1

T19.2   CPSA sch 7 para 6; DAR 16(1) and sch; NICPSA sch 7 para 6; NIDAR 16(1) and sch
         Beltekian v Westminster CC [2004] EWCA Civ 1784, reported as R(H) 8/05 www.bailii.org/ew/cases/EWCA/Civ/2004/1784.html

- The frequency of payment of a rent allowance (paras 16.21-22)
- Making payment to a person entitled (para 16.31-32)
- Paying outstanding HB after a death (para 16.33)
- Suspending or restoring HB (paras 17.71-73)

Appealable

- Adjusting HB to correct a payment on account (para 16.28)
- Who HB is to be paid to (e.g. claimant or landlord/agent) (paras 16.34-53);
- Whether the landlord/agent is a 'fit and proper person' (paras 16.54-56)
- Terminating HB (para 17.75)

Decisions about overpayments

Non-appealable

- What 'an overpayment' means (para 18.1)
- The exercise of discretion to recover or not (paras 18.27-28)
- The method of recovery (paras 18.40-57)

Appealable

- The decision which caused the overpayment (para 18.3)
- Whether an overpayment is recoverable (paras 18.11-15)
- The amount of the overpayment (paras 18.16-26)
- Who an overpayment can be recovered from (paras 18.29-39)

Other decisions

Non-appealable

- LHA figures and areas (paras 8.22-34)
- Rent determinations in rent referral cases (but see paras 19.99-110)
- The DWP's assessed income figure or 'AIF' (table 13.3) – though modifications to it are appealable (para 13.15)
- Whether to run a local scheme for pensions for war disablement and war bereavement (paras 13.18)
- A refusal to correct a mistake out-of-time (Beltekian v Westminster CC reported as R(H) 8/05)
- Any figure laid down in the law (e.g. the capital limit or the amount of the HB benefit cap)

Appealable

- All other HB decisions

Appeals that do not meet the conditions

19.29   If your appeal is incomplete, the authority can accept it if it contains enough information. If it doesn't, the authority must write to you requesting further details, or return it for completion, and allow you 14 days to reply, or longer if the authority directs. If you do not reply within that time, the authority must send the documents to the tribunal (including any other documents it has received) for the tribunal to determine whether the appeal should go ahead.

Time limit for appealing

19.30   Your appeal should normally get to the authority within one month of the date on which its decision notice was sent out. If you have requested a statement of reasons within that time (para 19.8) then the time limit is 14 days after the end of that month, or after the date on which the authority provides the statement, whichever is later. If you have made an unsuccessful revision request, then the time limit is one month after the authority sends out notice of that decision. If the time in which you can make an appeal runs out on a non-working day, your appeal is still in time if it gets to the authority on the next working day. Appeals should normally get to the authority at the latest by 5pm on the final day.

19.31   If the authority's decision notice is invalid because it fails to meet the relevant legal requirements (paras 16.7-9, 18.68-70 and table 18.6) your time for appealing does not start until the authority issues a valid notice: CH/1129/2004. The authority should refer disputes about this, or any other question about whether the appeal was within the time limit, to the tribunal.

Requesting acceptance of a late appeal

19.32   If you are outside the time limit you may write requesting the authority to accept a late appeal. Give your reasons for lateness, including details of any special circumstances. You must sign the request and it must get to the authority within an absolute time limit of 12 months after the end of the last 'normal' day for appealing (19.30). You can only make an application for a late appeal once (for that appeal).

Accepting a late appeal

19.33   The authority may grant your request for a late appeal if it is in the interests of justice to do so. If it does not, it must forward your request to the tribunal. In Great Britain the First-tier Tribunal may grant your application for a late appeal under its case management powers in the context of the overriding objective to deal with cases fairly and justly, but must not extend the maximum time limit. In Northern Ireland a panel member must be satisfied that your appeal has reasonable prospects of success or that it is in the interests of justice for the late appeal application to be granted.

19.29   DAR 20(2)-(8); NIDAR 20(2)-(8)

19.30   FTPR 12,23, sch 1; NIDAR 18

19.32   DAR 20(1); NIDAR 20(1); FTPR 23(3)-(5)

19.33   DAR 19(5),(6),(8); FTPR 2(1),(3),5(3)(a),7(2),23(5),(8); NIDAR 19(3),(5),(6),(8),(10),(11)

'Interests of justice'

19.34   When the authority, or a tribunal in Northern Ireland, is determining whether to accept your request for a late appeal, only the following count as being in the interests of justice – and only if they meant that it was not practicable for you to make the appeal within the normal one month:

(a) you or a partner or a dependant has died or suffered serious illness; or

(b) you are not resident in the UK; or

(c) normal postal services were disrupted; or

(d) some other special circumstances exist which are wholly exceptional and relevant to the application.

19.35   Ignorance of the law or of the time limits is ignored, as is any change in how the law is interpreted as a result of a decision of the Upper Tribunal, NI Commissioners or a court; and the longer you delay (beyond the one month time limit), the more compelling your special circumstances need to be.

Withdrawing your appeal

19.36   You or your representative may withdraw your appeal (or any part of it) at any time before the tribunal decides it by giving notice in writing of withdrawal to the First-tier Tribunal (in Northern Ireland, the authority). In Great Britain the tribunal may direct that notice of withdrawal will take effect only with the tribunal's consent and withdrawal of an appeal at a hearing always requires the tribunal's consent.

Death of a party to an appeal

19.37   If you die, the authority may appoint someone to proceed with the appeal in your place. A grant of probate or letters of administration, etc, has no effect on this appointment.

The authority's actions on getting your appeal

19.38   When the authority gets your appeal, it should consider revising the appealed decision (para 19.21). If it revises it in a way which is advantageous to you, the appeal lapses and it takes no further action.

19.39   In all other cases, the authority sends HMCTS/Appeals Service (NI):

(a) a notice of appeal completed by the authority (form AT37) along with your submissions; and

(b) the authority's response to your appeal (this is often referred to as its submission).

The authority also sends its response (with a covering letter) to you and any other person affected (para 19.18). This should be done as soon as reasonably practicable.

19.34   DAR 19(5A)-(9); NIDAR 19(6)-(9)

19.35   DAR 19(8)-(9); NIDAR 19(8)-(9)

19.36   FTPR 17(1)-(3); NIDAR 20(9)

19.37   DAR 21; NIDR 21

19.39   FTPR 24(1)(b)

19.40   The authority should tell HMCTS/Appeals Service (NI) (on form AT37) if eviction proceedings have begun against you so that the case can be heard urgently, and also if there are special reasons which may delay your reply (para 19.42).

The pre-hearing enquiry form

19.41   On getting the above, HMCTS/Appeals Service (NI) sends a pre-hearing inquiry form to you and a similar form to any other person affected [www]. The form asks you whether you:

(a) want to withdraw your appeal;

(b) want a hearing (at which you and/or your representative can be present) or have no objection to the appeal being decided in your absence;

(c) have a representative and if so their name and contact details;

(d) agree to having less than 14 days notice if you have opted for a hearing;

(e) have dates that you would not be able to attend a hearing; and/or

(f) need an interpreter or signer.

19.42   You should normally return the completed form within 14 days – a period which may be extended for appropriate reasons.

The authority's response and your submission

19.43   In Great Britain the authority's response must include:

(a) its name and address;

(b) the name and address of the authority's representative (if any);

(c) an address where documents for the authority may be sent or delivered;

(d) the names and addresses of any other persons affected (para 19.18) and their representatives (if any);

(e) whether the authority opposes your case and, if so, any grounds which are not set out in the documents before the tribunal; and

(f) any further information or documents required by a direction (para 19.63).

19.44   With its response, the authority must provide copies of:

(a) any written record of the disputed decision, and any statement of reasons for the decision, if not sent with the notice of appeal;

(b) all documents relevant to the case in the authority's possession unless a direction (para 19.63) says otherwise; and

(c) your notice of appeal, and any documents you provided with your notice of appeal.

If the authority wishes to submit redacted evidence, the tribunal decides whether it is to be disclosed: [2012] UKUT 472 (AAC). Additional DWP guidance for authorities on responses may be found in GM paras. C7.280-309.

19.41   (GB) Example enquiry form – hmctsformfinder.justice.gov.uk/courtfinder/forms/appellant-enquiry-form-eng.pdf

19.42   FTPR 5(3)(a); NIDAR99 39(2),(3)

19.43   FTPR 24

19.45　You and any other respondent may make a written submission and supply further documents in reply to the authority's response. Unless directed otherwise, this should normally be done within one month of the authority sending out its response. Submissions, etc, are often submitted later than this. If relevant they should be considered by the tribunal but if other parties have not been given adequate time to consider the material this may lead to the adjournment of a hearing.

How quickly is your appeal dealt with?

19.46　The authority should send its response to the tribunal as soon as reasonably practicable, but the law does not set a time limit. The DWP suggests to authorities a normal time scale of four weeks except for more complex cases (DWP A20/2003 appendix B annex C para A65). In cases of significant delay by the authority, you or your representative may make a written application to the First-tier Tribunal for a direction to be given requiring the authority to produce its response or listing the appeal for hearing (R(H)1/07 paras. 27-34). The law also does not say how quickly an appeal is heard once HMCTS/Appeals Service (NI) get the authority's response. The First-tier Tribunal has a responsibility to deal with cases 'fairly and justly'. This includes avoiding delay so far as compatible with proper consideration of the issues. In cases of urgency you or your representative may write to the First-tier Tribunal requesting that it give a direction requiring an early hearing of the appeal.

The appeal tribunal

Membership of the tribunal

19.47　All tribunal members are independent of the authority. The tribunal normally consists of just one person, a judge or in Northern Ireland a panel member, who is legally qualified. In rare instances where difficult financial questions are raised (e.g. about company accounts) there may also be a member with relevant qualifications. An additional member may also be present to provide experience or to assist with the monitoring of standards. Tribunal judges should be referred to as 'Sir' or 'Madam'.

Venues

19.48　The hearing normally takes place at your nearest venue. HMCTS has around 152 venues across England, Wales and Scotland. You can find information on venue locations and facilities on the web [www]. The Appeals Service (NI) currently holds appeal hearings at 18 venues in towns and cities throughout the province [www].

Functions

19.49　The tribunal's task is to reconsider the decision you have appealed and either change it or confirm it. It should reconsider the decision in a way that is fair and just. The tribunal may give directions on its own initiative or you or any of the other parties may request that

---

19.46　FTPR 2(2)(e),5,6,24(1)(b)

19.47　SI 2008/2835; SI 2008/2692; NIDAR 22(1),(2)

19.48　www.justice.gov.uk/tribunals/sscs/venues
　　　　www.dsdni.gov.uk/index/taser-appeals_service.htm

specific directions be issued on a wide range of case management matters (para 19.63). It does not have to consider any issue that has not been raised, but it does have the power to do so. The Tribunal should not shut its eyes to things if to do so would cause an injustice. In certain instances, this could mean that you end up with a decision that is even less favourable than the one you have appealed. The Tribunal can't take account of any factual matters that didn't exist at the time the original appealed decision relates to but it can consider evidence that was not available to the original decision maker that relates to those facts. The tribunal cannot alter the law but must interpret and apply the law to the facts of your case to arrive at a reasoned decision. It cannot award compensation or costs in relation to a HB appeal. The First-tier tribunal also has the power to make a decision in the form of a consent order. This ends the proceedings and makes such other provisions as you, the authority and any other parties have agreed to. This may be done at the request of the parties if the tribunal considers it appropriate.

The appeal hearing

Notice

19.50 HMCTS should give you notice of the time and place of the (oral) hearing. This should be given at least 14 days before the hearing (beginning with the day on which the notice is given and ending on the day before the hearing takes place). If you or someone else has not been given notice of the hearing it may go ahead only with everyone's consent or in urgent or exceptional circumstances. Where you, the authority and any other party have all chosen not to have a hearing, and the tribunal also thinks that it is able to decide the matter without a hearing, you won't be notified of the date on which the appeal is considered on the papers. You need to make sure that all your submissions and documents are with the tribunal before this happens.

Postponement

19.51 The tribunal may postpone the hearing at any time before it starts but need not do this. If you want a postponement, write to HMCTS giving the reasons for your request. If it is too late to ask for a postponement you may request an adjournment at the hearing. The tribunal may grant or refuse this request as it thinks fit.

Public or private hearings

19.52 Your hearing is normally in public but usually only the people involved are present. The tribunal may decide that the hearing (or part of it) should be in private if, for example, sensitive or family matters are to be considered. In Northern Ireland the rules set out that this may be done:

19.49   CPSA sch 7 para 6(9); NICPSA sch 7 para 6(9); FTPR 2,5,6,32

19.50   FTPR 27-29; NIDAR99 49(2)

19.51   FTPR 5; NIDAR99 51(1)

19.52   FTPR 30; NIDAR99 49(6)

(a) in the interests of national security, morals, public order or children;

(b) for the protection of the private or family life of one of the parties; or

(c) in special circumstances, if publicity would prejudice the interests of justice.

19.53 Certain people such as trainee members or clerks may be present (whether or not the hearing is in private), but they must not take part in the proceedings.

Deciding to proceed in someone's absence

19.54 If you or someone else who has a right to be present at the hearing fails to attend, the tribunal may, having regard to all the circumstances including any explanations offered, go ahead with the hearing if:

(a) it is in the interest of justice to do so; and

(b) it is satisfied that the absent person was told about the hearing or that reasonable steps were taken to do this.

19.55 In Northern Ireland if you have waived the right to be given 14 days notice of the hearing, the tribunal may proceed with the hearing despite your absence.

Your rights at the hearing

19.56 The tribunal decides its own procedure at the hearing, but you and the other parties have the right to be present, to be heard and to be represented.

19.57 You may be able to attend the hearing by telephone or via a live link, e.g. a video conference facility, but only where the judge gives permission. You should contact HMCTS about this.

19.58 Someone else, for example a relative or friend, may accompany you to the hearing. Someone else may also represent you at the hearing whether they have professional qualifications or not. With the tribunal's permission, the person that accompanies you can help you present your case or act as your representative.

19.59 For the purposes of the proceedings at the hearing your representative has all the rights and powers that you have (except signing a witness statement). Once the tribunal and the other parties have been notified that you have appointed a representative they must provide your representative with any documents they should provide to you and don't also have to provide you with them. They may also assume that your representative remains authorised to act for you until they get written notification from either you or the representative that this is not the case.

19.54   FTPR 31; NIDAR99 49(4)

19.55   NIDAR99 49(5)

19.56   FTPR 2,5,28; NIDAR99 49(1),(7)

19.57   FTPR 1(3) def of 'hearing';

19.58   FTPR 11; NIDAR 49(8)

19.59   FTPR 11(5)-(6); NIDAR99 49(8)

19.60   You may:

(a)   address the tribunal;

(b)   give evidence;

(c)   call witnesses; and

(d)   put questions directly to any other person called as a witness.

Order and conduct of the hearing

19.61   The tribunal determines the procedure for the hearing within the framework set in the law, e.g. the need to ensure that you (and the other parties) have the opportunity to put your case. If the tribunal fails to observe proper procedures or the rights of the parties its decision may be open to appeal on grounds of natural justice (GM para C7.309) or the right to a fair hearing (CJSA/5100/2001).

19.62   The way the tribunal conducts itself varies according to the issues it has to decide. You should expect to have those present introduced and their role explained at the start. The tribunal should also tell you about the procedure it wishes to follow and seek your, and any other parties', agreement to going ahead in this way. You may be asked to start by explaining why you think the decision is wrong. If the authority's presenting officer is present (they are not always), they may be asked to explain the basis of the decision. At some point the tribunal is likely to question you. This questioning may be assertive and inquisitorial. You may be offered the opportunity to have the final word before the tribunal goes on to consider its decision.

Directions

19.63   The tribunal may at any stage of the proceedings:

(a)   give the directions it thinks necessary or desirable for the just, effective and efficient conduct of the proceedings; and

(b)   direct you, or any other party, to provide items or documents that may be reasonably required.

The tribunal may, for example, direct the postponement of a hearing or the adjournment of a hearing to allow new evidence to be obtained or considered. The tribunal can decide to do this itself, or you or any other party may make a written application giving reasons for a direction to the clerk before a hearing or by an oral request during the hearing. If you are dissatisfied with a direction you may apply for it to be amended, suspended or set aside. But if you fail to comply with one that is in force there is a possibility that your appeal may be struck out (if you have been warned about this). If the authority fails to comply there is a possibility that it may be barred from the proceedings and may have all issues decided against it.

19.60   NIDAR99 49(11)

19.61   FTPR 5,6; NIDAR99 49(1)

19.62   FTPR 2,5,6,8; NIDAR99 38(2)

19.63   FTPR 2,5,6;7,8; NIDAR99 38(2)

Adjournment

19.64   The tribunal may (or may not) adjourn your hearing at any time on your (or another party's) application or of its own motion. This might be, for example, to allow it to consider new evidence.

Withdrawing your appeal at the hearing

19.65   You may withdraw your appeal at the hearing (in Great Britain this requires the tribunal's consent). If this happens the clerk must send a notice in writing to any party who is not present informing them that the appeal has been withdrawn.

The tribunal's decision

19.66   The tribunal reaches a decision once it has considered all the evidence. In reaching its decision the tribunal should:

(a)   consider the relevant law including any applicable case law;

(b)   identify the relevant facts on the basis of the available evidence; and

(c)   where the facts are in doubt or dispute, establish them (if necessary on the balance of probability); and

(d)   apply the law to the relevant facts to arrive at a reasoned decision.

Duty to follow precedent

19.67   The tribunal has a duty to follow the legal points held in past decisions of: the Upper Tribunal, the Commissioners and the courts (para 19.91) unless the case before the tribunal is distinguishable (R(U)23/59). Northern Ireland decisions are not binding in England, Wales or Scotland but may assist the tribunal (they are said to be of persuasive authority) (R(I)14/63) and vice versa. Decisions of the First-tier Tribunal in Great Britain or Appeal Tribunals in Northern Ireland do not set any precedent.

19.68   There is an order of precedence to Upper Tribunal decisions (and the former Commissioners' decisions) (R(I)12/75(T) and [2009] UKUT 4 (AAC) para 37), as follows:

(a)   decisions of the Upper Tribunal where a Three Judge Panel (formerly a Tribunal of Commissioners) heard the case are the most authoritative – whether reported or unreported;

(b)   reported decisions come next. For many years these were given serial numbers by the year and identified by having the prefix 'R', e.g. R(H)1/02. However, since 1st January 2010 these are known as the Administrative Appeals Chamber Reports and are indicated (after a reference to the parties) by the year of reporting, e.g. [2010], the abbreviation AACR, and the consecutive reporting number within that year's series, e.g. [2010] AACR 40: this is the 'neutral citation';

(c)   then come other decisions. These are identified by the file number, e.g. CH/1502/2004, or, since 1st January 2010, by a reference to the parties and a neutral citation e.g. JD v Leeds City Council [2009] UKUT 70 (AAC).

19.64   FTPR 5,6; NIDAR99 51(4)

19.65   FTPR 17; NIDAR99 40(1)(a),(2)

19.69 If there appears to be conflict between two or more decisions the tribunal should apply the above hierarchy. If the conflicting decisions are of equal rank, the tribunal is free to choose between them. More recent decisions should be preferred to older decisions. If a more recent unreported decision has fully considered all the earlier authorities, and given reasons for disapproving one or more earlier reported decisions, the tribunal should generally follow the more recent unreported decision (R(IS) 13/01).

19.70 Most decisions of the Upper Tribunal and NI Commissioners (and their predecessors) are online [www]. Reported cases are kept at tribunal venues but unreported cases are not. If you want to use an unreported decision in support of your case you should supply a copy, where possible, in advance, otherwise an adjournment may be necessary.

The tribunal's written decision notice

19.71 If you attend the hearing you may be given the decision on the day. It should be confirmed in writing as soon as practicable after the hearing by the judge or (in NI) the legally qualified tribunal member or chair.

Communicating the decision

19.72 As soon as practicable after the tribunal has decided your appeal, a copy of the decision notice must be sent or given to you and every other party to the proceedings. You must also be informed about:

(a) your right to apply for a statement of reasons (para 19.74); and

(b) the conditions governing appeals to the Upper Tribunal or (in NI) the Commissioners (para 19.90).

Implementing the decision

19.73 The tribunal's decision notice is the legal document that enables the authority to correct and pay (or recover) HB in line with the tribunal's decision. The authority should action the tribunal's decision as soon as practicable and normally within four calendar weeks (DWP A20/2003 appendix B annex C para A70). An exception to this is where an appeal is pending against the tribunal's decision, in which case the authority has the discretion to suspend payment in whole or in part (para 17.72).

19.70   www.osscsc.gov.uk/Aspx/default.aspx
       www.dsdni.gov.uk/index/law_and_legislation/nidoc_database.htm
       www.bailii.org/form/search_cases.html

19.71   FTPR 33(1)-(2); NIDAR99 53(1),(2),(5)

19.72   FTPR 33(2); NIDAR99 53(3)

19.73   CSPSA sch 7 para 13(3); DAR 11(2)(b); NICPSA sch 7 para 13(3); NIDAR 11(2)(b)

A 'statement of reasons'

19.74   A statement of reasons sets out the tribunal's findings of fact and the reasons for the decision. If you are considering an appeal to the Upper Tribunal/NI Commissioners you must ask for a statement of reasons.

Time limit for application for statement of reasons

19.75   You may apply to the clerk at the hearing for a statement of the reasons for the decision. Otherwise you must normally make your application within one month of the date the tribunal's decision notice is given or sent. If not made in time, your chance of appeal may be lost.

19.76   In Great Britain the First-tier Tribunal does have power to extend the one-month time limit in which your request for a statement of reasons may be made if it would be fair and just to do so. If you make a late request it should include information as to why this is the case but it may be easier to get an extension where the request relates to reasons for a decision on a preliminary issue rather than a final decision.

19.77   In Northern Ireland your late application for a statement of reasons can only be accepted if it is made in writing to the clerk within three months of the date the tribunal's decision note was sent to you. Where a correction is made, or where set-aside is refused (para 19.85), the three month period is counted from the day notice of the correction or refusal is given. Your application should explain why it is late, including details of any relevant special circumstances.

Requirement to supply written statement of reasons

19.78   When the tribunal gets your accepted application for a written statement of reasons it must send or give a copy of that statement to you and every other party to the proceedings within one month of the date it gets the application or as soon as practicable after that.

The tribunal's record of proceedings

19.79   The tribunal must make a record of the proceedings at an oral hearing, which is sufficient to indicate the evidence taken (Senior President's Practice Statement, 30th October 2008) [www]. This record, together with the decision notice, and any statement of the reasons for the tribunal's decision, must be preserved for six months from the date it was created. You or any other party to the proceedings may apply in writing within that six month period for a copy, which should be supplied on request.

19.75   FTPR 34(2)-(4); NIDAR99 53(4)

19.76   FTPR 2, 5(3)(a), 34(4)

19.77   NIDAR99 54(1),(3)

19.78   FTPR 34(5); NIDAR99 54(11)

19.79   NIDAR99 55(1),(2)
        www.judiciary.gov.uk/publications/record-of-proceedings-in-social-security-and-child-support-cases-
        in-the-social-entitlement-chamber-on-or-after-3-november-2008/

If a tribunal's decision is wrong

19.80   Once a tribunal has made and communicated its decision, the decision may be:

(a) altered if the authority supersedes it;

(b) corrected, where there is an accidental error;

(c) set aside on certain limited grounds;

(d) appealed on a point of law to the Upper Tribunal or in Northern Ireland the NI Commissioners.

When may the authority supersede the tribunal's decision?

19.81   You may apply for the decision to be superseded, or the authority on its own initiative may make such a change where:

(a) the decision was made in ignorance of a material fact; or

(b) the decision was based on a mistake as to a material fact; or

(c) there has been a relevant change of circumstances since it had effect.

When may the tribunal correct its decision?

19.82   The tribunal may correct clerical mistakes, accidental errors such as a typing mistake or omissions at any time. A correction made to a decision or to a record of it is treated as part of the decision or record. You can ask for a correction to be made. The tribunal should provide a written notice of the correction as soon as practicable to every party. You do not have a right of appeal against the tribunal's decision to make a correction or a refusal to make a correction. A First-tier Tribunal may not revise its own decision on its own initiative: [2014] UKUT 43 (AAC) except following an application for permission to appeal (para 19.92).

When may the decision be set aside? (Great Britain)

19.83   If a tribunal's decision is 'set aside' this means that it is cancelled and a new tribunal hearing must be arranged. You or any other party can apply for a decision to be set aside. The tribunal may set aside a decision if it considers that it is in the interests of justice to do so; and

(a) a document relating to the proceedings was not sent to, or was not received at an appropriate time by you or your representative;

(b) a document relating to the proceedings was not sent to the tribunal at an appropriate time;

(c) you or your representative, were not present at a hearing; or

(d) there has been some other procedural irregularity.

19.84   If you want to apply for a decision to be set aside you must make a written application to the tribunal that gets to it within one month of the date on which its decision was sent to you. The tribunal may extend this time limit where it is fair and just to do so.

19.81   DAR 7(2)(a),(d); NIDAR 7(2)(a),(c)

19.82   FTPR 36; NIDAR99 56(1),(2)

19.83   FTPR 37; 5(3)(a); NIDAR99 57(1)

19.84   FTPR 37(3);

Other parties to the appeal should be notified of your application and given the right to make representations. In Great Britain there is a right of appeal (para 19.90) against a decision to set aside: [2013] UKUT 170 (AAC).

When may the decision be set aside? (Northern Ireland)

19.85   In Northern Ireland a tribunal's decision may be set aside where it appears just to do so in the first three circumstances set out above (para 19.83). In deciding to set aside a decision on the ground that you or your representative were absent, the tribunal must consider whether you gave notice that you wished to have an oral hearing. If not, the tribunal can't set aside the decision unless it is satisfied that the interests of justice support the decision being set aside.

19.86   Your application for a set aside must:

(a) be made within one month of the date on which a copy of the decision notice is sent or given to you, or the statement of the reasons for the decision is given or sent, whichever is the later;

(b) be in writing;

(c) be signed by you or, where you have provided written authority to a representative to act on your behalf, signed by your representative;

(d) contain the detailed grounds on which it is made; and

(e) be sent to the clerk to the appeal tribunal.

19.87   You can make a late application for set aside up to one year after the end of the one month time limit (but you can only make one such application per decision). Your application must give the reasons for the lateness. It is determined by a legally qualified panel member. The other parties must be sent a copy and given a reasonable opportunity to make representations on it before it is determined. A late application for set aside is accepted if:

(a) it is in the interests of justice to do so (as described in paras 19.34-35); and

(b) there are reasonable prospects of success in the application to set aside.

19.88   You and every other party must be sent a written notice of the decision on your set aside application as soon as practicable. The notice must contain a statement giving the reasons for the decision.

19.89   In Northern Ireland, you have no right of appeal against the decision on your set aside request. If the request is refused, however, the time limit for appealing to the NI Commissioners does not start until the notice of the set aside decision has been issued. The application to set aside may be treated as an application for a statement of the reasons, subject to the normal time limits (paras. 19.75-77).

19.85   NIDAR99 57(2)

19.86   NIDAR99 57(3)

19.87   NIDAR99 57(2),(4),(6)-(8),(9)-(12)

19.88   NIDAR99 57(5)

19.89   NIDAR99 57A(2)

Appeals to the Upper Tribunal/NI Commissioners

19.90 You can appeal against a tribunal decision but only if it contains an error of law (para 19.95). If the decision was in your favour you should be aware that the authority and any other party to the proceedings could apply for permission to appeal.

19.91 The Upper Tribunal/NI Commissioners give interpretations of the law which are binding on all decision makers and tribunals. Their judges/commissioners are barristers, solicitors or advocates of not less than ten years' standing who are specialists in social security law, and have a legal status comparable to that of a High Court judge in their specialised area.

The DWP provides guidance on appeals to the Upper Tribunal (GM paras C7.560 - 928). Further advice and copies of the appeal forms may be found online [www].

Getting permission to appeal and the appeal itself

19.92 If, having considered the tribunal's statement of reasons, you think that its decision contains an error of law you can apply to it for permission to appeal. Your application should identify the decision in question and the errors of law in it. You should get it to the tribunal within one month from the date the statement of reasons was sent to you. This tribunal may extend the time limit but you cannot rely on this. If you are making a late application you should request an extension of time and include the reason why the application is late. When it gets your application for permission to appeal the tribunal may:

(a) decide to review the decision without the need to refer the case onwards – if it is satisfied that there was an error of law in the decision. The case may be re-decided or heard again by a different tribunal;

(b) give permission for the appeal – in which case you will be able to send it on to the Upper Tribunal/NI Commissioners;

(c) refuse permission together with a statement of reasons for refusal – in this case you may then apply (normally within one month) directly to the Upper Tribunal/NI Commissioners for permission to appeal.

19.93 You should make a direct application for leave or appeal to the Upper Tribunal/NI Commissioners on the appropriate forms (UT1, or UT2 for authorities, and the NI equivalent OSSC1) [www]. You should normally make a direct application for leave to appeal within one month of refusal of leave by the tribunal but this may be extended. If leave is given then the appeal goes ahead.

19.94 Most appeals to the Upper Tribunal/NI Commissioners are determined on paper without a hearing. You make your submission in writing. However, you may ask for a hearing. These take place in London, Edinburgh and Belfast and can be arranged elsewhere.

19.90 CPSA sch 7 paras 8(1),(2),(7)(c),(8); NICPSA sch 7 paras 8(1),(2),(7)(c),(8); FTPR 38,39; UTPR 21; NIDAR99 58(1),(3); SSCPR 9,10,12,13; NISSCPR 9,10,12,13

19.91 https://www.gov.uk/administrative-appeals-tribunal
www.courtsni.gov.uk/en-GB/Tribunals/OSSC/Pages/OSSC.aspx

19.92 TCEA s9; FTPR 38-40; NIDAR 58

19.93 UTPR 21; 5(3)(a); NISSCPR 9
http://hmctsformfinder.justice.gov.uk/HMCTS/FormFinder.do
www.courtsni.gov.uk/en-GB/Tribunals/OSSC/Pages/OSSC.aspx#Downloads

What is an error of law?

19.95   You can only make an appeal to the Upper Tribunal/NI Commissioners on an error of law. An error of law is where the tribunal did one or more of the following:

(a) failed to apply the correct law;

(b) wrongly interpreted the relevant Acts or Regulations;

(c) followed a procedure that breached the rules of natural justice;

(d) took irrelevant matters into account, or did not consider relevant matters, or did both of these things;

(e) did not give adequate reasons in the full statement of reasons (para 19.74);

(f) gave a decision which was not supported by the evidence;

(g) decided the facts in such a way that no tribunal properly instructed as to the law, and acting judicially, could have reached that decision.

These are examples, not an exhaustive list (R(IS) 11/99).

Who can apply for leave to appeal?

19.96   Other people who can apply for permission to appeal are:

(a) any other 'person affected' by the decision the appeal was about or by the tribunal's decision on that appeal;

(b) the authority whose decision the appeal was about;

(c) the Secretary of State (the DSD in Northern Ireland).

Appeals against the Upper Tribunal's/NI Commissioner's decision

19.97   There is a right to appeal against a decision of the Upper Tribunal/NI Commissioners to the Court of Appeal or the Court of Session in Scotland. An appeal can only be made on a point of law. Leave to appeal must be obtained from the Upper Tribunal/NI Commissioners or, if they refuse, from the relevant court. The time limit for applying for leave to appeal is three months, but it may be extended. If leave to appeal is refused the application may be renewed in the relevant court within six weeks.

19.98   Separately from the above, if your appeal involves European Union law it can be referred by the Upper Tribunal straight to the European Court of Justice.

19.95   TCEA s11(2); NICPSA sch 7 para 8(1)

19.96   CPSA sch 7 para 8(2); NICPSA sch 7 para 8(2)

19.97   TCEA s.13(1); CPSA sch 7 para 9(3); NICPSA para 9(1)-(3)

Appeals against rent officer decisions in rent referral cases

Appeals and errors in Great Britain

19.99   This section deals with appeals to the rent officer in rent referral cases (paras 9.31-72) in Great Britain. (For Northern Ireland see para 19.110.) You do not have a right of appeal to a tribunal against the rent officer's determinations (para 9.50). Instead, the following procedures apply. An earlier version of these arrangements was considered to be sufficiently independent to comply with the Human Rights Act: R (on the application of Cumpsty) v The Rent Service.

Your appeal against a rent officer decision

19.100   To appeal against a rent officer determination (not LHA related determinations) you should write to the authority within one month of the date it notified you of its HB decision. Include any representations you wish to make regarding the rent officer's determinations and sign the appeal. Within seven days of getting your appeal the authority should apply to the rent officer for a redetermination and include with its application any representations/ evidence you provided. The authority should also make an application for a redetermination if you don't specifically request a rent officer redetermination but your appeal is made within the one month and the points you make relate, in whole or in part, to a rent officer's determination.

19.101   For any claimant and any dwelling, the authority may only make one application to the rent officer in respect of any determination (plus one in respect of any substitute determination: para 19.107). This applies whether or not the authority itself has previously made an application for a re-determination (para 19.103).

19.102   If you consider that the authority should or should not have made a referral in the first place, or that the authority has provided the wrong information to the rent officer, you have the right to use the ordinary HB appeals procedure to challenge this (para 19.9). This is because the decision to refer a case to the rent officer and what information to provide is made by the authority ([2010] UKUT 79 (AAC), [2010] AACR 40).

Appeals by the authority

19.103   The authority may itself choose to apply to the rent officer for a re-determination. For any particular claimant and any particular dwelling, it may do this only once in respect of any particular determination (plus once in respect of any substitute determination: para 19.107); unless a re-determination is subsequently made because of your appeal (para 19.100), in which case the authority may do this once more.

19.99   R (on the application of Cumpsty) v Rent Service [2002] EWHC 2526 (Admin)
          www.bailii.org/ew/cases/EWHC/Admin/2002/2526.html

19.100   HB 16; HB60+ 16

19.101   HB 16; HB60+ 16

19.103   HB 15; HB60+ 15

Rent officer re-determinations

19.104   In each of the cases described above (paras 19.100-103), the rent officer must make a complete re-determination. Even if the application for a re-determination relates only to one figure, the rent officer has to reconsider all matters pertaining to the case in question. All the assumptions, etc, applying to determinations (para 9.50 onwards) apply equally to re-determinations. The rent officer should make the re-determinations within 20 working days or as soon as practicable after that. The period begins on the day the rent officer gets the application from the authority or (if he or she has requested this) on the day he or she gets further information needed from the authority.

19.105   The rent officer making the re-determination (called a 're-determination officer') must seek and have regard to the advice of one or two other rent officers. In England, rent officers have set up independent re-determination units. The rent officers should always supply reasons for their re-determinations to you and the authority [www]. Similar arrangements are in place in Wales and Scotland.

Rent officer errors

19.106   Where the rent officer discovers an error (other than one of professional judgment) in any determination, redetermination, etc, the authority should be notified as soon as is practicable. The authority must then apply to the rent officer for a substitute determination though this is unnecessary if the authority has completed a standard agreement enabling the rent officer to send substitute determinations without the authority making an individual request (DWP G5/2005 and Annex A).

19.107   The authority must apply, on a case by case basis, to the rent officer for a substitute determination (or substitute re-determination) if the authority discovers that it made an error in its application as regards: the size of the dwelling, the number of occupiers, the composition of the household or the terms of the tenancy. In all such cases, the authority must state the nature of the error and withdraw any outstanding applications for rent officer determinations in that case.

19.108   All the assumptions, etc, applying to determinations (paras 9.50 onwards) also apply to substitute determinations/re-determinations.

19.104   ROO 4, sch 3

19.105   www.voa.gov.uk/corporate/publications/Manuals/RentOfficerHandbook/HousingBenefitReferral/Determination/
r-roh-reasons-for-decision.html

19.106   ROO 7A; HB 17; HB60+ 17

19.107   HB 17; HB60+ 17

19.108   ROO 4A(2)

The date the re-determination affects your HB

19.109   Whenever the rent officer issues a re-determination, substitute determination, or substitute re-determination (for the reasons in paras 19.104-108), the new rent officer figures apply as follows.

(a) If the new figures increase the eligible rent, the authority alters its original decision from the date it took effect (or should have). So you get your arrears of HB.

(b) If the new figures reduce the eligible rent, the authority alters its original decision from the Monday following the date of the new determination. If the authority acts promptly you should not suffer from an overpayment.

Appeals and errors in Northern Ireland

19.110   In Northern Ireland the NIHE makes the determinations needed in rent referral cases (para 9.34). You cannot appeal these determinations to a tribunal, but you can ask the NIHE to reconsider in the normal way (para 19.10). The new figures apply as follows:

(a) If the new figures increase your eligible rent, and you made the request within one month of the original decision (or longer in special circumstances: paras 19.11 and 19.14), the NIHE alters its original decision from the date it took effect (or should have). So you gets your arrears of HB.

(b) If the new figures increase your eligible rent, and the request was outside the time limit, the NIHE alters its original decision from the date of your request (paras 17.68-69).

(c) If the new figures reduce your eligible rent, the normal practice (except perhaps in the case of misrepresentation) is to treat your request as a change of circumstances (i.e. a change in the housing market) and alter its original decision from the date of the request (paras 17.68-69).

19.109   DAR 4(3),7(2)(c),8(6),10
19.110   NIDAR 4(1), sch para 1

Chapter 20 **Migrants and recent arrivals**

- The rules that apply to migrants: see paras 20.1-8.
- How the decision is made: see paras 20.9-22.
- The immigration control test, asylum seekers and refugees: see paras 20.23-37.
- The habitual residence test: see paras 20.38-52.

20.1   This chapter is about when you are eligible for HB if you are a person from abroad. It covers everyone, whether you are from the British Isles, Europe or the rest of the world, and whether you are arriving in the UK for the first time or returning after a time abroad.

Which rules apply

20.2   If you have recently arrived in the UK, there are three main rules which affect whether you are eligible for HB:

- the immigration control test;
- the right to reside test; and
- the habitual residence test.

Table 20.1 shows when each of those rules apply to you. There are also further rules if you are seeking asylum or a refugee.

Table 20.1 **Migrants and recent arrivals: eligibility for HB**

A national of	Test you have to satisfy
The British Isles (para 20.5)	Habitual residence
The EEA including Croatia (table 20.2)	Right to reside (and in some cases also habitual residence)
Macedonia and Turkey	Right to reside and habitual residence
The rest of the world	Immigration control and habitual residence

20.3   For clarity, this guide treats the above three tests as separate (though in the law they are intertwined: paras 20.17-21). The guide also avoids the term 'person from abroad', because it is often used informally to describe someone who has recently arrived in the UK (whereas in the law it has a narrower meaning).

Eligibility of nationals of different parts of the world

20.4   This section identifies which rules apply to you depending on your nationality, followed by a straightforward example of each.

Nationals of the British Isles (the Common Travel Area)

20.5   The 'British Isles' (a geographical term, roughly meaning all the islands off the North-West of the continent) is also known in immigration law as the 'Common Travel Area'. They both mean:

- the United Kingdom (England, Wales, Scotland and Northern Ireland);
- the Republic of Ireland;
- the Isle of Man; and
- the Channel Islands (all of them).

If you are a national of any part of the British Isles you only have to satisfy the habitual residence test (paras 20.38-52) to be eligible for HB.

Nationals of the European Economic Area

20.6   Table 20.2 lists all the countries in the European Economic Area (EEA) plus Switzerland, which UK law treats as being part of the EEA. The EEA includes all of the European Union (EU) states and some others. The EEA includes Croatia, which joined the EU on 1st July 2013. If you are an EEA national, the rules for eligibility are described in chapter 21.

Table 20.2 **The European Economic Area (EEA)**

The EEA states (apart from Ireland and the United Kingdom) are:

Austria	Belgium	Bulgaria
Croatia	Cyprus	Czech Republic
Denmark	Estonia	Finland
France	Germany	Greece
Hungary	Iceland	Italy
Latvia	Liechtenstein	Lithuania
Luxembourg	Malta	Netherlands
Norway	Poland	Portugal
Romania	Slovakia	Slovenia
Spain	Sweden	Switzerland

Nationals of the rest of the world

20.7   In this guide this means any country not mentioned above (paras 20.5-6). It also applies to you if you have applied for asylum or to enter the UK solely on humanitarian grounds, whether or not your application has been determined.

20.6 and T20.2   EEA 2(1)

20.8 If you are a national of the rest of the world you have to satisfy the immigration control test (paras 20.23-37) and also the habitual residence test (paras 20.38-52) to be eligible for HB.

Examples: Eligibility for HB

1. A British citizen

A British citizen has been living abroad for 12 years. During that time she gave up all her connections in the UK. She has now just come 'home' and has rented a flat here.

The only test that applies to a UK national is the habitual residence test. As described later, it is unlikely that the above claimant satisfies that test to begin with (unless she was living and working in an EEA state). She might well satisfy that test in (say) three months time. So for the time being she is not eligible for HB.

2. National of the EEA

An Italian national has been working in the UK for several years. He has recently taken a more poorly paid job.

He passes the right to reside test because he is working. So he is eligible for HB.

3. National of the rest of the world

An Indian national arrived in the UK six months ago to be with her family. She was given leave to enter and remain, and was granted leave by the Home Office without any conditions, in other words her leave did not include a 'no recourse to public funds' condition, so she is able to claim benefits. She now claims HB.

The two tests that apply to a national of the rest of the world are the immigration control test and the habitual residence test. As described later, she passes both tests. So she is eligible for HB.

Decision-making

20.9 This section covers general matters relevant to this chapter and chapter 21, including decision-making and claims, and how the law and terminology work.

DWP and authority decisions: passport benefits

20.10 If you receive any of the following benefits you are exempt from the habitual residence test (para 20.38-52) and right to reside test (chapter 21):

- ■ income-based jobseeker's allowance (but see para 21.27 for exceptions);
- ■ income-related employment and support allowance;
- ■ income support;
- ■ any kind of state pension credit (guarantee credit or savings credit).

The above is true only if the DWP has decided (in full possession of the facts) that you are eligible for one of the benefits mentioned (and not, say, in a case where you wrongly continued to receive one of the benefits).

20.10 HB 10(3B)(k); HB60+ 10(4A)(k); NIHB 10(5)(l); NIHB60+ 10(5)(l)

20.11   If the DWP has decided that you are not eligible for one of the above benefits, this decision is not binding on the authority – but a considered decision by the DWP carries weight.

Claims and couples

20.12   If you are a couple, it can matter which partner is the HB claimant. The rules in this chapter apply to each partner individually. So if partner A is eligible under the rules, but partner B is not, it is necessary for partner A to be the claimant (for you to get HB at all). If the 'wrong' partner claims the authority must give you a 'not entitled' decision; in such a case it would be good practice to explain this and invite a claim from your partner.

20.13   Once a claim is made by the 'correct' partner, the claim is assessed (e.g. income, applicable amount, etc) in the usual way.

Partners and national insurance numbers

20.14   Normally both members of a couple must have or have applied for a national insurance number (para 5.16), but an exception applies if one of you requires 'leave' from the Home Office (table 20.3 and paras 20.24-26) but does not have it (for example if they have not applied for leave or it has expired). In these cases, the normal rule does not apply to that member. In such cases the DWP advises authorities that they should assign a dummy number (Circular A9/2009).

20.15   The above is a rule only about eligibility for HB. This guide cannot guarantee that it is safe, in immigration terms, for that partner to be part of your HB claim.

HB claim forms

20.16   Most HB claim forms ask you (the claimant): (a) your nationality and (b) whether you have entered the UK within the past two years. These two questions are intended to act as a trigger for further investigation in appropriate cases. If you

(a)   are a British citizen, and

(b)   did not enter the UK within the past two years,

you are unlikely to fall foul of these rules (since two years in the UK is almost always sufficient to pass the habitual residence test).

Law, terminology and how the tests overlap

20.17   The tests used in deciding your eligibility for HB are contained in a mixture of immigration, European and HB law as follows.

20.18   The 'immigration control test' (para 20.23) may stop you from getting HB (and many other benefits) if you are from outside the EEA depending on your immigration status.

20.12   HB 8(1)(b), 10(1); HB60+ 8(1)(b), 10(1); NIHB 8(1)(b), 10(1); NIHB60+ 8(1)(b), 10(1)

20.14   HB 4(c); HB60+ 4(c); NIHB 4(c); NIHB60+ 4(c)

20.18   Immigration and Asylum Act 1999 s115 (applies to the whole of the UK)

20.19 HB law (constrained by European law) then stops certain other people including EEA nationals from getting HB (and many other benefits):

(a) The 'habitual residence test' (para 20.38) is in HB law and applies regardless of your nationality. It treats you as not being liable for rent/rates – which means you do not qualify for HB.

(b) The 'right to reside test' applies if you are an EEA national (table 20.2). It is also in HB law, but what the right to reside means is in the Immigration (European Economic Area) Regulations 2006 (which apply to the whole of the UK). HB law says that if you do not pass this test then you do not pass the habitual residence test (and so, as described in (a), you cannot get HB).

20.20 If you pass the immigration control test then you also pass the right to reside test. There is only one exception: if you are a national of Macedonia or Turkey (para 20.28) you pass the immigration control test but do not pass the right to reside test unless you have 'leave' – 'temporary admission' (table 20.3) is not sufficient (Yesiloz v LB Camden). But without exception if you have a right of abode, right to reside or leave from the Home Office (table 20.3) you pass both tests.

20.21 If you pass the right to reside test then in most cases you also pass the habitual residence test – but there are a few exceptions: mainly if you are not in work or if you have retired without having worked in the UK (see paragraphs 21.26-32).

Immigration law terms

20.22 A basic understanding of immigration law terminology is useful (particularly in relation to the immigration control test). Table 20.3 lists the key terms and defines them in a way that is useful for HB decision making.

Table 20.3 **Simplified immigration law terminology**

Immigration rules

The legal rules approved by parliament which UKIV officers use to decide whether a person should be given permission ('leave') to enter the UK.

UK Immigration and Visas (UKIV)

The Home Office agency responsible for immigration control and determining asylum applications (including asylum support).

Leave and temporary admission

Leave is legal permission to be in the UK. Leave can be for a fixed period (limited leave) or open ended (indefinite leave). Both can be granted with or without a 'no recourse to public funds' condition, and this nearly always applies if you have been given limited leave. Leave can be varied provided the application is made before it has expired (para 20.26).

20.19   HB 10(1)-(3); HB60+ 10(1)-(3); NIHB 10(1)-(3); NIHB60+ 10(1)-(3)

20.20   Yesiloz v Camden LBC 01/05/09 CA [2009] EWCA Civ 415 www.bailii.org/ew/cases/EWCA/Civ/2009/415.html

A person who has been granted open ended leave without any conditions is said to have 'indefinite leave to remain', also known as settled status.

Temporary admission is not in itself a form of leave, it is merely the discretion allowed by UKIV which allows time for you to do something – such as apply for asylum or leave – without falling foul of the law. Since it is not a form of leave, it does not confer a right to reside.

Public funds

Nearly all tax credits and non-contributory benefits (including HB and passport benefits) count as public funds. So does a local authority homelessness duty or acceptance on its housing waiting list.

Sponsorship and maintenance undertaking

These terms go together. Someone (typically an elderly relative) may be granted leave to join a family member on the understanding that this 'sponsor' will provide for their support and/or accommodation.

Some (but not all) sponsors are required to sign a written agreement (a maintenance undertaking) as a condition of granting leave and if they do the person they sponsor is excluded from HB (but see para 20.28 for exceptions).

Illegal entrant and overstayer

These both refer to someone who needs leave to be in the UK but does not have it and has not been granted temporary admission. An illegal entrant is someone who entered the UK without applying for leave and an overstayer is someone who was granted leave which has since expired.

Right of abode and right to reside

'Right of abode' is a term that describes someone who is entirely free of any kind of immigration control. It applies to all British citizens and some citizens of Commonwealth countries, but not necessarily to other forms of British nationality. Non-British nationals can apply to have this status confirmed in their passport.

'Right to reside' is a wider term that describes anyone who has legal authority to be in the UK. It therefore includes everyone with the right of abode, plus anyone who has any form of leave (including if your leave is granted with 'no recourse to public funds') or if you are from the EEA and have a right of residence. 'Right to reside' is sometimes used informally to mean right of abode (because it sounds less archaic).

The immigration control test

20.23 If you are from a country outside the EEA you have to pass the immigration control test to get HB. (You also have to pass the habitual residence test: paras 20.38-52.)

20.24 The purpose of the test is to stop you getting benefit if:

■ you require 'leave' (table 20.3) but do not have it – e.g. you are an illegal entrant or overstayer; or

■ you have been granted leave but with a 'no recourse to public funds' condition (but see paras 20.27-28 for exceptions); or

■ you have been granted temporary admission while your application to the Home Office is being decided – for example if you are an asylum seeker.

People who pass the immigration control test

20.25 You pass the immigration control test regardless of your nationality if:

■ you hold a passport containing a certificate of entitlement to the 'right of abode' (table 20.3) in the UK;

■ you have 'indefinite leave to remain' (also called settled status);

■ you have any form of leave whether limited or indefinite (table 20.3), but only if it is not subject to a public funds condition or a maintenance undertaking (table 20.3) – although certain exceptions apply (paras 20.27-29);

■ you applied for asylum and you have been granted refugee status, humanitarian protection or discretionary leave (paras 20.33-34);

■ you are not an asylum seeker and you have been granted permission to claim HB as a victim of domestic violence by UK Immigration and Visas (para 20.37).

The authority normally needs to see your passport or other Home Office documentation to confirm the above.

20.26 If you have limited leave you can apply for it to be extended before it expires. Provided your application is made in time and in the correct form, you are still treated as having leave until 28 days after the decision is made on your application, and so you pass the immigration control test until then. Authorities often wrongly terminate benefit in these cases.

People with no recourse to public funds who are entitled to HB

20.27 The general rule is that if your UK visa is subject to a public funds condition or a maintenance undertaking (table 20.3) you fail the immigration control test (para 20.24). The only exceptions are in paragraph 20.28.

20.24   IAA99 115(9)

20.26   IAA99 3

20.28   You are not affected by the general rule (para 20.27) and pass the immigration control test (and see also paras 20.20 and 20.29) if:

- ■ you are a national of Macedonia or Turkey (but see para 20.20);

- ■ you were admitted to the UK as a result of a maintenance undertaking (a 'sponsored immigrant'), but you have been resident for five years or more;

- ■ you were admitted to the UK as a 'sponsored immigrant' and have been resident for less than five years and your sponsor (or all of your sponsors if there are more than one) has died;

- ■ you are the former partner of a British citizen or of a person with settled status (table 20.3) and have been granted permission to claim HB under the Domestic Violence Concession (paras 20.37 and 20.40).

20.29   In the first three cases you must also be habitually resident to be entitled to HB but not in the fourth (para 20.40).

Asylum seekers

20.30   You are an asylum seeker if you have applied to be recognised as a refugee (para 20.33) under the United Nations Convention because of fear of persecution in your country of origin (typically on political or ethnic grounds).

20.31   While your asylum application is being processed you fail the immigration control test and are disqualified from HB, although there are some limited exceptions (para 20.32). If you are disqualified you may be able to get help with your maintenance and accommodation from the Home Office asylum support scheme.

20.32   If you are an asylum seeker the general rule in paragraph 20.31 does not apply and so you may be eligible for HB (although all of these cases are rare) if:

- ■ you are a couple where your partner is eligible (para 20.12) – in this case any Home Office support counts as income (GM para C4.128);

- ■ if you have been granted discretionary leave (para 20.33) (e.g. if you are aged under 18 and unaccompanied by an adult);

- ■ if you are a national of an EEA state (para 20.6) in which case the rules in chapter 21 apply.

Refugees and others granted leave on humanitarian grounds

20.33   Following your asylum application the Home Secretary may:

- ■ recognise you as a refugee (i.e. accept your claim for asylum) and grant leave; or

- ■ refuse asylum but grant humanitarian protection (which is a form of leave) or discretionary leave (see circular HB/CTB A16/2006 for details of when these might apply); or

- ■ refuse asylum and not grant leave.

20.28   IAA99 115(1),(3),(9); SI 2000 No. 636 sch; SI 2013 No 458; NISR 2000 No. 71 sch

20.34 If leave is granted it is normally for a period of five, six or ten years, after which you can normally apply for settled status. If you have been granted refugee status, humanitarian protection or discretionary leave you pass the immigration control test and the habitual residence test. So you are eligible for HB from the date your status is confirmed. If you are granted refugee status (but not in other cases), then your dependants are granted leave as well so they are also eligible for HB.

Evacuees

20.35 Evacuees are people granted exceptional leave to enter the UK in response to a specific humanitarian crisis (e.g. war, famine, natural disaster). They are often British nationals without full UK citizenship. In appropriate circumstances, the UK government may grant discretionary leave to those affected, normally on a temporary basis.

20.36 Evacuees are only eligible for HB if or when they become habitually resident. Temporary exceptions have been made in response to a specific crisis (e.g. the programme for vulnerable British citizens living in Zimbabwe and Montserrat residents fleeing the volcanic eruption) but there are none that currently apply.

Destitution domestic violence concession

20.37 If you were originally granted a temporary visa as the partner of a British citizen but your relationship has broken down because of domestic violence, you can apply for permission to claim public funds (benefits) for up to three months while the Home Office considers your application to settle in the UK. This is known as the Victims of Domestic Violence Concession (or 'Destitution Domestic Violence Concession' (DDVC)) [www]. If you have been granted this concession you are entitled to HB (i.e. you are exempt from the habitual residence test). The DDVC is not available to EEA family members but in certain circumstances you have a right to reside under the EEA regulations if you have suffered domestic abuse: see chapter 21.

20.34   HB 10(1),(3B)(g),(h); HB60+ 10(1),(4A)(g),(h); NIHB 10(1),(5)(g),(h); NIHB60+ 10(1),(5)(g),(h)

20.37   10(3B)(h)(iii); HB60+ 10(4A)(h)(iii); NIHB 10(5)(h)(iii); NIHB60+ 10(5)(h)(iii); rule 289A of the immigration rules
www.gov.uk/government/publications/application-for-benefits-for-visa-holder-domestic-violence

The habitual residence test

Who has to pass the habitual residence test

20.38   The habitual residence test applies if you are a national of:

- the British Isles; or
- the rest of the world (apart from the EEA).

It does not normally apply if you are an EEA national unless you are not active in the labour market (e.g. not working or looking for work). All the rules that apply if you are an EEA national including these exceptions are dealt with in chapter 21.

20.39   The purpose of the test is to stop someone claiming benefit immediately they enter the UK (for example, if you have a right of abode in the UK but have never lived here or have not lived here for a long time).

Domestic violence concession and displaced persons

20.40   If you have been granted temporary permission to stay in the UK under the domestic violence concession (para 20.37) you are exempt from the habitual residence test and entitled to HB. A person who requires temporary protection as a displaced person is also exempt (but at the time of writing this power has not been used).

People deported to the UK from another country

20.41   If you are a British citizen or a person with a right of abode or settled status (table 20.3) who is deported to the UK from another country you are exempt from the habitual residence test and are entitled to HB.

The meaning of habitual residence

20.42   To be eligible for HB you must be 'habitually resident' in the British Isles (para 20.5). What counts as habitual residence is a 'question of fact' (a phrase used to mean that the term is not defined in the regulations). It is decided by looking at all the facts in your case; no list of considerations can be drawn up to govern all cases. The DWP gives general guidance on this (GM paras C4.87-106).

20.43   There are two elements to 'habitual residence':

- 'Residence': You must actually be resident, a mere intention to reside being insufficient; and mere physical presence is not residence.
- 'Habitual': There must also be a degree of permanence in your residence in the British Isles (GM C4.80), the word 'habitual' implying a more settled state in which you are making your home here. There is no requirement that it must be your only home, nor that it is permanent, provided it is your genuine home for the time being.

20.38   HB 10(2); HB60+ 10(2); NIHB 10(2); NIHB60+ 10(2)

20.40   HB 10(3B)(h); HB60+ 10(4A)(h); NIHB 10(5)(h); NIHB60+ 10(5)(h)

Losing habitual residence

20.44   Habitual residence can be lost in a single day. This applies if you leave the UK intending not to return but to take up long-term residence in another country.

Gaining habitual residence

20.45   You cannot gain habitual residence in a single day. If you have left another country with the intention to settle in the UK you do not become habitually resident immediately on arrival. Instead there are two main requirements (R(IS) 6/96):

■ your residence must be for an 'appreciable period of time'; and

■ you must have a 'settled intention' to live in the UK.

'Appreciable period of time' and 'intention to settle'

20.46   There is no fixed period that amounts to an appreciable period of time (CIS 2326/1995). It varies according to the circumstances of your case and takes account of the 'length, continuity and nature' of your residence (R(IS) 6/96).

20.47   Case law (CIS 4474/2003) suggests that, in general, the period lies between one and three months, and that a decision maker needs 'powerful reasons to justify a significantly longer period'. That time would have to be spent making a home here, rather than merely studying or on a temporary visit.

20.48   As suggested by the DWP (GM C4.85-86), factors likely to be relevant in deciding what is an appreciable period of time, include:

■ the length and continuity of your residence;

■ your reasons for coming to the UK;

■ your future intentions;

■ your employment prospects (para 20.49); and

■ your centre of interest (para 20.50);

although no one factor is absolutely decisive in every case.

20.49   In considering your employment prospects, your education and qualifications are likely to be significant (CIS 5136/2007). An offer of work is also good evidence of an intention to settle. If you have stable employment here it is presumed that you reside here, even if your family lives abroad.

20.50   Your centre of interest is concerned with the strength of your ties to this country and your intention to settle. As suggested by the DWP (GM C4.105), this can be shown by:

■ the presence of close relatives;

■ decisions made about the location of your family's personal possessions (e.g. clothing, furniture, transport);

■ substantial purchases, such as furnishings, which indicate a long term commitment; and

■ the membership of any clubs or organisations in connection with your hobbies or recreations.

Temporary absence and returning residents

20.51   Once your habitual residence has been established, the following general principles apply (in each case unless other circumstances over-ride them):

- if you are a UK or EEA national (only), it resumes immediately on return from a period of work in another EEA member state (Swaddling v Chief Adjudication Officer);

- and, in all cases, it resumes immediately on your return from a single short absence (such as a holiday or visiting relatives).

20.52   In considering whether you regain your habitual residence following a longer absence, or repeated absences, the following points need to be considered:

- the circumstances in which your habitual residence was lost;

- your intentions – if your absence was always intended to be temporary (even in the case of longer absences) you are less likely to lose your habitual residence than someone who never originally had any intention of returning;

- your continuing links with the UK while abroad;

- the circumstances of your return. If you slot straight back into the life you had before you left, you are likely to resume habitual residence more quickly.

20.51   Swaddling v Chief Adjudication Officer 25/02/99 ECJ C-90/97
www.bailii.org/eu/cases/EUECJ/1999/C9097.html

Chapter 21 **EEA nationals**

Introduction

21.1   This chapter is about when you are entitled to HB if you or a member of your family is a citizen of an EEA member state (an 'EEA national'). EEA member states are listed in table 20.2. This chapter does not apply if you are a citizen or a settled person of the UK, Republic of Ireland or any other part of the British Isles (para 20.5) or if you are a citizen of a European country which is not part of the EEA (para 20.6).

21.2   If you are an EEA national you are entitled to HB if:

(a) you are 'economically active' (para 21.3) and you have a right to reside (paras 20.21 and 21.7-23); or

(b) you are not economically active, and

■ you have a right to reside; and

■ you are habitually resident in the British Isles.

If you are a Croatian national further rules apply that restrict your rights to work and your entitlement to HB when you are out of work (paras 21.34-41). If you are a couple see paragraphs 20.12-13 for how these rules apply to you.

21.3   'Economically active' means you are working or you are temporarily out of work due to sickness or unemployment. In certain circumstances you can be treated as if you are working if you have worked in the UK for at least one year. See also paragraph 21.8

Decision making and terminology

21.4   If you are an EEA national general matters such as making your claim, how the law works, decision making and an explanation of the technical terms used in the law and administration are in paragraphs 20.9-22. In particular, it describes how decision making is carried out if you receive a passport benefit, but see also paragraph 21.27 if you receive JSA(IB).

21.5   The law about entitlement to HB if you are an EEA national is very complex so case law develops rapidly. How the rules are interpreted is likely to continue changing.

21.6   If you are an EEA national you have to show you have a 'right to reside' in the UK to get HB. The purpose of this rule is to stop you acquiring the right to HB (and passport benefits) solely by living here if you have no intention to work. If you are an EEA national and you are a worker, a former worker (including if you are temporarily unemployed or retired), self-employed or the family member of someone who is any of these (paras 21.9-23) you are exempt from this test and entitled to HB.

EEA nationals and the right to reside

21.7   This section (paras 21.8-33) is about whether you are entitled to HB if you are an EEA national. However, if you are a Croatian the rules in this section only apply if:

(a)   you are self-employed (paras 21.9 and 21.36);

(b)   you have completed one year employed in authorised work (para 21.39).

in any other case, see the rules in paragraphs 21.34-41.

Who has a right to reside

21.8   If you are an EEA national (para 20.6) you have a right to reside and are entitled to HB if you:

(a)   are self-employed;

(b)   are a worker;

(c)   are self-employed but temporarily unable to work due to sickness;

(d)   are a worker who has retained your worker status while temporarily out of work;

(e)   have acquired a permanent right of residence;

(f)   are, in certain circumstances, a family member of the above; or

(g)   are, in limited circumstances, a parent, a work seeker or a self-sufficient person.

Details of each of these categories are given in the following paragraphs. In immigration law, the first four groups are sometimes called 'economically active' because you are engaged in the labour market. The requirement to have a right to reside does not violate your right to family life (Mirga v SSWP) and although it constitutes discrimination it is justifiable and so is not unlawful (Patmalniece v SSWP).

Self-employed people

21.9   If you are an EEA national and you are self-employed you have a right to reside and you are entitled to HB (including if you are a Croatian national, see para 21.36).

21.10   Your self-employment must be 'real', and have actually begun, but unlike the requirement for workers it seems that the ten-hour threshold (para 21.15) does not apply and your self-employed status can continue even where there is no current work, provided you continue to look for it: [2010] UKUT 451 (AAC). A seller of *The Big Issue* who buys the magazine at half price and sells it has been found to be in self-employment: [2011] UKUT 494 (AAC).

21.11   If you are self-employed you have a legal duty to register with HMRC within three months of starting your business – even if you think you won't earn enough to pay tax/ national insurance. However, just because you are registered it does not necessarily mean that HMRC accepts you are self-employed (since their job is to collect money, without perhaps worrying unduly about the niceties of its origins). On the other hand, the fact that you have not registered does not mean that you are not self-employed: CIS/3213/2007.

21.5   HB 10(3B)(a)-(f); HB60+ 10(4A)(a)-(f); NIHB 10(5)(a)-(f); NIHB60+ 10(5)(a)-(f)

21.8   EEA 6(1), 14(1); HB 10(3B); HB60+ 10(4A); NIHB 10(5); NIHB60+ 10(5);
           Mirga v SSWP 04/12/12 CA [2012] EWCA Civ 1952 www.bailii.org/ew/cases/EWCA/Civ/2012/1952.html;
           Patmalniece v SSWP 16/03/11 UKSC [2011] UKSC 11 www.bailii.org/uk/cases/UKSC/2011/11.html

Workers

21.12   If you are an EEA national you have a right to reside and you are entitled to HB if you are a 'worker' (para 21.13). But if you are a Croatian national, see paragraph 21.34.

21.13   You are a worker if you are currently engaged in remunerative work in the UK, which is

(a) 'effective and genuine'; and

(b) not 'on such a small scale as to be purely marginal and ancillary'.

'Remunerative' here has its ordinary English meaning: broadly payment for services you provide. (It does not have the same technical meaning as in paragraph 6.19.)

21.14   The following are relevant to whether your work is 'effective and genuine':

(a) the period of employment;

(b) the number of hours worked;

(c) the level of earnings; and

(d) whether the work is regular or erratic.

21.15   The number of hours worked is not conclusive of your worker status but it is relevant: CH/3733/2007. Ten hours may not be enough when the other factors here are considered – and not doing ten hours does not automatically exclude you. The factors always have to be considered together.

21.16   The fact that your job is poorly paid or the fact the that you have to claim, say, tax credits, is not enough on its own to stop you from qualifying as a worker. You can be a 'worker' even if your work is paid 'cash in hand': [2012] UKUT 112 (AAC).

Examples: Right to reside as worker

A Spanish national works in the UK as a cleaner in a garage for two hours a night on two nights a week. He is mainly in the country to study English. So he probably does not pass the right to reside test as a worker.

An Icelandic national works in the UK as a legal translator doing variable hours (depending on whether it is term time or holiday time) but averaging six hours a week over the year. She has been doing this for three years, and her hourly rate is substantial. It is therefore quite possible that she passes the right to reside test as a worker.

Retaining worker/self-employed status while out of work

21.17   If you are an EEA national (but see para 21.36 if you are Croatian) you can retain your worker or self-employed status (and therefore your right to reside and entitlement to HB) if:

(a) you are temporarily unable to work due to sickness or injury. 'Temporarily' is decided objectively (rather than solely by reference to your subjective intention): De Brito v Home Secretary. This excludes maternity, an exclusion which does not constitute unlawful discrimination: JS v SSWP;

21.17   De Brito v Home Secretary 30/05/12 CA [2012] EWCA Civ 709 www.bailii.org/ew/cases/EWCA/Civ/2012/709.html
        JS v SSWP 13/07/11 CA [2011] EWCA Civ 806 www.bailii.org/ew/cases/EWCA/Civ/2011/806.html

(b) you are on sick leave or maternity leave, with the right to return under their contract;

(c) you have worked for more than one year and are registered unemployed at the Jobcentre;

(d) you have worked for less than one year and are registered unemployed at the Jobcentre in which case your retained status lasts for only six months (after which you become a jobseeker: para 21.26)

(e) you are involuntarily unemployed and have started vocational training; or

(f) you are voluntarily unemployed in order to follow vocational training relating to your previous employment.

Item (a) includes self-employment but items (b)-(f) only apply only to former employees who have worked in the UK. In the case of items (c) and (d) (registered unemployed with the Jobcentre), you must provide evidence that you are seeking work and have a genuine prospect of being engaged; and in the case of item (c), after six months unemployment you must provide 'compelling evidence' of this.

21.18   You do not necessarily have to be entitled to ESA to qualify as being 'unable to work due to sickness or injury' (CIS 4304/2007). Likewise you don't have to qualify for JSA or national insurance credits to be 'registered unemployed' (CIS 184/2008). Small gaps between leaving your employment and registering as a jobseeker can be ignored: [2013] UKUT 163 (AAC).

EEA nationals with the permanent right of residence

21.19   If you are an EEA national you have a right to reside and you are entitled to HB if you have a 'right of permanent residence' in the UK, as defined by the EEA regulations. You have this right if:

(a) you have lawfully resided in the UK for a continuous period of five years (para 21.20); or

(b) you retired from working in the UK in a way which meets one of the conditions in paragraph 21.21.

21.20   For the first rule above, 'residence' means residence arising from an EEA right to reside (and not, for example, as a British citizen): McCarthy v Secretary of State for the Home Department. And a period of residence counts as 'continuous' despite absences, so long as:

(a) in any one year, the total length of your absence(s) from the UK is no more than six months, and this can be longer if your absence is due to compulsory military service; or

(b) the total period of absence is not more than 12 months – so long as the reason is pregnancy, childbirth, serious illness, study, vocational training, a posting in another country, or some other important reason.

Once you have acquired a permanent right of residence it can only be lost after an absence from the UK of more than two years.

21.17   EEA 6(2),(2A),(3)-(7); HB 10(3B)(c); HB60+ 10(4A)(c); NIHB 10(5)(c); NIHB60+ 10(5)(c);
         De Brito v Home Secretary 30/05/12 CA [2012] EWCA Civ 709 www.bailii.org/ew/cases/EWCA/Civ/2012/709.htm;
         JS v Secretary of State for Work and Pensions 13/07/11 CA [2011] EWCA Civ 806 www.bailii.org/ew/cases/EWCA/Civ/2011/806.html

21.19   EEA 5, 15(1)(a)-(f); HB 10(3B)(e); HB60+ 10(4A)(e); NIHB 10(5)(e); NIHB60+ 10(5)(e)

21.20   EEA 3; McCarthy v Secretary of State for the Home Department 25/11/10 ECJ C-434/09
         http://eur-lex.europa.eu/LexUriServ/LexUriServ.do?uri=CELEX:62009CC0434:EN:HTML

21.21   For the rule in paragraph 21.19(b) above, you must:

(a) have retired (at retirement age or at early retirement) after working in the UK for at least 12 months – and have been continuously resident in the UK for more than three years. In counting this 12 months, any period of involuntary unemployment registered with the Jobcentre, or period out of work due to illness, accident or some other reason 'not of [your] own making', is counted as a period of employment; or

(b) have retired (at retirement age or at early retirement) and your spouse or civil partner is a UK national; or

(c) have ceased working as a result of permanent incapacity; and either

■ the incapacity is the result of an accident at work or an occupational disease which entitles you to ESA, incapacity benefit, industrial injuries benefit or some other pension payable by a UK institution; or

■ you have continuously resided in the UK for more than two years; or

■ your spouse or civil partner is a UK national.

EEA family member rights

21.22   If you are the 'family member' of an EEA national who has acquired the right to reside you may also acquire a right to reside (and therefore a right to HB) through them. You are an EEA family member if you satisfy the conditions in table 21.1. You do not need to be an EEA national yourself (although you can be): instead your rights depend on the status of the person you are accompanying (e.g. worker, self-employed, student). If you are an EEA family member (table 21.1) you have a right to reside if:

(a) the person you are accompanying is a worker, self-employed person, student or a self sufficient person;

(b) the person you are accompanying is a person with a permanent right to reside (para 21.19) (whether through residence or retirement);

(c) you have lived in the UK for a continuous period of five years under a right to reside (whether as a family member or otherwise);

(d) the person you accompanied is a worker or self employed person who has died, and

■ you were living with them immediately before their death, and

■ either the worker or self-employed person had lived continuously in the UK for at least the two years immediately before their death or their death was a result of an accident at work or occupational disease; or

(e) you are a family member with a retained right of residence (para 21.23).

21.21   EEA 5(2),(3)

21.22   EEA 14(2), 15(1)(b),(d),(e); HB 10(3B)(d); HB60+ 10(4A)(d); NIHB 10(5)(d); NIHB60+ 10(5)(d);

Table 21.1 **Who is an EEA family member**

You are an EEA family member if you accompany an EEA national who is self-employed, a worker, a student or a self-sufficient person and you are:

(a) their spouse or civil partner (until divorce/dissolution, not mere separation or estrangement);

(b) a direct descendant of that person (e.g. a child or grandchild) or of their spouse or civil partner, and you are

- aged under 21; or

- dependent on him/her or their spouse or civil partner (for example, because you are studying or disabled;

(c) a dependent direct relative in ascending line (e.g. a parent or grandparent) or of their spouse or civil partner;

(d) some other family member who has been admitted to the UK on the basis that you are:

- their partner (in the benefit sense, instead of being their spouse or civil partner); or

- a dependent household member of that person in their country of origin; or

- a relative who is so ill that you strictly require personal care from that person.

Note:

If the EEA national you accompany is a student:

- if you are not their dependent child you do not count as a family member during the first three months of their (i.e. the student's) first three months of residence; and/or

- if you only fall within category (d) you only count as a family member if you have been issued with a residence card, family permit or registration certificate by the Home Office.

Former EEA family members with retained rights

21.23　　If you are a former EEA family member you nevertheless retain your family member rights if you:

(a) are the child of a former EEA worker who is in education in the UK;

(b) are the parent who is the primary carer of a former EEA worker's child that is in education in the UK;

(c) the EEA national you accompanied has died, and

- you were living with them as their family member for at least one year immediately before they died; and

- you are not an EEA national yourself;

T21.1　　EEA 7(1),(2),(4), 8(2)-(5)

(d) are the separated spouse or registered civil partner of an EEA worker who is living in the UK but you have not yet divorced (or dissolved your civil partnership);

(e) are a non-EEA national former spouse/civil partner who has divorced (or had your partnership dissolved) and either:

- your marriage/civil partnership lasted at least three years and you both lived in the UK for at least a year before the marriage ended, or

- there was domestic violence, or

- there is a child from the relationship and either custody or access (you must have one or the other) needs to take place in the UK.

Generally, if you are a partner who is not married or in a civil partnership you lose your family member rights if the relationship ends. However, if the relationship has ended because of domestic violence and your former partner is an EEA national you may be able to get leave to remain or a right to reside: this is a new and complicated area of law.

Primary carer of a child in education in the UK

21.24   If you are the child of an EEA migrant worker and in education in the UK or you are their primary carer (parent, grandparent, guardian) you have a right to reside and are entitled to HB provided that you are also habitually resident. This right to reside is sometimes called an 'Ibrahim/Teixeira' right (after the case that first established it) and you qualify for it as a child/primary carer if:

(a) the child has started a course of education in the UK, (e.g. primary or secondary school, or beginning a college or university course); and

(b) a parent of that child has been, at some time, an EEA worker (including a Croatian while working on the worker authorisation scheme).

The child has the right to reside while finishing the course of education, and the primary carer of the child (whether an EEA citizen or not) also has the right to reside. But you can only acquire this right through being a worker and not as a self employed person: [2014] UKUT 401 (AAC). But if you are subject to immigration control and the other parent has a right to reside in the UK and can care for your child you do not acquire the right to reside through being the primary carer: Hines v Lambeth LBC.

Non-EEA parents of a child who is a UK citizen

21.25   If you are a non-EEA national who is the parent of a child who is a UK citizen you have a right to reside in the UK under the EEA regulations. This right is sometimes referred to as a 'Zambrano' right after the case that first established it. However, this right to reside

---

21.23   EEA 10(2)-(6)

21.24   EEA 15(A)(1)-(4),(5); HB 10(3); HB60+ 10(3); NIHB 10(3); NIHB60+ 10(3);
Harrow LBC v Ibrahim and Secretary of State for the Home Department 23/02/10 ECJ C-310/08)
www.bailii.org/eu/cases/EUECJ/2010/C31008.html
Teixeira v Lambeth LBC and Secretary of State for the Home Department 23/02/10 ECJ C-480/08
www.bailii.org/eu/cases/EUECJ/2010/C48008.html
Hines v Lambeth LBC 20/05/14 CA [2014] EWCA Civ 660
http://www.bailii.org/ew/cases/EWCA/Civ/2014/660.html

21.25   EEA 15A(4A); HB 10(3A)(bb),(e); HB60+ 10(4)(bb),(e); NIHB 10(4)(bb),(e); NIHB60+ 10(4)(bb)(e);
Sanneh v SSWP [2015] EWCA Civ 49 www.bailii.org/ew/cases/Civ/2015/49.html

(unlike the others above) cannot be used to help you qualify for HB. (The HB regulations prohibit this and have been upheld as valid by the Court of Appeal but you may qualify for other financial support from social services: Sanneh v SSWP.)

EEA job seekers

21.26   You count as an EEA job seeker (as defined by the EEA regulations) if:

(a) you entered the UK seeking work, or you are seeking work immediately after your retained worker status as a registered unemployed person (para 21.17) has expired; and

(b) you can provide evidence that they are seeking employment and have a genuine chance of being engaged.

21.27   If you are an EEA job seeker you are not entitled to HB nor any of the other passport benefits except JSA(IB). If you meet the conditions in paragraph 21.26 you are entitled to register as unemployed and claim JSA(IB) but no award can be made during your first three months' residence in the UK. After three months' residence you are entitled to JSA(IB) but it does not entitle you to HB so long as you remain an EEA jobseeker (para 21.26) unless you have some other right to reside (i.e. other than as a jobseeker) described above (paras 21.7-24). However, you are protected from this rule if you were getting both JSA(IB) and HB on 31st March 2014, in which case you remain entitled to HB until such time as either your JSA(IB) ends or you make a new claim for HB (paras 2.2 and 17.22).

Students and other economically inactive but self-sufficient people

21.28   You have a right to reside as an EEA national if you were admitted to the UK on the basis that you were self-sufficient. The rules about self-sufficiency apply if you are 'economically inactive', including if you are a student (but with some differences). If you have a right to reside as self-sufficient (paras 21.29-32), whether or not you are a student, you must also be habitually resident (paras 20.38-52) to be entitled to HB. You must have your own resources to be considered self sufficient: [2014] UKUT 32 (AAC).

21.29   If you are an EEA student you have the right to reside if:

(a) you are currently studying on a course in the UK;

(b) you signed a declaration at the beginning of the course that you were able to support yourself without social assistance (which means HB and any passport benefit); and

(c) the declaration was true at the time it was signed and for the foreseeable future; and

(d) you have comprehensive health insurance for the UK (access to NHS treatment is not enough: [2014] UKUT 32 (AAC)).

21.30   In practice, this means that if you are an EEA student you are unlikely to be entitled to HB. However, it is possible to qualify for HB if your circumstances have changed since you started your course (e.g. your source of funds has unexpectedly dried up) – but you will also have to satisfy the rules for students in chapter 22.

21.26   EEA 6(1),(4)-(6)

21.27   HB 10(3A)(b),(l); HB60+ 10(4)(b); NIHB 10(4)(b),(m); NIHB60+ 10(4)(b); SI 2013/3196 Reg 2; SI 2014/539 Reg 3; NISR 2013/308 Reg 2; NISR 2014/98 Reg 3

21.29   EEA 4,6(1),14(1); HB 10(3); HB60+ 10(3); NIHB 10(3); NIHB60+ 10(3)

21.31   If you are economically inactive but not a student you have a right to reside if you:

(a) have sufficient resources not be an 'unreasonable burden' on the social assistance system; and

(b) have comprehensive health insurance.

21.32   The fact that your income is so low that you qualify for social security benefits does not automatically disqualify you but in practice you are likely to be refused HB. However, whether you are an 'unreasonable burden' is a matter of judgment and discretion (paras 1.52-53). DWP guidance acknowledges this and suggests that if you have been resident in the UK for some time, the fact that you have been self-sufficient until now is a relevant factor in deciding whether you are an 'unreasonable burden' as is the length of time you are likely to be claiming (GM paras C4.123). For example, if your funds have been temporarily disrupted you may still qualify.

Transitional exceptions

21.33   If you are an EEA national (including if you are a Croatian) you do not need a right to reside to qualify for HB if you were entitled to HB on 30th April 2004; and have since remained continuously entitled to one or more of the following benefits: HB, IS, JSA(C),JSA(IB), state pension credit or council tax benefit (prior to its demise on 31st March 2013). This is now rare.

Croatian nationals

21.34   The remainder of this chapter only applies if you are from Croatia. These rules apply from 1st July 2013 when Croatia joined the European Union. If you are from Croatia you must have a right to reside to get HB, but unlike other EEA nationals the circumstances in which you can have a right to reside are more limited because there are restrictions on your right to work and you have limited rights if you lose your job.

Right to reside

21.35   If you are a Croatian national you have a right to reside (and so are eligible for HB) if you:

(a) are self-employed (para 21.36);

(b) are employed in authorised work (para 21.37);

(c) have completed your one year qualifying period in authorised work (para 21.39) and have a right to reside that would qualify you for HB if you were from any other EEA country (paras 21.7-33) (for example, if you were working);

(d) are in paid employment and exempt from worker authorisation in any of the ways listed in table 21.2; or

(e) are, in limited circumstances, a primary carer of a child in education (para 21.24).

21.31   EEA 6(1),(3),14(1); HB 10(3B)(a),(b); HB60+ 10(4A)(a),(b); NIHB 10(5)(a),(b); NIHB60+ 10(5)(a),(b)

21.33   CPR sch 3 para 6(4); NICPR sch 3 para 6(3)

21.35   EEA 4(1)(a),(b), 6(1)(b),(c); SI 2013 No 1460 Reg 2(3),(4),(5), 5

Self-employed people

21.36   If you are a Croatian who is self-employed you qualify for HB in exactly the same way as any other EEA national (paras 21.9-11). There are no further conditions and you do not need Home Office authorisation to run your business. However, you must be currently self-employed; it is not enough that you were self-employed in the past: R (Tilianu) v Secretary of State for Work and Pensions. But you may remain self-employed despite the fact that your work has currently dried up ([2010] UKUT 451 (AAC)) – even, in the short term, if you have claimed JSA: [2011] UKUT 96 (AAC).

Authorised work

21.37   If you are a Croatian you can usually only take up work (as an employee) which has been 'authorised' by the Home Office until you have completed 12 months in continuous lawful employment (para 21.40). Authorised work is limited to certain specified occupations and in most cases you must meet other further conditions. Unless the work you propose to do falls into the 'highly skilled' category, the numbers of places that are authorised by the Home Office are subject to strict quotas.

21.38   If you are a Croatian it is not enough for you to have been a worker in the past to get HB, you must meet one of the conditions in paragraph 21.35.

Completing the 12 month qualifying period

21.39   After you have completed your 12 month qualifying period in lawful employment you are no longer required to be authorised to work and you can acquire the right to reside in exactly the same way as any other EEA national (paras 21.8-33).

21.40   During your qualifying period your employment only counts as 'lawful' if you hold the appropriate authorisation document and are complying with any conditions set out in it (CIS/3232/2006 and CJSA/700/2007).

21.41   You are treated as having completed your 12 month qualifying period if you were in lawful employment at the beginning and end of that period and any intervening periods in which you were not do not, in total, exceed 30 days.

21.36   R (Tilianu) v SSWP 18/12/10 CA [2010] EWCA Civ 1397 www.bailii.org/ew/cases/EWCA/Civ/2010/1397.html

21.37   SI 2013 No 1460 Reg 5

21.40   SI 2013 No 1460 Reg 2(3),(4),(5)

21.41   SI 2013 No 1460 Reg 2(5)

Table 21.2 **Croatians exempt from worker authorisation**

You are a Croatian national who is exempt from worker authorisation if:

(a) you have leave to enter the UK (table 20.3) which is not subject to any condition restricting your employment;

(b) you have worked in the UK in lawful employment for an uninterrupted period (para 21.39) of 12 months (whether that period started on, before or after 1st July 2013 when the work authorisation rules started);

(c) you have dual nationality either as a British citizen or a citizen of another EEA state, other than Croatia;

(d) your spouse, civil partner or partner is either a British citizen or a person with settled status (table 20.3);

(e) you have acquired a permanent right of residence (para 21.19);

(f) you are a family member (para 21.22) of an EEA national (other than a Croatian who is subject to worker authorisation) who has a right to reside in the UK;

(g) you are the spouse/civil partner/partner or a child aged under 18 of a person who has 'leave' to enter the UK (table 20.3) provided the terms of that leave allows them to work;

(h) you are the spouse/civil partner/partner or direct descendant of a Croatian who is subject to worker authorisation, provided that in the case of a direct descendant you are aged under 21 or dependent on that worker;

(i) you meet the Home Office criteria to enter the UK under the highly skilled migrant programme and hold a registration certificate that states that you have unrestricted access to the UK labour market;

(j) you are a student who works for no more than 20 hours per week and you hold a registration certificate which allows you to work for up to 20 hours per week;

(k) you have been posted to work in the UK by an organisation that is based in another EEA member state; or

(l) you are a diplomat or the family member of a diplomat.

T21.2   SI 2013 No 1460 Reg 2(2)-(20); HB 10(3B)(f); HB60+ 10(4A)(f); NIHB 10(5)(f); NIHB60+ 10(5)(f)

Chapter 22 **Students**

■ General rules and who counts as a student: see paras 22.1-8.

■ Which students can get HB: see paras 22.9-18.

■ How student loans, grants and other income are assessed: see paras 22.19-32.

General rules

22.1   This chapter explains the HB rules which apply if you are a student or your partner is. They apply in addition to the rules in the rest of this guide.

Working age HB

22.2   In working age HB claims:

(a) you can get HB if you are an eligible student;

(b) you can get HB if your partner is a student but you are not;

(c) eligible students include:

■ part-time students;

■ students under 21 who are not in higher education;

■ students with a child or young person in their family;

■ many students with a disability; and

■ some others (see table 22.1);

(d) your income from a student loan, grant and so on is taken into account (unless you are on a passport benefit).

This chapter gives the details of these and related rules.

Pension age HB claims

22.3   In pension age HB claims:

(a) all students and partners of students can get HB;

(b) all the kinds of student income in this chapter are disregarded.

But see paras 22.11 and 22.14 for rules that can apply to you.

Who is a student

22.4   You count as a student if:

(a) you are 'attending or undertaking a course of study at an educational establishment'. This could be a university, college or school, and the DWP says it can include any other educational establishment 'used for the purposes of training, education or instruction' (GM C2 annex A para C2.04); or

(b) you are on JSA and attending or undertaking an employment-related course.

You do not have to be getting a student loan or grant to count as a student, but you do not count as a student if you are getting a government training allowance.

22.5   You count as a student from when your course begins to when it ends, or you abandon it or are dismissed from it. This includes:

(a)   all term-times and vacations within the course (but not the vacations after it ends, or between two different courses);

(b)   periods of work experience in a sandwich course; and

(c)   absences while you remain registered with your educational establishment (for example, because you are sick or caring for someone, or for other personal reasons): O'Connor v Chief Adjudication Officer.

Full-time and part-time students

22.6   You count as a full-time student if you are on the following courses:

(a)   sandwich courses (courses with a period of work experience);

(b)   in England and Wales, courses funded by the Department for Education, Welsh Ministers, or Skills Funding, which require more than 16 hours per week of guided learning;

(c)   in Scotland, courses up to and including Scottish Higher level or SCOTVEC level 3 at a college of further education, which require more than:

■   16 hours per week of classroom or workshop based programmed learning; or

■   21 hours per week of those and other structured learning supported by teaching staff.

Information relating to (b) and (c) should be in the learning agreement (or a similar document) signed by you and your educational establishment.

22.7   For other courses there is no all-embracing definition of who counts as a full-time or part-time student. Your council should decide this by considering the nature of the course, the number of hours you are required to attend, how the educational establishment describes the course, and the amount and nature of any student loan or grant you receive (GM chapter C2 annex A para C2.08). Information about student courses and qualifications is available online [www].

22.8   But if you are on a modular course, you only count as full-time during the periods you are registered as full-time, or re-taking an exam or module from a full-time period.

22.4   HB 2(1) definition – 'training allowance', 53(1) definitions – 'course of study', 'sandwich course', 'student', 'qualifying course';
          HB60+ 2(1) definition – 'student'; NIHB 2(1), 50(1); NIHB60+ 2(1)

22.6   HB 53(1) definitions – 'college of further education', 'full-time course of study', 'full-time student', 'higher education'

22.7   https://www.gov.uk/what-different-qualification-levels-mean

22.8   HB 53(2)-(4); NIHB 50(2)-(4);

Eligibility for HB

22.9   The basic conditions for getting HB are summarised in para 2.2. This section explains the additional student rules. Table 22.1 gives the list of eligible students.

Table 22.1 **Eligible students**

Working age HB claims

In working age HB claims, you are an eligible student if you are in one or more of the following groups:

(a)   you are on JSA (IB), ESA (IR) or IS;

(b)   you are in supported accommodation and on UC (see para 2.7);

(c)   you are on a part-time course (see paras 22.6-8);

(d)   you are under 21 and are on a course which is not higher education (in other words your course is up to and including GCSE A level or BTEC/SCOTVEC National Diploma or Certificate level 3), or you are aged 21 and you are continuing such a course;

(e)   you are a lone parent (see para 4.7);

(f)   you are in a couple and are responsible for one or more children or young persons (see paras 4.31-38);

(g)   you are a single claimant and are responsible for a foster child placed with you by a local authority or voluntary organisation;

(h)   you quality for a disability premium or severe disability premium (see paras 12.25, 12.32 and 12.38);

(i)   you would qualify for a disability premium except that the DWP has disqualified you from incapacity benefit because you are treated as capable of work;

(j)   you are accepted by the DWP as having had limited capacity for work for ESA purposes for 28 weeks or more (ignoring breaks of up to 12 weeks), or as having been incapable of work for incapacity benefit purposes for 28 weeks or more (ignoring breaks of up to eight weeks);

(k)   you have a UK grant which included an amount for deafness (this applies from the date you requested this);

(l)   you are unable to get a student loan or grant following an absence from your studies which was due to sickness or to providing care, and was agreed by your educational establishment. But this only applies from when your sickness or caring responsibility ends to the day before you resume your studies, and only for a maximum of one year.

Pension age HB claims

In pension age HB claims, all students are eligible for HB.

T22.1   CBA 130(1)(a); HB 56; NICBA 129(1)(a); NIHB 53

Single claimants and lone parents

22.10 If you are a single student:

(a) in working age HB claims, you can only get HB if you are an eligible student. All lone parents and some single claimants are eligible students: see table 22.1;

(b) in pension age HB claims, all students can get HB.

22.11 The following rules apply when your term-time accommodation is different from your normal home:

(a) if you are liable for mortgage interest on your normal home, you cannot get HB (even if you pay rent on your term-time accommodation);

(b) if you are liable for rent on your normal home, you can only get HB there (even if you also pay rent on your term-time accommodation);

(c) if you are liable for rent on your term-time accommodation but are not liable for rent or mortgage interest on your normal home (for example because it is your parent's home), you can only get HB on your term-time accommodation. (See also para 22.15.)

Couples

22.12 If you are a couple:

(a) in working age HB claims, you can only get HB if at least one of you is:

■ an eligible student: see table 22.1; or

■ not a student.

You cannot get HB if you are both ineligible students;

(b) in pension age HB claims, all students and partners of students can get HB.

22.13 In working age HB claims, if one of you is an ineligible student the other one has to be the HB claimant (see para 5.4 for how to change which partner in a couple is the claimant). In other working age HB claims, and all pension age HB claims, either of you can be the HB claimant (see para 5.3). In all cases the calculation of your HB takes into account the income (including student income) and capital of both of you.

22.14 You can get HB on two homes if:

(a) one of you is an eligible student;

(b) the other one is also an eligible student, or is not a student;

(c) having two homes is unavoidable; and

(d) paying HB on two homes is reasonable.

For example, this could be because one of you is renting term-time accommodation for a course which is a long way from your normal rented home.

22.10   HB 54,56; NIHB 51,53

22.11   HB 7(1),(3); HB60+ 7(1),(3); NIHB 7(1),(3); NIHB60+ 7(1),(3)

22.12   HB 54,56; NIHB 51,53

22.13   CBA 136(1); HB 8(1)(e), 56(1); HB60+ 8(1)(e); NICBA 132(1); NIHB 8(1)(e), 53(1); NIHB60+ 8(1)(e)

22.14   HB 7(6)(b); HB60+ 7(6)(b); NIHB 7(6)(b); NIHB60+ 7(6)(b)

Examples: Student eligibility for HB

The examples are about working age HB claims, and the claimants meet the basic conditions for getting HB (see para 2.2).

1. A single student

A single student does not fall within any of the groups in table 22.1.

■ She cannot get HB: see para 22.10.

2. A single student with a disability

A single full-time student is registered as blind, so he qualifies for a disability premium.

■ He can get HB: see table 22.1(h).

3. A lone parent student

A student is a lone parent with two children.

■ She can get HB: see table 22.1(e).

4. A couple: one is a student

One partner in a couple works. The other is a full-time student and does not fall within any of the groups in table 22.1.

■ They can get HB, but the non-student has to be the HB claimant: see paras 22.12-13.

5. A couple: both are students

A couple are both full-time students. Neither of them falls within any of the groups in table 22.1.

■ They cannot get HB: see para 22.12.

6. The couple have a baby

The couple in example 5 have a baby.

■ They can get HB, and either of them can be the HB claimant: see paras 22.12-13.

Exceptions for term-time accommodation

22.15 Paragraphs 22.11 and 22.14 describe when you can get HB on term-time accommodation which is not your normal home. But in working age HB claims, if you are a full-time student you cannot get HB there while you are absent from it in your summer vacation (see para 22.18), unless the absence is due to hospital treatment or is less than one complete benefit week.

Exceptions for student accommodation

22.16 You can get HB on student accommodation (see para 22.17), for example a hall of residence. But in working age HB claims, if you are a full-time or part-time student you cannot get HB there during your 'period of study' (see para 22.18), unless you are in one or more of groups (c) to (k) in table 22.1. And if you are the partner of a full-time or part-time student, the same applies during their period of study.

22.15   HB 55; NIHB 52

22.16   HB 53(1) definition – 'education authority', 57,58; NIHB 50(1), 54,55

22.17   Student accommodation means:

(a) accommodation you rent from the educational establishment you are attending. This includes accommodation it in turn rents from another educational establishment, an education authority, or under a long tenancy (a tenancy with a lease of more than 21 years), but not accommodation it rents from someone else; or

(b) accommodation an educational establishment has arranged to provide to you in order to 'take advantage of' (abuse) the HB scheme.

Period of study and summer vacation

22.18   Your 'period of study' means:

(a) all the period you count as a student (see para 22.5) apart from summer vacations; but

(b) in courses requiring more than 45 weeks of study in a year (for example many postgraduate courses), all the period you count as a student. In these cases you do not count as having summer vacations.

Student income

22.19   The rules about how income is assessed are in chapters 13 and 14. This section gives the additional rules for student loans, grants and other income. Information about the amounts of loans, grants and so on is available online [www].

22.20   In pension age HB claims, all the kinds of student income in this section are disregarded. The rest of this chapter applies only to working age HB claims. But all your income is disregarded if you are on a passport benefit (see paras 13.3 and 13.5).

Student loans

22.21   A student loan can include:

(a) a fee loan towards your fees. This is disregarded; and/or

(b) a maintenance loan towards your living expenses. Part of this is counted as your income: see paras 22.22-24.

22.22   Most UK students in higher education are eligible for a maintenance loan. Higher education means degree courses, teacher training courses, training courses for youth and community workers, BTEC/SCOTVEC Higher National Diploma or Certificate, and other courses at level 4 and above. The main groups who cannot get a maintenance loan are:

22.18   HB 53(1) definitions – 'last day of course', 'period of study'; NIHB 50(1)

22.19   England: www.gov.uk/student-finance
         www.practitioners.slc.co.uk/policy-information/student-support-information-notices.aspx
         Scotland: www.saas.gov.uk/
         Wales: www.studentfinancewales.co.uk
         NI: www.studentfinanceni.co.uk/
         NHS & Social Work: www.nhsbsa.nhs.uk/Students.aspx

22.20   HB 54; HB60+ 29(1); NIHB 51; HB60+ 27(1)

22.21   HB 64(1), 64A; NIHB 61(1), 62

(a) part-time students;

(b) students on nursing and midwifery diploma courses (who can get a reduced maintenance loan);

(c) postgraduate students (but PGCE students can get a maintenance loan);

(d) students aged 60 or over at the start of the course; and

(e) students in Scotland aged 50 or over at the start of the course (unless you are under 55 and intend to work after completing the course).

22.23 If you are eligible for a student maintenance loan:

(a) you are counted as receiving it at the maximum level applicable to you for the year. This includes:

■ any additional loan you could get for extra weeks and so on;

■ any contribution you, your partner or your parents have been assessed as being able to make (see also para 22.27);

■ in Scotland, a young student's bursary;

(b) it is taken into account as your income (not capital) as described in table 22.2.

22.24 The rules in para 22.23 apply if you get a maintenance loan. They also apply if you could get a maintenance loan by 'taking reasonable steps' to do so. Religious beliefs are unlikely to be accepted as preventing you from doing so (CH/4422/2006).

Table 22.2 **Assessing student maintenance loans**

If you are eligible for a student maintenance loan (see paras 22.22-24), your income from it is calculated as follows.

(a) Start with the maximum amount of student maintenance loan you could receive for the year (see para 22.23).

(b) Subtract £693. This is a standard annual disregard of £303 towards travel and £390 towards books and equipment.

(c) Average the result over the weeks in the period from:

■ the first Monday in September,

■ or in Scotland, the first Monday in your academic year if it begins in August;

to:

■ the last Sunday in June,

■ or in your final year (or only year in a one-year course), the last Sunday in your course.

In 2014-15 there are 43 weeks from 1.9.14 to 28.6.15, but in 2015-16 there are 42 weeks from 7.9.15 to 26.6.15.

22.23 HB 53(1) definition – 'contribution', 'student loan', 56(1),(3),(4); NIHB 50(1), 53(1),(3),(4);

22.24 HB 56(3); NIHB 53(3)

T22.2 HB 40(7)-(9), 53(1) definitions – 'academic year', 'last day of course', 64; NIHB 37(3)-(7), 50(1), 61

(d)   Then subtract £10. This is a standard weekly disregard (see also para 13.45).

(e)   This gives your income for each of the weeks described in step (c).

(f)   But in your first year, the income calculated as above is not taken into account until your course begins (CIS/3735/2004).

Notes

■   If you are a couple and are both eligible for a student maintenance loan, the calculation applies separately for each of you (you each get the disregards at steps (b) and (d)).

■   If your course does not start in the autumn, the period used in step (c) is all of your academic year apart from weeks falling wholly or partly in the 'quarter' containing your longest vacation. But the 'quarters' are January to March, April to June, July to August, and September to December (even though these aren't all three months).

■   If you abandon or are dismissed from your course, any student loan you have received continues to be taken into account as calculated above, but the £10 disregard in step (d) does not apply after you have left.

Example: A student assessment (2014-15 academic year)

One partner in a couple is a full-time student in the first year of a degree course at a university outside London. He receives a student maintenance loan of £5,330 (£5,150 plus £180 for two extra weeks), which is the maximum he could receive as an English student. He also receives a fee loan. The other partner is self-employed for an average of 35 hours per week, and has net profit of £90 per week. They are eligible for HB because the non-student is the claimant (see para 22.12-13). They have no other income, and their capital is below £6,000. Their eligible rent is £130 per week.

Student income

The fee loan is disregarded (see para 22.21). The maintenance loan is assessed as follows (see 22.2):

(a)   He receives £5,330, which is the maximum amount applicable to him.

(b)   Subtract £693, leaving £4,637.

(c)   Average over the 43 weeks from 1.9.14 to 28.6.15: £4,637 ÷ 43 = £107.84.

(d)   Subtract £10, leaving £97.84.

(e)   This is his weekly income from the maintenance loan.

(f)   It is ignored from 1st September 2014 to when his course begins. It is then his income until 28th June 2015.

Amount of HB

From when the course begins to 28th June 2015 (unless their circumstances change) their HB is calculated as follows (see paras 6.2-8):

■	Student maintenance loan	£97.84 pw
■	Self-employed net profit (£90) minus standard earned income disregard for a couple (£10) and additional earned income disregard (£17.10)	£62.90 pw
■	Total income	£160.74 pw
■	Applicable amount (for a couple aged 18 or over but under SPC age)	£113.70 pw
■	Excess income (£160.74 – £113.70)	£47.04 pw
■	Eligible rent	£130.00 pw
■	Minus 65% of excess income (65% of £47.04)	£30.58 pw
■	Amount of HB	£99.42 pw

Student grants

22.25 A student grant means any kind of educational grant, award, scholarship, studentship, exhibition, allowance or bursary, whether it is paid by a local authority, a government department, an employer or someone else.

22.26 If you receive a grant:

(a) the amount you receive is taken into account as your income. This includes:

- ■ a maintenance grant towards your living expenses,
- ■ any amounts for the living expenses of a child or adult dependant,
- ■ any additional amounts you get for extra weeks and so on,
- ■ any contribution you, your partner or your parents have been assessed as being able to make (see also para 22.27);

(b) but some kinds of grant, and most amounts for extra expenses are disregarded.

The details are in table 22.3.

Table 22.3 **Assessing student grants**

If you receive a grant (see paras 22.25-26), your income from it is calculated as follows.

Disregard amounts

(a) Disregard the whole amount of the following grants:

- ■ special support grant (awarded to students on means-tested benefits),
- ■ education maintenance allowance (EMAs), and 16-19 bursary fund payments which replaced EMAs in England (awarded to students in non-advanced education). These are also disregarded in the assessment of your capital,
- ■ parent's learning allowance (awarded for dependants),
- ■ higher education bursary (awarded to care-leavers).

22.25 HB 53(1) definition – 'grant'; NIHB 50(1)

22.26 HB 53(1) definitions – 'contribution', 'grant income'; NIHB 50(1)

T22.3 HB 40(7)-(9), 53(1) definition – 'grant income', 59; NIHB 37(3)-(7), 50(1), 56

(b) For other grants, start with the total amount of grant you receive for the year (see para 22.26).

(c) If you are not eligible for a student maintenance loan (see para 22.22), subtract £693. This is a standard annual disregard for travel and books and equipment (it applies even if amounts for these are deducted at step (d)).

(d) Subtract all amounts included in your grant for:

- any disability you have,
- child care costs,
- travel,
- books and equipment,
- tuition or examination fees,
- maintenance of two homes,
- term-time residential establishment,
- anyone outside the UK who is not included in your application amount.

(e) The result counts as your income over the period(s) described below.

(f) Amounts for child or adult dependants.

(g) If you are eligible for a student loan (see para 22.22), apart from the reduced loan for an NHS-funded degree student, average amounts in your grant for a child or adult dependant over the same period as the student loan (see table 22.2).

(h) But if you are:

- a nursing and midwifery diploma student, or
- an NHS-funded degree student,

average amounts in your grant for a child or adult dependant over the whole academic year (52/53 weeks).

(i) In any other case, the rules in steps (j) and (k) apply.

Other amounts

(j) Average other amounts in your grant (apart from disregarded amounts) over the weeks from the first Monday to the last Sunday in the period they cover:

- for many grants this means your 'period of study' (see para 22.18),
- for a leaver's grant it means your summer vacation.

(k) But if you are a sandwich student, omit any weeks wholly or partly in your period of work experience.

Notes

- If you are a couple and both receive a grant, the calculation applies separately for each of you.
- If you abandon or are dismissed from your course, any amount you have received which falls within step (g) continues to be taken into account as calculated above.

Making contributions to your student loan or grant

22.27 If you or your partner have been assessed as being able to contribute to your student loan or grant, the contribution is:

(a) included when the loan or grant is assessed (see paras 22.23 and 22.26);

(b) disregarded from your or your partner's other earned or unearned income.

Parental contributions are also included when your loan or grant is assessed (see also para 13.43).

Using other income to supplement a student loan or grant

22.28 If you have income from a student loan or grant, you may qualify for an extra disregard towards your expenditure. This is calculated as follows:

(a) work out your expenditure for the year on the items in table 22.3(d), but only include expenditure which is necessary for you to attend your course;

(b) add together the following figures:

■ £693,

■ your higher education bursary (if you get one),

■ the amounts subtracted from your grant (if you get one) for the items in table 22.3(d);

(c) if the total of (a) is greater than the total of (b), you qualify for a disregard equal to the difference. In practice this is averaged over the year (or a more appropriate period) to give the weekly amount of the disregard.

But this disregard can only be made from income 'intended' for this purpose (CIS/3107/2003), for example if you have to take a part-time job to pay for your travel. It cannot be made from the student loan or grant, or from income you would have anyway.

Repaying a student loan

22.29 If you are repaying a student loan, your repayments cannot be deducted in the assessment of your income. But in England, Scotland and Wales, payments you receive from the Teacher Student Loan Repayment Scheme are wholly disregarded.

Access funds, learner support funds and financial contingency funds

22.30 Educational establishments can make payments to students from 'access funds' or 'learner support funds', and Welsh Ministers can make payments to students from 'financial contingency funds'. These are sometimes called hardship payments. They are assessed as follows:

22.27 HB 64(1),(4)(a)(iii),(b)(ii), 66,67; NIHB 61(1),(4)(a)(iii),(b)(ii), 64,65

22.28 HB 63; NIHB 60

22.29 HB 40(1), sch 5 para 12; NIHB 37(1)

22.30 HB 53(1) definition – 'access funds', 65,68(2),(4); NIHB 50(1), 63,66(2),(4)

(a) payments towards your living costs (see para 22.31) are counted as your income or capital as appropriate. But if they are income (in other words regular payments):

■ the whole amount is disregarded if they are paid before your course begins, or to tide you over until you receive your student loan,

■ £20 per week is disregarded in other situations (see also para 13.45);

(b) payments for anything else (for example course-related expenses) are disregarded as income and as capital for 52 weeks.

22.31 In paras 22.30 and 22.32, your living costs mean rent (other than any part of the rent which is not eligible for HB, or not met by HB because of a non-dependant deduction), council tax (in Northern Ireland rates), water charges, household fuel, food or ordinary clothing or footwear.

Sports Council awards

22.32 Sports Council awards are assessed as follows:

(a) payments towards your living costs (see para 22.31) are counted in full as your income or capital as appropriate;

(b) payments for anything else (including vitamins, minerals or performance-enhancing dietary supplements) are disregarded as income, and as capital for 26 weeks.

22.32   HB 2(1) definition – 'sports award', sch 5 para 59, sch 6 para 50; NIHB 2(1), sch 6 para 61, sch 7 para 49

Chapter 23 **Subsidy**

- General rules about subsidy for HB expenditure, local schemes, and administration: see paras 23.1-8.
- The effect of HB overpayments on subsidy: see paras 23.9-25.
- The effect of high rents etc on subsidy: see paras 23.26-37.

General rules

23.1 This chapter explains how much the DWP pays councils in Great Britain to run the HB scheme. This is called subsidy. (For the separate rules about grants towards discretionary housing payments see paras 24.16-18.)

23.2 The DWP pays councils subsidy for each financial year (1st April to 31st March) towards their:

(a) HB expenditure: see paras 23.2-4; and

(b) HB administration: see para 23.5.

The balance of the council's costs are met from the council's general fund in England and Scotland, or its council fund in Wales.

Subsidy for HB expenditure

23.3 The DWP pays each council subsidy towards the HB it pays in the financial year:

(a) this equals 100% of all HB lawfully paid;

(b) except that a lower amount (or no subsidy) is paid for:

- additional HB paid under a local scheme: see para 23.4,
- some overpayments of HB: see paras 23.9-25, and
- some payments of HB relating to high rents etc: see paras 23.26-37.

Lawfully paid HB includes rebates, allowances and payments on account (see chapter 16). It also includes payments made in the financial year for an earlier financial year. But each amount of HB can only get subsidy once.

Subsidy towards local schemes

23.4 If the council runs a local scheme for war disablement and bereavement pensions (see paras 13.18-19):

(a) first the council's annual subsidy is calculated (see para 23.3), but including only the HB that would be awarded if it did not run a local scheme;

23.3   AA 140(6), 140B(1); SO 11(2),(3), 12(1)(a), 13, 14, 19(1)(h), 20

23.4   SO 12(1)(c),(4)

(b)   then this is increased to take account of the local scheme. The increase equals the lower of:

  ■   0.2% of the council's annual subsidy,

  ■   75% of the additional HB awarded in the year as a result of the local scheme.

Subsidy for HB administration

23.5   The DWP also pays each council subsidy towards part of its HB administration costs in the financial year (for example staffing, accommodation, training and computers). The amounts for 2015-16 are in Circular HB SX/2014. The DWP calls this a 'cash-limited specific grant'. It is separate from the grant for council tax rebate (CTR) administration, which is paid to councils by the DCLG in England, or by the Scottish or Welsh Government.

Subsidy claims, payments and overpayments

23.6   To get subsidy, councils have to claim it from the DWP. They may not get their full amount of subsidy if they do not:

(a)   claim it on time using the correct procedures;

(b)   provide the information and evidence required by the DWP; and

(c)   get their final subsidy claim certified by their auditor by 30th November.

The Secretary of State for Work and Pensions has a discretion to recover subsidy which was overpaid, or was claimed in breach of the subsidy rules: R (Isle of Anglesey County Council) v SSWP, R (Lambeth LBC) v SSWP.

Subsidy law and guidance

23.7   The law about HB subsidy is in:

(a)   sections 140A-140G of the Social Security Administration Act 1992 (which gives the legal framework); and

(b)   the Income-related Benefits (Subsidy to Authorities) Order 1998, SI 1998 No.562 (which gives the detailed rules).

When the subsidy rules change in relation to a financial year, the Order is usually amended at the end of that year, but DWP guidance usually gives advance warning. DWP guidance is in its Subsidy Guidance Manual (which is reissued each year) and the 'S' series of circulars [www].

Subsidy and HB decision-making

23.8   When councils make decisions about awarding HB, or recovering overpaid HB, they have a duty to apply HB law fairly, objectively and impartially. If a decision means the council has to use its judgment (see para 1.52), it must not allow the subsidy rules to affect this. For example, although backdated HB qualifies for 100% subsidy, decisions about 'good cause'

23.5   AA 140B (4A),SO 12(1)(b), sch 1

23.6   SO part II
         R v Anglesey CC v SSWP 30/10/03 QBD [2003] EWHC 2518 Admin www.bailii.org/ew/cases/EWHC/Admin/2003/2518.html
         R (Lambeth LBC) v SSWP 20/04/05 QBD [2005] EWHC 637 Admin www.bailii.org/ew/cases/EWHC/Admin/2005/637.html

23.7   www.gov.uk/government/publications/hb-and-ctb-subsidy-guidance-manual
         www.gov.uk/government/collections/housing-benefit-for-local-authorities-circulars

(see paras 5.55-57) are subject to certification by the council's external auditor (DWP subsidy Guidance Manual paras 307-308). But if a decision allows the council to use its discretion (see para 1.53), it may take its own financial position (including the effect of the subsidy rules) into account as one factor: R v Brent LBC HBRB ex parte Connery. For examples see paras 9.30, 18.27-28 and 23.12.

Overpayment of HB

23.9   This section describes how much subsidy the DWP pays councils towards overpayments of HB.

Subsidy categories

23.10   For subsidy purposes, HB overpayments fall into the categories shown in table 23.1. The table also summarises the amounts of subsidy paid. The details for each category are in paras 23.13-25.

23.11   The rules about which HB overpayments are recoverable do not always correspond to the subsidy categories, but in broad terms:

(a) departmental error and authority error/administrative delay overpayments may or may not be recoverable: see the rules about official error overpayments in paras 18.10-14;

(b) other overpayments are usually recoverable: see paras 18.11-12 and 18.15.

Table 23.1 **Overpayments subsidy categories**

Subsidy category	Amount of subsidy
(a) Departmental error overpayments	100%
(b) Payment on account overpayments	100%
(c) Duplicate payment overpayments	25%
(d) Technical overpayments	Nil
(e) Authority error/administrative delay overpayments	100%, 40% or nil depending on certain thresholds
(f) Claimant error, fraudulent and other overpayments	40%

Notes

In broad terms:

▪ subsidy in categories (a) to (c) is paid only on unrecovered overpayments;

▪ subsidy in categories (e) and (f) is paid whether the overpayments are recovered or not.

Detailed rules about the categories, amounts etc are in paras 23.13-25.

23.8   R v Brent LBC ex p Connery 20/10/89 QBD 22 HLR 40

T23.1   AA 140(6); SO 11(2), 13, 18, 19(1)(e)-(i)

Deciding subsidy categories

23.12　The council decides which category each HB overpayment falls into for subsidy purposes. To ensure councils do this correctly, and claim the correct amount of subsidy, their external auditors are instructed that 'testing of overpayments needs to provide assurance that overpayments are correctly classified and fairly stated, recognising that there is a subsidy incentive to misclassify overpayments, for example, to code a technical error overpayment (nil subsidy) as an eligible [claimant error, etc] overpayment (40% subsidy) or, at or near one of the [authority error/administrative delay] thresholds, not to code a local authority error at all' (Audit Commission, Certification Instruction BEN01 (06-07) para 35).

Departmental error overpayments

23.13　For subsidy purposes, a 'departmental error overpayment' means one caused by a mistake of fact or law (whether in the form of an act or omission):

(a) by the DWP or HMRC or someone providing services to them; or

(b) in a decision of a First-tier or Upper Tribunal.

This does not include an overpayment to which the claimant, or someone acting on the claimant's behalf, or the payee, materially contributed (see para 23.24(c)). And it does not include an overpayment counted because a court interprets the law differently from how the DWP or HMRC or a tribunal interpreted it (see para 23.24(d)).

23.14　Subsidy on these overpayments is 100% of:

(a) the total departmental error overpayments in the year;

(b) minus the total departmental error overpayments recovered in the year (whether they were overpaid in the year or in a previous year).

This means the council does not qualify for subsidy towards the amount it recovers.

Payment on account overpayments

23.15　A 'payment on account overpayment' means one caused when a payment on account is greater than the amount of HB a claimant qualifies for (see paras 16.23-28).

23.16　Subsidy on these overpayments is 100% of:

(a) the total payment on account overpayments in the year;

(b) minus the total payment on account overpayments recovered in the year (whether they were overpaid in the year or in a previous year).

23.12　SO 18(4)

23.13　SO 18(4)

23.14　SO 18(b)(i),(2),(3), 19(1)(e)

23.15　SO 18 (7B)

23.16　SO 18(1)(f)

Duplicate payment overpayments

23.17 A 'duplicate payment overpayment' means one caused when:

(a) a duplicate payment of HB is issued because the first one was (or was alleged to have been) lost, stolen or not received; but

(b) the first one is in fact cashed.

23.18 Subsidy on these overpayments is 25% of:

(a) the total duplicate payment overpayments in the year;

(b) minus the total duplicate payments recovered in the year (whether they were issued in the year or in a previous year).

Technical overpayments

23.19 A 'technical overpayment' means one caused because:

(a) a council tenant's liability for rent ends (for example their tenancy ends) or reduces; but

(b) HB has already been credited to their rent account for a period after it ended or reduced.

23.20 No subsidy is paid on these overpayments.

Authority error/administrative delay overpayments

23.21 For subsidy purposes:

(a) an 'authority error overpayment' means one caused by a mistake of fact or law (whether in the form of an act or omission) by the council;

(b) an 'administrative delay overpayment' means one caused by a delay (rather than a mistake), but only when the council:

- is notified of a change of circumstances, and

- has the information and evidence it needs to make a decision on it, but

- fails to make the decision before the next HB payment date.

These do not include an overpayment to which the claimant, or someone acting on the claimant's behalf, or the payee, materially contributed (see para 23.24(c)). And they do not include an overpayment caused because a court interprets the law differently from how the council interpreted it (see para 23.24(d)).

23.22 These overpayments are combined for subsidy purposes. The amount of subsidy (see para 23.23) depends on:

(a) the total authority error and administrative delay overpayments in the year;

(b) as a percentage of the total HB paid in the year. (This means HB which qualifies for 100% subsidy: see para 23.3.)

23.17   SO 18(1)(a)

23.18   SO 18(1)(a), 19(1)(i)

23.19   SO 18(7),(7A)

23.20   SO 18(2)(b)

23.21   SO 18(6),(6ZA)

23.22   SO 18(1)(e),(6A)

23.23   If the above percentage is:

(a)   not more than 0.48% (the lower threshold), 100% subsidy is paid on all authority error and administrative delay overpayments in the year;

(b)   more than 0.48% but not more than 0.54% (the higher threshold), 40% subsidy is paid on all these overpayments;

(c)   more than 0.54%, no subsidy is paid on any of these overpayments.

In cases (a) and (b), the council qualifies for this subsidy even if it recovers some or all of these overpayments.

Example: Subsidy for authority error and administrative delay overpayments

A council's annual expenditure on correctly paid HB is £10,000,000.

So its lower threshold is £48,000 and its higher threshold is £54,000 for that year (see para 23.23).

If the total authority error and administrative delay overpayments in that year are:

■   £45,000, the council gets subsidy of 100% of this, which is £45,000;

■   £50,000, the council gets subsidy of 40% of this, which is £20,000;

■   £55,000, the council gets no subsidy for this.

Claimant error, fraudulent and other overpayments

23.24   Any other overpayment qualifies for 40% subsidy, whether it is:

(a)   a 'claimant error overpayment'. This means one caused by the claimant, or someone acting on the claimant's behalf, failing to provide required information or evidence;

(b)   a 'fraudulent overpayment'. This means one where the claimant has been found guilty of an offence, made an admission under caution, or agreed to pay a penalty as an alternative to prosecution (see para 18.73);

(c)   an overpayment that would count as departmental error (see para 23.13) or authority error/administrative delay (see para 23.21), except that the claimant, someone acting on the claimant's behalf, or the payee, materially contributed to it;

(d)   an overpayment caused because a court interprets the law differently from how the DWP, HMRC, a tribunal or the council interpreted it (see paras 23.13 and 23.21);

(e)   an overpayment caused by a third party, for example a landlord, whether or not they are the payee; or

(f)   any other overpayment not included in paras 23.13-23.

23.23   SO 18(1)(e),(6A)

23.24(a)   SO 18(4A)

23.24(b)   SO 18(5),(5A)

23.24(c),(d) SO 18(4),(6)

23.24(e),(f) SO 18(1)(b)(iii),(2)

23.25 Subsidy is 40% of the total of these overpayments in the year. The council qualifies for this subsidy even if it recovers some or all of these overpayments.

High rents etc

23.26 This section describes the subsidy limitations which apply when HB is paid for:

(a) exempt accommodation: see paras 23.28-31;

(b) temporary accommodation for homeless people: see paras 23.32-35;

(c) council tenants in certain circumstances: see para 23.36; and

(d) rent referral cases which the council fails to refer to the rent officer: see para 23.37.

23.27 The DWP pays councils 100% subsidy on all other payments of HB (see para 23.3) regardless of how high the claimant's eligible rent is, so long as it is correctly assessed. In practice this applies in most HB cases, because most HB cases do not fall within any of the rules in para 23.26. In particular, local housing allowance (LHA) cases never fall within these rules. (For how eligible rent is assessed, see chapters 7 to 10.)

Exempt accommodation

23.28 'Exempt accommodation' is defined in paras 9.4-7. The rules for exempt accommodation are as follows:

(a) details of the claimant's eligible rent are referred to the rent officer (see para 9.10);

(b) the rent officer's determinations are not binding on the assessment of the claimant's eligible rent (see paras 9.12 and 23.8);

(c) but the subsidy limitations in paras 23.29-30 apply if:

■ the rent officer's determinations include a 'significantly high rent' or 'exceptionally high rent' determination (see paras 9.55 and 9.57), and

■ the claimant's eligible rent is higher than these.

For exceptions for registered housing associations see para 23.31.

Subsidy limitations for exempt accommodation

23.29 The subsidy limitations for exempt accommodation apply to the part of the claimant's HB which is attributable to:

(a) the excess of the claimant's eligible rent;

(b) over the exceptionally high rent (EHR) determination (if there is one); or

(c) over the significantly high rent (SHR) determination (if there is no EHR).

23.30 Subsidy on HB attributable to this excess is:

(a) 100% when the claimant falls into the protected groups of people who:

■ could formerly afford their accommodation (see paras 7.66-67), or

■ have had a death in their household (see paras 7.68-69);

23.25   SO 18(1)(b)(iii),(c),(d),(2), 19(1)(ea),(f)

23.28-31   SO 13, 16, section 4

(b) 40% when:

- the claimant or someone in their household falls into the protected group of vulnerable people (see para 9.25), and

- there is no suitable cheaper alternative accommodation the claimant can reasonably be expected to move to (see paras 9.26-27);

(c) nil in any other situation. For example, when there is no suitable alternative accommodation to make a comparison with (see paras 9.15-17), or when the amount by which the council has restricted the claimant's eligible rent still leaves an excess (see paras 9.28-30).

In all these cases, 100% subsidy is paid on HB not attributable to the excess. The example illustrates this.

Example: Subsidy for exempt accommodation

A claimant is renting exempt accommodation. The rent officer has provided an exceptionally high rent (EHR) determination of £170 per week. But the council decides her eligible rent is £200 per week. This is because she falls into a vulnerable group and there is no suitable cheaper alternative accommodation she can move to. The claimant is not on a passport benefit and qualifies for HB of £80 per week.

Subsidy is calculated as follows (see paras 23.29-30):

- the excess of how eligible rent over the EHR is £30 per week.
- First subsidy is calculated on the HB attributable to this excess: this is 40% of £30   £12 pw
- Then subsidy is calculated on the HB not attributable to the excess: this is 100% of £50   £50 pw
- Total   £62 pw

The council gets subsidy of £62 per week.

Note: If the landlord was a registered housing association and the council did not consider the rent unreasonably high, the council would get subsidy of 100% of the claimant's HB (see para 23.31), which is £80 per week.

Registered housing association exempt accommodation

23.31   The following exceptions apply when the landlord of exempt accommodation is a registered housing association (see para 7.8):

(a) the subsidy limitations in paras 23.29-30 only apply if the council considers:

- that the claimant's rent is unreasonably high, or

- in pension age HB claims, that other accommodation is unreasonably large.

This is because details of the claimant's rent can only be referred to the rent officer in these circumstances (see paras 9.35-37);

(b) when exempt accommodation is used as temporary accommodation for homeless people, the rules in paras 23.32-35 apply (instead of those in paras 23.29-30).

Temporary accommodation for homeless people

23.32   The subsidy limitations in para 23.33 apply to the types of temporary or short-term accommodation in table 23.2, when they are provided:

(a) by a council or a registered housing association (see para 7.8);

(b) in order to meet a homeless duty under part 7 of the Housing Act 1996 or part 2 of the Housing (Scotland) Act 1987 (or for old cases, part 3 or the Housing Act 1985).

Subsidy limitations for temporary accommodation

23.33   Subsidy for HB paid on temporary accommodation is limited on a weekly basis to the lowest of:

(a) the claimant's entitlement to HB in the week;

(b) the 'maximum weekly subsidy' amount shown in table 23.2;

(c) the weekly 'cap' limit of:

■ £500 if the accommodation is one of the following London broad rental market areas: Central, Inner East, Inner North, Inner South East, Inner South West, Inner West, and Outer South West,

■ £375 if the accommodation is elsewhere.

The rules are described in detail in DWP circulars SI/2011, S5/2011 and G10/2012.

Table 23.2 **Maximum weekly subsidy amounts for temporary or short-term accommodation**

Type of accommodation	Maximum weekly subsidy amount
(a) LA or HA board and lodging accommodation.	The January 2011 LHA figure for one-bedroom self-contained accommodation
(b) LA or HA licensed accommodation:	
(1) not self-contained	one-bedroom self-contained accommodation;
(2) self-contained	the appropriate size of dwelling.
(c) LA or HA leased accommodation, or HA owned accommodation:	90% of the January 2011 LHA figure for:
(1) not self-contained	(1) one-bedroom self-contained accommodation;
(2) self-contained	(2) the appropriate size of dwelling; plus (in either case) £40 if the placing LA is in London or £60 if it is outside London (as a contribution towards management costs).

23.32-35   SO 11(1), 13, 17-17C, sch 7, sch 8

T23.2   SO 11(1), 13, 17-17C, sch 7, sch 8

Notes

LA: Local authority (council).

HA: Registered housing association.

Board and lodging accommodation: Accommodation

- where the charge includes at least some meals which are cooked or prepared, and also consumed, in the accommodation on or in associated premises; or

- provided in a hotel, guest house, lodging house or similar establishment;

but not accommodation in a hostel, or residential care or nursing home (see paras 2.30 or 2.34).

Licensed accommodation: Accommodation which the LA or HA holds under a lease. But in the case of English LAs, it must be outside the LA's housing revenue account, and the lease must be longer than ten years.

Self-contained or not self-contained: For subsidy purposes the accommodation in (b) and (c) is not self-contained if the claimant has to share a kitchen, bathroom or toilet with another household.

Maximum weekly subsidy amount: See para 23.33.

January 2011 LHA figures: See para 23.34.

Appropriate size of dwelling: See para 23.35.

The use of January 2011 LHA figures

23.34   The maximum weekly subsidy amounts in table 23.2 are based on the January 2011 LHA (local housing allowance) figure for the broad rental market area in which the accommodation is situated. The DWP intends to 'reform' arrangements to support people living in temporary accommodation. But it is expected that the January 2011 LHA figures (and the other rules in the table) will continue to apply in 2015-16.

23.35   Where table 23.2 refers to 'the appropriate size of dwelling', this means a self-contained dwelling with up to five bedrooms (because in January 2011 the LHA rules allowed for dwellings up to this size). But the following special rule applies when deciding this. If the total number of bedrooms and living rooms in the claimant's accommodation is:

(a)   two to five, one of these must be counted as a living room;

(b)   six or more, two of these must be counted as living rooms.

For example, if a claimant has five bedrooms and one living room, there are six rooms in total. But two of these must be counted as living rooms, so the January 2011 LHA figure is the one for a four-bedroom dwelling.

Example: Subsidy for short-term leased accommodation

A council outside London houses a family in a short-term leased three-bedroom house in London. The claimant is entitled to HB of £260 per week. The January 2011 LHA figure for a three-bedroom dwelling in that area is £180 per week.

Subsidy is calculated as follows (see table 23.2(c)):

■ 90% of the January 2011 LHA figure	£162 pw
■ Plus (because the placing authority is outside London)	£60 pw
■ Total	£222 pw

The council gets subsidy of £222 per week.

Council tenants

23.36   The following subsidy limitations can apply to council tenants (see para 7.5), but in practice they are rare. The DWP's Subsidy Guidance Manual gives further details and exceptions:

(a) The 'rent rebate subsidy limitation scheme' applies in England and Wales only. If the council increases its tenants' rents by more than its central government guideline rent increase, no subsidy is payable on the HB attributable to the excess (DWP circulars S2/2012 and S3/2013). (Rents on local authority homes provided under the Affordable Rents model are exempt from this control.)

(b) The 'disproportionate rent increase rule' applies in Wales and Scotland only. If a council increases rents to its tenants on HB more than it increases its other rents, subsidy on the difference is restricted.

(c) Limitations on 'modular improvement schemes' apply throughout Great Britain. If a council offers its tenants the right to select optional services, no subsidy is payable on the amount of HB attributable to these.

(d) Limitations on 'rent payment incentive schemes' apply throughout Great Britain. If a council makes payments (in cash or kind) to reward tenants for paying their rent on time, the total value of such payments is deducted from the amount of subsidy paid to the council.

Failure to make a rent referral

23.37   'Rent referral cases' are described in paras 9.31-72. If the council:

(a) is required to refer an HB case to the rent officer during the year;

(a) but fails to do so before the date its final subsidy claim has to be submitted for that year,

no subsidy is paid for any of the HB awarded in the year for that case. Some councils have lost a significant amount of subsidy for this reason: R (Isle of Anglesey County Concil) v SSWP, R (Lambeth LBC) v SSWP.

23.36   SO 11(2), 13, 15, 15A, 19(1)(a),(c),(2),(3), 20A, sch 4A

23.37   SO 13, 16, sch 4 para 6; R (Anglesey) v SSWP and R (Lambeth) v SSWP see footnote 23.6

Chapter 24 **Discretionary housing payments and DWP direct payments for rent arrears, etc**

■ Discretionary housing payments (DHPs): see paras 24.1-18.

■ The DWP scheme for third party payments by deductions from specified benefits for rent arrears, ineligible hostel charges and other payments: see paras 24.19-38.

Discretionary housing payments (DHPs)

Legislation

24.1　In Great Britain the UK government has the power to:

(a) make regulations providing for a scheme of discretionary housing payments (DHPs) – see the Discretionary Financial Assistance Regulations 2001/1167;

(b) pay grants to authorities for the cost of the scheme and in England and Wales impose a limit on the amount of each authority's total payments under the scheme – see the Discretionary Housing Payments (Grants) Order 2001/2340.

24.2　From 2014-15 onwards Scottish Ministers have had the power to set the limit on the total amount of expenditure that Scottish authorities may incur in making discretionary housing payments. They have chosen not to apply a limit in the expectation that the additional monies will be used by Scottish authorities to mitigate the impact of the reductions in HB or UC due to the social sector size rules [www].

24.3　In Northern Ireland the DSD has similar powers to run a DHP scheme – see the Discretionary Financial Assistance Regulations (NI) 2001/216.

24.4　DHPs are an independent scheme administered by authorities that also administer HB but they are not a form of HB. The HB appeals procedures (chapter 19) do not apply. You may however ask an authority to look again (review) any decision it has made. Payment of DHPs is discretionary but in its consideration of your circumstances the authority should not take into account any mobility component of disability living allowance (DLA) you or any partner get and should not have a fixed rule or policy requiring it to take into account any DLA care component received: Hardy R (on the application of) v Sandwell MBC. Authorities vary in their willingness to award DHPs. While it is worth asking about and/or claiming DHPs, you should not rely on an authority making an award.

24.1　CPSA 69,70; SI 2001 No 1167; SI 2001 No 2340

24.2　SI 2014 No. 2918, SSI 2014 No. 298 http://tinyurl.com/mql2p9t

24.3　NICPSA 60,61; NISR 2001 No 216

24.4　CBA 73(14), Hardy, R (on the application of) v Sandwell MBC [2015] EWHC 890 (Admin) (30th March 2015) www.bailii.org/ew/cases/EWHC/Admin/2015/890.html

DWP guidance

24.5   Guidance for authorities on the administration of DHPs is set out in the DWP's *Discretionary Housing Payments Guidance Manual* (April 2014) [www], referred to in this chapter as 'DHPGM'. The DWP has updated the guidance to reflect: changes to the LHA rules from April 2011 onwards, the introduction of universal credit, the abolition of CTB, the introduction of the benefit cap and the social sector size rules.

Circumstances in which DHPs may be made

24. 6   You may be able to get a DHP if you are:

(a)   in GB and entitled to HB or UC, have a rent liability, and 'appear to [the] authority to require some further financial assistance… in order to meet housing costs';

(b)   in Northern Ireland and entitled to HB in respect of your rent which has been restricted as a rent referral case or under LHA rules and 'appear to require some further financial assistance… in order to meet housing costs'.

There is no requirement for your family's circumstances to be 'exceptional', nor does there have to be 'hardship'. The DWP (paras 1.15-1.17 of DHPGM) says that there is no legal definition of the phrase 'further financial assistance' but that usually the claimant 'will need to demonstrate that they are unable to meet housing costs from their available income or that they have a shortfall as a result of the welfare reforms'.

Housing costs

24.7   The term 'housing costs' is not defined in the regulations. The DWP (para 1.12 of DHPGM) says that the term may be interpreted to include not just rent (with certain exclusions) but also:

(a)   rent in advance,

(b)   deposits, and

(c)   other lump sum costs associated with a housing need such as removal costs.

24.8   You can't get a DHP to meet your council tax liability or make up any shortfall between your council tax liability and your CTR. In England and Wales, however, an authority has a separate and wide discretionary power to reduce your council tax liability whether or not you qualify for HB or CTR.

Uses for DHPs

24.9   By way of examples the DWP (paras 2.3-2.4 of DHPGM) says that authorities may use DHPs to cover such matters as:

(a)   reductions in HB or UC where the benefit cap has been applied (see also DWP circular HB A15/2013 para 70);

24.5   www.gov.uk/government/publications/discretionary-housing-payments-guidance-manual

24.6   SI 2001 No. 1167 reg 2; NISR 2001 No. 216 rule 2

24.8   LGFA 13A(1)(c),(6),(7)

24.9   www.gov.uk/government/statistics/use-of-discretionary-housing-payments-april-to-september-2014
          www.scotland.gov.uk/Resource/0046/00463850.pdf

(b) reductions in HB or UC due to the social rented sector size rules;

(c) reductions in HB or UC because of local housing allowance restrictions;

(d) rent shortfall to prevent a household becoming homeless while the housing authority explores other options;

(e) rent officer restrictions such as local reference rent or shared room rate;

(f) non-dependant deductions;

(g) income tapers;

(h) a rent deposit or rent in advance for a property you have yet to move into if already entitled to HB/UC for your present home.

If you are on UC and move into supported accommodation (para 17.31) it would also be reasonable for an authority to use a DHP to cover a gap between the end of UC housing costs and the beginning of HB. The DWP's and the Scottish Government's analysis of the actual use of DHPs between April and September 2014 revealed that the highest proportion of DHP expenditure is the result of HB reductions due to the social sector size rules [www].

24.10   You can't get a DHP to help you with any of the following:

(a) service or support charges that are ineligible for HB/UC (para 10.40 onwards);

(b) any council tax liability;

(c) charges for water, sewerage or allied environmental services;

(d) in Northern Ireland any liability to meet rates;

(e) increases to cover rent arrears which are not eligible for HB (para 10.59);

(f) a reduction in the amount of benefit due to recovery of an HB/UC overpayment;

(g) reductions in any benefit because of Jobseeker's sanctions, Child Support sanctions or sanctions following certain benefit related offences.

Maximum amount of DHP and period of award

24.11   Where you are on HB the total weekly amount of a DHP, taken together with your award of HB, must not exceed your eligible rent calculated on a weekly basis. Where you are on UC the amount of the DHP (if calculated as a monthly amount) must not be greater than the UC housing cost element for renters or, where you are in exempt accommodation, the relevant rent and service charge payments calculated on a monthly basis.

24.12   The Court of Appeal has held that 'the limit placed on DHPs… does not prevent the Council from exercising its discretion to make DHPs for past housing costs (arrears of rent) on the ground that the applicant is currently receiving full housing benefit.' (Gargett, R (on the application of) v Lambeth LBC para 32). The authority may award a DHP for any period (i.e. for a fixed period or indefinitely) that is appropriate for the circumstances of your case.

24.10   SI 2001 No. 1167 reg 3; NISR 2001 No. 216 rule 3

24.11   SI 2001 No. 1167 reg 4; NISR 2001 No. 216 rule 4

24.12   R (on the application of Gargett) v Lambeth LBC [2008] EWCA Civ 1450, www.bailii.org/ew/cases/EWCA/Civ/2008/1450.htm

24.13 The maximum amount only applies where the authority calculates DHP as a weekly sum – for example to meet a shortfall. Where the DHP is for a lump sum payment such as a deposit or rent in advance these limits do not apply (DWP paras 2.10-2.11 of DHPGM) but the authority does have to take account of its overall DHP budget.

Claims, decisions, payments and overpayments

24.14 You may claim a DHP or someone acting on your behalf may make the claim if this appears reasonable to the authority. The authority may accept a claim in such form and manner as it approves. Some authorities have a separate DHP claim form. The authority should provide you with a written notice of its decision on your claim and the reasons for it as soon as is reasonably practicable. The authority may pay DHPs to you or to someone else it thinks appropriate. You (and the person getting the DHPs if different) must provide the authority with details of the grounds of claim, information on any changes of circumstance that may be relevant and any other information required by the authority. The authority may stop making payments of DHP when it thinks fit.

24.15 The authority has the discretion to recover DHP payments when it decides that someone has misrepresented, or failed to disclose, a material fact and, as a consequence, a payment was made. The authority may also recover DHPs where it decides that an error was made in deciding the application for payment which would not have been made but for that error.

DWP's contribution to DHP expenditure

24.16 The DWP partly reimburses an authority's DHP expenditure through a system of grants (and both Scottish and Welsh Governments have also provided additional support).

24.17 Because DHPs are separate from the HB scheme they do not qualify for HB subsidy. Instead the DWP pays each council a grant towards its DHP expenditure. The total grant for all councils in 2015-16 is £125 million (see DWP circular HB S1/2015), a reduction of £40 million from the previous year (HB S1/2014). The DWP grant contribution to each authority is set out in the circulars.

24.18 The authority has to claim this grant by 30th April in the following financial year (the claim does not have to be audited). Its expenditure on DHPs does not have to equal the amount of the grant. It can be less or more. But in the case of English and Welsh authorities their annual DHP expenditure must not be more than 2½ times the amount of the grant.

24.14   SI 2001 No. 1167; NISR 2001 No. 216

24.15   SI 2001 No 1167 reg 8; NISR 2001 No 216 rule 8

24.17   CPSA 70; SI 2001/2340

24.18   SI 2001/2340 art 3(2)(f), 7(1)

DWP rent arrears etc direct payments

24.19   This section describes how the DWP/DSD can pay part of your IS, JSA, ESA or pension credit directly to your landlord or mortgage company – usually to cover rent or mortgage arrears, or if you are a hostel resident other items included in your rent (para 24.24). The different rules that apply in the case of deductions and alternative payment arrangements from UC are described in the companion volume.

What is the scheme called?

24.20   Payments made under this scheme are called 'rent arrears direct' or 'direct payments' (usually by claimants or advisors and in this guide) or officially 'third party payments' (by the DWP).

The law and guidance on direct payments

24.21   The law about direct payments is found in:

(a)   schedule 9 of the Social Security (Claims and Payments) Regulations SI 1987/1968 (as amended); or

(b)   in Northern Ireland, schedule 8A of the Social Security (Claims and Payments) Regulations NISR 1987/465 (as amended).

The DWP/DSDNI have produced guides for new creditors on *How to Apply for Third Party Payments* [www] and a handbook for organisations and individuals that get Third Party Payments *(Third Party Payments Creditor/Supplier Handbook)*. The DWP also issues guidance to authorities about the scheme (GM D1.570-689). The description of the arrangements set out below applies to England, Scotland and Wales. While similar arrangements apply in NI, the detailed rules differ and the interested reader should consider the relevant NI legislation and guidance.

What is the scheme for?

24.22   The purpose of the scheme is to provide your landlord or lender with an incentive not to evict you from your home (and therefore it cannot be used for arrears on your former home). It acts as a safety net to make sure that if you are on a passport benefit you have access to essential services (housing, water, fuel) even if you get into payment difficulty.

24.23   For similar reasons the same scheme can be used to secure the continued supply of essential utilities to your home (fuel and water) – the details for this part of the scheme are beyond the scope of this guide except where payment of water or fuel is part of your rent.

24.24   If you are a hostel resident the scheme may also cover those payments included in the hostel's charge for essential services that are ineligible for HB such as fuel, water and meals – whether or not you are in arrears (para 24.27).

24.21   SI 1987/1968 35(1) & sch 9, NISR 1987/465 34A(1) & sch 8A
          www.gov.uk/government/uploads/system/uploads/attachment_data/file/236163/tpp-new-creditor-guide.pdf
          www.dsdni.gov.uk/dsd-tpp-guide.pdf
          www.gov.uk/government/uploads/system/uploads/attachment_data/file/417640/third-party-payments-handbook-march-2015.pdf
          www.dsdni.gov.uk/dsd-tpp-handbook.pdf
24.24   SI 1987/1968 sch 9 para 4A

Relationship to HB/SMI

24.25   The rules are additional to the rules about paying HB to your landlord (paras 16.34-53) or, if you are a homeowner with a mortgage, the rules about the payment of SMI to your lender (para 25.60). Indeed, they are not HB/SMI rules at all, but they so often arise in HB/SMI cases that they are included here for reference.

24.26   Although not part of the HB scheme itself, direct payments have consequences for the way that your HB is paid – they trigger mandatory payment of HB to your landlord (para 16.38).

Qualifying conditions for direct payments

24.27   The power to make direct payments is discretionary even if all the qualifying conditions are met. The qualifying conditions are that you or your partner must be:

(a) getting a 'specified benefit' (para 24.29); and

(b) getting HB/SMI (or have claimed HB if you are a hostel resident); and

(c) in occupation of the home for which payments are to be made; and either you

- have arrears of mortgage payments and have paid less than eight weeks full housing costs as eligible for SMI (chapter 25) in the last 12 weeks; or

- have rent arrears and meet the rent arrears condition (para 24.31); or

- live in a hostel (para 2.30) and (regardless of whether there are rent arrears or not) for which the overall charge includes payment for one or more of the following services: water; a service charge for fuel; meals; laundry or cleaning (other than communal areas); and the DWP determines that direct payments should be made.

24.28   Note that because of the requirement for residence direct payments cannot be made towards arrears on your former home.

Specified benefits for direct payments

24.29   When the DWP makes direct payments, it deducts an equivalent amount from your specified benefit. The specified benefits are:

(a) income support;

(b) state pension credit (savings credit or guarantee credit or both);

(c) income-based JSA;

(d) income-related ESA;

(e) contribution-based JSA if there would be entitlement to income-based JSA but for the fact that contribution-based JSA is being paid at the same rate;

(f) contribution-based ESA if there would be entitlement to income-related ESA but for the fact that contribution-based ESA is being paid at the same rate.

24.29   SI 1987/1968 sch 9 para 1(1) definition of 'specified benefit', para 1(2), 1(3),

24.30   In addition, in the case where any of the first three qualifying benefits (para 24.29) are in payment and the amount is insufficient for deductions to be made, deductions can also be made from any contribution-based jobseekers' allowance, incapacity benefit, retirement pension or severe disablement allowance that you also get (whether or not it is paid in a combined payment with the qualifying benefit).

What is the rent arrears condition

24.31   There must be 'rent arrears' (para 24.33) of at least four times the gross weekly 'rent' or, in the case of hostels, the arrears exceed £100.00, and either:

(a)   the rent arrears have accrued or persisted over a period of at least eight weeks and the landlord requests that deductions are made; or

(b)   the rent arrears have accrued or persisted over a period of less than eight weeks but in the opinion of the DWP it is in the overriding interests of the family that payments should be made; or

(c)   the dwelling is a hostel (para 2.30) and the rent includes a charge for services that is eligible for direct payments (para 24.27).

24.32   In calculating the four weeks' arrears and any period over which those arrears have accrued, the DWP must ignore any arrears which have arisen due to your failure to pay a non-dependant charge.

What counts as 'rent' and 'rent arrears'

24.33   For the purpose of determining whether you meet the rent arrears condition (para 24.31) 'rent' and 'rent arrears' includes:

(a)   any charge which is covered by HB;

(b)   any water charges or service charges payable with the rent which are ineligible for HB;

(c)   fuel charges included in the rent provided the charge does not vary more than twice a year;

(d)   any other inclusive charge paid with the rent, whether or not it is eligible for HB, except any unpaid non-dependant charge.

Rate of payment

24.34   In the case of direct payments for a hostel, the amount of the payment equals whatever amount of the charge is ineligible for HB for those services in paragraph 24.27 (e.g. laundry, cleaning, etc) as they are calculated for HB (chapter 10). If the application is made before your HB is awarded, the DWP should estimate the figure.

24.30   SI 1987/1968 sch 9 para 1(1) definition of 'specified benefit'

24.31   SI 1987/1968 sch 9 para 5(1)-(1A);

24.32   SI 1987/1968 sch 9 para 5(2),

24.33   SI 1987/1968 sch 9 paras 1(1) definition of 'rent', 5(7),

24.34   SI 1987/1968 sch 9 paras 4A(3),

24.35　　In the case of direct payments for rent arrears or mortgage arrears the rate of payment is (subject to any maximum amount: para 24.37):

(a)　the standard weekly deduction (para 24.36) plus, if it applies,

(b)　in the case of mortgage arrears, the weekly ongoing cost; or

(c)　in the case of rent arrears, any fuel or water charged as part of the rent, provided that the specified benefit is at least equal to that charge.

When all of the arrears are cleared, the weekly ongoing cost or amount for fuel or water can continue if it is in the 'interests of the family'.

24.36　　The standard weekly deduction for 2015-16 is £3.70. In subsequent years the rate is calculated as being equal to 5% of the personal allowance for a single claimant aged 25+ (table 12.1) rounded up to the nearest 5p.

Maximum deductions for rent arrears cases

24.37　　The maximum amount for rent arrears (para 24.35) that the DWP can deduct from your specified benefit is as follows:

(a)　There must be at least 10p of any qualifying benefit(s) remaining after any deduction.

(b)　If the standard amount together with any ongoing fuel/water payment exceeds 25% of your qualifying benefit applicable amount (or where child tax credit is payable, 25% of your applicable amount plus child tax credit and child benefit) then the deduction cannot be made without your consent.

(c)　If there are standard deductions for several items such as rent, fuel, water, council tax, child maintenance and fines, the total cannot exceed three times the standard weekly deduction (i.e. for 2015-16, £11.10).

(d)　If there are deductions for various other debts such that the total would reduce the qualifying benefit to less than 10p, then they are paid in the order shown in paragraph 24.38.

24.38　　The order of priority is:

(a)　mortgage (SMI) arrears or rent arrears (as appropriate);

(b)　fuel;

(c)　water;

(d)　council tax;

(e)　unpaid fines;

(f)　child support;

(g)　repayments of a refugee integration loan;

(h)　loan repayments to certain qualifying affordable credit lenders (e.g. credit unions);

(i)　tax credit overpayment debts and tax self-assessment debts.

24.35　SI 1987/1968 sch 9 paras 2, 5(6)-(7),

24.36　SI 1987/1968 sch 9 paras 1(1) definition of '5%', 3(2), 5(6)

24.37　SI 1987/1968 sch 9 paras 2(2), 8

24.38　SI 1987/1968 sch 9 para 9

Chapter 25 **Support for mortgage interest**

- Common rules and differences from the HB scheme, and terminology used in this chapter: see paras 25.1-9.
- The basic eligibility rules for JSA(IB)/ESA(IR)/IS/guarantee credit and how housing costs are calculated: see paras 25.10-26.
- What are eligible housing costs: see paras 25.27-45.
- Waiting periods and time limiting rules: see paras 25.46-56.
- Other matters, such as moving home, two homes and appeals: see paras 25.57-61.

25.1 This chapter sets out the rules for help with mortgage interest or similar costs that are excluded from the HB scheme (paras 2.17-36). Help with these costs is available through JSA(IB)/ESA(IR)/IS/guarantee credit which are paid by the DWP.

25.2 There are many complicated transitional rules for help with mortgage interest if you have a long-standing claim. This chapter only describes the rules for claims made on or after 1st October 2010.

25.3 Certain other housing costs apart from mortgage interest are also payable through JSA(IB)/ESA(IR)/IS/guarantee credit (such as rent for Crown tenants) but are not described in this chapter.

25.4 The rules described in this chapter stand alone and are not part of the HB scheme. In some cases the rules are identical to HB and reference is made to these as and when they arise.

Terminology and common rules with HB

25.5 Help with housing costs such as mortgage interest are paid as part of JSA(IB)/ESA(IR)/IS/guarantee credit – in this chapter we also refer to these as qualifying benefits. Although help with housing costs is an integral part of each of these benefits, the rules for each type of claim are similar enough to be referred to generically. Any differences between each of these qualifying benefits are identified as they arise.

What this type of support is called

25.6 Although a number of different types of housing costs are eligible for help, in the vast majority of cases help is for mortgage interest on a home loan. For that reason and because there are many common rules (para 25.5), this type of support is generally referred to as Support for Mortgage Interest (SMI), and this is the term used in this chapter.

Differences from and similarities to the HB scheme

25.7 There are many features of the SMI scheme that are similar – or even identical – to the HB scheme, such as how each item of your income is assessed. But there are many differences too. It is beyond the scope of this guide to describe them all in detail but the main differences are set out in the next paragraph and described further in this chapter.

25.8   The main differences from the HB scheme are:

■   administration and assessment is by the DWP rather than by your local council/NIHE;

■   eligible housing costs (together with any personal allowances and additional amounts) form part of your applicable amount;

■   no support is payable if your assessed income (including income from capital) exceeds your applicable amount;

■   there is no upper capital limit if you are claiming pension credit;

■   there are other numerous small differences in the assessment of income and capital and the applicable amount;

■   if you are working age, support is only available if you are out of work;

■   if you are working age there is a waiting period at the start of your claim during which help with your housing costs is excluded;

■   if you are claiming JSA, SMI is time limited (i.e. all support ends after a set time period).

25.9   In addition, your eligible housing costs are based on a standard rate, rather than what you actually pay and are also subject to an overall limit. As in the HB scheme, not all housing costs are eligible so the amount of SMI payable may not reflect what you pay.

Eligibility for SMI qualifying benefits

25.10   To be entitled to SMI you must be in receipt of a qualifying benefit – or would be once your housing costs have been included. The qualifying benefits are JSA(IB), ESA(IR), IS and guarantee credit. Therefore, to be entitled to SMI you must meet the qualifying rules for the particular benefit you are claiming.

Basic qualifying rules for JSA/ESA/IS/guarantee credit

25.11   It is beyond the scope of this guide to describe in full the conditions for each of these qualifying benefits. The basic rule is that your income and capital must be low enough (paras 25.17-21) and either:

■   you (or your partner if you have one) must have attained state pension credit age (para 1.24); or

■   you (and your partner if you have one) must be under state pension credit age:

   ■   you (or your partner) must not be in remunerative work (para 25.13); and

   ■   you must be in one of the qualifying groups entitled to claim JSA, ESA or IS.

Note that even if you meet these basic conditions you can nevertheless be excluded from entitlement (para 25.12).

25.12   If you are a migrant or recent arrival in the UK, or if you are a student, you might be excluded from IS/JSA/ESA/PC: the rules are similar to those that apply to HB but there are some differences (chapters 20-22).

25.13   If you are the claimant, remunerative work has the same meaning as it does for HB (para 6.19), or if your partner is the claimant the same meaning except that the minimum number of hours is 24 instead of 16.

Who is entitled to JSA and ESA

25.14   To qualify for JSA you (and in some cases both you and your partner) must meet the labour market conditions. Broadly these are that you must be 'available for work' and 'actively seeking work' and not be disqualified (for example if you gave up a job without good reason). To qualify for ESA you must be accepted by the DWP as having limited capability for work (para 12.20).

Who is entitled to Income Support

25.15   You can only get Income Support if you are capable of work (with some exceptions) but if you are in one of the groups listed below, you are not expected to meet the labour market conditions for JSA. You can claim income support if you are:

- entitled to statutory sick pay;
- a lone parent with a youngest child aged under 5;
- not a member of a couple and fostering a child aged under 16;
- pregnant and either incapable of work due to the pregnancy or there are 11 weeks or less before the baby is due;
- a woman who has given birth to a baby not more than 15 weeks ago;
- a person aged under 19 (in some cases aged under 21) in non-advanced full-time education who has no-one acting as parent for you or if, in certain circumstances, you are unable to live with your parents;
- a carer entitled to carer's allowance, or caring for a person who has claimed attendance allowance or disability living allowance in the last 26 weeks;
- a refugee learning English (in certain circumstances);
- a prisoner on remand or awaiting sentence (only eligible for the housing costs element of IS);
- a juror or witness required to attend court or a tribunal.

This is not an exhaustive list: there are other less common categories, such as if you are sick or disabled and met the qualifying conditions prior to April 2011 (i.e. transitional cases).

How to start a claim for JSA/ESA/IS/guarantee credit

25.16   You can start your claim for a qualifying benefit by a telephone call to the national number: 0800 055 6688 for JSA/ESA/IS; 0800 99 1234 for pension credit. A claim for JSA/ESA/IS can also be started online [www]. In Northern Ireland, claims for these benefits must be made in writing at the local Social Security Agency office.

26.16   www.dwp.gov.uk/eservice

Assessing income and applicable amounts

The capital limits and how capital is assessed

25.17 You cannot get JSA/ESA/IS if your capital exceeds the upper capital limit. If your capital exceeds the lower capital limit but not the upper limit a tariff income applies. The upper and lower limits and tariff income are the same as for working age HB claims (para 15.4).

25.18 If you are getting pension credit, there is no upper capital limit but if your capital exceeds the lower capital limit a tariff income applies. The lower limit and tariff income are the same as for pension age HB claims (para 15.4). Capital is assessed in a similar way to HB (chapter 13) although there are some differences.

How income is assessed

25.19 Your income is assessed in a similar way to HB (chapters 13-15) – although there are some differences. The main ones are identified in table 25.1.

Table 25.1 **Assessment of income: main variations from HB**

This table sets out the main variations in the assessment of your income and capital from the rules as set out in the rest of this guide. Except where otherwise stated, rules that apply to working age claims apply if you get IS/JSA/ESA and pension age claims if you get pension credit.

Earned income

■ Your self-employed earnings are averaged over one year or a more appropriate period. Reasonable expenses include debts.

Earnings disregards

■ There is no child care disregard or additional disregard (paras 14.63 and 14.68). The lone parent disregard is £20 (IS/JSA/PC). For ESA, the main disregard is £20 (work as a councillor, partner works part-time or in one of the special occupations (table 14.5(f)) and some other rare cases) but the higher £101.00 disregard may apply if your are in permitted work. If you are pension age you cannot qualify for the £20 disregard through long-term incapacity or limited capability for work (i.e. national insurance credit cases).

Income from social security benefits and tax credits

■ For working age claims only, statutory sick pay, statutory maternity pay, etc (table 14.1) count as unearned income and therefore do not attract an earnings disregard. Arrears of any benefits only count from the moment they are paid for the same length of time as the period they cover. For pension age claims (including pension age claims for JSA/IS) the rules are the same as for HB.

- Child tax credit is disregarded in full. There is no carry over of any unused earnings disregard to working tax credit (para 14.61(c),(d)).
- Only £10 is disregarded from widowed parent's allowance (table 13.2(n)).

Other income

- Maintenance for an adult counts in full.
- Payments made by a mortgage protection policy to cover costs not covered by SMI are ignored completely.

Low income and the size of the award

25.20 Your assessed income is compared with your applicable amount to determine whether or not you are entitled to benefit. Your applicable amount is calculated in a similar way to HB (chapter 12) – but with the following important differences:

- there are no personal allowances or additional amounts payable in respect of any child, and there is no family premium (this is because children are covered by your child tax credit which is not counted as income);
- if you or your partner have attained state pension credit age (para 1.24), your applicable amount is always the same rate, equivalent to the HB personal allowance for a single person/couple aged over pension age but under 65 (adjusted as follows);
- the only premiums you can get are the carer and severe disability premiums plus if you get JSA/ESA/IS any amounts identified in table 25.2 that apply;
- your claimant's eligible housing costs form part of your JSA/ESA/IS/PC applicable amount (in other words, it is added to your personal allowance and premiums, etc);
- deductions are made from your eligible housing costs in respect of any non-dependant in your household; the same rules apply as for HB (paras 6.15-17). The deduction rates are the same as for HB in table 6.4 except where the non-dependant is on ESA in which case:
  - if you get JSA/ESA/IS/PC and the non-dependant is under 25 no deduction is made except where they get ESA(IR) paid with a work related activity or support component;
  - if you get ESA and the non-dependant is on ESA(IR) no deduction is made except where it is paid with a work-related activity or support component.

25.21 The rules about converting income into a weekly figure are the same as for HB (para 6.44) except that annual payments are always divided by 52 (i.e. including if you are working age).

Table 25.2 **Additional amounts in JSA/ESA/IS**

This table sets out the amounts (in addition to those set out in paragraph 25.20) used to calculate your applicable amount for JSA/ESA/IS. The weekly rates and qualification rules are the same as in chapter 12.

Income support and income-based JSA

- Disability premium.
- Enhanced disability premium (adults only).

Income-related ESA

- Work related activity component (except for pension age claims).
- Support component (except for pension age claims).
- Enhanced disability premium (adults only).

Deciding which period a payment belongs to

25.22   The rules that determine which week a particular item of your income belongs to are broadly the same as for HB (para 15.11) but there are some differences. Payments are generally treated as paid on the first day in your benefit week in which it is due, or the date it was due if this was before your claim.

25.23   Your benefit week is the seven days ending on your JSA pay day, or the day before pay day if you get ESA(IS). If you get pension credit your benefit week is the seven days ending on the day your pension credit is paid if it is paid in arrears, or starting on that day if it is paid in advance. Your pay day is determined by the last two digits of your national insurance number as follows (although there are some exceptions for older claims):

- 00 to 19 – Monday
- 20 to 39 – Tuesday
- 40 to 59 – Wednesday
- 60 to 79 – Thursday
- 80 to 99 – Friday

The amount of JSA/ESA/IS/guarantee credit payable

25.24   The amount of your JSA/ESA/IS/guarantee credit award is your applicable amount less your assessed income. If your assessed income is equal to or exceeds your applicable amount there is no entitlement. Note that in some cases it is possible that the award you qualify for is less than your eligible housing costs (i.e. your income exceeds your personal allowance and premiums).

Minimum benefit

25.25   The minimum payment for JSA/IS/PC is 10p per week – although if you claim pension credit and the amount is less than 10p you have underlying entitlement and so are entitled to maximum CTR.

Differences in overall support levels between HB/CTR and SMI

25.26   Even a small award can make a significant difference: the payment acts as a passport benefit for council tax rebate (CTR) and the amount of CTR could be significantly more as a result because:

- ■   your eligible housing costs are not taken into account in CTR and so they do not reduce your CTR excess income (see example);

- ■   if you get pension credit but you have more than £16,000 capital, your entitlement to CTR would otherwise be zero.

However, because of major differences between the HB/CTR and SMI calculations, the total amount of support you receive varies according to your household type. Broadly, if you have children you can often still qualify for maximum CTR even if your income is too high to qualify for IS/JSA/ESA/pension credit: see example.

Examples: Calculation of SMI and effect on CTR (2015-16)

Maximum housing costs covered: ESA(IR)

A claimant and his wife are homeowners. They are buying their home with a mortgage of £71,625. The SMI standard interest rate is 3.63%. The claimant is on ESA(C) of £109.30 per week which includes the support component. His wife has no income. Their council tax is £26.95 per week.

Their income for ESA(IR) is £109.30.

Their applicable amount for ESA(IR) is calculated as follows:

Personal allowance:	£114.85
Enhanced disability premium	£22.60
Support component	£36.20
Eligible housing costs	£50.00
Total:	£223.65

The housing costs element is calculated as follows:

£71,625 x 3.63% = £2599.99 a year. Divide by 52 = £50.00 (rounded).

They are entitled to £114.35 ESA(IR) (£223.65 – £109.30) which includes £50.00 housing costs. Getting ESA(IR) means they are entitled to maximum CTR.

Partial housing costs covered: ESA(IR)

The claimant's wife starts part-time work for 12 hours per week at £10.50 per hour (too low for tax and national insurance).

Their income is now £109.30 + £126.00 – £20.00 disregard = £215.30.

They are now entitled to £8.35 ESA(IR) and even though it is solely on account of their housing costs they are still entitled to maximum CTR of £26.95 per week.

Ineligible for SMI

The claimant's wife increases her hours from 12 to 13 per week. Their assessed income is now £109.30 + £136.50 – £20.00 disregard = £225.80. Their income exceeds their ESA(IR) applicable amount by £2.15 so they do not qualify for any ESA(IR).

Their applicable amount for CTR is the same as for ESA(IR) except that it would not include a housing costs element so would be £173.65.

For CTR the excess income is not £2.15 but £52.15 so their CTR will be £26.95 – 20% of £52.15 = £16.52.

Note, however, that if they had one child they would still be entitled to maximum CTR because their CTR applicable amount would include a child personal allowance and family premium (£66.90 + £17.45) which would more than offset the £2.15 plus the maximum possible income from child tax credit of £63.94 which counts as income for CTR (para 13.12 and table 17.5).

Eligible housing costs

25.27   Your qualifying benefits can cover three types of eligible housing costs. These are:

■   interest on a loan taken out to purchase your home (e.g. a mortgage or other loan);

■   interest on a loan taken out to pay for certain repairs and improvements on your home;

■   other miscellaneous housing costs not eligible for HB (ground rent, rent for Crown tenants, certain service charges payable by leaseholders etc: paras 2.17-36).

The following paragraphs (paras 25.28-37) set out these rules in more detail.

Eligible mortgages and home loans

25.28   Your loan is eligible if:

■   it is taken out to buy the home you and your family normally occupy (para 3.2) or to increase your share of the equity (such as buying out the share of your former partner or a sitting tenant or purchasing the freehold of a leasehold property); or

■   it is taken out to repay a loan that would have qualified as above.

However, even if your loan meets these requirements, all or part of it may be disqualified (para 25.29).

Disqualified home loans

25.29   All or part of your qualifying loan is disqualified if:

■   any part of it was more than you needed to buy the home (e.g. any part of the loan was used to purchase other goods, or to repay accrued interest); or

■   the loan was taken out or increased while you were on benefit (para 25.30) though in this case there are some exceptions (paras 25.32-34).

Taking out or increasing a loan while on benefit

25.30   If your loan was taken out during a 'relevant period' it is disqualified from help. A relevant period is a period:

■   when you were entitled to JSA(IB)/ESA(IR)/IS/pension credit;

■   when you were living as a member of a family of someone who was entitled to JSA(IB)/ESA(IR)/IS/pension credit; or

■   up to 26 weeks between two of either of the above periods.

The above rule is modified according to the type of qualifying benefit you received, as described in the next paragraph.

25.31   The rule about a relevant period is modified as follows:

■   if you are claiming IS it does not include periods on pension credit;

■   if you are claiming JSA(IB) it does not include periods on pension credit, but it also includes periods on JSA(C) (although DWP guidance suggests it should not when you or the family member you were living with was entitled to JSA(C));

■   if you are claiming ESA and PC, 'member of family' means your partner only.

However, some new or increased loans are eligible even if if you took them out during a relevant period (para 25.32).

Eligible new or increased loans

25.32   Certain new or increased loans are eligible for assistance even if you take one out during a relevant period (para 25.30). Your new or increased loan is eligible if:

■   it was used to buy a home that is better suited than your former home to the special needs of a disabled person. The disabled person need not be a member of your family but they must have qualified as disabled at the time the loan was taken out;

■   it was used to buy a new home because it was needed to provide separate sleeping accommodation for two children of the opposite sex aged 10 or over but under 20 who are members of your family;

■   it was used to pay off your original loan (e.g. a remortgage);

■   the original home was sold to pay off an eligible loan and the loan was taken out to buy a new home even if this was some time later; or

■   it was used to buy a home and in the week before, you were in receipt of HB or 'other' housing costs on your JSA/ESA/IS/pension credit that were not for a home loan (e.g. ground rent, etc: para 25.27).

In the case of the last three items, although the loan is eligible, the amount of SMI you can receive is subject to the maximum limit (paras 25.33-34).

25.33   If the loan was taken out to repay your original loan or after your original home was sold then any increase in housing costs is not eligible. For example, if your original loan was for £50,000 and your new loan is for £60,000 then only £50,000 of housing costs are eligible.

25.34   If the loan was taken out immediately after being on HB or help with other housing costs, then to begin with the amount of help is limited to the amount of support you were previously receiving (e.g. if you were getting £50.00 HB per week this would be the maximum help you could receive). However, if the standard rate of interest subsequently increases you become entitled to a proportional increase.

Loans for repairs and improvements

25.35   You cannot get help to cover the cost of repairs or improvements (i.e. any bills for those repairs), nor for variable service charges in leasehold accommodation.

25.36   However, if your loan was taken out to cover the cost of certain qualifying repairs and improvements (including a loan to cover a leasehold variable service charge) it is eligible. Any type of borrowing is eligible but you must have used it to pay for the repairs or improvements within six months of taking it out.

Qualifying repairs and improvements

25.37   If you took out a loan for repairs and improvements it only qualifies for help if the repairs and improvements were for one or more of the types listed in table 25.3 and the works were undertaken to maintain the fitness of the home for human habitation. If a loan is also for other repairs and improvements not listed in table 25.3, only the proportion that is in respect of qualifying items is covered.

Table 25.3 **Qualifying repairs and improvements**

The following items are qualifying repairs and improvements for the purpose of para 25.37.

Measures to provide

- a bath, shower, wash basin, sink or lavatory, and necessary associated plumbing, including the provision of hot water not connected to a central heating system;
- ventilation and natural lighting;
- drainage facilities;
- facilities for preparing and cooking food;
- insulation;
- electrical lighting and sockets;
- storage facilities for fuel or refuse.

Repairs

- to an existing heating system;
- of unsafe structural defects.

Other measures

- damp proofing measures;
- the first two bullet points in paragraph 25.32.

The amount of eligible housing costs

25.38   Once your eligible housing costs have been identified the weekly amount is calculated and included as part of your applicable amount. The calculation is as follows:

- Any eligible loans are added together (e.g. separate loans for home purchase and eligible repair).
- A restriction is made if the total exceeds the upper limit (para 25.39) or if the costs are otherwise considered excessive. If there is more than one eligible loan and together they exceed the upper limit the restriction is applied proportionately to each.

- Each loan (or each restricted loan) is multiplied by the standard rate of interest and then divided by 52 to give a weekly amount and, if there is more than one, they are added together.

- From this total the appropriate deductions (if any) are made for any non-dependants (para 25.20).

- The resulting figure is included in the calculation of your applicable amount (i.e. added to your personal allowance and premiums, etc) (para 25.20).

The upper limit on eligible loans

25.39 The upper limit on eligible loans is:

- £200,000 in the case of claims for JSA, ESA or IS.

- £100,000 in the case of claims for pension credit.

Prior to 4th January 2009, the upper limit was also £100,000 for JSA/ESA/IS and the rules are expected to revert to this position from 1st April 2016.

Restrictions on excessive costs

25.40 Whether or not the upper limit applies, your housing costs can be restricted if:

- the home you occupy is larger than is reasonably required by you and your family (including any foster children) and any non-dependants, having regard to any suitable alternative accommodation;

- the area in which your home is located is more expensive than other areas in which suitable alternative accommodation exists; or

- the amount that is eligible is higher than the cost of suitable alternative accommodation in your area.

When the DWP is making a decision about any of the above, the area over which the comparison is made should not be too wide and the capital value of your home must be ignored. In certain circumstances, a restriction cannot be applied or must be delayed (paras 25.41-43).

25.41 A restriction cannot be made even if suitable accommodation is available, if it is not reasonable to expect your household to look for other accommodation. In deciding this, similar considerations apply as in HB exempt accommodation cases (paras 9.26-27).

25.42 If it is reasonable to expect your household to move, your housing costs cannot be restricted for the first 26 weeks if you were able to meet the repayments when they were entered into. This can be extended for a further 26 weeks if you are using your 'best endeavours' to find somewhere cheaper. In calculating the 26 week period, the 12 week linking rule applies (para 25.53).

25.43 If a restriction applies, any excess over the amount of loan you would need to obtain suitable alternative accommodation is disallowed. So if the equity in your home is sufficient to buy a new home outright, there may be no entitlement.

The standard rate of interest

25.44   As at 1st April 2015 the standard rate of interest is 3.63% (and has been since 1st October 2010). The standard rate of interest is set in line with the Bank of England average mortgage rate. Future changes will only be triggered when the standard rate and the Bank of England published average mortgage rate differ by at least 0.5%.

25.45   The standard rate applies to all claims covered in this chapter, regardless of whether the actual interest rate paid by you is more or less. If the standard rate is more than the actual interest rate, any excess payments are nonetheless credited to your mortgage account.

Waiting periods and time limit of awards

What the waiting period is and when it applies

25.46   If you are claiming JSA/ESA/IS, even if there is entitlement you will not normally receive any help with these costs during the first 13 weeks of your claim (known as the 'waiting period').

25.47   Prior to 4th January 2009, the waiting period was 39 weeks (in certain rarer cases 26 weeks). It is expected that the waiting period will revert to the pre-January 2009 position from April 2015 (as announced in the 2012 Autumn Statement).

25.48   The waiting period does not apply if:

■   your partner has attained the qualifying age for state pension credit or, for JSA only, you have;

■   your claim is for payments as a Crown tenant, under a co-ownership scheme or for a tent (para 25.27).

25.49   If you are entitled to JSA/ESA/IS during your waiting period without your housing costs included (i.e. because your income is less than your personal allowance plus any premiums and components) then your award is superseded when the waiting period ends.

25.50   If you are only entitled to JSA/ESA/IS once your housing costs are included then your 'nil award' can be superseded at the end of your waiting period and your housing costs included provided you are treated as entitled, otherwise you will have to make a fresh claim. You are treated as entitled if throughout that period you were entitled to contribution-based JSA/ESA, incapacity benefit or statutory sick pay or awarded national insurance credits for sickness or unemployment – but there are also other exceptions.

Time limiting for JSA claims

25.51   If you are claiming JSA, your award of housing costs is time limited unless your claim (or linked claim) began before 4th January 2009: para 25.53.

25.52   If your JSA claim began on or after 4th January 2009, the maximum length of your housing costs award is 104 weeks. In calculating the 104 week limit the 13 week waiting period is ignored. Any two or more periods that are linked to an award that first began on or after 4th January 2009 will count as a continuous award (see example).

Linking rules (JSA, ESA, IS)

25.53 If you are claiming JSA/ESA/IS, breaks in your claim can affect entitlement to SMI when you reclaim (paras 25.46 and 25.51). However, there are special rules (known as the 'linking rules') which treat you as having a continuous award. There are two main linking rules (and a number of less common linking rules) that affect your award of SMI. These are:

■ where a repeat claim for a qualifying benefit is made within 12 weeks (104 weeks in certain circumstances if you were claiming ESA and returned to work), your claims are linked and treated as being continuous (whether or not your waiting period had been served when your previous claim ended);

■ where SMI was previously in payment and the claimant or their partner moves into work (or certain kinds of training such as New Deal) a 52 week linking period applies, and they are treated as having been continuously in receipt of SMI from day one of any repeat claim.

25.54 In addition to the main rules above, any periods you spend on JSA(IB), IS and ESA(IR) are treated as entitlement to each other; so, for example, if you moved off ESA(IR) and onto JSA(IB), any time spent on ESA(IR) would be treated as time on JSA(IB). Likewise, any periods spent on these benefits by your partner or former partner also count. There are a number of other more obscure linking rules which are beyond the scope of this guide.

25.55 The linking rules affect your entitlement to SMI as follows:

■ your linked claim counts as time served towards the waiting period and if SMI was already in payment at the end of your previous claim it can be paid immediately; and

■ if you are a jobseeker who has exhausted your 104 weeks' entitlement you cannot re-qualify for a further 104 weeks' by simply breaking your claim and reclaiming.

25.56 If you are claiming JSA the only way you can can re-qualify for SMI once your 104 week entitlement has been exhausted is to:

■ leave JSA for over 12 weeks if you are not working, or over 52 weeks if you move off benefit and into work; and

■ make a new claim for JSA and serve a new 13 week waiting period for SMI.

If both of these conditions are met you qualify for a fresh 104 week period of entitlement.

Other matters

Moving home, two homes and temporary absence

25.57 As with HB, there are rules about when you can claim for two homes, during a temporary absence and during a move into a new home:

■ SMI can be paid in certain circumstances for a period before you move into a new home. The rules are the same as in paragraphs 3.17-22 (waiting for disability adaptation or social fund payment, and leaving care);

■ SMI can be paid for up to 13 or, in some cases, 52 weeks when you are temporarily absent. The rules are the same as in paragraphs 3.31-34 and table 3.1;

■ SMI can be paid in certain circumstances if you have commitments on two homes. The rules are same as in paragraphs 3.7-16 and 3.26-27 (unavoidable liability, fear of violence, students and trainees).

Mortgage interest run-on

25.58 The mortgage interest run-on scheme mirrors extended payments if you get help with your housing costs through JSA/IS/ESA instead of HB (paras 17.46-53). The qualifying conditions are the same as for 'qualifying income related benefits' in table 17.7 except that, instead of the fourth bullet, any qualifying benefit received must include an amount for housing costs within your applicable amount. Payment is automatic provided you have notified the DWP/Jobcentre Plus office that you have started full-time work.

25.59 If you are entitled, the run-on is for four weeks. The amount paid is the same as any housing costs award you were previously being paid, or the amount of JSA/ESA/IS you received if lower (para 25.24). Payment counts as an award of JSA/ESA/IS, so maximum CTR is payable.

Payment

25.60 Your SMI is normally paid direct to your lender – except in the case of an SMI run-on which is paid to you instead. Your lender can opt out of the direct payment scheme but this is virtually unheard of.

Appeals

25.61 Most decisions about your SMI can be revised or appealed to a tribunal. The rules about appeals – including the basic one month time limit – are similar to those described in chapter 19, although there are many minor differences that are beyond the scope of this guide.

Appendix 1 **Legislation**

England, Wales and Scotland

Main primary legislation (Acts)

The Social Security Contributions and Benefits Act 1992

The Social Security Administration Act 1992

The Child Support, Pensions and Social Security Act 2000

The Welfare Reform Act 2007

The Welfare Reform Act 2012

Main secondary legislation (Regulations and Orders)

SI 2006/213	The Housing Benefit Regulations 2006
SI 2006/214	The Housing Benefit (Persons who have attained the qualifying age for state pension credit) Regulations 2006
SI 2006/217	The Housing Benefit and Council Tax Benefit (Consequential Provisions) Regulations 2006
SI 1997/1984	The Rent Officers (Housing Benefit Functions) Order
SI 1997/1995	The Rent Officers (Housing Benefit Functions) (Scotland) Order
SI 2001/1002	The Housing Benefit and Council Tax Benefit (Decisions and Appeals) Regulations
SI 2001/1167	The Discretionary Financial Assistance Regulations

Recent secondary legislation (Regulations and Orders)

The following is a list of amendments etc made (or otherwise relevant) to the main regulations from 1st April 2014. This list is up to date as at 1st April 2015.

SI 2014/852	The Child Arrangements Order (Consequential Amendments to Subordinate Legislation) Order 2014
SI 2014/902	The Social Security (Habitual Residence) (Amendment) Regulations 2014
SI 2014/1230	The Universal Credit (Transitional Provisions) Regulations 2014
SI 2014/1452	The Welfare Reform Act 2012 (Commencement No 9, 11, 13, 14 and 16 and Transitional and Transitory Provisions (Amendment)) Order 2014
SI 2014/1626	The Universal Credit (Transitional Provisions) (Amendment) Regulations 2014
SI 2014/1667	The Income-related Benefits (Subsidy to Authorities) and Discretionary Housing Payments (Grants) Amendment Order 2014

SI 2014/1923   The Welfare Reform Act 2012 (Commencement No 9, 11, 13, 14, 16 and 17 and Transitional and Transitory Provisions (Amendment) (No 2)) Order 2014

SI 2014/2103   The Special Educational Needs (Consequential Amendments to Subordinate Legislation) Order 2014

SI 2014/2888   The Universal Credit and Miscellaneous Amendments (No 2) Regulations 2014

SI 2014/3094   The Welfare Reform Act 2012 (Commencement No 20 and Transitional and Transitory Provisions and Commencement No 9 and Transitional and Transitory Provisions (Amendment)) Order 2014

SI 2014/3117   The Jobseeker's Allowance (18-21 Work Skills Pilot Scheme) Regulations 2014

SI 2014/3126   The Rent Officers (Housing Benefit and Universal Credit Functions) (Local Housing Allowance Amendments) Order 2014

SI 2014/3229   The Marriage and Civil Partnership (Scotland) Act 2014 and Civil Partnership Act 2004 (Consequential Provisions and Modifications) Order 2014

SI 2014/3255   The Shared Parental Leave and Statutory Shared Parental Pay (Consequential Amendments to Subordinate Legislation) Order 2014

SI 2015/6   The Housing Benefit and Housing Benefit (Persons who have attained the qualifying age for state pension credit) (Income from earnings) (Amendment) Regulations 2015

SI 2015/30   The Welfare Benefits Up-rating Order 2015

SI 2015/33   The Welfare Reform Act 2012 (Commencement No 21 and Transitional and Transitory Provisions) Order 2015

SI 2015/67   The Social Security (Miscellaneous Amendments) Regulations 2015

SI 2015/202   The Social Security (Penalty as Alternative to Prosecution) (Maximum Amount) Order 2015

SI 2015/457   The Social Security Benefits Up-rating Order 2015

SI 2015/478   The Social Security (Miscellaneous Amendments No 2) Regulations 2015

SI 2015/499   The Social Security (Overpayments and Recovery) Amendment Regulations 2015

SI 2015/634   The Welfare Reform Act 2012 (Commencement No 23 and Transitional and Transitory Provisions) Order 2015

SI 2015/643   The Care Act 2014 (Consequential Amendments) (Secondary Legislation) Order 2015

SI 2015/740   The Welfare Reform Act 2012 (Commencement No 23 and Transitional and Transitory Provisions) (Amendment) Order 2015

SI 2015/971   The Deregulation Act 2015 (Consequential Amendments) Order 2015

Northern Ireland

Main primary legislation (Acts and Acts of Northern Ireland Assembly)

The Social Security Contributions and Benefits (Northern Ireland) Act 1992

The Social Security Administration (Northern Ireland) Act 1992

The Child Support, Pensions and Social Security Act (Northern Ireland) 2000

The Welfare Reform Act (Northern Ireland) 2007

Main secondary legislation (Statutory Rules and Orders)

NISR 2006/405   The Housing Benefit Regulations (Northern Ireland) 2006

NISR 2006/406   The Housing Benefit (Persons who have attained the qualifying age for state pension credit) Regulations (Northern Ireland) 2006

NISR 2006/407   The Housing Benefit (Consequential Provisions) Regulations (Northern Ireland) 2006

NISR 2008/100   The Housing Benefit (Executive Determinations) Regulations (Northern Ireland) 2008

NISR 2001/213   The Housing Benefit (Decisions and Appeals) Regulations (Northern Ireland) 2001

NISR 2001/216   The Discretionary Financial Assistance Regulations (Northern Ireland) 2001

Recent secondary legislation (Statutory Rules and Orders)

The following is a list of amendments etc made (or otherwise relevant) to the main regulations from 1st April 2014. This list is up to date as at 1st April 2015.

NISR 2014/105   The Social Security (Miscellaneous Amendments) Regulations (Northern Ireland) 2014

NISR 2014/133   The Social Security (Habitual Residence) (Amendment) Regulations (Northern Ireland) 2014

NISR 2014/150   The Jobseeker's Allowance (Schemes for Assisting Persons to Obtain Employment) Regulations (Northern Ireland) 2014

NISR 2014/275   The Social Security (Miscellaneous Amendments No 2) Regulations (Northern Ireland) 2014

NISR 2015/2   The Housing Benefit (Executive Determinations) (Amendment) Regulations (Northern Ireland) 2015

NISR 2015/19   The Housing Benefit (Income from earnings) (Amendment) Regulations (Northern Ireland) 2015

NISR 2015/34   The Social Security (Miscellaneous Amendments) Regulations (Northern Ireland) 2015

NISR 2015/124   The Social Security Benefits Up-rating Order (Northern Ireland) 2015

NISR 2015/146   The Shared Parental Leave and Statutory Shared Parental Pay (Consequential
                Amendments to Subordinate Legislation) Order (Northern Ireland) 2015

NISR 2015/163   The Social Security (Miscellaneous Amendments No 2) Regulations
                (Northern Ireland) 2015

Appendix 2 **Selected benefit rates from April 2015**

	£
Attendance allowance	
Higher rate	82.30
Lower rate	55.10
Bereavement benefits	
Widowed parents allowance (standard rate)	112.55
Bereavement allowance (standard rate)	112.55
Reduction in standard rate for each year aged under 55 (approx)	7.88
Child benefit	
Only or older/oldest child	20.70
Each other child	13.70
Carer's allowance	
Claimant	62.10

Disability living allowance/Personal independence payment

Care component	*Daily living*	£
Highest rate	Enhanced	82.30
Middle rate	Standard	55.10
Lowest rate	–	21.80
Mobility component	*Mobility component*	
Higher rate	Enhanced	57.45
Lower rate	Standard	21.80

Employment and support allowance

Personal allowances	£
Under 25/lone parent under 18	57.90
18 or over/under 25 (main phase)	73.10
Couple both under 18 with child	87.50
Couple both over 18	114.85
Components	
Work-related activity	29.05
Support	36.20

	£
Guardian's allowance	16.55

Incapacity benefit

Short-term lower rate (under pension age)	79.45
Short-term higher rate (under pension age)	94.05
Long-term rate	105.35
Spouse or adult dependant (where appropriate)	61.20
Increase for age higher rate (under 35)	11.15
Increase for age lower rate (35-44)	6.20

Industrial disablement pension

20% disabled	33.60
For each further 10% disability up to 100%	16.80
100% disabled	168.00

Jobseekers allowance (contribution-based)

Aged under 18 to 24	57.90
Aged 25 or more	73.10

Maternity and paternity pay and allowance

Statutory maternity, paternity and adoption pay	139.58
Maternity allowance	139.58

Retirement pension

Single person (basic rate)	115.95
Couple (basic rate)	185.45

Severe disablement allowance

Basic rate	74.65
Age-related addition	
Higher rate	11.15
Middle rate	6.20
Lower rate	6.20

Statutory sick pay

Standard rate	88.45

For details of other benefit rates from April 2015 (including means-tested benefits, tax credits and war pensions) see Circular A18/2014.

Appendix 3 **Qualifying age for state pension credit**

Date of birth	Date qualifying age for state pension credit is reached
Before 6th April 1950	On reaching age 60
6th April 1950 to 5th May 1950	6th May 2010
6th May 1950 to 5th June 1950	6th July 2010
6th June 1950 to 5th July 1950	6th September 2010
6th July 1950 to 5th August 1950	6th November 2010
6th August 1950 to 5th September 1950	6th January 2011
6th September 1950 to 5th October 1950	6th March 2011
6th October 1950 to 5th November 1950	6th May 2011
6th November 1950 to 5th December 1950	6th July 2011
6th December 1950 to 5th January 1951	6th September 2011
6th January 1951 to 5th February 1951	6th November 2011
6th February 1951 to 5th March 1951	6th January 2012
6th March 1951 to 5th April 1951	6th March 2012
6th April 1951 to 5th May 1951	6th May 2012
6th May 1951 to 5th June 1951	6th July 2012
6th June 1951 to 5th July 1951	6th September 2012
6th July 1951 to 5th August 1951	6th November 2012
6th August 1951 to 5th September 1951	6th January 2013
6th September 1951 to 5th October 1951	6th March 2013
6th October 1951 to 5th November 1951	6th May 2013
6th November 1951 to 5th December 1951	6th July 2013
6th December 1951 to 5th January 1952	6th September 2013
6th January 1952 to 5th February 1952	6th November 2013
6th February 1952 to 5th March 1952	6th January 2014
6th March 1952 to 5th April 1952	6th March 2014
6th April 1952 to 5th May 1952	6th May 2014
6th May 1952 to 5th June 1952	6th July 2014
6th June 1952 to 5th July 1952	6th September 2014
6th July 1952 to 5th August 1952	6th November 2014

6th August 1952 to 5th September 1952 . . . . 6th January 2015

6th September 1952 to 5th October 1952 . . . . 6th March 2015

6th October 1952 to 5th November 1952 . . . . 6th May 2015

6th November 1952 to 5th December 1952 . . . . 6th July 2015

6th December 1952 to 5th January 1953 . . . . 6th September 2015

6th January 1953 to 5th February 1953 . . . . 6th November 2015

6th February 1953 to 5th March 1953 . . . . 6th January 2016

6th March 1953 to 5th April 1953 . . . . 6th March 2016

6th April 1953 to 5th May 1953 . . . . 6th July 2016

6th May 1953 to 5th June 1953 . . . . 6th November 2016

6th June 1953 to 5th July 1953 . . . . 6th March 2017

6th July 1953 to 5th August 1953 . . . . 6th July 2017

6th August 1953 to 5th September 1953 . . . . 6th November 2017

6th September 1953 to 5th October 1953 . . . . 6th March 2018

6th October 1953 to 5th November 1953 . . . . 6th July 2018

6th November 1953 to 5th December 1953 . . . . 6th November 2018

6th December 1953 to 5th January 1954 . . . . 6th March 2019

6th January 1954 to 5th February 1954 . . . . 6th May 2019

6th February 1954 to 5th March 1954 . . . . 6th July 2019

6th March 1954 to 5th April 1954 . . . . 6th September 2019

6th April 1954 to 5th May 1954 . . . . 6th November 2019

6th May 1954 to 5th June 1954 . . . . 6th January 2020

6th June 1954 to 5th July 1954 . . . . 6th March 2020

6th July 1954 to 5th August 1954 . . . . 6th May 2020

6th August 1954 to 5th September 1954 . . . . 6th July 2020

6th September 1954 to 5th October 1954 . . . . 6th September 2020

6th October 1954 or after . . . . On reaching age 66

App 3   Pensions Act 1995 schedule 4; Pensions Act 2011 s1; SI 1995 No. 3213 (NI 22) schedule 2; Pensions Act (Northern Ireland) 2012 s1

Index

References in the index are to paragraph numbers (not page numbers), except that 'A' refers to appendices, 'T' refers to tables in the text and 'Ch' refers to a chapter.